Tantra

Tantra

Sex, Secrecy, Politics, and Power in the Study of Religion

Hugh B. Urban

UNIVERSITY OF CALIFORNIA PRESS
Berkeley · Los Angeles · London

University of California Press
Berkeley and Los Angeles, California

University of California Press, Ltd.
London, England

Library of Congress Cataloging-in-Publication Data

Urban, Hugh B.
Tantra : sex, secrecy, politics, and power in the study of religion / Hugh B. Urban.
p. cm.
Includes bibliographical references and index.
ISBN 0-520-23062-0 (alk. paper).—
ISBN 0-520-23656-4 (pbk. : alk. paper)
1. Tantrism. 2. Tantric Buddhism. I. Title.
BL1283.84 U73 2003
294.5'514—dc21 2002073270

Manufactured in the United States of America

12 11 10 09 08 07 06 05 04 03
10 9 8 7 6 5 4 3 2 1

The paper used in this publication meets the minimum requirements of ANSI/NISO Z39.48–1992 (R 1997) (*Permanence of Paper*).⊗

In memory of Hugh Bayard Urban, Sr.
(1926–2001)

Contents

Illustrations

FIGURES

TABLES

Preface and Acknowledgments

The Extreme Orient and the Quest for Ecstasy

O Mother! At your holy lotus feet I pray that I have not transgressed all the Veda and Artha Śāstras and destroyed your worship; with this fear, I have revealed many profound matters. Please forgive me for whatever sins I have incurred by revealing these secret things. . . . Forgive me, for, with an ignorant heart, I have revealed the most secret things of your *tantra*s.

Kṛṣṇānanda Āgamavāgīśa,
Bṛhat-Tantrasāra (sixteenth century)

For the last 150 years . . . we have been orientalizing; in reality, it is precisely because the whole world is Westernizing that the West is becoming more permeable to Indian philosophy, to African art . . . to Arabic mysticism. Hindu philosophy, African art acquire a consciousness of self by virtue of those structures through which Western civilization assimilates them.

Michel Foucault, interview,
"Who Are You, Professor Foucault?" (1967)

This book was born in large part out of my own long and deeply ambivalent relationship to the phenomenon of "Tantra" or "Tantrism" and its role in the contemporary Western imagination.[1] It is the product of my own fascination with this most tantalizing aspect of the "exotic Orient"—this brand of Indian spirituality that seemingly could combine sexuality, sensual pleasure, and the full range of physical experience with the religious life. Coming as I do from a fairly strict and conservative middle-class Episcopalian background, and generally bored with that brand of Christianity, I was drawn naturally to Tantra—an enticing and wonderfully *Other* form of religion that seemed in every way the perfect opposite of the stodgy religion of my childhood. Many years ago, as a college freshman sitting in on an "Introduction to Eastern Religions" class, I was captivated by accounts of sexual rituals, the use of alcohol and other intoxicants, and the explicit violation of conventional social laws, all in the name of a powerful, ecstatic religious experience. In Tantra, it seemed, I had discovered the ideal alternative to (and wonderfully liberating inversion of) everything I thought "religion" was supposed to be about; it seemed the embodiment of everything my upbringing was *not*.[2]

My own first immersion in the world of Tantra occurred many years later, as a graduate student, when I undertook a detailed study of the role of secrecy in one particular sect—the Kartābhajās, or "Worshipers of the Master"—which emerged in the Calcutta area at the end of the nineteenth century. The focus of my work at that time was the difficult question of how one could—and indeed whether one *should*—study a tradition such as Hindu Tantra, which is emphatically esoteric, meant to be understood only by initiated insiders.[3] However, in the course of my study, I was faced by an even more difficult, self-reflective question: why was I, a middle-class, Episcopalian, white kid, so fascinated with a bunch of poor, lower-class Bengalis performing secret rituals and engaging in illicit sexual activities? Still more broadly, why has Tantra now assumed such a central place in American popular culture, with pop stars like Sting practicing seven-hour-long Tantric sex and New Age gurus offering Tantric workshops such as the "Path to Total Ecstasy"? Is this part of what Marianna Torgovnick called our "primitive passion" and our "quest for ecstasy"—that is, the contemporary Western search for an irrational, mystical, or ecstatic experience that we feel we have lost amid a rationalized, demystified, modern world? Torgovnick writes: "Westerners seem like Adam and Eve banished from the Eden of the primitive, convinced that some ecstatic primal emotions have been lost, almost as penalty for being Western. Yet . . . what is now sought in the primitive is really a reflection or projection of something . . . in the West."[4]

In the course of my probing into the mysteries of Tantra, I interviewed, studied under, and became friends with a number of Tantric practitioners in West Bengal, Assam, Himachal, and Uttar Pradesh. Like many curious travelers, both Western and Indian, I was fascinated by the aura of secrecy, power, and danger that surrounds great Tantric centers, such as the cremation ground at Tārāpīṭh, West Bengal, or the temple of Kāmākhyā in Assam, where rather grisly animal sacrifices are still performed on a regular basis. And I encountered a wide variety of responses and reactions to my curiosity. In Tārāpīṭh for example, I tried to question one skeptical and worldly older Aghorī about the infamous "fifth M" of Tantric practice—*maithuna,* or sexual union with a female partner. After my repeated prodding, he finally lost his patience and exclaimed, "All you Americans want to know about is sex. Don't you get enough of that in your own country? Go back home to your 'pornography' and your 'free love.'" On the other hand, I also met a wide range of gurus who were quite proud of their powerful esoteric knowledge and seemed more than happy to "advertise their secrets" to a well-funded Western researcher. For many self-proclaimed *tāntrika*s, the claim to possession of such knowledge appears to be closely related to their aspirations for status, prestige, money, and even a possible trip to the United States.[5]

This book thus represents a moment of intense self-reflection, self-scrutiny, and self-criticism, one that I think has larger implications for the field of South Asian studies and the history of religions as a whole. It raises the question of just why so many intellectuals in the West are fascinated by this hitherto obscure and esoteric Indian religion. Why has Tantra come to saturate American pop culture, with slick paperbacks promoting it as *The Art of Sexual Ecstasy* and web sites offering Tantric advice for the "multiorgasmic Man"? Is this simply a case of cross-cultural voyeurism? Or are we in fact caught up in networks of neocolonial or neoimperialist exchange, the ultimate impact of which we have not yet begun to fathom?[6]

Troubled by these questions, I set out to try to unravel the complex genealogy of Tantra and our contemporary fascination with this most "extreme" of all Oriental traditions. It was an investigation that led me from ancient Sanskrit manuscripts in Calcutta and Kathmandu to the annals of British colonial rule, to the revolutionary writings of the Bengal nationalists, to the scandalous antics of contemporary New Age neo-Tantric gurus and the techno-Tantra of the World Wide Web. In the process, I found this genealogy to be far more complicated than I had ever imagined, and surely far more interesting than a simple imperialist imposition of a Western category onto a colonized subject. On the contrary, "Tantra" appears to me a densely tangled web of intersecting threads, both Eastern and Western, ancient and modern, woven through the intricate cross-cultural interplay of scholarly and popular imaginations, and creatively reimagined in each new historical era.

A brief note on transliteration: I have followed a Sanskritic model of transliteration for most of the South Asian terms in this text. There are, however, a few exceptions, particularly in the case of Indian authors whose names have been rendered by themselves or their disciples into English, often with little consistency. Names and titles that I have translated directly from Sanskrit or other languages will therefore be rendered with Sanskrit diacritics (e.g., Svāmī or Śrī). But names and titles that have been published in English without diacritics will be left as printed (Swami, Svami, Shri, or Sri). All translations in this book are mine unless otherwise stated.

Because Tantra is such a lively and controversial topic, it was perhaps inevitable that new works would appear that I would be unable to incorporate into this book. At least three important studies were published during the very late stages of this book's production, which I feel I should note but which I cannot discuss in any detail here. The first is David Gordon White's *The Kiss of the Yoginī,* an excellent study of the role of sexual rituals and sexual fluids in Tantric practice. The second is Ronald M. Davidson's *Indian Esoteric Buddhism,* an original and impressively thorough new look at the social context of early Buddhist Tantric movements in India. And the third is Martine van Woerken's *The Strangled Traveler,* arguably the best and most comprehensive study of the "Thuggee" myth and its role in the British colonial imagination. I regret being unable to discuss these important texts here, and I encourage interested readers to use them as a supplement to this book.

I am deeply indebted to the following people for their help in the research and writing of this book: first, the various gurus, *sādhaka*s (practitioners), and devotees I have encountered in the course of my wanderings in the Orient; second, my various American gurus, most importantly, Wendy Doniger and Bruce Lincoln; third, my fellow *sādhaka*s and *sādhikā*s on the strange path of the Western study of Tantra, above all, Jeffrey J. Kripal, Rachel Fell McDermott, and Glen A. Hayes; fourth, the various scholars who have offered me feedback and criticism on this book in its various manifestations, including André Padoux (who kindly shared with me his own observations on the construction of "Tantrism" as a modern category), Narendra Nath Bhattacharyya (who kindly allowed me to interview him regarding his life, politics, and scholarship), Paul Muller-Ortega, and David Gordon White; and finally and perhaps most importantly, my personal *bhairavī*-guru, Nancy, and the more fully enlightened members of our doga lineage, Shakti and Moses.

Abbreviations

AV	*Atharva Veda,* with the commentary of Sāyaṇa. Calcutta: Bibliotheca Indica, 1896. Trans. William Dwight Whitney. Cambridge, Mass.: Harvard University Press, 1905.
BP	*Bhāgavata Purāṇa.* Bombay, 1832. Trans. Ganesh Vasudeo Tagare. New Delhi: Motilal Banarsidas, 1976–78.
GST	*Guhyasamāja Tantra: A New Critical Edition.* Ed. Yukei Matsunaga. Osaka: Toso Shuppan, 1978.
HT	*Hevajra Tantra: A Critical Study.* Trans. David Snellgrove. London: Oxford University Press, 1959.
KT	*Kulārṇava Tantra.* Ed. Arthur Avalon. New Delhi: Motilal Banarsidas, 1965.
LP	*Śrīśrīrāmakṛṣṇalīlāprasaṅga,* by Svāmī Sāradānanda. Calcutta: Udbodhan Kāryālay, 1965.
MT	*Mahānirvāṇa Tantra.* Calcutta: Ādi Brāhma Samāj, 1876. Trans. Arthur Avalon, *The Tantra of the Great Liberation: Mahānirvāṇa Tantra.* New York: Dover Publications, 1979.
NUT	*Niruttara Tantra.* Ed. Kulabhūṣana Rāmadatta Śukla. Prayāg: Kalyāna Mandir Prakāśana, 1979.

RV	*The Ṛg Veda,* with the commentary of Sāyaṇa. 6 vols. London: H. Frowde, 1890–92. Trans. Wendy Doniger O'Flaherty. New York: Penguin Books, 1981.
SvT	*Svacchanda Tantra,* with commentary by Kṣemarāja. Ed. M. K. Śāstrī. Śrīnagar: Kashmir Series of Texts and Studies, 1921–35.
TA and TAV	*Tantrāloka* of Abhinavagupta, with the commentary, *vivaraṇa,* of Jayaratha. Ed. M. K. Śāstrī. Śrīnagar: Kashmir Series of Texts and Studies, 1921–38.
VST	*Vīṇāśikhatantra: A Śaiva Tantra of the Left Current.* Trans. Teun Goudriaan. New Delhi: Motilal Banarsidas, 1985.

Introduction

Diagnosing the "Disease" of Tantra

> If at any time in the history of India the mind of the nation as a whole has been diseased, it was in the Tantric age, or the period immediately preceding the Muhammadan conquest of India. . . . The story related in the pages of . . . Tantric works is so repugnant that excepting a few, all respectable scholars have condemned them wholesale. . . . No one should forget that the Hindu population of India as a whole is even today in the grip of this very Tantra in its daily life; . . . and is suffering from the same disease which originated 1300 years ago and consumed its vitality. . . .
>
> Someone should take up the study comprising the diagnosis, etiology, pathology and prognosis of the disease so that more capable men may take up its treatment and eradication.
>
> Benyotosh Bhattacharyya,
> *An Introduction to Buddhist Esoterism* (1932)

The category "Tantra" is a basic and familiar one today in the vocabulary of most scholars of religions and generally considered one of the most important and controversial forms of Asian religion. In academic discourse, Tantra usually refers to a specific brand of religious practice common to the Hindu, Buddhist, and Jain traditions since at least the seventh century; above all, it is identified as a particularly radical and dangerous practice that involves activities normally prohibited in mainstream society, such as sexual intercourse with lower-class partners and consumption of meat and wine. Not surprisingly, given the rather racy nature of the subject, interest in Tantra has skyrocketed in the past two decades in both the popular and scholarly imaginations. On the academic level, Tantra has become one of the hottest topics in the field of South

Asian studies, generating a large body of provocative (and often controversial) new scholarship.[1] Still more strikingly, Tantra has also become an object of fascination in the popular imagination, where usually it is defined as "sacred sex" and often is confused with Eastern sexual manuals such as the *Kāma Sūtra* and Western occult traditions such as Aleister Crowley's "sex magick." As we can see on the shelves of any bookstore, Tantra pervades Western pop culture, appearing in an endless array of books, videos, and slick web sites. Indeed, the phrase "American Tantra" is now even a registered trademark, representing a whole line of books, videos, and "ceremonial sensual" merchandise.[2]

And yet, as André Padoux points out, the category "Tantrism"—as a singular, coherent entity—is itself a relatively recent invention, in large part the product of nineteenth-century scholarship, with a tangled and labyrinthine history.[3] When it was first discovered by Orientalist scholars and missionaries in the eighteenth century, Tantra was quickly singled out as the most horrifying and degenerate aspect of the Indian mind. Identified as the extreme example of all the polytheism and licentiousness believed to have corrupted Hinduism, Tantra was something "too abominable to enter the ears of man and impossible to reveal to a Christian public," or simply "an array of magic rites drawn from the most ignorant and stupid classes."[4] Yet in our own generation, Tantra has been praised as "a cult of ecstasy, focused on a vision of cosmic sexuality," and as a much needed celebration of the body, sexuality, and material existence.[5]

This ambivalence has grown even more intense in our own day. On the one hand, the scholarly literature often laments that Tantra has been woefully neglected in the study of Asian religions as "the unwanted stepchild of Hindu studies."[6] On the other, if we peruse the shelves of most popular bookstores or scan the rapidly proliferating web sites on the Internet, it would seem that Tantra is anything but neglected in modern discourse. As we see in endless publications, bearing titles like *Tantric Secrets of Sex and Spirit* or *Ecstatica: Hypno Trance Love Dance,* Tantra has become among the most marketable aspects of the "exotic Orient." Borrowing some insights from Michel Foucault and his work on sexuality in the Victorian era, I will argue that Tantra has by no means been repressed or marginalized; on the contrary, like sex itself, Tantra has become the subject of an endless proliferation of discourse and exploited as "the secret."[7] Indeed, one might say even that Tantra represents the ideal religion for contemporary Western society. A religion that seems to combine spirituality with sensuality, and mystical experience with wine, women, and wealth, Tantra could be called the ideal path for spiritual consumers in the strange world of "late capitalism."[8]

But despite the contradictory and wildly diverse constructions of Tantra, both popular and scholarly, there is still one key element that all of these imaginings share, namely, the very *extremity* of Tantra, its radical Otherness, the fact that it is considered to be the most radical aspect of Indian spirituality, the one most diametrically opposed to the modern West. As Ron Inden has argued, the India of Orientalist scholarship was constructed as the quintessential Other in comparison to the West. Conceived as an essentially passionate, irrational, effeminate world, a land of "disorderly imagination," India was set in opposition to the progressive, rational, masculine, and scientific world of modern Europe.[9] And Tantra was quickly singled out as India's darkest, most irrational element—as the Extreme Orient, the most exotic aspect of the exotic Orient itself.[10]

This book traces the complex genealogy of the category of Tantra in the history of religions, as it has been formed through the interplay of Eastern and Western, and popular and scholarly, imaginations. What I hope to achieve is by no means just another anti-Orientalist critique or postcolonial deconstruction of an established category—an exercise that has become all too easy in recent years. Rather, I suggest that Tantra is a far messier product of the mirroring and misrepresentation at work between both East and West. It is a dialectical category—similar to what Walter Benjamin has called a *dialectical image*—born out of the mirroring and mimesis that goes on between Western and Indian minds.[11] Neither simply the result of an indigenous evolution nor a mere Orientalist fabrication, Tantra is a shifting amalgam of fantasies, fears, and wish fulfillments, at once native and Other, which strikes to the heart of our constructions of the exotic Orient and of the contemporary West.

I hope that this book will offer not only a valuable contribution to our knowledge of South Asian religions, but also, more important, a keen insight into the very nature of cross-cultural dialogue, the mutual re- and misrepresentations of the Other that occur in every cross-cultural encounter. In the chapters that follow I explore a series of reciprocal exchanges between East and West, played out in several key historical encounters—from the severe criticisms of Tantra by early European scholars and the reactions of Hindu reformers, to the paranoid imaginings of British authorities and the uses of Tantra by the revolutionary Indian nationalists, to the wildly exoticized representations of Tantra in English and Indian fiction, to the role of Tantra in contemporary New Age and New Religious movements. Finally, I explore some possible ways to redefine and reimagine Tantra in a more useful form in contemporary discourse.

THE "DIALECTICAL IMAGE" OF TANTRA

> The moment one hears the word "Tantrism," various wild and lurid associations spring forth in the Western mind which add up to a pastiche of psychospiritual science fiction and sexual acrobatics that would put to shame the most imaginative of our contemporary pornographers.
>
> Jacob Needleman, *The New Religions* (1970)

But just what is Tantra? Few terms, it would seem, are at once so pervasive, so widely used, and yet so ill-defined in contemporary discourse, both popular and academic. As Herbert Guenther put it, Tantra is perhaps "one of the haziest misconceptions the Western mind has evolved."[12] It is a term that permeates literature, movies, and the Internet, as we now find alternative-rock groups described as "Tantric" and pop stars like Sting claiming to have achieved seven-hour orgasms by means of Tantric sexual techniques.[13] Yet it is a term that most people would be hard pressed to define.

As we will see in more detail, the Sanskrit word *tantra* has appeared since Vedic times with an enormous diversity of meanings; it has been used to denote everything from a warp or a loom (e.g., AV 10.7.42), to the "chief potion or essence of a thing," to simply "any rule, theory or scientific work" (*Mahābhārata* 13.48.6).[14] Probably derived from the root *tan,* "to weave or stretch," *tantra* is most often used to refer to a particular kind of text, which is "woven" of the extended threads of many words. Yet, as Padoux points out, such texts may or may not contain materials that we today think of as "Tantric."[15]

For most American readers today, Tantra is usually defined as "sacred sexuality," "spiritual sex," or "sex magic"—that is, the unique synthesis of religion and sexuality, which is also often identified with diverse spiritual traditions from around the world, such as European sexual magic, Wicca, Kabbalah, and even certain Native American practices. "Tantra is the only spiritual path that says that sex is sacred and not a sin," as one recent author, Swami Nostradamus Virato, defines it. "The art of Tantra . . . could be called *spiritual hedonism,* which says '*eat drink and be merry but with full awareness.'* . . . Tantra says yes! to sex; yes! to love."[16] According to an even more explicit New Age appropriation—the "American Tantra" espoused by California eros-guru Paul Ramana Das—the sexual magic of Tantra has now become a hyperorgasmic event of truly cosmic proportions:

> American Tantra (tm) is a fresh eclectic weaving of sacred sexual philosophies drawn from around the world, both ancient and modern. . . . Making love is a galactic event! . . . We intend to co-create neo-tribal post-dysfunctional sex and spirit positive . . . generations of gods and goddesses in the flesh. On the Starship Intercourse we greet and part with: ORGASM LONG AND PROSPER![17]

Thus, according to many popular accounts, such as that of the great "neo-Tantric" master, the notorious Osho-Rajneesh, Tantra is not even a definable religion or philosophy; it is more of a nonreligion, an antiphilosophy, which insists on direct experience, not rational thought or dogmatic belief: "The Tantric attitude . . . is not an attitude. It has no concepts, it is not a philosophy. It is not even a religion, it has no theology. It doesn't believe in words, theories, doctrines. . . . It wants to look at life as it is. . . . It is a non-attitude."[18]

Unlike many recent scholars, however, I do not think that the popular American and New Age versions of Tantra can be dismissed as the mere products of "for-profit purveyors of Tantric sex," who "peddle their shoddy wares."[19] Rather, I see these contemporary neo-*tāntrika*s (however absurd they might appear to those in the academy) as important representations of the ongoing transformations of Tantra in culture and in history.

Not surprisingly, given the vast semantic range of the term and the diversity of texts and traditions using it, modern scholars struggled for generations to come up with some kind of usable definition for Tantrism. Not only is the very notion of Tantrism, as a unified, singular, abstract entity, itself largely the product of modern scholarship, but it has been subjected to an enormous variety of conflicting and contradictory interpretations. As Benyotosh Bhattacharyya commented in 1932, "Many scholars have tried to define the Tantras; but every one of their descriptions is insufficient. . . . The definitions of Tantra given by students of Sanskrit literature are not unlike the descriptions of an elephant given by blind men."[20]

At one end of the scholarly spectrum, as we see in the earliest Orientalist and missionary accounts, Tantrism was defined as the most debased form of Hindu idolatry and the most shocking confusion of sexuality with religion. The "so-called Tantric religion," as Talboys Wheeler defined it in 1874, is essentially a cult wherein "nudity is worshipped in Bacchanalian orgies which cannot be described."[21] At the complete opposite end of the hermeneutic spectrum, however, there is Sir John Woodroffe's highly apologetic, sanitized definition, which largely excises or rationalizes Tantra's alleged sexual content: indeed, in Woodroffe's redefinition, far from being a decline into depraved licentiousness, Tantra becomes a noble and orthodox tradition in continuity with the most ancient teachings of the Vedas and Vedānta: indeed, "Tāntrikism is nothing but the Vedic religion struggling . . . to reassert itself."[22]

In more recent years, there appears to have been a remarkable shift *back* to the opposite end of the spectrum, toward an emphasis on Tantra's sexual and scandalous aspects—though this time in a far more positive, even celebratory sense. As we see in the more romantic definitions of Mircea Eliade and other European historians of religions, Tantra represents a much needed affirmation of sexuality and bodily existence, much older than the Vedic Aryan tradition with its patriarchal ideology; it is a "great underground current of autochthonous and popular spirituality," centering around the worship of the Mother Goddess, which later burst forth into mainstream Hindu and Buddhist traditions.[23] For other, still more enthusiastic authors like Philip Rawson, Tantra is nothing less than "a cult of ecstasy" that "offers a uniquely successful antidote to the anxieties of our time."[24] As we will see, it is in large part through the dialectical play between these extremes—from Victorian horror at Tantric licentiousness, to Woodroffe's sanitization and defense of Tantric philosophy, to the neoromantic celebration of Tantric sexual liberation—that the notion of Tantrism has been formed in the modern imagination.

In the face of this intense confusion and contradiction, many scholars have abandoned the very idea of asserting a singular, monothetic definition for Tantra.[25] As Douglas Brooks argues, Tantra is not something that can be defined as a singular, unified category; rather, it can only be described by what Jonathan Z. Smith calls a "polythetic classification," in which a large number of characteristics are possessed by a large number of class members. Various scholars have offered different enumerations of such characteristics, ranging from six (Jeffrey Kripal) to eighteen (Teun Goudriaan).[26] Brooks, for example, suggests the following ten properties of Tantric phenomena: (1) they are extra-Vedic; that is, not part of the conventional canon of Hindu scriptures; (2) they involve special forms of physical discipline, such as kuṇḍalinī yoga; (3) they are at once theistic and nondualistic; (4) they contain elaborate speculations on the nature of sound and the use of mantras; (5) they involve the use of symbolic diagrams, such as yantras or *maṇḍalas*; (6) they place special stress on the importance of the guru; (7) they employ the bipolar symbolism of the god and goddess; (8) they are secret; (9) they prescribe the use of conventionally prohibited substances (e.g., wine, meat, sexual intercourse); (10) they require special forms of initiation in which caste and gender are not the primary qualifications.[27] Unfortunately, however, Brooks gives no indication as to just how many or which of these characteristics a given phenomenon must have to be usefully identified as Tantric; nor does he account for the large number of traditions that share most or all of these characteristics and yet would deny vehemently that they have anything to do with the "scandal and smut" of Tantrism.[28]

In sum, as Donald Lopez puts it, *tantra* has long been and still remains one of the most elusive terms in the study of Asian religions—a kind of "floating signifier . . . gathering to itself a range of contradictory qualities, a zero symbolic value, marking the necessity of a supplementary content over and above that which the signified contains."[29] Yet the reasons for this difficulty in defining Tantra are not far to seek. As I will argue, Tantra is a highly variable and shifting category, whose meaning may differ depending on the particular historical moment, cultural milieu, and political context. We might say that Tantra serves as a kind of Rorschach test or psychological mirror of the changing moral and sexual attitudes of the past two hundred years. As N. N. Bhattacharyya comments:

> Most of the modern writers on this subject insist solely on its sexual elements, minimal though they are compared to the vastness of the subject, and purport to popularize certain modern ideas pertaining to sex problems in the name of Tantra. Thus the historical study of Tantrism has been handicapped, complicated and conditioned by the preoccupation of those working in the field.[30]

For this very reason, however, the various definitions of Tantra also offer us a fascinating window onto the history of the history of religions, revealing the particular historical moments and political contexts of those who have defined it.

We "Post-Victorians"

Tantrism . . . is India's most radical contribution to spirituality. The underlying idea of Tantrism is that even the most mundane occurrence can serve as a means of

> transcendence. . . . Sex is no longer feared as a spiritual trap but is employed as a gateway to heaven.
>
> Georg Feuerstein, *Holy Madness* (1990)

> In the United States, sex is everywhere except in sex.
>
> Roland Barthes, *Empire of Signs* (1982)

One of the most pervasive themes in contemporary literature on Tantra—in both its popular and scholarly forms—is the notion that this tradition has been ignored, marginalized, and repressed consistently by Western scholarship. As Brooks argues, this "unwanted stepchild of Hindu Studies" has been a persistent source of embarrassment to scholarship. Brooks presents his own work as an act of retrieval and restoration that will completely revise our prejudiced and distorted understanding of Hinduism: "The Tantric traditions . . . are routinely treated as trivial or tangential to the mainstreams. . . . Just as our previously deficient understanding of Christianity has been corrected by considering mysticism . . . so our understanding of Hinduism will be revised when Tantrism . . . [is] given appropriate scholarly attention."[31]

While I have great respect for Brooks's work on South Indian Tantra, I must point out that this claim is, so far as I can tell, quite inaccurate. It is true that the body of texts known as *tantra*s have long been misunderstood by Western scholars; yet even in the nineteenth century, Western scholars and popular writers appear not to have trivialized or marginalized the *tantra*s, but in fact to have been fascinated by, often preoccupied and obsessed with, the seedy, dangerous world of the Tantras. And surely, since the pioneering work of John Woodroffe, and continuing with historians of religions like Mircea Eliade, Heinrich Zimmer, Agehananda Bharati, and many others, Tantra has become one of the most popular and pervasive topics in contemporary discourse about Indian religions. In short, far from being denied and ignored in modern literature, Tantra has arguably become one of the most widely discussed, fashionable, and marketable forms of South Asian religion. As Guenther remarked as early as 1952, "There is hardly any other kind of literature that has met with so much abuse . . . or has so much fascinated those who . . . thought the Tantras to be a most powerful and hence strictly guarded means for the gratification of biological urges."[32]

This fascination with the Tantras—and this complex mixture of prudish repugnance and tantalizing allure—has only grown all the more intense in recent years. According to one of the most common tropes in recent

New Age and popular religious literature, our sexuality has been repressed and denied by the stifling institutions of Christianity; therefore, to realize our true potential, we must turn to the ancient arts of the Orient—above all to the sexual magic of Tantra—to liberate the immense wellspring of power within us. So reads an article on the tantra.com web site:

> Sex as an art form has yet to mature in the West. Social repression and internalized guilt have prevented Westerners from a frank and joyous exploration of sexuality. . . . The Orient did not consider sex apart from . . . spirituality. . . . All variations of sexual postures were . . . venerated. Sex was given a place of honor. . . . The parameters of sexual behavior in the East extend way beyond the West's narrow spectrum of normalcy.[33]

Surely few other forms of Hinduism or Buddhism have generated as much literature in the past twenty years, both scholarly and popular, as the Tantras. One need only peruse the shelves of any bookstore or surf the Internet to see that Tantra has come to capture the Western popular imagination no less than it has the academic. Now books such as *Ecstasy through Tantra* and *Tantra: The Art of Conscious Loving* are commonly available; as are any number of videos on "Tantric massage," workshops such as "Extended Orgasms: A Sexual Training Class," and web sites where we encounter the "Church of Tantra," the "alchemy of ecstasy," and so on.[34] Indeed, we now also can order a wide range of sexual-spiritual commodities from the online "Tantra gift shop," including herbs, aphrodisiacs, and other stimulating elixirs. In short, as Rachel McDermott aptly observes in her study of the recent explosion of interest in the Tantric goddess Kālī: "Interest in Tantra, while strong in the last decade, has skyrocketed in recent years, with magazines championing it, Web sites whose sole purpose is to explicate and illustrate it, and newsgroups whose conversations center around its use."[35]

A similar narrative of "repression" and the present need for "liberation" centers around the role of women in the Tantras. From its origins, discourse on Tantra has focused particularly on the role of women in Tantric practice, and above all, their alleged role in sexual rituals. Yet many recent authors, such as Miranda Shaw, have fiercely argued that the role of women in Tantra has been consistently ignored, repressed, or marginalized by the (mostly male) scholars in the academy. According to Shaw, this is nothing other than a lingering residual effect of European colonialism and prudish Victorian attitudes: "The scholarly characterizations of the Tantric Buddhist yoginis as 'lewd,' 'sluts,' 'depraved and debauched' betray a vestige of Victorian indignation not only at nonmarital sexual activity of women but also at the religious exaltation . . . of women."[36]

At this point, I must wonder whether Shaw has been reading the same scholarship as I have. The available literature seems to me to demonstrate that the role of women by no means has been ignored or excluded but, on the contrary, often has been celebrated and exaggerated. While it is true that some authors have pointed out the exploitative use of women in Tantric ritual, the majority of modern scholars appear to have celebrated the status of women in Tantra as a much needed affirmation of femininity, motherhood, and the forces of nature. Consider, for example, the works of some of the most influential scholars like Mircea Eliade and Heinrich Zimmer: "Tantrism," Eliade suggests, represents nothing less than "a religious rediscovery of the mystery of woman, for . . . every woman becomes the incarnation of the Śakti. . . . Woman incarnates both the mystery of creation and the mystery of Being, of everything that *is,* that becomes and dies and is reborn. . . . We must never lose sight of this primacy . . . of the Divine Woman . . . in Tantrism."[37] And of course, even more audacious assertions of the freedom and power of women in Tantra can be found in the seemingly endless array of New Age and popular religious literature in the contemporary West. In one recent and very enthusiastic work, *Tantra: The Cult of the Feminine,* the Woman of the Tantras is now praised as "the Erotic Champion," holding a role far greater than that offered by any contemporary feminist movement.[38]

In sum, it would seem that neither Tantrism nor the women of Tantra have been marginalized or repressed in Western discourse: it is perhaps more accurate to say that Tantra has been exaggerated and, ultimately, commercialized—celebrated as the sexiest, most tantalizing offering of the exotic Orient. Despite the claims to liberate and redeem Tantra, much of the recent literature on the subject in fact only *continues* the worst tendencies of Western "Orientalism" and exoticism identified by Said and other postcolonial critics: the long-held image of India as the quintessential, irrational "Other" of the West.[39]

In this sense, Tantra would appear to play much the same role in the modern imagination as did "sexuality" during the Victorian era, as Michel Foucault has described it. Far from being simply prudish and repressive—as the predominant modern rhetoric would have it—the Victorian era was in fact pervaded by a deeper interest in and endless discourse about sexuality: "What is peculiar to modern societies . . . is not that they consigned sex to a shadow existence, but that they dedicated themselves to speaking of it *ad infinitum*, while exploiting it as *the* secret."[40] Conversely, our own generation—the generation of we "other Victorians"—is seemingly obsessed with the rhetoric of "unveiling" and "liberation," of coming out of the closet and freeing itself of the prudish bonds of the Victorian era.

> If sex is repressed, that is, condemned to prohibition . . . then the mere fact that one is speaking about it has the appearance of a deliberate transgression . . . we are conscious of defying established power . . . we know we are being subversive.
>
> What stimulates our eagerness to speak of sex in terms of repression is doubtless this opportunity to speak out against the powers that be, to utter truths and promise bliss, to link together enlightenment, liberation and manifold pleasures.[41]

So too, I would argue, much of the contemporary rhetoric about the repression of Tantra reflects an obsession with the scandalous, seedy, sexy side of Tantra, and a similar claim to "liberate" it from the prudish Victorian biases of our scholarly forefathers.

Oh No—It's Something "Postcolonial"

> "Oh it's something post-colonial" . . . the latest catchall term to dazzle the academic mind.
>
> Russel Jacoby, "Marginal Return" (1995)

From the outset of a study like this, however, I feel I need to address a few of the anticipated objections of my readers. No doubt, some will groan in tired dismay at the very suggestion of this project—a project that might appear, at first glance, to be just one more of the many Saidian critiques of Orientalism or another clever deconstruction of a familiar category. Let me make it clear, first of all, that my aim is by no means to prove that Tantra "never existed" or that it is purely a colonialist fantasy or a "Western category imposed upon Asian traditions."[42] Rather, I aim to reveal the complexity, plurality, and fluidity of the many varied traditions that we now call Tantra. The abstract concept of Tantrism, like "Hinduism," is a relatively recent creation. Like religion itself, as Jonathan Z. Smith reminds us, it is the product of human imagination and our own "imaginative acts of comparison and generalization."[43] But it is not *solely* the product either of the Western mind or the scholarly imagination; rather, it is a complex hybrid creation of Eastern and Western and scholarly and popular imaginings. Moreover, this does not mean that we cannot still speak of Tantric texts, Tantric people, and Tantric practices. In short, rather than constructing abstract monolithic isms, it is perhaps more fruitful to look at specific forms of discourse, ritual acts, and historical actors, located in particular social, political, and economic contexts, which we, as scholars "imagining religion," find it useful to label as Tantra.

Thus, what I hope to do here is something a bit more subtle and nuanced than a just another postcolonial white-male-bashing. In fact, I am in many ways skeptical of the recent proliferation of postcolonial discourse in the academy. As critics like Aijaz Ahmad have pointed out, there are a number of troubling problems inherent in the discourse of postcolonialism. First, it tends to oversimplify the colonial situation, portraying it as a simple Manichean binarism of colonizer and colonized, imperial oppressor and native victim.[44] By overemphasizing the radical impact of Western power on the rest of the world, much postcolonial discourse, dividing global history into pre- and postimperial epochs, risks lapsing into a more subtle form of imperialism, viewing all human history from the standpoint of European expansion and the progress of modern capitalism.[45]

As Benita Parry and others argue, much of the anti-Orientalist discourse tends to place more or less all of the agency, knowledge, and power on the side of the colonizer. In so doing, it tends to reduce the colonized to a mere passive *materia* to be reformed in the imperial gaze, a helpless victim lacking the possibility to resist, challenge, and subvert Western representations.[46] What we need, in short, is a more complex and interactive model of the encounter between East and West. This does not, however, have to be a simple romantic celebration of the colonized Other in its noble struggle to resist colonial domination—a cause that has become increasingly popular in recent years. Rather, we must examine *both* the ability of indigenous cultures to resist or contest *and* their tendency to mimic, cooperate, or collude with Western representations of the exotic Orient. Instead of a simple process of imperial domination and native resistance, we seem to find "a dense web of relations between coercion, complicity, refusal, mimicry, compromise, affiliation and revolt."[47]

Finally and perhaps most problematically, much of the recent postcolonial literature tends to ignore, elide, or gloss over the more subtle forms of neocolonialism and cultural imperialism still very much at work in the West's dealings with formerly colonized (and yet to be colonized) peoples in the Third World. As Ahmad has powerfully argued, much of the postcolonial literature is in fact complicit with a new form of economic imperialism, as consumer capitalism now spreads to virtually every corner of the globe. Just as capitalist industries have appropriated the material resources of Third World peoples and mass-marketed them to a Western audience, so too postcolonial theorists have capitalized upon the exotic cultural goods of formerly colonized peoples, packaged them in sexy, attractive wrappings, and marketed them to a host of intellectual consumers in the Western academy.[48]

We need to move beyond a predictable, postcolonial, anti-Orientalist reading of Tantra, to examine the more interesting ways in which this category has functioned in precolonial, neocolonial—and also quite *noncolonial*—contexts alike.

Theory and Method: From History of Religions to Genealogies of Religion

> Genealogy does not pretend to go back in time to restore an unbroken continuity that operates beyond the dispersion of forgotten things; its duty is not to demonstrate that the past . . . continues secretly to dominate the present. . . . Genealogy does not resemble the evolution of a species. . . . On the contrary, to follow the complex course of descent is to maintain events in their dispersion; it is to identify the accidents, the minute deviations—or the complete reversals—the errors . . . and the faulty calculations that gave birth to those things that continue to exist and have value for us.
>
> Michel Foucault, "Nietzsche, Genealogy, History" (1984)

My approach to the problem of Tantra will be that of an historian of religions, in the full sense—that is, an historian who critically interrogates those phenomena claiming to be eternal or transcendent, in the light of their most concrete social and political contexts. Here, I understand the task of the historian of religions to go beyond a simple Eliadean quest for universal symbolic patterns or a search for the sui generis essence of religion as the product of *homo religiosus;* rather, we must also examine myths and symbols as the works of living, historically situated human beings, as products of *homo faber,* inextricably enmeshed in social, political, and material struggles.[49] The history of religions, as Bruce Lincoln points out, therefore bears a deep tension at its very heart: for the historian of religions must examine the most material, human, and temporal aspects of those phenomena that claim to be suprahuman and ahistorical: "To practice history of religions . . . is to insist on the temporal, contextual, situated, interested, human and material dimensions of those discourses . . . that represent themselves as eternal, transcendent, spiritual and divine."[50]

Going still further, however, I will also approach the problem of Tantra as an *historian of the history of religions;* that is, I will trace the genealogies of (this particular category of) religion by critically examining the ways in which we scholars have constructed and manipulated our own objects of inquiry, grounding our own imaginings of Tantra firmly in their unique social, historical, and political contexts.[51] The genealogy of Tantra will therefore turn out to be something of a political history of the history of the history of religions, tracing the ways in which both Western and Indian authors have defined and redefined "Tantra" in relation to specific scholarly, ideological, and political interests.

The imagining of Tantra, we will find, has been anything but a simple process or the result of a straightforward, linear narrative. Rather, it is the result of a tangled genealogy, as conflicted and contested as the history of encounters between India and the West over the past several hundred years. To trace this genealogy is not a matter of reconstructing a tidy historical progression leading up to our own era, but rather of piecing together the fragmented, contradictory, and often quite *erroneous* tangle of discourses that have given birth to this strange hybrid construction. It is a matter of tracing, as Foucault puts it, "the accidents . . . the complete reversals—the errors, the false appraisals and the faulty calculations that gave birth to those things that continue to have value for us."

The Dialectical Image:
A Cross-Cultural Play of Mimesis and Misrepresentation

> Where thought comes to a standstill in a constellation saturated with tension, there appears the dialectical image, it is the caesura in the movement of thought. It is to be sought at the point where the tension between the dialectical oppositions is the greatest.
>
> Walter Benjamin,
> "Erkenntnistheoretisches, Theorie des Fortschritts" (ca. 1937)

If my general method is that of an historian of religions, the various hermeneutic tools I employ to make sense of this category are drawn from a wide range of disciplines, employing a number of comparative insights borrowed from many cultures and fields. Above all, I hope to use some of the insights of Michael Taussig, specifically the key notions of the "dialectical image" and the cross-cultural play of "mimesis," which he in turn adapts from Walter Benjamin. As a dialectical category, Tantra is a complex, shifting fusion of both Western and Indian discourse, a composite construction of Orientalist projections, indigenous counterprojections, and the play of misrepresentation between them.

On one side, the image of Tantra clearly has been the result of a certain displacement of many deep-seated fears, anxieties, and desires within the Western imagination, projected onto the screen of the exoticized Other of India. As Gustavo Benevides comments in his study of Giuseppe Tucci, one of Europe's greatest scholars of Buddhist Tantra, "The vision of the Orient nurtured by these intellectuals was in most cases a screen upon which they could project their own understanding of the Occident: either the triumphant discovery that the West was superior to the East, or the melancholy realization that the East possessed a magic no longer present in West."[52] Richard King has recently explored a similar dynamic in his study of Western scholarship on mysticism and the construction of India as the "mystic East" in the Orientalist imagination. Rather strangely, however, King makes absolutely no reference either to the role of sexuality in mysticism or to Tantra—a category that was a key, I will argue, in the Western imagining of India, and a crucial part of the modern imagining of mysticism, particularly in its most dangerous and aberrant forms.[53]

In this sense, the image of Tantra is closely related to the broader construction of "the primitive" or "savage" in modern anthropological and popular discourse. As Torgovnick puts it, "the primitive is the screen upon which we project our deepest fears and desires"; indeed, "the West seems to need the primitive as a precondition and supplement to its sense of self: it always creates heightened versions of the primitive as nightmare or pleasant dream."[54]

Yet surely it would be a mistake to assume that this has been an entirely one-way process of projection, an imaginal creation of the Western mind. The category of Tantra is every bit as much a product of the Indian imagination's counterimagining, mimicry, and mirroring. As Wilhelm Halbfass has argued, Indian intellectuals have consistently redefined themselves in the face of the encounter with the West—often by adapting Western categories and constructions: "Indians reinterpreted key concepts of their traditional self-understanding, adjusting them to Western modes of understanding. By appealing to the West, by using its conceptual tools they tried to defend the identity of their tradition."[55] Since at least the mid-nineteenth century, the category of Tantra has been reappropriated and reinterpreted by Indian authors as a basic part of the ways in which they understand their own traditions. The idea of Tantra—with all its immoral and scandalous connotations—has become a basic part of the way in which many Indians now interpret their own history: "We cannot look at Tantrism as mere perversion without at the same time looking at ourselves as a nation of perverts. . . . It is necessary to know how our ancestors had such absurd beliefs in order to understand how we have become what we are today."[56] The imagining of Tantrism is thus very similar to that of "Lamaism" in the case of Tibetan Buddhism. As Donald Lopez observes in his incisive study of the modern imagining of Shangri-La, "the abstract noun, coined in the West, has become naturalized as if it were an empirical object, the manipulation of which has effects beyond the realm of rhetoric."[57]

Thus the construction of Tantra is neither a simple indigenous fact nor the mere product of Western projection and fantasy: it is the complex result of a long history of mutual misrepresentation and mirroring at work between both Western and Eastern imaginations—a kind of "curry effect" (to play on Agehananda Bharati's metaphor of the "pizza effect") or a game of cross-cultural Ping-Pong.[58] This is an especially acute example of what Friedrich Max Müller long ago called "that world wide circle through which, like an electric current, Oriental thought could run to the West and Western thought returns to the East."[59]

It is in precisely this sense, I would suggest, that Tantra can be understood as a unique example of a dialectical image, to borrow Walter Benjamin's apt phrase. As a "constellation saturated with tension," the dialectical image brings together past and present, ancient myth and contemporary meaning in a single, highly charged, symbolic form.[60] In contrast to the romantic notion of the "symbol"—imagined as a unified, coherent cipher of some hidden meaning—the dialectical image is a powerful juxtaposition of conflicting and contradictory elements that "crystallizes antithetical elements by providing the axes for their alignment."[61] The image of Tantra is precisely this kind of juxtaposition of conflicting forces—or rather, a complex series of such juxtapositions—which brings together sex and spirituality, hedonism and transcendence, the profane and the sacred, even consumer capitalism and mystical ecstasy, in a variety of shifting configurations.

This dialectical image of Tantra, in turn, lies at the pivot of a complex play of representations and imaginary projections—a play of mimesis. As Michael Taussig defines it, elaborating upon Benjamin's essay "On the Mimetic Faculty," mimesis is the basic human power of imitation and representation of the Other. It is our capacity to grasp alterity, to make sense of the foreign or unknown, which takes place in all cultures and historical periods. But it becomes especially intense in periods of colonial contact, when cultures are dramatically confronted with a radical Otherness that brings domination and imperial control. The colonizing powers, for their part, construct a variety of imaginary representations of native peoples—as savage, primitive, feminine, emotional, or violent, rather than rational or scientific. Projecting their own deepest fears of disorder or subversion, together within their own repressed desires and fantasies, the colonizers construct a kind of negative antitype of themselves within the mirror of the colonized Other.[62]

And yet, particularly in cases of colonial contact, mimesis is a two-way street. Colonized peoples also have their own forms of mimesis, their own ways of imaginatively representing the colonial Other. Not only do they frequently mimic, parody, and satirize their colonial rulers in various ways, using the mimetic faculty to appropriate the mysterious power of the white man, but they also seize upon the imaginings of the colonizers, often by turning those notions on their heads and manipulating them as a source of "counterhegemonic discourse." The play of mimesis is, in short, a complex back-and-forth dialectic of interlocking images, a "circulation of imageric power between selves and antiselves, their ominous need for and their feeding off each other's correspondence."[63]

It is just this kind of circular play of images between Eastern and Western imaginings, I would suggest, that has given birth to the complex category of Tantra. And it is the ongoing dialectic of images that has led to the constantly shifting nature of the category, which assumes new valences in changing historical and social contexts. Like the concept of the primitive or the shaman, Tantra is a profoundly Janus-faced category: attacked in some historical periods as uncivilized or subhuman, and celebrated in other periods (particularly our own) as a precivilized "unsullied original state, a sort of Eden before the fall when harmony prevailed," when sex was free and unrepressed, when the body had not yet been subjected to modern Western prudishness and hypocrisy.[64] As we see, for example, in the strikingly "dialectical" image of Kālī (figures 1–3), Tantra lies at a nexus of contradictory forces at work between India and the West. For European Orientalists and colonial authorities, the image of Kālī was singled out as the most extreme example of the dangerous immorality

Figure 1. Illustration for Kālī Cigarettes, a nationalist brand. Calcutta Art Studio (1879).

and depravity that were running rampant in the subcontinent; yet for the radical leaders of the revolutionary movement in Bengal, this same image could be seized and exploited, transforming the Tantric goddess into a symbol of Mother India in violent revolt against her colonial masters (see chapter 2). In our own day, Kālī has been taken up by feminist writers, in both India and in the West, as a radical symbol of women's liberation and empowerment (see chapter 6). I hope, then, to trace the tangled genealogy of these dialectical imaginings of Tantra as they have been transformed and reconfigured over the last several hundred years.

Structure and Outline of the Book: A Dialectical Argument

There is no privilege to the so-called exotic . . . it is all history. There is no "other." . . . Nevertheless the historian of religion will . . . gain insight from the study of materials which at first glance appear uncommon or remote. For there is extraordinary cognitive power in . . . "defamiliarization"—making the familiar seem strange *in order to enhance our perception of the familiar.*

Jonathan Z. Smith, *Imagining Religion* (1986)

We penetrate the mystery only to the degree that we recognize it in the everyday world, by virtue of a dialectical optic that perceives the everyday as impenetrable, the impenetrable as everyday.

Walter Benjamin, "Surrealism" (1929)

Mirroring the dialectical, hybrid, and shifting nature of the category of Tantra, this book will proceed in a dialectical fashion, tacking back and forth between Western and Indian imaginations. Each chapter will be structured around the reciprocal exchanges, the reactions and counter-reactions, between East and West, as they have been played out in a series of key historical encounters. In so doing we will discover that the various discourses surrounding Tantra may not always tell us much that is terribly useful about any particular form of Asian religion, but they do tell us a great deal indeed about the concrete social, political, and moral contexts in which these discourses emerged. Indeed, the discourses about Tantra are an integral part of larger cultural and governmental issues—the ruling of British India, the regulation of the colonial body and its sexuality, the construction of a reformed Hindu identity, the fight for In-

Figure 2. Kālī, goddess of destruction. From Augustus Somerville, *Crime and Religious Belief in India* (Calcutta: Thacker, Spink, 1931).

dian independence, the politics of scholarship in the modern study of religions, and the global spread of consumer capitalism at the start of the millennium.

I begin, later in this introduction, with a brief genealogy of the term *tantra* in Indian literature, retracing the many tangled ways in which the "thread" of *tantra* has been stretched and interwoven throughout Indian history. Chapter 1 will then discuss the age of Orientalism, examining the first British depictions of Tantra and the ways in which they played into the colonial political programs and the sexual-moral ideals of Victorian culture. At the same time, I will also explore the many ways

Figure 3. A modern Kālī. Cover illustration, by Mary Wilshire, for Trina Robbins, *Eternally Bad: Goddesses with Attitude* (Berkeley, Calif.: Conari Press, 2001). Courtesy of the artist.

in which these images were in turn reappropriated and transformed by nineteenth-century Indian authors, for example, Rāmmohun Roy and the leaders of the Bengal Renaissance.

In chapter 2, I will explore the political role of Tantra in the imaginations of the British authorities, particularly in their fears of criminal activity and the association of secret Tantric cults with revolutionary agitation. Indian revolutionaries of the early twentieth century in turn played upon and exploited those very fears, using Tantric imagery to express nationalist ideals and terrorist violence.

Chapter 3 will delve into the realm of the popular imagination, examining the often wildly exaggerated and exoticized image of Tantra in Victorian novels and Indian popular literature. Here I will explore the rich confluence of Orientalist constructions, colonial paranoia, and poetic license that fed into the literary portrayals, both Eastern and

Western, of the seedy Indian underworld in the nineteenth and twentieth centuries.

In chapter 4, I will examine the various attempts, on the part of both Western and Indian authors, to deodorize, sanitize, or reform Tantra. The most famous of these is the eccentric Supreme Court judge and secret *tāntrika* (practitioner of Tantra), Sir John Woodroffe, who is regarded as the founding father of Tantric studies. His legacy of reform and sanitization of Tantra would be mirrored and echoed in various ways by a great many Indian authors, such as Swami Vivekenanda and the disciples of Sri Ramakrishna.

Chapter 5 will then look at the "revalorized" place of Tantra—and perhaps even Tantro-centrism—in the work of twentieth-century historians of religions, such as Mircea Eliade, Heinrich Zimmer, and Julius Evola. As we will see, there were often many political—and in Evola's case, explicitly fascist—ramifications in their scholarly reconstructions of Tantrism. However, we will also examine the role of Tantra in modern Indian scholarship, where it likewise has become a key part of various cultural and political discourses surrounding Indian national identity and even the rise of communism in regions like West Bengal.

Finally, chapter 6 will engage the increasing fusion between East and West, as in our own time Tantra becomes more and more a part of popular culture and New Age religion. I will examine the widespread popular impact of Tantra as manifest in the Tantrik Order in America, the "sex magick" of Aleister Crowley, the cult of Osho-Rajneesh, and the growing the search for Tantric ecstasy online, in the strange new world of cyber space. We might even say that the contemporary appropriation of Tantra—with its fusion of spirituality and materialism, sacred transcendence and this-worldly profit—has in many ways become the ideal religion of late-twentieth-century Western consumer culture, or perhaps even the "spiritual logic of late capitalism."

In the conclusion I try to go beyond a mere deconstructive genealogy, offering instead some constructive comments as to how we might begin to reimagine the category of Tantra in contemporary discourse. Above all, I will argue, we need to move beyond both the early Orientalist horror of Tantra as a scandalous perversion and the contemporary celebration of Tantra as an affirmation of sensual pleasure. Instead, I will argue for a more historical, contextual, socially, and politically embodied approach to Tantra that roots these traditions solidly in their material circumstances and lived contingencies.

STRETCHING THE TRUTH: "TANTRA" AND THE TANTRAS IN INDIAN HISTORY

A very common expression in English writings is "the Tantra"; but its use is often due to a misconception. For what does Tantra mean? The word denotes injunction *(vidhi),* regulation *(niyama), śāstra* generally or treatise. . . . A secular writing may be called Tantra.

We cannot speak of "the Treatise" nor of "the Tantra," any more than we can or do speak of the Purāṇa, the Saṃhitā. We can speak of "the Tantras" as we do of "the Purāṇas."

Sir John Woodroffe, *Shakti and Shākta* (1918)

. . . as in spinning a thread we twist fibre by fibre . . .

Ludwig Wittgenstein, *Philosophical Investigations* (1958)

Given the profound ambiguity of the category and the conflicting Western interpretations of its content, perhaps we should begin with a brief analysis of the term *tantra* in Indian literature. Not only is *tantra* a kind of "floating signifier . . . gathering to itself a range of contradictory qualities"; but to use perhaps a more fitting Indian metaphor, *tantra* is a tangled "thread" that has been spun out, intertwined, and often snarled in myriad complex ways throughout the dense history of Indian religions.[65]

The historical origins of the vast body of traditions that we call Tantra are today lost in a mire of obscure Indian history and muddled scholarly conjecture. As Padoux observes, "the history of Tantrism is impossible to write" based on the sheer poverty of data at present.[66] In what follows, I will by no means attempt to reconstruct this history—a formidable, perhaps hopeless task that has already been attempted by more capable scholars. Instead, I will try to retrace the complex genealogy of the term *tantra* itself, in order to show the diverse and heterogeneous body of concepts and traditions this term has been used to designate. For the sake of simplicity, I will focus here primarily on Indian, Sanskrit, and vernacular uses of the term *tantra;* I will not engage the interesting problem of related terms in other languages, such as the Tibetan *rgyd,* the Chinese *mi-chiao,* or the Japanese *mikkyo,* or the complex genealogy of *tantra* outside the Indian context.[67]

There is of course no lack of myths and legends about the origins of particular *tantras*. Many of the Hindu *tantras* offer their own narrative of a mythic origin, often in the form of the *tantrāvatāra* or "descent of the text," in which Lord Śiva or the Goddess reveals the scripture. According to the narrative of the *Tantrarāja Tantra,* for example, the teaching was originally revealed by Śiva to the supreme Śakti at the dawn of the first cosmic age; it was then transmitted through a series of nine Nāthas, or perfected masters, who descended in a chain from Śiva's realm to earth, through whom the *tantra* was revealed to humankind: "by these nine, the *tantra* was spread throughout this world; the Primordial Supreme Śakti revealed it in the *Kṛta Yuga.*"[68]

Meanwhile, contemporary scholars have come up with a variety of quasi-mythical origin-narratives of their own. The two most common ones are (a) the pre-Aryan/tribal–origin narrative and (b) the Vedic-origin narrative. The former had its origins in nineteenth-century Orientalist literature, was later popularized by historians of religions like Mircea Eliade, and has now become a standard trope in most New Age versions of Tantra. According to this view, Tantra is rooted in the ancient Indus Valley civilization, which is alleged to have been a matriarchal culture centering around goddess worship and fertility cults. With the coming of the Indo-Europeans or "Aryan invaders," sometime around 1700 B.C.E., the story goes, sexual practices and goddess worship were pushed underground, where they survived as the "autochthonous substratum" of later Hinduism; only a millennium later did they resurface and work their way into the textual record. At the same time, Eliade and others have argued that Tantra is closely tied to non-Hindu, indigenous, and "aboriginal" traditions, such as the many tribal groups that survive today, above all in the marginal areas like Bengal, Assam, and the northwest mountains.[69]

The other common scholarly narrative takes the opposite stance. Since the time of Woodroffe, many defenders of the Tantras have argued that they are not only in continuity with Brahmanical Vedic traditions, but that they are in fact the very essence and inner core of Vedic teachings.[70] This emphasis on the elite, nonpopular, and Sanskritic side of Tantra continues in a more nuanced form in much of the recent scholarship on Tantra. Downplaying its antinomian, radical, and transgressive aspects, many authors appear to have followed Woodroffe in trying to present a version of Tantra that is "not based upon a popular movement but was the outgrowth of the specialized position of an intellectual elite of religious functionaries from the upper classes, as a rule, of Brahmans."[71]

Yet the genealogy of *tantra,* I think we will find, turns out to be far messier, more ambiguous, and more interesting than either of these scholarly narratives. In keeping with its etymological meaning of "stretching" and "weaving," *tantra* will perhaps turn out to be less a unified singular entity than a series of complex threads that have been woven, spread out, and extended in manifold ways throughout the rich fabric of Indian history.

Weaving the Web of Words and Worlds: Tantra in Early Indian Literature

> The poets stretched forth the seven threads to weave
> the warp and woof [of the ritual].
>
> *Ṛg Veda* (RV 1.164.4–5)

The Sanskrit word *tantra* can be found in the earliest known texts of ancient India, appearing as a key term in the hymns of the *Ṛg* and *Atharva* Vedas (ca. 1500–1000 B.C.E.), and woven throughout the later history of Indian literature. Yet its meaning is by no means either simple or fixed. A number of authors have suggested possible etymologies for the term, some defining it as "shortening" or "reduction," others tracing it to the noun *tanu* (body), and still others deriving it from *tantrī* (to explain) or *tatrī* (to understand).[72] However, most scholars seem to agree (with Pāṇiṇi, a Sanskrit grammarian) that the term probably derives from the root *tan,* which means basically to stretch, to spread, or to weave, and, metaphorically, to lay out, to explain, or to espouse.[73] As William Mahony suggests, the imagery of thread and weaving is one of the most evocative themes throughout the early Vedic literature; it is used to describe both the language of the Vedic poets, who "weave their words out of the fabric of a timeless language," and the creation of the universe out of the supreme Brahman, which is likened to "the finely drawn thread on which creatures are woven" (AV 10.8.38).[74] Perhaps most significantly, *tan* is a key verb used in the classic cosmogonic hymn (RV 10.90), which describes the origin of the universe out of the sacrificial dismemberment of the primordial man, Puruṣa. The body of Puruṣa is divided up and "spread out" into the parts of the universe, just as a thread is spun and woven by a loom: "When the gods spread out *[atanvata]* the sacrifice with the Man as the offering, spring was the clarified butter, summer the fuel, autumn the oblation. . . . [T]he gods, spreading the sacrifice, bound the Man as the sacrificial beast" (RV 10.90.6, 15). Hence, as Wendy Doniger O'Flaherty notes, this key verb *tan* is used simultaneously to refer to the performance of the sacrifice, which is spread out over the ritual ground, and to the origin of the universe, which is "spread upon the cosmic waters, or woven, like a fabric."[75]

The Upaniṣads (700–400 B.C.E.) continue this play upon the imagery of weaving evoked by the root *tan,* adding to it the metaphor of the spider spinning its threads *(tantu).* Just as a spider covers itself with its own web, so too "the one God covers himself with things issuing from the primal source . . . as a spider with the threads *[tantubhiḥ].*"[76] "As a spider sends forth its thread . . . so do all the vital functions, all the worlds, all the gods and all beings spring forth from this Self."[77] Thus all of reality, along with the sacred language that reflects it, is the product of this stretching out of the One into the variegated fabric of the universe.

Derived from this seminal root *tan,* the noun *tantra* is thus first used in the Vedic hymns to denote a kind of weaving machine, a loom or, specifically, the warp and woof (RV 10.71.9; AV 10.7.42). Even here, however, it often has the extended meaning of the "weaving" of speech: the visionary poets who composed the Vedas wove them with the threads of words as if upon a loom. However, as J. C. Heesterman points out, *tantra* as "loom" is also a metaphor standardly used for the sacrificial ritual, which is similarly stretched and spread out through the many interwoven threads of the ritual acts.[78] As the *Ṛg Veda* puts it:

> The sacrifice that is spread out with threads on all sides, drawn tight with a hundred and one divine acts, is woven by these fathers as they come near: Weave forward, weave backward, they say as they sit by the loom that is stretched tight. The Man stretches the warp and draws the weft; the Man has spread it out upon this dome of the sky. (RV 10.130.1–2)

Later, in the Brāhmaṇas (ca. 1200–900 B.C.E.), *tantra* is extended from the sense of "weaving words" and "weaving rituals" to a more abstract level, whereby it refers to the essential part of a thing, the main point or characteristic feature of a given system.[79] And by the period of the great Sanskrit epic the *Mahābhārata* (ca. 500 B.C.E.–500 C.E.), the range of *tantra* has been expanded to refer simply to "any rule, theory, or scientific work" (13.48.6). Thus, later authors like the great philosopher Śaṇkara use *tantra* simply to refer to any system of thought (e.g., Kapilasya Tantra, meaning the Sāṃkhya system).[80] However, according to Sir Monier-Williams, the term would eventually be extended and used throughout Sanskrit literature in an almost infinite variety of ways, to denote everything from "an army, row, number or series" (BP 10.54.15), to a magical device or diagram (often synonymous with *yantra*) to "a drug or chief remedy."[81]

But perhaps most commonly, *tantra* is used much like the term *sūtra,* which derives from the verb *suc,* "to sew," to designate a particular kind of discourse or treatise. According to one common definition, a *tantra* is simply "a scripture by which knowledge is spread" *(tanyate vistāryate jñānam anena iti tantram)*—a text, however, that may or may not contain any of the secret and transgressive materials that today we think of as Tantric (for example, the *Pañcatantra,* a popular collection of fables).[82]

In sum, as Padoux observes, the substantive noun "Tantrism" appears nowhere in Indian literature prior to the modern period. It is "assuredly a Western creation," with a fairly recent history.[83] However, we do find the adjective *tāntrika,* which has been used sometimes as a counterpart and contrast to the adjective *vaidika* (Vedic, pertaining to the Vedas). One of the passages most often cited by modern scholars is a brief one in Kullūka Bhaṭṭa's commentary on the Laws of Manu, "revelation *[śruti]* is twofold, *vaidika* and *tāntrika.*"[84] In other words, revealed scripture can be classified into that which belongs to the traditional canon of the Vedic texts and that which appeals to an extra-Vedic source of authority. Yet, rather oddly, despite the frequency with which this passage is cited by modern scholars, Bhaṭṭa does not elaborate this point at all beyond this one terse statement and provides no further explanation of what *tāntrika* means. Moreover, this *vaidika/tāntrika* distinction by no means resolves the semantic muddle presented by *tantra.* If anything, it only compounds it a hundredfold, for now *tāntrika* seems to be a generic term referring not just to what we today think of as Tantra, but to *all* non-Vedic texts that claim revealed status. So we are left wondering how to distinguish Tantra as a category apart from any other Indian literature that claims an extra-Vedic origin and authority.

Some of the Purāṇas also use the *vaidika/tāntrika* distinction to describe the primary ways of worshiping of the deity, in accordance with different social and spiritual types (see BP 11.3.47). According to the *Padma Purāṇa, vaidika* worship is prescribed for Brahmans and the other twice-born classes, while *tāntrika* offers even lowly *śūdra*s a way to worship God: "The worship of Viṣṇu is of three kinds: as laid down in the Vedas, as laid down in the Tantras, and mixed. The *vaidika* or the mixed one is laid down for *brāhmaṇa*s and others. The *tāntrika* is enjoined for even a *śūdra* who is Viṣṇu's devotee."[85] Yet quite strikingly, these texts *do not* associate *tāntrika* with any of the sexy, scandalous, or transgressive practices that we associate with the term; nor do they identify *tāntrika* worship with those deviant sects—such as the Kāpālikas, Pāśupatas, and Vāmas—who are, elsewhere in the Purāṇas, vilified as dangerous and deluded cults, and who are typically identified by modern scholars as quintessential *tāntrika*s.

Continuing the Search: Tantra and the First Texts Called Tantras

> Since it is unalterably present, like the sky (in everything) beginning with sentient beings and ending with Buddhas, it is termed "Tantra as actuality" because of its continuousness.
>
> Padma dkar-po (trans. Guenther, *The Tantric View of Life*)

> As for the smile, the gaze, the embrace, and the union, even by the *tantra*s the secret language of these four is not mentioned.
>
> *Hevajra Tantra* (HT 2.3.53–54)

Given the incredible semantic polyvalence of the term *tantra* in Sanskrit literature, we might wonder if we can find any clearer definition of the term within the *tantra*s themselves. There is of course a vast body of texts called *tantra*s, as well as related texts called *yāmala*s, *āgama*s, *nigama*s, and *saṃhitā*s, which spread throughout the Hindu, Jain, and Buddhist communities over the past twelve hundred years. The Tibetan canon, for example, preserves almost five hundred such texts, along with over two thousand commentaries and interpretive works. Within the Hindu tradition, we find *tantra*s composed by the Vaiṣṇava Pāñcarātra school, the lost *tantra*s of the Sauras, as well as the more famous *tantra*s of the Śaivites and Śāktas. *Tantra*s are found in more or less every corner of the subcontinent, with powerful strongholds in the northeast (Bengal, Orissa, and Assam) and the northwest (Kashmir), and later spreading to the far south (Tamilnadu and Kerala). Buddhist *tantra*s would eventually spread not only throughout India, but also to Nepal, Tibet, China, Japan, and parts of Southeast Asia.[86]

Yet precisely when or where these texts emerged is largely a mystery. In fact, we cannot find any concrete reference to Hindu texts called *tantra*s until the ninth century, at the earliest; the *tantra*s are nowhere mentioned in the *Mahābhārata,* which claims that there is nothing in the world that is not contained within it; nor do any of the early Chinese pilgrims to India make any reference to the *tantra*s. Even more striking is the fact that none of the great compendiums of Indian philosophical systems—such as Mādhava's *Sarvadarśanasaṃgraha* (fourteenth century) or the

Sarvasiddhāntasaṃgraha—contains any section on Tantra, even though they *do* contain discussions of specific traditions such as *āgama, pratyabhijñā,* and so on.[87]

The earliest known reference to texts called *tantra*s seems to lie in Bāṇabhaṭṭa's classic fantasy tale, *Kādambarī* (seventh century), where we meet a strange, crazy, and rather comical old *sādhu* (holy man) from South India, who "had a collection of palm-leaf manuscripts, *tantra*s and mantras." Yet we are told virtually nothing about these manuscripts, nor is it clear exactly what *tantra* means in this context.[88] Thus, as Gupta and Goudriaan admit, "the existence of the Hindu Tantras cannot as yet be proved for the period before 800," when we find the oldest epigraphic mention of specific *tantra*s. According to an inscription of Sdok kak Thom in Cambodia, at the beginning of the ninth century (802?), King Jayavarman II's court priest Śivakaivalya installed a royal cult based on the doctrine of four *tantra*s brought from elsewhere. Of these texts, named as the *Śirascheda, Nayottara, Sammohana,* and *Vīṇāśikha Tantra*s, only the last survives.[89]

There has also been a long, heated, and never resolved debate over the question of the primacy of Hindu or Buddhist Tantra. Scholars on both sides have argued fiercely for either a Buddhist or Hindu basis for Tantra, with some arguing for Vedic origins and others for inherently non-Vedic roots within the Buddhist tradition.[90] But in any case, it seems likely that the oldest known texts called *tantra*s are the Buddhist *Guhyasāmaja Tantra* and *Hevajra Tantra.* The older of these, the *Guhyasamāja,* has been dated anywhere from the third to the eighth century.[91] Even here, however, the use of the term *tantra* is by no means either clear or particularly helpful in understanding the category of "Tantrism."[92]

In one terse and cryptic passage, we are told that *tantra* can be defined as *prabandha.* This term *prabandha,* in turn, is one that carries a wide range of meanings, denoting everything from a "ligament" to a "poetic composition"; but here it seems to mean something like "continuity" or "continuous series." And this continuous series consists of three things: "*Tantra* is explained as 'continuity'; that continuity is threefold, divided into Ground *[ādhāra],* Nature *[prakṛti],* and Inviolability *[asaṃhārya].* Nature is the Cause; Inviolability is the Fruit; and Ground is the Means—thus the threefold meaning of *tantra*" (GST 18.34–35).[93] According to the interpretations of later Tibetan commentators, the threefold "continuous series" here is the progress of the initiate along the path to *nirvāṇa.* It is the path that leads from the unenlightened state, through the means of spiritual practice, to the fruit of awakening or Vajradhāra ("diamond bearer"): "The Tantra shows the continuous progress of a candidate (Tantra of Cause) along the Tantric Path (Tantra of Means) to the high goal of Vajradhāra (Tantra of Fruit)."[94] Tantra thus seems to be the "thread of continuity" that carries the disciple along the path from ignorance to liberation.

When we turn to the second early Buddhist *tantra,* the *Hevajra,* which probably reached its final form by the eighth century, we find other occasional uses of the term *tantra.* Indeed, the *Hevajra* itself claims to be the revelation of the inner core of all the *tantras*—"That which is concealed in all the *tantras* is here finally made manifest" (HT 2.5.66), now revealed by Lord Buddha as the heart of all the most esoteric practices: "Then the adamantine Lord spoke to the *yoginīs* of the Means, which are the basis of all *tantras [sarvatantranidānam],* of the Union, of consecrations, and of secret language, of the different Joys and moments, of feasting and the rest" (HT 2.3.1). Yet it seems clear that in both the *Guhyasamāja* and in the *Hevajra, tantra* is not used to refer to a unique religious movement or overarching category; it simply refers to a kind of text, and thus to one of the many elements that comprise the path to liberation, neither more nor less important than the other meditations, rites, or initiations.[95]

In general, it would seem that the term *tantra* is not the one most often used in Buddhist literature; much more common are the terms Vajrayāna (diamond or thunderbolt vehicle) or Mantrayāna (mantra vehicle), which designate a new spiritual path, going beyond both the Hīnayāna (lesser vehicle) and the Mahāyāna (great vehicle) (GST 5). Yet even these are by no means easily defined terms. As Dasgupta comments, all we get from the Buddhist literature are "mere cursory descriptions, none of which suggests any correct definition of Vajrayāna. In fact, Vajrayāna cannot be defined; for it incorporated so many heterogeneous elements that any attempt at strict definition would be futile."[96]

Eventually, the Vajrayāna Buddhists would elaborate a hierarchical classification of texts into four kinds of *tantras.* This is often traced back to one cryptic passage in the *Hevajra Tantra,* which speaks in very elusive terms of the four gestures—the "smile," "gaze," "embrace," and "union"—which are said to be even more secret than all the *tantras:* "What may be said of the secret language, that great convention of the *yoginīs,* which the *śrāvakas* (disciples) and others cannot unriddle? . . . As for the smile, the gaze, the embrace, and the union, even by the *tantras* the secret language of these four is not mentioned" (HT 2.3.53–54).

Although it is by no means clear what the precise meaning of this verse might be, it had become common by the time of the great Tibetan theologian and founder of the dGe lugs pa school, Tsong-ka-pa (1357–1419), to associate these enigmatic "gestures" with four classes of *tantras*. Thus we have a progression of *kriyā* (action), *caryā* (practice), *yoga,* and *anuttara-yoga* (supreme yoga) *tantras*, revealed through a series of increasingly esoteric consecrations. However, as Tucci points out, this well-known fourfold division of the dGe lug school was by no means the only way of carving up the vast body of Vajrayāna literature; rather, there were a variety of fourfold, fivefold, sixfold, and other divisions common in different schools.[97]

In sum, it would seem that the Buddhist literature provides us neither with a clear definition of *tantra* nor with a simple or consistent classification of all the many texts called *tantras*. As Lopez concludes in his own insightful deconstruction of the term in the Buddhist tradition, *tantra* perhaps cannot be understood as any kind of substantive, unified category by itself; rather, it seems to function in a contrastive relation to the term *sūtra*. The path of the *tantras* is thus a kind of "supplement" to the path of the *sūtras*, just as the Vajrayāna imagines itself to be the supplement to the Hīnayāna and Mahāyāna traditions.[98]

Spreading the Knowledge That Saves: Tantra in the Hindu Tantras

A *tantra* always spreads and saves . . .
[tanute trāyate nityaṃ tantramithaṃ . . .]

Piṅgalāmata (1174)

It should be carefully kept secret, this essence of the *tantras* which is difficult to obtain *[gopitavyaṃ prayatnena tantrasāraṃ sudurlabham]*.

Vīṇāśikhatantra (VST 312)

When we turn to the Hindu tradition, we find little help in discerning a clear or simple definition of *tantra.* It is true, of course, that many Hindu texts do speak of the "essence of the *tantras*" *(tantrasāra),* the "essential meaning discussed in the *tantras*" *(tantrapratipādyam arthatattvaṃ),* and the "established truth of the *tantras*" *(tantra-siddhānta)* (NUT 1.1; VST 100). Yet one is hard pressed to find any clear definition of *tantra* in these texts, much less any notion of larger movement or tradition conceived as "Tantrism."

The Vaiṣṇava Pāñcarātra tradition, for example, produced a large body of esoteric ritual and philosophical texts beginning around the fifth century. As F. Otto Schrader points out, the Pāñcarātras use *tantra* interchangeably with the more common term *saṃhitā* to refer to particular compositions; both terms, moreover, are used rather generically to refer to "the main topics of a philosophical or religious system"; for example, "Pāśa Tantra," meaning the Pāśupata school of Śaivism. Thus the Pāñcarātra text *Ahirbudhnya Saṃhitā* (AS 60.20) describes itself as *tantrasāra,* which Schrader renders simply as "the essence of philosophy."[99]

Many later texts of the Śaiva and Śākta schools do give us occasional hints as to possible definitions of the term *tantra*. According to one often-cited definition that appears in the *Kāmika Āgama,* "It is called '*tantra*' because it promulgates great knowledge concerning Truth and *mantra,* and because it saves *[tanoti vipulān arthāṃs tattvamantrasamāśritān/trāṇaṃca kurute yasmāt tantram ityabhidhīyate].*"[100] Other texts, such as the *Svacchanda Tantra,* also give some partial definition of the adjective *tāntrika*. For example, one who pursues the *tāntrika* method or way *(tāntriko nyāyah)* is described as follows: "He by whom the senses are conquered and whose mind is fixed . . . he whose intellect is still with regard to his own affairs or those of others . . . this, in short, is said to be the *tāntrika* method" (SvT 10.71–73). The *Niruttara Tantra* also uses the *vaidika/tāntrika* distinction to contrast the consecration ceremony of kings with that of the truly wise *(jñānins*). Whereas royal consecration is based on Vedic injunctions, the esoteric consecration of truer knowers is concealed in the *tantras*. "The consecration of kings follows the *vaidika* procedures; but the consecration of the truly wise is hidden within all the *tantras*. The wise perform the consecration by preparing the *kula cakra*" (NUT 7.2–3). Yet none of these definitions indicates that these authors think of themselves as belonging to a particular school, movement, or religious tradition called "Tantrism." And the definitions they provide of *tantra,* as a text which spreads knowledge and saves, or *tāntrika,* as a method based on conquering the senses and stilling the mind, do little to distinguish this from any other yogic path aimed at spiritual liberation.

However, if the authors of the *tantras* don't seem to think of themselves as belonging to a "Tantric tradition" or to Tantrism as a distinct movement, they *do* think of themselves as belonging to *other* sorts of traditions and lineages: that is, they describe themselves as Śākta (worshipers of

Śakti), Śaiva (worshipers of Śiva), Krama (literally, "gradation," "method," or "way"), or Trika ("triadic"), but not typically as "Tantric." Among the most important of these schools is the Kula, which is often identified with the semimythical Siddha Matsyendranāth (see TA 29.32).[101] Thus the classic *Kulārṇava Tantra,* one of the most influential *tantra*s of the medieval period, speaks frequently of the *kula* path *(kulamārga), kula* dharma, *kula* scriptures *(kulaśāstra),* and "Kaula" is used as a substantive noun for the tradition as a whole (KT 1.119, 12.43, 2.23, 11.98). In several places we find a hierarchy of schools, ascending from the Vedic, to the Vaiṣṇava, to the Śaiva, to the highest path of Kaula:

> Vedic worship is greater than all others. But greater than that is Vaiṣṇava worship; and greater than that is Śaiva worship; and greater than that is Dakṣiṇācāra. Greater than Dakṣiṇācāra is Vāmācāra; and greater than Vāma is Siddhānta; greater than Siddhānta is Kaula—and there is none superior to Kaula. Devī, this Kula is more secret than secret, more essential than the essence, greater than the supreme, given directly by Śiva, proceeding from ear to ear. (KT 2.4–9; cf. NUT 1.13, 1.25)[102]

Yet nowhere here do we find "Tantrism" imagined as a coherent movement or school.

Many later works would eventually attempt to construct some sort of classificatory schema in order to organize all of the various literature proliferating under the titles of *āgama, nigama, tantra, yāmala,* and so on. Thus, we find a number of varying lists of the major texts: for example, the *Navamīsiṃha* mentions forty-nine *tantra*s, seventeen *saṃhitā*s, eight *yāmala*s, four *cūḍāmaṇi*s, three *pāñcarātra*s, and more. However, probably the most common way of carving up the vast territory covered by these various traditions is the threefold division into *saṃhitā, āgama,* and *tantra.* Thus the *saṃhitā*s of the Pāñcarātra school are traditionally said to be 108 in number, the *āgama*s of the Śaivas said to be 28, and the usual number for the *tantra*s is held to be 64 (VST 9). Yet there is significant disagreement as to precisely which texts belong among these *tantras*.[103] Such formalized lists of texts are quite common in Hindu literature, and can also be seen in the enumerations of the principle Upaniṣads or the lists of the eighteen major Purāṇas.[104] However, as Woodroffe pointed out, this by no means indicates existence of a distinct religious movement or tradition; no one, for example, would use a term like "Purāṇism" to describe the wide range of philosophical systems and devotional traditions covered in the vast body of literature called Purāṇas.

The Essence of the Tantras? *Abhinavagupta and the Kashmir School*

Just as stars, remaining in the clouds, do not shine in the sunlight, so too the *tantra*s of the *siddhānta*s do not shine in the *kula āgama [siddhāntatantrāṇi na vibhānti kulāgame].*

Jayaratha (TAV 1.6)

Perhaps the most logical place to look for some kind of coherent internal definition of Tantra would be in the work of the great theologians and systematizers, such as the later Bengali Śākta digests[105] or the works of Kashmir Śaivite school. Foremost among these are the works of the monumental Kashmiri philosopher and aesthetician Abhinavagupta (ca. 950–1050). In his classic works, the *Tantrāloka* (Light on the *tantra*s) and *Tantrasāra* (Essence of the *tantra*s), Abhinava sought to create a grand synthesis and hierarchical ordering of all the known schools of Śaivism, ultimately placing his own school of the Trika (Triad) at the summit, as their culminating goal. Thus we find a gradation of the orthodox Śaiva Siddhānta and Āgamic Śaivisim, followed by the left- and right-hand paths (Vāma and Dakṣiṇa), and then the schools of the Mata, the Kula, and finally the Trika: "The essence of all the *tantra*s, present in the right and left traditions, which has been unified in the Kaula, [is to be discovered] in the Trika" (TA 37.26).[106] This is perhaps the closest we come to an idea of "Tantra" as a singular, comprehensive category that embraces most of the traditions that we now identify by the term.

In other places, however, Abhinava uses the term *tantra* very differently. According to his commentator, Jayaratha, all the many schools covered in the *Tantrāloka* can be divided into two main groups: the *tantraprakriyā* (tantra method or mode) and the *kulaprakriyā.* In fact, he suggests that the *kula* is actually a higher path than the *tantra* (see TAV 1.6). Here *tantra* is used to refer primarily to the more conservative monistic Śaiva tradition, while *kula* is used for the more radical, transgressive, and antinomian tradition, which tend toward the extremes of sexual and amoral activities: "the [Tantra] prohibits the following of the religious practices such as the worship of the external phallic form, keeping of matted hair, visiting sacred places, etc., but the [Kula] allows perfect freedom in regard to them."[107] Yet strangely, despite his otherwise meticulous analysis of terms and categories, Abhinavagupta nowhere appears to state any clear definition of *tantra.* As Rastogi observes, "It is disquieting to see that Abhinava, even though subjecting his observations to the minutest analysis, nowhere mentions 'his' conception of *Tantra-Prakriyā* in contrast with *Kula Prakriyā*. It remains for his students to make their own conclusion."[108] There are, to be sure, a few places where Abhinavagupta offers brief passing glosses on the meaning of *tantra;* yet as Rastogi concludes, these are really quite vague and do little to help us distinguish Tantra from any other of the other main Śaiva schools:

> Such descriptions fail to enlighten us about the precise nature and subject matter of *tantra*. . . . "Unswerving mind control and controlled senses—these two things are said to constitute the essential features of the *tantras*" (SvT 10.71–72). . . . This is all that we find expressly mentioned in the essentials of Tantric culture. But this, too, does not give us insight into the bases of the Tantric way of thinking.[109]

Later commentators, such as Kṣemarāja, attempted to resolve these apparent contradictions and confusions in Abhinava's work by trying to differentiate, organize, and hierarchize the various schools of *tantra, krama, kula, trika,* and so on, in a somewhat clearer way. Yet interestingly enough, for Kṣemarāja, *tantra* actually becomes an inferior and limited position that is ultimately surpassed by both the *kula* and the *trika* philosophies: "The *tāntrika*s say the Self-Essence is transcendent; those who adhere to the *kula* tradition say it is immanent; but the followers of the *trika* philosophy hold it to be both transcendent and immanent."[110] In short, for Abhinavagupta and his followers *tantra* is neither a clear, consistent category nor one that is applied generically to a larger body of traditions conceived as "Tantrism." Its meaning is not only ambiguous, but also often defined as an inferior or limited spiritual path—as Padoux puts it, one that is "more general, more exoteric, shall we say less 'tantric'?"[111]

*Texts of Delusion to Protect the Deluded: Perceptions of Tantra by Non-*Tāntrikas

> There are various non-Vedic texts in the world, such as the Vāma, Kāpālika, and Bhairavāgama. They were expounded by Śiva for the sake of delusion and have no other cause. They were taught because of the curses of Dakṣa, Bṛghu, and Dadhica.
>
> *Devībhāgavata Purāṇa* (7.39.26 ff.)

One of the most insightful ways to try gain an understanding of any religious concept or tradition—particularly one as elusive as *tantra*—is to examine the ways in which nonmembers and critics of the tradition have viewed it. How, in other words, has it been negatively defined by its opponents? Yet even here, we are left at something of a loss, since there is no recorded reference even to texts called *tantra*s until the seventh or eighth century; and there is no reference to Tantrism as a distinct tradition in any Indian literature prior to the modern era. What we *do* find, however, is a large number of interesting descriptions of various *sects* and *individuals,* who would much later come to classified as "Tantric."

Perhaps the earliest reference to such groups is a passage from a fourth century C.E. portion of the *Mahābhārata* (12.335.40), which names the Pāśupatas and the Pāñcarātras as "non-Vedic." However, far more colorful and vivid descriptions appear in the Purāṇas, which often identify Śiva as the founder of specifically non-Vedic and transgressive sects, such as the Kāpālikas, Pāśupatas, and Vāmas. According to the *Kūrma Purāṇa,* for example, Śiva is said to have taught these false and heretical non-Vedic paths in order to help save certain individuals from still *worse* heresies by which they had been deluded. Assuming his terrible form, covered in ashes and adorned with skulls, Śiva revealed the Kāpālika, Vāma, Pāśupata, and other texts as lures to attract certain people away from even more dangerous teachings, using them as stepping stones to lead them ultimately back to the Vedas:

> When Viṣṇu learned that Gautama had cursed the sages to be outside the pale of the Vedas he went to Śiva and said, "There is not even a drop of merit in a man who is beyond the Vedas. Nevertheless . . . we must protect them. . . . Let us make texts of delusion to protect and delude the evil ones beyond the Vedas." Śiva agreed and they made the Kāpāla, Pāśupata, Vāma and other texts. . . . Śiva descended to earth . . . and begged for alms from those who were outcaste, deluding them as he came . . . saying you will go to hell, but then you will be reborn and gradually work your way to the place of merit.[112]

A similar narrative appears in the *Bhāgavata Purāṇa* which tells us that the non-Vedic, antinomian Śaivite sects were created as a kind of spiritual antidote to the teachings of the Buddha. Because of the Buddha's austere teachings about suffering and renunciation, the story goes, so many people had become monks that civilization and government had ground to a halt. Thus, in order to counteract this excessive austerity and set the world back on its proper course, "Lord Śiva taught the path of indulgence in wine, meat and sex. Let the foolish and impure men who wear long hair, apply ashes and carry bones be admitted in the *Śiva-dīkṣā* in which intoxicating drink is held sacred" (BP 4.2.2).

Finally, as we will see in more detail in chapter 3, there are also many lively and often quite hilarious descriptions of these non-Vedic sects in Sanskrit drama and fiction. For example, the *Mattavilāsa*, a comic farce attributed to the Pallava ruler Mahendra-varman (ruled 600–630 C.E.), centers around a drunken Kāpālika named Satyasoma. Primarily interested in alcohol and sex, Satyasoma describes the liquor shop as a kind of sacred space, comparable to the sacrificial enclosure, and the liquor to the sacred Soma beverage of the Vedic rite. As he indulges all the senses, he sings, "Drink up to intoxication, Look deep into your lover's eyes, Wear fancy clothes from every nation."[113] Bāṇabhaṭṭa's famous Sanskrit tale *Kādambarī* contains an equally amusing description of a demented old ascetic whom some have identified as very "Tantric" in appearance. A devotee of the goddess Caṇḍīkā, he is parodied for his useless magical charms and his hypocritical attitudes toward sex: "Though he had taken a vow of celibacy he often threw powder that was thought to make women sexually active on the old female ascetics who had come from foreign lands. . . . Not being refined, he did whatever he pleased."[114]

Yet as vivid and entertaining as these accounts are, they nowhere speak of Tantra as a distinct sect, school, or religious tradition. While they clearly conceive of Kāpālikas, Pāśupatas, and other extreme groups as distinct traditions, they do not identify them as *tāntrika* (even though, as we have seen, the Purāṇas and other texts *do* identify *other* non-Vedic forms of worship as *tāntrika*); nor does there appear to be any concept of Tantrism as a singular tradition in the early Indian imagination.

Black Magic and Fulfillment of All Desires: Tantra in the Indian Popular Imagination

> With the help of the *mantras* and *yantras* written in this book, you can perform many un-do-able deeds. Not only will you turn your hard times into good times, but you will attain the sight of hidden wealth, prosperity in business, victory in litigation . . . the quick marriage of sons and daughters . . . healing illness, success in exams, the six acts of immobilization, killing, etc."
>
> Śrī Brahmānanda, *Sarvva Manaskāmanā Siddhi Pustaka*

All of the sources discussed thus far have been Sanskrit texts—and hence primarily the domain of well-educated, upper-class men, generally Brahmans. However, one finds a rather different, often neglected, yet no less important perspective on *tantra* when one looks to the living vernacular languages of India, the "mother tongues," as opposed to the patriarchal and typically elitist tongue of Sanskrit.[115] One often need only mention the word *tantra* to many Indians (as I did to my Bengali teacher in Calcutta) to elicit responses of "ooph!" "Mā go!" (literally, "Oh, mother!" used as an emphatic expression) and a clucking of tongues. In most vernacular languages today, the term *tantra* is typically associated with a whole range of intense associations, usually relating to the darker realms of the magical, the immoral (sometimes the illegal), and the occult. "The word 'Tantra' in vernacular languages . . . is frequently used to conjure notions of black magic, illicit sexuality, and immoral behavior. It is also clear . . . that Tantrics are considered 'powerful' people."[116]

In the case of modern Bengal, for example, *tantra* has come to carry particularly dark and nefarious implications. For the great Bengali saint and national hero Sri Ramakrishna, for example, Tantra was something fraught with an aura of danger and power, surrounded by "shame, disgust, and fear," and considered at once a very rapid but also rather seedy and scandalous path to liberation. "Everything they do is a secret," Ramakrishna declares, for "that which in the Vedas . . . is said, 'Don't do this, this shouldn't be done,' in the Tantras is called good."[117] In my own research in Bengal, I encountered a similar attitude toward the dark, frightening world of Tantra. In my exploration of the Kartābhajā sect, which emerged in the Calcutta area at the turn of the nineteenth century, I found that Tantra is consistently associated with moral depravity, criminal behavior, and illicit sexual practices such as *parakīyā* love, or intercourse with another man's wife. By the late nineteenth century, the Kartābhajās had become a kind of laughingstock throughout Calcutta society, attacked as a degenerate Tantric sect and widely satirized for their fraud, trickery, and licentiousness. As the satirist Dāśarathī Rāy parodied them in his humorous poem "Kartābhajā,"

> They have a separate *tantra;* abandoning the *mantra*s of all other gods,
> they are initiated by a human *mantra.*
> Religion is mixed up with all irreligion;
> they turn every deed into the enjoyment of sensual pleasure.
> In all their teachings there is deception and fraud.[118]

Even today, this mysterious and scandalous notion of Tantra survives in the Indian popular imagination. During a recent trip through north India, I happened to pick up a colorful Hindi book at a roadside stall, entitled *Śābara Tantra Mantra Śāstra,* whose cover shows a black-robed figure holding a flaming skull. Seeing the book in my hands, a curious

Figure 4. Billboard for *Shaitan Tantrik,* directed by A. Kumar. Photo by the author (Cuttack, Orissa, January 2000).

passerby smiled knowingly at me and exclaimed, "Ooh! Śaitān indrajāl! [Satanic black magic]." In January 2000, I saw a film playing in Orissan theaters, entitled *Shaitan Tantrik,* starring a ghoulish and grinning, fat, bald Tantric priest whose main goal is to abduct beautiful women in order to perform human sacrifice and other nefarious rites (see figure 4). The poster advertising the film depicts the villainous Tantric priest surrounded by young maidens whom he carries away to sacrifice to the bloodthirsty goddess Kālī. In sum, if *tantra* in the Sanskrit texts simply means a particular treatise that "spreads knowledge and saves," *tantra* in the popular imagination means something quite different indeed—a frightening, dangerous path that leads to this-worldly power and control over the occult forces on the dark side of reality.

From Tantric Sects to Tantric Sex: Is Tantra Really All That "Sexy"?

Sexual union is the libation; the sacred precept is the shedding of semen. . . . The pleasure derived from sexual union is of the nature of the Supreme Bliss.

Kṛṣṇānanda Āgamavāgīśa, *Bṛhat-Tantrasāra* (sixteenth century)

> Most of you [in America] . . . believe that the sexual element in Tantra is somewhat *nice* and *romantic* and lovely and full of nice warm love-making. Nonsense. The sex of Tantra is hard-hitting, object-using manipulative ritual without any consideration for the other person involved.
>
> Agehananda Bharati,
> "The Future (if Any) of Tantrism" (1975)

If it is true that there is no singular monolithic category of "Tantrism" prior to the modern period, but only a wide array of specific historical texts called *tantra*s, which in turn contain different and conflicting definitions of *tantra,* the next question then becomes: do these texts really contain any of the scandalous, sexy, and transgressive materials that we today associate with the category of "Tantra"?

The short answer to this question is: yes, of course they do. Many *tantra*s do indeed contain explicit descriptions of sexual rituals, the manipulation of sexual fluids, consumption of wine and meat, and other transgressive practices (such as the infamous five M's, or five forbidden substances of meat *[māṃsa],* fish *[matsya],* wine *[madya],* parched grain *[mudrā],* and sexual intercourse *[maithuna]*). "No one succeeds in attaining perfection by employing difficult and vexing operations; but perfection can be gained by satisfying all one's desires," as the *Guhyasamāja* puts it (GST 7.3). In the Hindu *tantra*s, the union of the male and female is commonly used as the supreme symbol of the eternal union of Śiva and Śakti, the primordial masculine and feminine, passive and active principles that lie at the foundation of all reality (see TA 29.110–11).[119] For the Buddhist *tantra*s, conversely, this union typically symbolizes the wedding of the passive wisdom *(prajñā)* and the active skill-in-means *(upāya),* which together are the essence of perfect liberation. In some cases, at least, this union is to be performed physically, through actual intercourse between male and female practitioners in a ritual context. As the *Kulārṇava Tantra* puts it, in fairly explicit terms, "Without thousands of pots of liquor, without hundreds of heaps of meat, and without the nectar of the vulva and penis, O Beautiful-Hipped One, I will not be pleased" (KT 8.107), and "The union of Śiva and Śakti by which procreation occurs, O Kālī, is the union of the *kula*-devotees; that is considered to be *samādhi*" (KT 8.109).

The longer and more accurate answer to this question, however, is that the meaning, role, and significance of these sexual practices is neither consistent throughout the *tantra*s nor anything like what most contemporary Western readers imagine them to be. As David Gordon White observes, sexual rituals clearly play an important role in many Tantric traditions from an early date; yet the interpretation of these rites has often been grossly misunderstood by Western authors, scholarly and popular alike. Moreover, there is tremendous difference of opinion within the *tantras* themselves as to precisely how such practices are to be performed and how they are to be interpreted. Within both the Hindu and Buddhist traditions, here has been a long and tangled debate over the question of whether sexual imagery in the *tantras* should be taken literally—as actual physical intercourse between males and females—or purely symbolically—as an internalized, spiritual union between the male and female principles of creation.[120]

Even in those traditions that do advocate a literal interpretation of sexual rites, there is enormous difference of opinion as to how and why such acts should be performed. The *tantras* disagree intensely over the most fundamental questions: Should the semen be ejaculated into the female body at the moment of orgasm? Or should it be sublimated and withdrawn upward into the male body?[121] Is the pleasure of orgasm something accidental to the ritual? Or is it the very essence of the act, as the manifestation of the supreme bliss of divine Consciousness?[122] What is the role of the sexual fluids? Are they to be manipulated physically and consumed by the practitioners as a sacramental meal? Or are they to be internalized and transformed into some nonphysical essence?[123] And what is the role of the female in all of this? Is she a necessary partner, who also achieves spiritual power from the union? Or is she a mere tool to be used by the male and then cast aside? ("What about the woman?" Bharati pointedly asks, "That's the most embarrassing question you can ask any Tantric").[124] There is no clear consensus on any of these questions, either within the *tantras* or among contemporary scholars. While for some, sex in its most literal sense lies at the heart of the *tantras*, for others, it is something that is only symbolic, secondary to the true essence of Tantra, which is philosophical, spiritual, and nonphysical.

Ultimately, anyone who wades through a few Sanskrit *tantras* soon realizes that, even when they do contain descriptions of sexual acts, they are usually buried beneath hundreds of pages of rather dull ritual details; typically, they are cast in terms that most modern readers would probably find disappointingly brief, general, and often quite "unsexy." "There is nothing glamorous about Tantric sexual intercourse," Feuerstein concludes.[125] As I will argue in what follows, the popular image of Tantra as something seedy, scandalous, and sexy is largely a creation of the modern age: it is the complex result of the demonization of Tantra by Orientalist authors and indigenous reformers, combined with the exoticization and sensationalization of Tantra in the modern popular imagination.

THE TANGLED THREADS OF TANTRA

I know the finely drawn thread on which all creatures are woven; I know the thread of that very thread; therefore, I know the great *brahman*.

Atharva Veda (AV 10.8.38)

. . . the strength of the thread does not reside in the fact that some one thread runs though its whole length . . .

Wittgenstein, *Philosophical Investigations*

What we have found in our brief genealogy of the term *tantra* in Indian literature is by no means the consistent linear narrative of the evolution of a coherent religious movement. Rather, it is the ongoing construction and reconstruction, deployment and redeployment of the "floating signifier" of *tantra* in a wide variety of historical contexts. As authors like Woodroffe and Snellgrove long ago pointed out, it makes little more sense to speak of "Tantrism" as a singular category of Asian religion than it does to speak of "Purāṇism," "Sūtra-ism," or "Textism," for that matter.[126] As such, the imagining of "Tantrism" is similar to the category of "mysticism" in the West, as described by recent authors like Grace Jantzen and Richard King. As Jantzen observes, the monolithic and ambiguous category of mysticism has been imagined in different ways in relation to different social, political, and spiritual interests over the last several hundred years, and it continues to be redefined in our own era: "The idea of mysticism is a social construction and . . . it has been constructed in different ways at different times. . . . The current philosophical construction of mysticism is therefore only one in a series of social constructions of mysticism, and like the others, is implicitly bound up with issues of authority and gender."[127]

So the question becomes: how are we to usefully describe the many texts and traditions that are now commonly lumped under the heading of Tantrism? Should we abandon the term altogether and substitute some other term or perhaps a series of terms (e.g., simply refer to the Śākta, Kaula, Trika, Vajrayāna, and other individual schools)? I will save a more complete statement of my own suggestions for a reimagining of Tantra in contemporary discourse for the conclusion of this book. For the time being, however, let it suffice to say that Tantra is perhaps best understood not as a unified or coherent movement; rather, in keeping with the etymology of the term, it is better understood using Wittgenstein's analogy of the thread, which he employs to explain the complex way in which all of our abstract concepts are formed. None of our concepts, such as "language" or "number," can be defined by the presence of a single unifying feature that runs through all languages and all numbers; rather they are comprised of many distinct fibers, "a complicated network of similarities overlapping and crisscrossing, sometimes overall similarities, sometimes similarities of detail," which are interwoven "as in spinning a thread we twist fibre by fibre." In contrast to the *Atharva Veda,* quoted above—and perhaps more in agreement with the Buddhist doctrine of *anātman* (no-self)—Wittgenstein sees no central unifying core or "thread of the thread" running through these overlapping fibers:

> The strength of the thread does not reside in the fact that some one thread runs though its whole length, but in the overlapping of many fibres. But if someone wished to say: "there is something common to all these constructions—namely, the disjunction of all their common properties"—I should reply, Now you are only playing with words. One might as well say, "Something runs through the whole thread—namely the continuous overlapping of those fibres."[128]

Similarly, I would argue for an equally decentered and pluralized view of Tantra. Rather than search for some single thread that runs through all the many traditions discussed above, perhaps it would be more useful to think of all of these as many overlapping fibers. This surely not to say that Tantra simply "doesn't exist"; rather, it suggests that it is best seen not as a coherent, unified tradition, but as a fluid and shifting collection of particular texts, practices, and traditions, woven and rewoven with a variety other traditions—not only with other texts called *yāmala, saṃhitā, āgama, nigama,* and so forth, but also with a host of other non-Sanskritic and vernacular texts and traditions. Just as the cosmos itself is "spread out" like the threads on a loom or like the web of a spider, so too Tantra extends like a network of overlapping, often tangled and contradicting threads that stretch throughout the dense fabric of Indian history. Most importantly, the meaning of Tantra is never fixed or singular, but is the complex result of the *encounter between* indigenous traditions and the scholarly imagination—an encounter that has from the beginning been closely tied to specific historical, intellectual, and political interests. But it is also an encounter through which both Indian and Western self-representations are transformed in the imaginal exchange.

CHAPTER I

The Golden Age of the Vedas and the Dark Age of Kālī

Tantrism, Orientalism, and the Bengal Renaissance

> The Tantras [exert] great influence in later days. . . . The worship assumes wild, extravagant forms, generally obscene, sometimes bloody. It is divided into two schools—that of the right and that of the left. The former runs into mysticism and magic in complicated observances, and the latter into the most appalling licentiousness. . . . We cannot go further into detail. It is saddening to think that such abominations are committed; it is still more saddening that they are performed as part of divine worship. Conscience, however, is so far alive that these detestable rites are practiced only in secret.
>
> J. Murray Mitchell and Sir William Muir, *Two Old Faiths* (1891)

> Now look at the trickery of these stupid *popes* that whatever is considered to be highly sinful and opposed to the Veda is regarded as virtuous. . . . The use of meat, wine . . . and copulation are considered as means of attaining salvation.
>
> Swāmī Dayānanda Saraswatī, *The Light of Truth* (1927)

The origins of "Tantra" or "Tantrism" as a scholarly category are ultimately inseparable from the unique historical encounter between Western and Indian imaginations that took place during the colonial era. Tantra as we know it is to a large degree a complex creation of what Mary Louise Pratt calls the "contact zone," that is, "the space of colonial encounters . . . in which peoples geographically and historically separated come into contact with each other . . . involving conditions of coercion, radical inequality and conflict."[1] To reiterate, however: this is surely *not* to say that Tantra is simply a colonialist fabrication or Orientalist projection onto the colonized Other. Rather, it is to say that the colonial era witnessed a clear "trend toward conceiving of a new entity called Tantrism as a specific modality of Indian religious experience,"[2] as the diverse body of texts known as *āgamas*, *nigamas*, *saṃhitās*, *tantras*, and so on, and the vast body of traditions known as Kāpālika, Pāñcarātra, Kula, Krama, Śākta, Śrīvidyā, and others, were gradually assimilated into a singular universal entity.

In this chapter I will examine the earliest discussions of Tantrism as a distinct entity, which appear in European missionary works, Orientalist scholarship, and the early Indian reform movements such as the Brāhmo Samāj and the Ārya Samāj. What we find here is a fairly consistent dichotomy between different conceptions of "Hinduism" and the "Indian mind": at one extreme, the ideal of an ancient, pure, and uncorrupted Golden Age, identified with the Vedas and Upaniṣads, and on the other extreme, the nightmare of a modern, perverse, and degenerate era, embodied in the licentious idolatry of the *tantras*.[3]

Discourse about Tantra, as we will see, was thus bound up with the construction of *Western* cultural identity, and above all with the problem of sexuality and sexual deviance in modern Europe. As early as the romantic era, the "mystic Orient" has been imagined as the exotic world of forbidden sexuality and dark sensuality, in both its most positive and negative forms.[4] However, this fetishization of the sexual, exotic Orient was only continued and intensified during the Victorian era in England. As Foucault has argued, nineteenth-century British men and women were by no means simply the repressed prudes we often imagine them to be; on the contrary, they were in many cases quite fascinated with sexuality, which they discussed in endless detail. Above all, this era witnessed a special fascination with sexuality in its most "deviant," antisocial forms: homosexuality, transvestism, nymphomania, and all manner of newly discovered psychosexual pathologies. The European fascination with Tantra, I will argue, was very much a part of this larger preoccupation with sexuality and its aberrations in the Western imagination. And just as the broader European discourse about sex, as Foucault has shown, was inseparable from larger issues of "biopolitics," population control, and national health, so the discourse about Tantra would become enmeshed in larger biopolitical issues of governance in Europe's colonies.[5]

But at the same time, the discourse surrounding Tantra would also became a key part of the conceptualization of India and "Hinduism."

When deployed by Indian elites and the leaders of the Bengal Renaissance, Tantra would also serve as a critical element in the reformation of Indian religious, cultural, and political identity in the nineteenth century. Indeed, discourse on Tantra became a central element in the narrative of Indian history: namely, the widely accepted narrative of the decline of medieval Hinduism, that it had become corrupted with Tantric immorality, a degeneration that had paved the way for the Muslim (and thereafter, British) conquest. Hence, one of the most necessary tasks in the reassertion of a strong and pure Hinduism would have to be the eradication of modern immorality, idolatry, and debilitating licentiousness, of which Tantra was the most notorious and embarrassing example.

HINDUISM AT ITS LAST AND WORST STAGE OF DEVELOPMENT: "TANTRISM" IN THE ORIENTALIST IMAGINATION

> Tantrism or Śāktism is Hinduism arrived at its last and worst stage of medieval development.
>
> Sir Monier Monier-Williams, *Hinduism* (1894)

> The tenets of the Śāktas open the way for gratification of all the sensual appetites; they hold out encouragement to drunkards, thieves and dacoits; they present the means of satisfying every lustful desire . . . and lead men to commit abominations which place them on a level with the beasts.
>
> "The Śāktas," *Calcutta Review* (1885)

It is probably no accident that the emergence of "Tantrism" as a distinct category of religion occurred at roughly the same time as the emergence of "Hinduism" itself in the Western imagination. Even as European scholars began to construct the abstract entity called Hinduism—itself largely "a Western inspired abstraction which until the nineteenth century bore little resemblance to the diversity of Indian religious belief and practice"[6]—they began to imagine Tantrism as one of its primary, though least admirable, components. As Bernard Cohn suggests, the detailed study and categorization of Indian society was a critical part of the colonizing project. In order to be governed, India had first to be analyzed, statistically evaluated, and categorized: "The conquest of India was a conquest of knowledge. . . . The vast social world that was India had to be classified, categorized and bounded before it could be hierarchized."[7]

Conceived as the quintessential Other of the West, as Ron Inden has persuasively argued, India came to be imagined as an essentially passionate, irrational, and erotic world—a land of "disorderly imagination" set in opposition to the progressive, rational, and scientific world of modern Europe.[8] As the widely read ethnographer Herbert Risley put it, "the Indian intellect has always reveled in the subtleties of a logic which undertakes to reconcile the most manifestly contradictory propositions."[9] At the same time, as Richard King argues, India was also typically imagined as the "mystic East" and the heartland of "mysticism"—the irrational, otherworldly and life-denying flight into transcendental bliss.[10] Tantra formed a critical part of the broader project of imagining India, precisely because Tantra was regarded as the most extreme, irrational embodiment of the worst tendencies in the Indian mind. Above all, we might say that it came to embody "mysticism" in its most dangerous and deviant form—a kind of mysticism that was not simply irrational and otherworldly, but also polluted with sexual desire and thirst for this-worldly power.

This Orientalist imagining of India, however, was neither monolithic nor static; rather, as Thomas Trautmann argues, the Orientalist vision of India underwent several important transformations. In the course of the eighteenth and nineteenth centuries, it gradually shifted from a benign, romantic vision of the kinship between India and Europe, as we find in early Orientalists like Sir William Jones, to an increasingly Indophobic view of barbarism and degeneracy, as we see in the work of James Mill.[11] This was a shift that probably was related closely to a larger change in British attitudes toward Indian culture as a whole, which took place in the first quarter of the nineteenth century. Up to the end of the eighteenth century, as Sumanta Banerjee observes, the British government had generally kept to a policy of nonintervention with regard to indigenous religious and cultural traditions; it was deemed more expedient, for the early leaders of the East India Company, to leave existing religious practices more or less alone and so avoid offending native sensibilities. During the period from 1790–1830, however, the British government began to turn from its original hands-off attitude. Under the influence of Evangelical and Utilitarian ideals in England, the British began active efforts at reform, at once religious, moral, and legal. Particularly in the years after 1813, when the Christian Evangelicals mounted a campaign to begin missionary work, we find growing exhortations to take strict measures against Indian social practices—above all, against infanticide, widow-burning, and "barbaric rituals" such as hook-swinging and animal sacrifice: "The conclusion was . . . that the natives needed to be emancipated socially and culturally."[12]

Tantra would become an important focus of these shifting attitudes toward Indian religions and was quickly singled out as one of the native customs most in need of reform. Both the early romantics and the later Indophobes agreed that the Tantras represented the worst and most decadent era in Indian history, the one furthest removed from the modern West. "The enduring legacy of Orientalism," as Kopf remarks, " is a contrasting set of images: the golden age, which is Indo-Aryan, classical brahminical and elitist versus a dark age which is medieval . . . orgiastic and corrupt."[13]

Yet the actual entry of "Tantrism" into Western discourse as a distinct category is surprisingly late. If we scan the various travelogues of the earliest Europeans to visit India or the first Jesuit missionary accounts, we find no mention of Tantra or anything even closely resembling it. It is true that as early as the eleventh century, Muslim travelers like Alberuni, and later European explorers like Marco Polo, had described various groups of yogis (*ciugi,* as Marco Polo calls them), as well as the alchemical art of *rasayana,* which aims at the goals of longevity and immortality.[14] Yet this is nowhere described as "Tantra." Indeed, up to the end of the eighteenth century, as we see in the works of the earliest British authors in India, such as John Holwell, Alexander Dow, or Nathaniel Halhed, Tantrism had not yet emerged as a distinct category or a definable body of texts.[15] Even James Mill's monument to imperialism, *The History of British India,* makes no mention of the Tantras. Though he does briefly mention the notorious phenomenon of the murderous brigands the "Thuggee," he does not link them to the nefarious practices of Tantrism, as would so many later authors.

The earliest Western references to a body of texts called *tantra*s come from the great Orientalist and pioneer in the study of Indian language Sir William Jones. In his essay "On the Literature of the Hindus" (1790), Jones makes a brief reference to a corpus of literature called *tantra*s, which are generally lumped together with "Mantra, Āgama and Nigama Śāstras," as an appendage to the Vedas, which consist "mainly of incantations."[16] In his essay on the gods of India, Greece, and Rome, Jones also briefly mentions the goddess "Cali" (Kālī), though his vision of the goddess, whom he compares to the goddess Diana "in the splendid opera of Iphigenia," is hardly a very Tantric one.[17]

H. T. Colebrooke—Jones's fellow pioneer Orientalist and Indo-Europeanist—appears to have had a somewhat greater familiarity with various texts called *tantras*, and cites the *Rudrayāmala Tantra, Kālī Tantra, Nirvāṇa Tantra,* and *Vīra Tantra,* among others.[18] However, for Colebrooke the *tantras* are only worth mentioning as the antipode of the Vedas. Whereas the Vedas embody everything that is noble, pure, and admirable in the Hindu tradition, its pristine monotheistic past, the *tantras* embody all the polytheism and idolatry that has corrupted Hinduism in modern times: "Most of what is taught [in the Vedas] is now obsolete; and in its stead . . . rituals founded in the *Purāṇas* and observances borrowed from a *worse* source, the *Tantras,* have . . . [replaced] the Vedas."[19]

Rather significantly, the first detailed discussions of the *tantras* come from Christian missionaries. One of the earliest and most influential of these was the widely read account of the French missionary Abbé Dubois, who worked for some thirty years in India following his ordination in 1792. After the defeat of Tipu Sultan in 1799, the Abbé was invited by Arthur Wellesley to come to Tipu's capital and reconvert the Christian community that had been swayed by Islam. Thereafter, he traveled across India, investigating Indian religious practices and recording them in his manuscript *Hindu Manners, Customs, and Ceremonies* (1807). Like many of his European contemporaries, the Abbé was immediately struck by the licentiousness and sexual explicitness of the Hindu religion; it seemed a lascivious religion aimed at stimulating the passions of an already overly passionate people: "The shameless stories about their deities . . . the religious ceremonies in which the principal part is played by prostitutes . . . all these things seem to be calculated to excite the lewd imagination of the inhabitants."[20] The Abbé also makes it clear that his primary motivation in exposing these perversions is to highlight the grandeur of Christendom, in the hope that "a faithful picture of the wickedness . . . of polytheism and idolatry would by its very ugliness . . . offset the beauties and perfections of Christianity."[21]

Nowhere was the Hindu's tendency toward the passionate and obscene more obvious than in the case of *Śakti-pūjā* or the secret worship of the Goddess as power. Interestingly enough, the Abbé does not identify this practice as "Tantra"; yet his vivid account of this nefarious rite would become a key part of most later European accounts and a key element in the early genealogy of "Tantrism":

> Among the abominable rites practiced in India is one which is only too well known; it called *śakti-pūjā*. . . . The ceremony takes place at night with more or less secrecy. The least disgusting of these orgies are those where they confine themselves to eating and drinking everything that the custom of the

> country forbids and where men and women . . . openly and shamelessly violate the commonest laws of decency. . . . When all the meat has been consumed, intoxicating liquors are passed round, everyone drinking without repugnance from the same cup. . . . When they are all completely intoxicated men and women . . . pass the rest of the night together, giving themselves up to the grossest immorality. . . . [T]he meeting winds up with the most revolting orgy.[22]

Indeed, one could imagine no greater contrast to the "perfection of Christianity" than this riotous orgy of drugs, liquor, gluttony, and sex.

But perhaps the most influential early description of the *tantra*s comes from the energetic Reverend William Ward, one of the leading figures in the spread of the Baptist Missionary Society in Bengal and one of the first Western authors to try to categorize the many diverse sects and castes of the "Hindoos." In Ward's eyes, Hinduism as a whole was "the MOST PUERILE, IMPURE AND BLOODY OF ANY SYSTEM OF IDOLATRY THAT WAS EVER ESTABLISHED ON EARTH," a religion of "idle, effeminate and dissolute people" with "disordered imaginations who frequent their temples for the satisfaction of their licentious appetites"; and the texts called *tuntra*s were the quintessence of this degenerate spirit.[23] Published in 1817, Ward's book recounts the insidious practices described in the *tuntra*s—practices that involve "things too abominable to be revealed to a Christian public" and caused even his Indian informant to blush with shame. In one particularly vivid account, Ward recounts the insidious ritual of the "Chukra" *(cakra),* or "circle" of Tantric worship:

> Many of the *tuntras* . . . contain directions respecting a most . . . shocking mode of worship, which is understood . . . by the name of Chukra. These shastrus direct that the person must, in the night, choose a woman as the object of worship . . . he must take . . . the daughter of a dancer, a kupalee, a washerman, a barber, a chundalu or a Musalman or a prostitute; and place her on a seat . . . and then bring broiled fish, flesh, fried peas, rice, spirituous liquor, sweetmeats, flowers and other offerings. . . . To this succeeds the worship of the . . . female, who sits naked* * * * * *
>
> Here things too abominable to enter the ears of man, and impossible to be revealed to a Christian public, are contained. . . . The learned brahmun who opened to me these abominations made several efforts—paused again, began again . . . before he could mention the shocking indecencies prescribed by his own shastrus. . . .
>
> [The woman] partakes of the offerings, even of the spirituous liquors, and flesh, though it should be that of a cow. The refuse is eaten by the persons present, however different their castes. . . . The priest then . . . behaves towards this female in a manner which decency forbids to be mentioned.[24]

Here we find the key elements that would later become the standard tropes in virtually all later discussion of the Tantras: (1) violation of caste and laws of purity; (2) consumption of normally prohibited substances; and above all, (3) sexual license. In Ward's opinion, the "sensual rites and black magic" of the Tantras were the clearest sign that the Hinduism of his time was indeed at low ebb, having degenerated sadly into immorality and idolatry. "At present, the persons committing these abominations are becoming more and more numerous. . . . They are performed in secret; but that these practices are becoming frequent is a fact known to all."[25]

The next stage in the development of the category begins in the second quarter of the nineteenth century, in the writings of Orientalist scholars such as H. H. Wilson (1786–1860). In Wilson's account of 1828, which would become among the most often cited in the later nineteenth century, a distinct set of texts called the *tantra*s really emerges as a clearly defined and relatively unified body of Indian literature. For Wilson, the *tantra*s are now considered a "*singular category*"; even though "they are infinitely numerous," they are all nonetheless "basically the same," such that a scholar need not read more than one or two *tantra*s to understand this (largely worthless) form of Hindu religion.[26] Like most Orientalist scholars, Wilson laments that the immoral and perverse practices of the *tantra*s are becoming more and more prevalent in his own day, that they "have been carried to more exceptionable extremes in modern times," and are a clear sign of the progressive degeneration of Hinduism in the present era. The "nonsensical extravagance and absurd gesticulations" of Tantric ritual have become "authorities for all that is abominable in the present state of Hindu religion."[27]

However, it is not until the last quarter of the nineteenth century that we find the abstract category of Tantrism as a true "ism," a unified body of beliefs and practices, emerging as a well-defined category in the Orientalist construction of "Hinduism." It was the Sanskritist Sir Monier-Williams who was the first to employ the term "Tantrism" as a singular, monolithic class, which he identifies with "Śaktism," and which he disparages as the most degenerate form of Indian religion: "The system [the Tantras] inculcate . . . for convenience may be called Tantrism or Śaktism. . . . Tantrism is Hinduism arrived at its last and worst stage of medieval development."[28] The classical tradition of the Vedas, Monier-Williams laments, had become, "in the Tantras, exaggerated and perverted," adulterated with "horrible things" such as "sanguinary sacrifices and orgies with wine and women."[29] Much of the Tantras are nothing more than "unmeaning sound," whose aim is to "acquire magical power and destroy one's enemies." As a whole, they may be summarized as mere "witchcraft, which to Europeans appears so ineffably absurd that the possibility of any person believing in it seems itself incredible."[30]

Finally, by the early twentieth century, as we see in histories of India like those of J. N. Farquhar or W. H. Moreland, and in popular works like D. L. Barnett's *Antiquities of India,* Tantrism had become infamous. It is now widely known as a scandalous teaching that makes it a "sacred duty to practice incest," engaging in "black art of the crudest and filthiest kind" in which "a veritable devil's mass is purveyed."[31] According to one of the most vividly imaginative accounts of the early twentieth century, Tantrism has now been conflated into a bizarre mixture of a Black Mass, a Roman Saturnalia, a scene from Dante's *Inferno,* and a Dionysian *sporagmos:*

> Shaktas usually meet in a forest glade where, by the light of a huge bonfire, they begin the ceremony by getting drunk and eating cow's flesh. On these nights everything is permissible; Untouchables jostle Kshatriyas, Brahmans dig knives into the remains of the cow, women come from the from the Zenana and discard their veils. . . . Stretched on the grass with her sari thrown off lies a young girl . . . who must allow herself to be embraced by all the adepts in turn. . . . The culminating act of this abominable orgy is the slaughter of a young man or woman who, while still alive is torn to pieces by frenzied Shaktas. . . . [I]t is priests and Black Magicians who lead the way . . . who promise happiness to these poor deranged people who, groaning and screaming, wallow in the bloodstained mire.[32]

Here we find that all of the darkest fears of colonial rule and all the most perverse fantasies of the Victorian imagination have been combined into a single fantastic image of sex, violence, and the transgression of every imaginable moral law.

The Tantric Parasite and the Degeneration of Buddhism

> With its adoption of Tantrism so-called, Buddhism entered on its most degenerate phase. Here the idolatrous cult of female energies was grafted upon the theistic Mahāyāna. . . . This parasite seized strong hold of its host and soon developed its monstrous growths which crushed and strangled most of the little life yet remaining of purely Buddhist stock.
>
> L. Austine Waddell, *The Buddhism of Tibet* (1895)

Tantra functions as a lamented supplement in the European construction of an original Buddhism.

Donald S. Lopez, Jr., *Elaborations on Emptiness* (1996)

Not only were the foul practices of the Tantras believed to have corrupted the Hindu tradition, causing the great decline from ancient Vedic rationalism to modern polytheism and idolatry, but they were also soon to be blamed for what Orientalists described as the historical degeneration of Buddhism. The dominant Orientalist narrative of Buddhist history is similar to that of the Golden Age of the Vedas described in Hindu studies. It begins with an original, sober, rational, even Socratic Buddhism, which was later progressively corrupted and perverted by various mystical-idolatrous and superstitious accretions. As Eugene Burnouf concluded in 1844, "It is certainly not without interest to see Buddhism, which in its first form had so little of what constitutes a religion, end in practices so puerile and superstitions so exaggerated."[33]

This process of deterioration and decadence, it was believed, had already begun with the rise of the Mahāyāna tradition, with all its celestial bodhisattvas, elaborate ritual, and theological speculation; and it would reach its final stage of perversion with the entry of the seemingly "un-Buddhist" Tantric influence. Running throughout the early discourse on Buddhism, the dominant metaphor is that of a disease or parasite, which somehow infected the Buddhist organism in India. As the widely read Tibetologist L. Austine Waddell recounts this narrative,

> About the end of the sixth century, Tantrism or Shivaic mysticism with its worship of female energies . . . began to tinge both Buddhism and Hinduism. Consorts were allotted to Celestial Bodhisatts . . . most of them were wild and terrible, and often monstrous. . . . Such was the distorted form of Buddhism introduced into Tibet about 640, and during the succeeding centuries Buddhism became still more debased.[34]

This theory of the decline of Buddhism was soon combined with the scholarly and popular imaginings about the mysterious, forbidden, inaccessible land of Tibet, the heartland of Buddhist Tantrism. Waddell describes the awesome strangeness of the land and its religion, which lies swathed in "barbaric darkness": "Tibet, the mystic Land of the Grand Lama, joint God and king of many millions, is still the most impenetrable country in the world. Behind its icy barriers its priests guard its passes jealously against foreigners."[35] The Tantric religion of the lamas is found to be a most "silly and debased belief," full of "puerile mysticism" and "hideous accretions," which hardly deserves to be considered a philosophy. In Waddell's opinion, it might be considered a sinister kind of devil worship, if it were not so childish or pathetically foolish: "The bulk of the Lamaist cults comprise deep-rooted devil worship and sorcery. . . . Lamaism is only thinly and imperfectly varnished over with Buddhist symbolism, beneath which the sinister growth of poly-demonist superstition appears."[36] Under the grip of such a debilitating spiritual illness, the people of Tibet can only be helped if they are liberated from parasitic priests and their oppressive religion: "They have fallen under the double ban of menacing demons and despotic priests. So it will be a happy day indeed for Tibet when its sturdy over-credulous people are freed from the intolerable tyranny of the Lamas and delivered from the evils whose ferocity and exacting worship weigh like a nightmare upon all."[37] Of course, this is precisely what the Chinese government attempted to achieve when it invaded Tibet and slaughtered thousands of monks during the communist invasion in 1959.

Polluting the Blood of the Noble Race: Tantra and the Aryan Myth

> . . . the purity of the race was soiled by marriage with native women . . . and the creed with foul Dravidian worships of Shiva and Kālī, and the adoration of the *liṅgam.*
>
> Isaac Taylor, *The Origin of the Aryans* (1889)

By the early twentieth century, Tantra thus had become a key part of the larger Orientalist narrative of South Asian history. In the process, it became a part of the increasingly accepted narrative of the Aryan or Indo-European race and its progressive conquest of the non-Aryan peoples of Asia and Europe. According to a wide range of scholars of the late nineteenth century, the development of Hinduism in the subcontinent was described as the result of a (perhaps bastard and unholy) union of the Aryan and the pre-Aryan cultures. The Aryan represented the "noble" Indo-European stock, an ancient people believed to have spread from central Asia, both northward into Europe, giving birth to Greek, Roman, Germanic, and Celtic cultures, and also southward into South Asia, giving birth to the ancient Persian and Vedic cultures. The pre-Aryan, conversely, was identified with the non-Indo-European or "Dravidian" race, which now populates most of south India. Finally, thanks to the work of Friedrich Max Müller, Gustav Oppert, and others, the "Aryan race" had emerged in the Western imagination as an essentially masculine, aggressive, patriarchal culture, which had progressively invaded and conquered the more passive, feminine, and goddess-worshiping non-Aryan or Dravidian peoples. According to Oppert's simultaneously racist, sexist, and elitist account, the Aryans worshiped primarily the inner, masculine, and intellectual forces, while the Dravidians worshiped primarily the external, feminine forces of nature; and this, in turn, "explains the higher status which characterizes the Aryan belief compared with the non-Aryan. It expresses the gulf which separates the Male from the Female principle and explains the superiority . . . maintained by the Aryan over non-Aryan divinities."[38]

Not surprisingly, the development of Tantra was quickly identified with this imagined non-Aryan, Dravidian, goddess-worshiping culture of pre-Vedic India. Tantra was the very essence of this "feminine," weak, and passive race that had initially been conquered by the invading Aryans but that was now causing the progressive decline of the noble Aryan spirit in India. Isaac Taylor recounted this narrative, in his *Origin of the Aryans* of 1889:

> The Aryan invaders . . . are found gradually advancing to the south and east in continual conflict with the Dasyu or dark skinned aborigines, who . . . worshipped strange gods . . . till finally the barbarians are subdued and admitted into the Aryan state as a fourth caste, called the blacks or Sudras. The higher civilization and superior physique of the northern invaders ultimately prevailed . . . but the purity of the race was soiled by marriage with native women . . . and the creed with foul Dravidian worships of Shiva and Kali, and the adoration of the lingam.[39]

In their own day, many Indologists felt, the "Male Aryan spirit was being strangled by the overheated female matter of India."[40] The purity of Aryan culture was being corrupted by indigenous elements like idolatry, polytheism, and above all Tantra. And this, in turn, naturally justified rule by a living and still virile civilization of good Aryan stock, namely, the British.

Classifying the Pathology of Tantrism: Sex, Secrecy, and Scandal in the Victorian Imagination

> In matters of sexuality, we are, all of us, the healthy as much as the sick, hypocrites nowadays.
>
> Sigmund Freud,
> "Sexuality in the Aetiology of Neuroses" (1898)

> Let us ponder all the ruses that were employed for centuries to make us love sex, to make the knowledge of it desirable and everything said about it precious. Let us consider the strategems by which we were induced to apply all our skills to discovering its secrets. . . . [O]ne day, perhaps . . . people will no longer understand how the ruses of sexuality and the power that sustains its organization, were able to subject us to that austere monarchy of sex, so that we became dedicated to the endless task of forcing its secret, of exacting confessions from a shadow.
>
> Michel Foucault, *The History of Sexuality* (1978)

In order to understand the notion of Tantra in the Western imagination, we must also place it against the backdrop of the broader programs of colonial morality and attitudes toward sexuality in the nineteenth century. The British interest in the sexual perversions of the Tantras was part of a much broader concern with sexuality and its aberrations in the Victorian era. The British upper and middle classes of the nineteenth century were fascinated by sexuality: "Paradoxically, it was during the nineteenth century that the debate about sexuality exploded. Far from the age of silence and suppression, sexuality became a major issue in Victorian social and political practice."[41] As Foucault argues, the categorization, classification, and control over sexuality was a key element in the regulation of society as a whole: "The array of sexual discourses . . . exploited sexuality's secrets. Sex began to be managed. . . . [P]erversion became codified. . . . Sexuality proliferated as power over it was extended."[42]

The Victorian era, in fact, witnessed a tremendous proliferation of medical treatises on sexuality, in both its proper and perverse forms. Viewing any deviation from "normal" sex as morally suspect, the Victorian imagination was obsessed with the identification and classification of sexual aberrations, with the detailed scientific descriptions of every imaginable perversion. Among the most popular works in late-nineteenth-century England was Richard von Krafft-Ebing's textbook *Psychopathia Sexualis* (1886), which became the most influential catalogue of deviations. Under the protective cover of "medical nomenclature" and the "posture of moral outrage," Victorian readers "could indulge in this 'medicoforensic' peep-show of sexual hyperaesthesia, paresthesia, aspermia, polyspermia, spermatorrhea, sadism, masochism, festishism, exhibitionism, psychic hermaphroditism, satyriasis, and nymphomania."[43]

Among the most sinister perversions were those which, under the guise of transcendental ideals, confused the religious and sensual spheres. British middle- and upper-class sensibilities of the late nineteenth century insisted on the proper separation of religion and sexuality: excessive religious celibacy and sexual licentiousness were both considered dangerous perversions. They came increasingly to regard only one form of sexual relation to be proper and healthy—namely, heterosexual marriage. Only the married life offered the *via media* between celibacy and licentiousness, which "repairs the Fall and leads from earth to heaven."[44] In an era that valued economic productivity, generation of capital, and restraint in consumption, healthy sex had to be useful, productive, and efficient: "normal heterosexuality appeared in one guise . . . attraction between men and women that led to marriage and family. Normal sex was consistent with the values of Victorian industrial society—it was another mode of production."[45]

The British interest in Indian sexual practices, and above all the practices of the Tantras, was a central part of this broader fascination with sexuality and its aberrations. Just as the imperial project involved a certain "colonization of the body"—a systematic analysis and diagnosis and institutional control of the bodies and diseases of colonized people—so it involved a certain "colonization of sexuality"—an investigation, classification, and control over the sexual practices and aberrations of those under imperial rule.[46]

As Said has observed, imperialism as a whole was very often a "gendered" project. The colonial West was consistently imagined as the masculine, rational, active power that penetrated and possessed the Orient, which was imagined as feminine, irrational, and passive: "The sexual subjection of Oriental women to Western men fairly stands for the pattern of relative strength between East and West and the discourse about the Orient. . . . Orientalism takes perverse shape as a 'male power fantasy' that sexualizes a feminized Orient for Western power and possession."[47] For many Orientalists, India was imagined as the "feminine" land par excellence, the land of weakness and passivity, in opposition to the strength and virility of the West. As Robert Orme described the Indian in 1782, "Breathing in the softest climates, having few wants and receiving the luxuries of other nations with little labor . . . the Indian must have become the most effeminate inhabitant of the globe."[48]

Not only was India commonly imagined as an inherently "feminine" land, but it was also conceived as a realm of sexual perversions and abnormal carnal desires. "Anything and everything that deals with sex, procreation and human passion is worshipped and glorified," George MacMunn concluded in his widely read account *The Underworld of India*.[49] While the Indian male was commonly portrayed as weak and effeminate, but also lascivious and morally corrupt, the Indian female was imagined to be excessively sexual and seductive, insatiable in her carnal appetites. Embodied in the horrific image of the violently sexual goddess Kālī, India was at once seductively mysterious and bound up with "debauchery, violence and death."[50]

With its obscene confusion of religion and sexuality, and its deliberate violation of caste and marriage, Tantra came to represent the epitome of this inherent tendency toward depravity. As Shaw suggests, the use of sexual practices in Tantric worship represented a phenomenon similar to that of the *devadāsī*s or temple courtesans: "an unfamiliar and disquieting sight to the colonial gaze."[51] But more than just disquieting, the licentious deeds of the Tantras were also—like sexual aberrations classified in the Victorian medical texts—objects of intense interest and often obsessive narration. In his study of the mystics of India, J. C. Oman makes this point quite clearly: with its depraved *tāntrika*s, India is the only country in the world where the bizarre pathologies and mental illnesses (so clearly analyzed and classified by Western psychologists) are not only widespread, but actually *made into religious cults:* "Cases, few and far between, of necrophilism, anthropophagy and coprology are not unknown to mental pathologists in Europe; but it is only in India that such perverted instincts could be made the basis of a *religious* sect."[52]

As Foucault suggests, the intense interest in sexuality in the Victorian era—and particularly the classification of sexual deviations—was more than a perverse fascination with the forbidden and obscene. Rather, it was part of the broader expansion of bio-power in modern Europe, a key element in the larger concern with population, national health, and the reproduction of the social body in the modern state: "sex was a political issue: It was at the pivot of the two axes along which developed the political technology of life. On the one hand it was tied to the disciplines of the body. . . . On the other hand it was applied to the regulation of populations."[53] So too, this concern with the sexual deviations of Tantra appears to have been a key element in the larger project of imperial bio-politics. The classification and categorization of sexual practices, particularly the most dangerous, antisocial forms, was a crucial part of the larger imperial project of knowing and thereby better controlling those under rule. At the same time, by diagnosing this demoralizing disease of Tantra, which had spread throughout the Indian social body, colonial authors also justified the need for a more rational, healthy foreign rule in the subcontinent—the prudent, moral administration of the British.

THE COUNTER-RENAISSANCE: TANTRA AND THE BENGAL RENAISSANCE

> Modern men could not but seek to get rid of the filth, superstition and corruption revealed by the searchlight of Christ. . . . There has been a serious attempt, on the part of the orthodox, to destroy, drive underground or deny the worst features of Left-hand Śāktism . . . and unclean superstition.
>
> J. N. Farquhar, *Modern Religious Movements in India* (1915)

> In the first era of the dissemination of English culture . . . Bengal resounded with opprobrious criticisms of the Tantras. No one among the educated in Bengal could praise them. . . . The educated Bengali of the age was bewitched by the Christian culture, and . . . any who attempted to study the Tantras ran the risk of exposing themselves to contumely from the educated community.
>
> Panchkori Bandyopadhyay, *Sāhitya* (1913)

The construction of Tantra in the nineteenth century was by no means a simple, one-way process, a mere projection of European fantasies onto the mirror of the exotic Other. It was also very much a product of the Indian imagination, responding to and interacting with that of its colonial masters and Orientalist educators. As David Kopf argues, the work of early scholars like Jones and Colebrooke, together with the college founded in Calcutta, provided a major intellectual stimulus to the leaders of the so-called Hindu Renaissance. At the same time, Orientalist constructions of Hinduism and Indian history also began to inform the ways in which Indian intellectuals understood their own traditions. As Halbfass observes, "Indians re-interpreted key concepts of traditional self-understanding, adjusting them to Western modes of understanding."[54] The leaders of the Hindu reform movements clearly assimilated many Orientalist paradigms, including the narrative of Indian history as a progressive devolution from the Golden Age of the Vedas to the modern, degenerate age of the Tantras.

The category of Tantra therefore played an important part in the modern Indian defense and reconceptualization of its own traditions, particularly during the period of Hindu reform in the nineteenth century. The more virulent defenders of traditional Hinduism, such as the founder of the Ārya Samāj, Swāmī Dayānanda Saraswatī (1824–83), undertook a "scathing attack on Tantra," which he identified as among the chief causes for the sad state of modern Indian culture.[55] Tantra is the epitome of all the "popery" that had corrupted the Hindu tradition with obscene ritual and sensual indulgence: "Now look at the trickery of these stupid *popes* that whatever is considered to be highly sinful and opposed to the Veda is regarded as virtuous. . . . The use of meat, wine . . . and copulation are considered as means of attaining salvation."[56] As we see in the following account, Dayānanda regards Tantra as the embodiment of everything that must be eradicated in order to restore Hinduism to its original purity; it was the inspiration for his reformist project:

> My eyes fell on such an amount of incredible obscenities, mistranslations of the most ancient texts and absurdity that I felt horrified. In these Tantras I found that incest was permitted even with mothers, daughters, sisters and low born maids. . . . They recommend worship of gods in a perfectly nude state, spirituous liquors, fish, and all kinds of animal foods are allowed for all. . . . By reading . . . the Tantras, I was fully convinced of the . . . viciousness of the authors of this disgusting literature.[57]

We find similar attacks on the Tantras appearing in other regions of India, such as Gujurat in the 1870s. In 1874, for example, an anonymous text was published in Ahmedabad, bearing the title *Exposition of the Āgamas, or That Portion of Hindoo Shastras Which Vamees or Left Hand Sect Follow as Their Books of Revelation, ie. Tantras, Yamalas, Rujusias, &c for the Use of Reformers in India.* The unknown author appears to have been an outspoken member of the newly emerging Swaminarayan movement. One of the most powerful reforming agents in nineteenth-century Gujarati society, the Swaminarayans opened their doors to all castes, argued strongly against *sati* and female infanticide, and promoted widow remarriage and other women's rights. Not surprisingly, many Swaminarayan reformers saw the *tantra*s as the clearest example of everything that was wrong with contemporary Indian society and the first thing that needed to be eradicated in any genuine social reform. With their "many immoral and horrible practices," the *tantra*s are "diametrically opposed to all religious or law books, morals and good customs."[58] The author makes it clear that the dangerous teachings of the *tantra*s need to be critically analyzed by leaders of the reform movements; for it is only by comprehending their dangerous threat that such evils can be eradicated from a moral Hindu society:

> They cannot be properly appreciated unless they are . . . unveiled and thrown open to the reformers who wish to introduce changes in order to establish a pure form of religion. The object of these pages is to hold up to light the most filthy, infernal and obscene superstitions . . . of Mantra Shastris who abound in every town in India. . . . It is hoped that this publication will induce all those who are concerned in the welfare of this great nation to unite in one common effort to put down the diabolical tenets inculcated by the Vami and Kowl sects.[59]

As Rhinehart and Stewart conclude, texts like these "reflect the climate of British colonial rule" and reveal the profound impact of Western values on the Hindus' self-perception of their own traditions; increasingly in the colonial era, categories like Tantra, with all their terrible connotations, were now internalized and applied by Indian authors to their own traditions.[60]

However, perhaps the most influential discussions of Tantra emerged in nineteenth-century Bengal, during the period of its so-called renaissance. We might even say that the category of Tantra served as a kind of counter-renaissance; that is, it came to represent the complete opposite of everything the renaissance stood for, the embodiment of all the idolatry and immorality that the reformers hoped to eradicate.[61] Following the lead of the Orientalists, the reformers looked back to the noble, rational religion of the Vedas as India's Golden Age, while they despaired of the modern "age of Kālī," in which the perverse rites of the Tantras ran rampant. As such, Tantra was foremost among those elements of modern Hinduism that would have to be uprooted if Hindus were to recover an authentic spiritual and national identity.

"Ceremonies Utterly Subversive of Every Moral Principle": Rāmmohun Roy, Tantra, and the Bengal Renaissance

> The stories . . . in the Tantras are of a nature that, if told of any man, would be offensive to the ears of the most abandoned of either sex.
>
> Rāmmohun Roy, "A Defense of Hindoo Theism"

Arguably the most important figure in the shaping of modern Indian understandings of Tantrism, and of Hinduism as a whole, was the Bengali reformer Rāmmohun Roy (1772–1833). Known today as the "father of modern India," often hailed as a kind of "Indian Martin Luther," Rāmmohun was the leading exponent of social and religious reform during the period of the Bengal Renaissance. Born to a Brahman family, Rāmmohun was a well-educated and ambitious entrepreneur—a successful businessman and real-estate agent, as well as a scholar who mastered Persian, Arabic, and English. Today, he is best known as the pioneer of liberal political consciousness and Indian nationalism, who first introduced "ethical and professional standards into Indian law, medicine, science . . . and civil administration."[62] It was Rāmmohun whom Max Müller praised as "the first who came from East to West . . . and completed that worldwide circle through which, like an electric current, Oriental thought could run to the West and Western thought return to the East."[63] However, as Kopf has argued, Rāmmohun exemplified a general pattern among many intellectuals of nineteenth-century Bengal: namely, their profound "psychological uncertainty" and ambivalence between the attempt to preserve ancient Hindu traditions and the desire to modernize India in imitation of the technologically superior West.[64] As Halbfass suggests, Rāmmohun stands out as a striking embodiment of this conflicted encounter and as a sort of "mirror of a hermeneutic situation in which the foreign came to be adopted as a means of *self-understanding and self-presentation.*"[65]

The primary goal of Rāmmohun's work was to purify Hinduism of what he saw as its modern, degenerate accretions and to restore it to its original pristine spirit. Against the unthinking dogmatism and blind ritualism of popular Hinduism, he hoped to substitute a liberal and rational religion; and against the polytheism and idolatry of the contemporary worship, he hoped to instill a monotheistic faith in the absolute, impersonal Brahman. Though largely rooted in the Upaniṣads and Vedānta, Rāmmohun's deity is not without a certain trace of Christian influence, conceived now as "a patriarchal God, the author and governor of the universe, he by whom the birth, existence and annihilation of the world is regulated."[66] As S. K. De suggests, one might even say that Rāmmohun in a sense "superimposed Western monotheism onto the monistic Vedānta of Śaṅkara."[67]

In opposition to the original monotheistic, rational spirit of ancient Hinduism, modern popular Hindu worship was, for Rāmmohun, a terrible degeneration and corruption. Influenced by Orientalist scholars like Jones and Colebrooke, Rāmmohun adopted the ideal of the Vedic Golden Age and its progressive decline, which he then adapted to the traditional Indian notion of the descending cycles of time. Like the Orientalists, he divided Indian history into an original era of rational monotheism and a later period of "Hindoo idolatry with its innumerable gods, goddesses and temples, which have since been destroying society."[68] As such, he envisaged his own mission as not unlike Luther's reformation in Europe, which had succeeded in purifying Christianity of its later accretions: "I began to think that something similar might have taken place in India and similar results might follow from a reformation of popular idolatry."[69]

Rāmmohun's works are filled with severe diatribes against the decadence of popular Indian traditions, and above all, the *śākta tantras*. Like so many nineteenth-century reformers, he saw the Tantras "as a horrendous and debased form of religious expression, representing a . . . radical departure from authentic . . . Hindu tradition."[70] At the same time, however, Roy also stands out as one of the most complex figures in the history of modern India. His own mother had in fact been a Śākta and a devotee of Kālī, the Tantric goddess par excellence. Yet Rāmmohun would eventually reject Śāktism and everything associated with it, decrying the idolatry of Kālī's worship and setting himself forever at odds with his own mother: "From this time onward his mother opposed and persecuted him."[71] For Rāmmohun, the dark mother Kālī was to become "the symbol of a treacherous mother eager to betray and prone to aggression. She came to be associated with all the other rituals cited as instances of the cultural decadence of the age, against which . . . every reformer fought."[72] As he wrote in his "Defence of Hindoo Theism," "In the worship of Kālī, human sacrifice, the use of wine, criminal intercourse and licentious songs are included. . . . Debauchery . . . universally forms the principal of the worship of her followers. Nigam and other Tantras may satisfy every reader of the horrible tenets of the worshippers of [Kālī]."[73]

This profound tension between personal inheritance of the Tantric tradition and public disavowal of it is a recurrent theme throughout Rāmmohun's life and in the reform movements as a whole. Indeed, given his seemingly radically anti-Śākta, anti-Tantric stance, it is all the more surprising that Rāmmohun should have had an especially close relationship with one particularly well-known Śākta Tantric text—the enigmatic text of the *Mahānirvāṇa Tantra*.

"A Woman's Tantra": The Strange Case of the Mahānirvāṇa Tantra

Our land of Bengal used to be ruled by Tantrik works
such as the *Śāradātilaka . . . Prānatoṣiṇī, Tantrasāra,* etc.
Then the *Mahānirvāṇa Tantra* did not have so great
influence. Considering the form into which, as a result

> of English education, the mind . . . of the Bengali has been shaped, the *Mahānirvāṇa* is a proper Tantra for the time. Raja Ram Mohan Roy endeavored to encourage the *Mahānirvāṇa* because he understood that . . . the English-educated Bengali community is without religion and devoid of the sense of nationality and caste. The *Mahānirvāṇa Tantra* alone is fit for the country at the present time.
>
> Bandyopadhyay, *Sāhitya*

Among all the strange, esoteric, and often seemingly incomprehensible works we call the Hindu *tantra*s, there are few more curious than the *Mahānirvāṇa Tantra.* Although it is probably "the *tantra* best known in the West,"[74] this text is extremely unusual and unlike virtually any other *tantra* in its conception of absolute reality, its description of ritual, its view of caste, and its attitude toward various social issues, such as marriage and women's rights. The *Mahānirvāṇa* is so unusually restrained in its description of Tantric ritual that at least one Bengali pundit referred to it rather disparagingly as a "woman's *tantra.*"[75] Moreover, the text has a rather suspicious history: mentioned nowhere prior to the late eighteenth century, it appears in very few manuscripts in a few select libraries of Bengal.

A wide range of scholars have suggested that the text is a recent creation, most likely from the late eighteenth century; in fact, some have even raised the possibility that it may have been fabricated by Rāmmohun Roy himself. The text was first published by the Ādi Brāhmo Samāj; two of the earliest manuscripts were contained in Rāmmohun's library and in a library of the Brāhmo Samāj; and Rāmmohun's own guru, Hariharānanda Bhārati, was an initiated *tāntrika* who wrote the first known commentary on the text.[76] When we look more closely at the doctrinal, ritual, and ethical content of the *Mahānirvāṇa,* moreover, we do indeed find many elements that have a strangely "modern" flavor.

Comprised of 2,303 verses, the text unfolds as a dialogue between Lord Śiva and Parvatī on Mount Kailāsa. Śiva begins his dialogue by first recounting the evils of this degenerate modern age, in which the traditional teachings of the Vedas are no longer adequate to feeble minds of human beings; hence, the once secret teachings of Tantras now must be revealed openly: "In this age the mantras of the Tantras are efficacious, yielding immediate fruit. . . . The Vedic rites . . . which were efficacious in the First Age have ceased to be so. . . . They are now powerless as snakes, the poison fangs of which are drawn" (MT 1.14–23). Unlike many *tantras*, however, the *Mahānirvāṇa* does not in any way devalue the authority of the Vedas; rather, it claims that its own teaching is already implicit within the Vedas and that it is the true fulfillment or inner core of the Vedic tradition itself (MT 1.10–13).

Unlike most Bengali *tantras*, moreover, the *Mahānirvāṇa* identifies the supreme reality not with the goddess Śakti or Kālī, nor with Śiva or any other personal deity; rather it is an unusually philosophical, abstract, Vedāntic view of the divine as the one impersonal, omnipresent Brahman, described "in Upaniṣadic terms."[77] "The Supreme Brahman . . . is ever Existent. . . . That which is changeless, existent only and beyond both mind and speech, which shines as the truth amidst the illusion of the three worlds is Brahman according to its real nature. That Brahman is known in samadhi yoga by those who look upon all things free of all illusion" (MT 3.5–8).

This monotheistic description of the divine was naturally attractive to most Western and anglicized Indian readers, who "admired its noble exposition of the worship of the Supreme Brahman."[78] For example, Ernest Payne—who elsewhere attacks Tantrism as the most debased side of Hinduism, a religion of "blind terror, of uncomprehended forces"—speaks highly of this text as a "noble passage on the worship of one eternal, omnipresent God."[79]

Chapter 7 of the *tantra,* it is true, contains a hymn addressed of the goddess Kālī as the object of personal devotion; however, in comparison to most other Śākta texts, which depict the goddess as a horrifying, violent power, the image of Kālī in the *Mahānirvāṇa* is remarkably benevolent and "sanitized." There is absolutely no mention of the violent, lustful, or cruel aspects of Kālī, with her love of cremation grounds, human corpses, or severed heads, so vividly portrayed in other Bengali texts like the *Bṛhat Tantrasāra.*[80] On the contrary, she is "the ocean of nectar of compassion . . . whose mercy is without limit" (7.13), the "possessor of beautiful ornaments, adorable as the image of all tenderness, with a tender body" (7.22). As McDermott has argued, the image of Kālī in Bengal appears to have undergone a general process of "sweetening" during the eighteenth and nineteenth centuries. Gradually, throughout the colonial period, she was domesticated and transformed from a wild, violent, and sexual deity into the approachable maternal goddess that we find today.[81] It seems likely that the *Mahānirvāṇa* was an important part of this progressive sweetening and transformation of the goddess in the colonial era.

Compared with many other *tantras*, the *Mahānirvāṇa* appears to be unusually sanitized also in its account of Tantric ritual. The infamous five M's are mentioned only in one chapter of the text, and the controversial fifth "M" is accorded only a single line (7.24–27). Even when such things are mentioned, it is only with "great euphemisms."[82] Moreover, unlike many other left-hand *tantras*, which prescribe ritual sex with lower-class partners like untouchables and menstruating prostitutes, this text is exceptional in proclaiming that *maithuna* should be performed only with one's own wife: "When the weakness of the Kali Age becomes great one's own wife alone should be known as the fifth *tattva*" (6.14). As various authors have observed, the text appears to represent a strong reforming tendency, which "endorses rituals that would not be threatening to a Western outlook."[83] As such, it is generally said to be less popular among many practicing *tāntrikas* than it is among Hindu reformers and Western scholars, precisely because of its "timidity and puritanical outlook."[84]

However, perhaps the most unusual feature of this text is the large amount of space that it devotes to the exoteric and seemingly "un-Tantric" matters of caste, social interaction, and domestic life. Chapters 8 through 12, which comprise nearly half (1,083 out of 2,303) of the total verses in the text, are concerned with social rules and practical matters, most of which are derived from the *Manusmṛti, Yājñavalkyasmṛti,* and *Dāyabhāga.* As J. Duncan M. Derrett observes, "The legal element in the *tantra* is very curious . . . and more extensive than genuine *śāstric* [law books] works allow."[85] Chapter 8, for example, gives detailed instructions for the role of the castes *(jātis),* the stages of life *(āśrama),* and the duties of the householder *(gṛhasta).* Devoted in all his actions to the supreme Brahman, the householder is the pillar of society, holding together the cohesion of family and society (8.23–36). The caste system is also emphatically upheld; all the traditional laws set forth by Manu regarding the duties of the four *varṇas* (classes) must be observed, along with the laws of initiation, ritual, family relations, diet, and business interactions. It is only within the strictly controlled environs of the Tantric circle that caste restrictions can be suspended; once the secret *cakra* is dissolved, normal social relations must be restored.[86]

Only in its attitudes toward women, marriage, and inheritance does the text depart significantly from orthodox doctrine. While by no means egalitarian, the *Mahānirvāṇa* has often been praised for its unusually generous attitude toward women.[87] Thus, it condemns the practice of *satī* or widow-burning, asserting that every woman is an image of the great

Goddess: "that woman who in her delusion ascends the funeral pyre of her lord shall go to hell" (10.79–80). More importantly, the text also diverges form the traditional ideals of marriage. According to orthodox law books like the *Manusmṛti* and *Dāyabhāga,* the most desirable form of marriage is "Brahma marriage," in which one weds only within his own caste. The *Mahānirvāṇa,* however, promotes "Śaiva marriage," in which there is no restriction of caste and age, and which is based on the mutual consent *(parasparecchā)* of man and woman (11.269–71). As Derrett comments, this probably represents "an attempt to reform the Hindu law of marriage from within," inspired largely by Muslim and Christian models.[88]

The text's attitude toward inheritance is equally idiosyncratic. According to the traditional *śāstric* rules that we find in the *Manusmṛti* or *Dāyabhāga,* a wife or father would normally inherit the property of a deceased male. The *Mahānirvāṇa,* conversely, advocates a very different form of inheritance, based on descent through male heirs; thus the property would be inherited by the eldest son, "by reason of his being a descendent" (12.19). As Derrett comments, such a "concept is quite foreign to Indian law" and not only has much in common with English concepts of the descent of property, but appears to be an attempt to translate English legal terms directly into Sanskrit.[89]

In short, it seems fairly clear that the strange case of the *Mahānirvāṇa Tantra* must be understood within the context of the social, political, and legal situation of early colonial Bengal. Derrett has argued convincingly that at least part of the text—namely, the large portions dealing with caste, domestic order, and property rights—can be explained by changes made in the British India legal system between 1773 and 1782. Up until 1772, the British had followed a system of dual government, allowing native administrators to govern while British authorities remained in the background. In 1774, however, the English Parliament set up a new system that created the Supreme Court. At this time, it appeared that British law would govern all Hindus in all aspects of life; and among the two most controversial issues were marriage and inheritance—precisely the two most unusual and idiosyncratic elements in the *Mahānirvāṇa.* But by 1782, the jurisdiction of the Supreme Court was curbed and Hindu law was restored in matters of marriage and inheritance. For these reasons, Derrett concludes that the *Mahānirvāṇa* was written some time in this eight-year period, most probably in 1775. It was, he thinks, an attempt to provide a source of ancient authority for thc new laws of marriage and inheritance, which would also be acceptable to the British administrators: "The Tantric religion could be called upon as a law for a community which would embrace more than caste Hindus. . . . The English would welcome a book . . . the tone and contents of which would be familiar to them."[90]

However, all of this still leaves unanswered a whole series of important questions. Why would a specifically left-hand Tantric text be chosen as the vehicle for these ideas, if they were purely legalistic in nature? Surely a more orthodox, less controversial sort of *śāstra* would have been a more appropriate vehicle? And what about the rest of the text, which is not concerned with legalistic matters, but rather with the nature of absolute reality and highly esoteric rituals?

In order to understand this text and its role in colonial Bengal, we need to examine its strange connections with Rāmmohun Roy and the Brāhmo Samāj. The *Mahānirvāṇa* was to become one of the most popular works among the reformers of nineteenth-century Bengal, and particularly among the early members of the Brāhmo Samāj. It is clear that Rāmmohun not only knew the *Mahānirvāṇa* well, but used it explicitly to support his own social and religious ideals. Rāmmohun owned a copy of the text and had studied various *tantra*s under Hariharānanda; some suspect that he may have received Tantric initiation during his stay in Varanasi in 1803.[91]

In many of his later writings, Rāmmohun draws upon the "ancient authority" of the *Mahānirvāṇa* in order to support his own reformed ideals, quoting or paraphrasing it in at least six treatises. In the *Cāri Praśner Uttara,* for example, he praises the "venerable *dharma* in the *Mahānirvāṇa.*"[92] Not only did he use hymns taken directly from the text (such as the one beginning "Nāmāste Sate" [MT 3.59]), in a short form of worship published in Bengali; more important, Rāmmohun cited the *Mahānirvāṇa* in support of many of his own key religious and social platforms, for example, its condemnation of widow-burning, which was one of his most important agendas. Perhaps most significantly, he referred explicitly to the Śaiva form of marriage taught in the *Mahānirvāṇa,* which, rather conveniently, conformed to his own liberal view of marriage, and which was in fact the only "ancient" authority he could cite in its support.[93]

From this discussion of the *Mahānirvāṇa* and the work of Rāmmohun Roy, we can see a number of significant parallels that might explain why this text was so popular among the leaders of the Bengal Renaissance. First, both Rāmmohun and the *Mahānirvāṇa* conceive of the divine being, not in the sectarian terms of Kālī, Śiva, or any other personal deity, but rather in terms of the impersonal, formless Brahman. Second, both place central emphasis on the doctrine of the degeneration of time: the Golden Age of Hinduism lies in the distant past, while the present modern age is filled with corruption, idolatry, and licentiousness. The return to the purity of original Hinduism therefore demands a recovery of the original monotheistic, rational spirit articulated in the Vedānta. Third, the *Mahānirvāṇa* and Rāmmohun also share a curious ambivalence toward caste: on the one hand, they both insist on the equality of all human beings, at least on the transcendent spiritual plane, and they both offer a hope for freedom for all castes, at least within certain prescribed ritual contexts. On the other hand, they both admit that the caste system should be observed in daily affairs. And finally, both agree on certain key legal issues, such as marriage, inheritance, and women's rights.

It may never be known who the actual author(s) of the *Mahānirvāṇa* were. Despite their close connection with the text, it seems unlikely that either Rāmmohun or Hariharānanda penned it.[94] What seems most probable is that the text was composed in late-eighteenth-century Bengal by some learned pundit who had extensive knowledge of the Sanskrit *tantra*s and of British Indian law. Nonetheless, now that we have placed it within its historical context, I do think we can begin to answer the perplexing question of why an upper-class, well-educated leader of the Bengal Renaissance like Rāmmohun would have been so interested in this enigmatic text.

The *Mahānirvāṇa,* I would suggest, played a strategic role in Rāmmohun's larger program of reform and his defense of Hinduism against its Western critics. As Dasgupta observes, Rāmmohun seemed to have picked and chosen those elements of the *Mahānirvāṇa*'s purified version of Tantra that agreed with his own reformist philosophy, while largely ignoring the rest of the text.[95] In this sense, the *Mahānirvāṇa* could perhaps be thought of as what Jonathan Smith calls a *"strategy for dealing with a situation"*—namely, the "incongruous situation" of Indian intellectuals under colonial rule.[96] As a kind of "purified Tantra," the *Mahānirvāṇa* offers a solution to the contradiction between the Golden Age of India's past and the immorality of modern Hinduism. For the *Mahānirvāṇa* presents a Tantric doctrine that is not idolatrous or immoral, but strongly monotheistic and really rather prudish.

David Haberman has examined an analogous phenomenon in the changing attitude toward Vaiṣṇava bhakti during the nineteenth century. In the eyes of the British Orientalists—who in turn determined the view of the British Indian Court—the erotic aspect of Vaiṣṇava bhakti was viewed much like the Tantric tradition: it represented a degraded corruption of the true Hindu spirit in the modern era. Through the rulings of the British court, and through the intellectual influence of the British Orientalists and Hindu reformers, there was a profound change in the understanding of love and devotion within the bhakti tradition of the nineteenth century: "The erotic traditions are wrong and should be eliminated. . . . The neo-Vedāntine religion of the reformers . . . is given the approval of the Supreme Court. Hindu theology must be in line with British morality, which is . . . founded on natural and eternal laws."[97] Much the same kind of interaction between British law and Hindu tradition appears to be reflected in the *Mahānirvāṇa Tantra.* The text is really something of a double-edged sword that accomplishes a twofold task. Not only does it attempt to reinterpret certain aspects of Indian culture according to the model of the *tantra*s, but it also attempts to relegitimize the Tantric tradition in light of a reformed, modernized Hinduism. Ironically, a *tantra* would in many ways appear to be the ideal medium for this kind of reformist agenda. For like other *tantra*s, the *Mahānirvāṇa* claims to be an ancient, revealed source of authority, but one that has been kept *secret,* hidden throughout the ages, revealed only now for this most decadent and dangerous modern age.

In sum, it seems unfair to dismiss the *Mahānirvāṇa,* as many have, as a modern fabrication or fraud. For *all* Tantric texts could be said to be fabrications, insofar as they claim to derive from some ancient or primordial time, and even to predate the Vedas. Instead, I would suggest that we regard this text, like all *tantra*s, as a product of the creative ingenuity of the human being as *homo faber*—and also, more importantly, as a striking example of the changing role of the *tantra*s under colonial rule. It is, in short, an original, though perhaps ultimately failed, attempt to deal with the "situational incongruities" that characterize the encounter between Hindu tradition and the ambivalent realities of colonial power.

CLASSIFYING, CONTROLLING, AND ERADICATING THE TANTRIC DISEASE

At one extreme there is the escape offered by abstraction . . . and at the other extreme there is wild debauchery. . . . The cultus includes the most barbaric distractions, drunken orgies, sexual promiscuity and all kinds of ugliness. . . . Among the Hindus we find the most

> beautiful poetry, but always with an element of utter irrationality: we are attracted by its grace, but . . . repelled by the sheer confusion and nonsense of it.
>
> G. W. F. Hegel, *Lectures on the Philosophy of Religion* (1827)

Despite the *Mahānirvāṇa*'s curious attempt to purify the image of the *tantras*, the category of Tantrism would only continue to grow more seedy, scandalous, and repugnant in both the British and Indian imaginations. By the late nineteenth century, European and Indian scholars alike appear to have reached a general consensus on the matter: the polytheistic and licentious *tantras* were fundamentally opposed to the pure, rational, monotheistic Vedas, and so lay at the farthest, most degenerate extreme of the progressive devolution of Indian history. One of the most common metaphors used to describe the destructive impact of Tantra was that it was a "disease"—a debilitating sickness that weakened the Indian spirit and made it prone to foreign attack. As Benyotosh Bhattacharyya traced this religious disease in 1932, Tantra was believed to have originally emerged in some more primitive, uncivilized, and barbaric world (perhaps Scythia?), from whence it penetrated into India and infected, first, Buddhism, giving birth to the "degenerate" Vajrayāna, and then Hinduism, fatally crippling India's religious and political structure.[98] Most importantly, Bhattacharyya associates the triumph of Tantra with the moral and political degeneration of the Indian people, which in turn opened the door to the Muslim conquest: "If at any time in the history of India the mind of the nation as a whole has been diseased, it was in the Tantric age, or the period immediately preceding the Muhammedan conquest of India. . . . The result was the destruction of Buddhism and the occupation of the country by the Muhammadans."[99] The original spirit of India was progressively sapped by the Tantric disease, making way for her inevitable conquest by foreign powers—first by the Muslims, and finally by the British. Therefore, if modern India is to recover her true spiritual, cultural, and political identity, it is precisely the diseased elements like Tantra that will have to be eradicated from the social body.

In short, the discourse surrounding Tantra was a key element of self-definition for both the British and Indian factions during the nineteenth century. For the British in India, the classification of Tantra and its pathologies was never a simple matter of intellectual curiosity about an exotic Eastern environment. It was also an important part of the classification of Indian religion, culture, and society as a whole, which was to a large extent carried out in the interest of more effective administration. For a majority of Orientalist authors, Tantra represented everything that was most dangerous about the land they hoped to rule. Yet at the same time, it offered a convenient justification for India's *need to be ruled,* its need to be colonized by a healthy, moral nation. Such a debased country, where psychological pathologies can become religious cults, is surely in need of rational administration by a foreign power.

For Indian elites, on the other hand, Tantra came to embody their nation's own weakness; it stood for everything that made India appear backward, uncivilized, and immoral in comparison to the West. For early reformers, the task was thus either to eradicate Tantra altogether, or else—as in the case of the mysterious *Mahānirvāṇa Tantra*—to bring it into line with British colonial and reformed Hindu values. As we will see in the following chapters, however, the discourse on Tantra would soon be played out, not just in the abstract realm of scholarly discourse, but in the concrete realms of social struggle and political action.

CHAPTER 2

Sacrificing White Goats to the Goddess

Tantra and Political Violence in Colonial India

Secrecy goes with savagery.

Sir George MacMunn, *The Religions and Hidden Cults of India* (1932)

Rise up, O sons of India, arm yourselves with bombs, dispatch the white Asuras to Yama's abode. Invoke the Mother Kali. . . . The Mother asks for sacrificial offerings. What does the Mother want? . . . A fowl or sheep or buffalo? No. She wants many white Asuras. The Mother is thirsting after the blood of the Feringhees. . . . [C]hant this verse while slaying the Feringhee white goat: with the close of a long era, the Feringhee Empire draws to an end, for behold! Kali rises in the East.

Jugantar, Bengali newspaper (1905)

Imagined as the most radical, dangerous, and transgressive of spiritual paths, in explicit violation of accepted ethical boundaries, Tantra was soon to be associated in both the Western and Indian imaginations with the possibility of political violence. If Orientalist authors began to shift from "Indophilia" to a more critical "Indophobia" in the years after 1833, this suspicious attitude was even more pronounced in the years following 1857, during the "crisis of the raj" in the wake of the Indian Mutiny. And it reached its peak in the tumultuous years of the early twentieth century, in the face of a growing, often violent nationalist movement whose struggle for independence was sometimes bloody.[1] Throughout the late nineteenth century, Tantra was increasingly identified with the most dangerous subversive movements, such as the criminal Thuggee and the political extremists of the nationalist movement. "Tantrism acquired a new political dimension as British fears about civil unrest and mutiny were excited and linked to the supposed degeneracy of the natives."[2] However, to use Taussig's terms, we might say that the colonial paranoia about Tantric savagery was as much a projection of the "barbarity of their own social relations" as it was a reflection of any actual Indian reality: "The magic of mimesis lies in the transformation wrought on reality by rendering its image. . . . In the colonial mode of production of reality . . . such mimesis occurs by a colonial mirroring of otherness that reflects back on the colonists the barbarity of their own social relations, but as imputed to the savagery they yearn to colonize."[3]

For Indian authors of the nineteenth century, conversely, the attitude toward the radical practices of Tantra was more complex and ambivalent. For the reformers and the more conservative members of the nationalist movement, Tantra was typically seen as a terrible embarrassment, a major reason for India's backwardness and lack of political power, one of the things most in need of eradication on the road to self-governance. Yet, remarkably, for the more radical, extremist wing of the nationalist movement, Tantric forms and symbols could also be used positively, as a source of revolutionary inspiration. Many Indian authors, such as the young Aurobindo Ghose, would appropriate and exploit the terrifying image of Tantra, and particularly the violent goddess Kālī, as the most powerful embodiment of their political cause. As a powerful dialectical category, Tantra could not only be employed by colonial authors as proof of Indian backwardness, barbarism, and savagery; it could also be turned around and redeployed as the symbol of India in violent revolt against her colonial masters.

In this chapter, I will explore, first, the paranoid fears of Tantric secrecy and violence that emerged in the colonial imagination, as we see in British descriptions of the goddess Kālī and the criminal gangs of the Thuggee. I will then examine the ways in which some Indian authors in turn appropriated the images of Kālī and Tantra as revolutionary weapons, exploiting their terrifying power in the colonial imagination. As we will see in the case of complex figures like Aurobindo, the Goddess could symbolize both Mother India, in violent rebellion against her colonial oppressors, and the Divine Mother, seeking some kind of harmony with the West in an age of postcolonial compromise.

THE PATHOS OF THE UNDERWORLD: TANTRA, CRIME, AND DISSENT

> It is just this presence of some ancient horror, existing beneath the surface of perfectly reasonable political aspirations, which has been a source of trouble to many a kind Viceroy desiring only India's good.
>
> Sir George MacMunn, *The Underworld of India* (1933)

Based in large part on the descriptions of Orientalist scholarship, British government officials and colonial administrators also began to take an interest in the *tantra*s and to contribute a new element to the imagining of Tantra. For the most part, Tantra was an object intense anxiety for the colonial authorities, who suspected it of revolutionary agitation and subversive plots. Throughout the European colonial imagination of the nineteenth and early twentieth centuries, the fear of subversive political activities often went hand-in-hand with the fear of immoral practices among the natives under their rule. As we see in the cases of the Mau Mau in Kenya or in various native uprisings in South America, political rebellion was often believed to be associated with immorality, sexual transgression, and the violation of social taboos. The rebellious colonial subject threatened not only to subvert colonial rule, but to unravel the moral fabric of society itself. As Nicholas Thomas observes, "Colonial rule was haunted by a sense of insecurity," terrified by the "obscurity of the native mentality" and overwhelmed by the indigenous societies' "intractability in the face of government."[4] Perhaps this was true nowhere more than in colonial India of the late nineteenth and early twentieth centuries.

Above all, India was imagined as a land where political activism and religious fervor were often wedded in the most dangerous form. In the insidious "Indian underworld," as M. Paul Dare described it, "crime, religious belief and magic are entangled . . . to a degree inconceivable to the western mind."[5] As Richard King suggests, the West has long held two powerful images of Indian religions: on one side, the detached, transcendent otherworldly mystic, and on the other, the "militant fanatic," the crazed devotee of mindless religion.[6] This association between political violence and religious extremism became increasingly acute after May 1857, the pivotal moment of the Indian Mutiny, when the Bengal Army revolted against its British officers, sparking a widespread violent bloodbath. Allegedly caused by specific religious reasons—the use of beef fat in gun cartridges—the mutiny probably had behind it a host of other cultural causes—such as Christian missionary activity, the prohibition of religious practices, and the introduction of Western education. Culminating in the Kanpur Massacre, with the grisly murder of British women and children prisoners, the mutiny became for the British authorities the epitome of all the "cruelty and impulsiveness" of their subjects and so the justification for the "moral and racial condemnation of native Indians."[7]

Tantra would come to represent the epitome of this dangerous fusion of religion with political action, a kind of perverse mysticism combining not just religion and sensuality, but criminal behavior and political unrest. As Valentine Chirol warned in *Indian Unrest,* there was an intimate connection between the sexual license of the Tantric secret societies and the subversive acts of the revolutionary political groups: "The Shakti cultus, with its obscene and horrible rites . . . represents a form of erotomania which is certainly much more common among Hindu political fanatics."[8] Above all, this erotomaniac fanaticism seemed to have reached its most extreme form in the violently sexual figure of the Tantric goddess.

An Orgy of Horrors: Kālī in the Colonial Imagination

> Kālī is wholly given over to cruelty and blood. She drinks the blood of her victims. She lives in an orgy of horrors.
>
> Rev. E. Osborn Martin, *The Gods of India* (1913)

> To know the Hindoo idolatry AS IT IS, a person must wade through the filth of the thirty-six pooranus. . . . [H]e must follow the brahmun through his midnight orgies before the image of Kalee.
>
> William Ward, *A View of the History, Literature, and Religion of the Hindoos* (1817)

Throughout the British and European literature of the colonial era, few figures held such a central role, as a source of mixed horror and fascination, as did the Tantric goddess Kālī (see figures 5 and 6). As Friedrich Max Müller put it, "nothing is so hideous as the popular worship of Kālī in India."[9] The goddess of time, darkness, and death *(kāla),* Kālī has been a powerful presence in the Hindu religious imagination since at least the early centuries of the common era. The first known account of Kālī as a wild, bloodthirsty goddess appears in the *Mahābhārata,* during Aśvatthāman's

Figure 5. "Procession of the Hindoo Goddess Kali." From Colin Campbell, *Narrative of the Indian Revolt: From Its Outbreak to the Capture of Lucknow* (London: G. Vickers, 1858).

night attack on the Pāṇḍavas (10.8.64). In the Purāṇas, Kālī emerges as a goddess of battle and war, often associated with lower-class people and non-Aryan tribals. However, her most famous appearance is found in the *Devī-Māhātmya*, a portion of the *Mārkaṇḍeya Purāṇa*, where she emerges as the wrathful projection of Durgā, a hideous, bloodthirsty creature, raging about the field of battle and slaying demons.[10] A goddess of military power and death, she is also the goddess of time itself, associated with destruction on a universal scale, the eschatological dissolution of the world at the end of the age. Portrayed as a "frightening hag with disheveled hair, pendulous breasts and a garland of skulls," she is "the embodiment of the fury which can be raised in the divinity under emergency conditions."[11]

Not surprisingly, given her extreme role in the Indian tradition, Kālī soon assumed an even more terrifying role in the colonial imagination. As Ward describes her, Kālī is the very epitome of that "puerile, impure and bloody system of idolatry" that is the Hindu faith. With her horrific violence and rampant sexuality, Kālī is the most explicit embodiment of this ghastly perversion that passes under the name of religion:

> The dark image of this goddess is a truly horrid figure. . . . [S]he holds in one hand a scimitar in another a giant skull. . . . [S]he stands upon her husband . . . to keep him in subjection till the time of the universal con-

Figure 6. Mahā Kālī. From Charles Coleman, *The Mythology of the Hindoos* (London: Parbury, Allen, 1832).

> flagration. . . . She exhibits the appearance of drunken frantic fury. Yet this is the goddess . . . upon whose altars thousands of victims annually bleed, and whose temple . . . is the resort of Hindoos from all parts of India.[12]

A similar, perhaps even more colorful, account is that of the Scottish missionary Alexander Duff, who describes Kālī's worship as a kind of Satanic delirium comprised of mindless violence and bloodshed: "Of all Hindu divinities, this goddess is the most cruel and vengeful. . . . The supreme delight of this divinity . . . consists in cruelty and torture; her ambrosia is the flesh of sacrificed victims; and her sweetest nectar, the copious effusion of blood."[13]

Throughout the accounts of British authors of the colonial era, the image of Kālī represents a kind of impenetrable, almost inconceivable mystery—a source of simultaneous horror and fascination, which the Western mind cannot fathom but which it feels compelled to describe in endless, almost obsessive detail. She is a "form to be remembered for its grotesqueness and startling ugliness," and "a hideous black woman . . . with a huge blood-red tongue hanging out of her mouth."[14] As such, she represents the most primitive substratum of the Indian mind itself:

> No one can tell in what age it was that divinity revealed itself to the vision of some aboriginal . . . seer in the grotesque form of Mother Kali, nor does any record exist regarding the audacious hand that first modelled . . . those awful features . . . crudely embodying . . . the very dread of femininity always working in the minds of a most sensuous people, too prone to fall before the subtle powers of the weaker sex. . . . [T]he strange shapes of Kali . . . date back to primeval times, and may be regarded as only the fantastic shadows of divinity seen . . . in the dim twilight of world's morning.[15]

Above all, the figure of Kālī and the secret rites of her Tantric devotees were regarded as manifestations of the fanatical side of the Indian mind and thus as a dangerous source of unrest: "This divinity is the avowed patroness of all the most atrocious outrages against the peace of society."[16] As Chirol observes in *Indian Unrest,* the worship of Kālī represents the worst example of the manipulation of religious superstition in the service of political agitation: "The constant invocation of the 'terrible goddess' . . . against the alien oppressors, shows that Brahminism . . . is ready to appeal to the grossest and most cruel superstitions of the masses."[17] Here, we see a kind of paranoia similar to that found in other situations of colonial domination. As Taussig observes in the case of colonial South America, the fear of native rebellion created all sorts of nightmarish fantasies of cannibals, head hunters, and shamans threatening to rise up against law and order: "The uncertainty surrounding the possibility of Indian treachery fed a colonially paranoid mythology in which dismemberment, cannibalism . . . body parts and skulls grinned wickedly."[18]

The Deceivers: Thugs, Kālī, and Criminal Activity in Colonial India

> Intense devotion to Kalee is the mysterious link that unites them in a bond of brotherhood that is indissoluble; and with secrecy which for generations has eluded the efforts of successive governments to detect them.
>
> Rev. Alexander Duff, *India and Indian Missions* (1839)

In a growing body of nineteenth-century literature, both factual and fictional, the figure of Kālī and her Tantric devotees began to be associated with criminal activity and the notorious gangs of robbers *(dacoits)* believed to thrive in the underworld of India. "Thieves pay their devotion to Kalee . . . to whom bloody sacrifices are offered under the hope of carrying on their villainous designs with success."[19] The most infamous of these groups, and the most sinister in the British imagination, were the gangs known as the Phansigars ("stranglers") or more widely as the Thuggee ("deceivers"). To what degree the Thuggee were a real organization or, rather, the fabrication of British imagination and colonial paranoia is difficult to say.[20] As Cynthia Humes has argued, the British authorities of the early nineteenth century initially regarded the Thuggee as clear evidence of the dangerous criminal elements within the subcontinent—and thus as a justification for the need of extensive British rule and the strict imposition of colonial law. Yet increasingly in the nineteenth century, and above all after the mutiny of 1857, the threat of the Thuggee began to intensify within in the colonial imagination, growing into a sinister nationwide organization, dedicated to the subversion of British colonial rule.[21]

The legends of the Thuggee first appeared when Dr. Richard Sherwood published a report on the Phansigars in the *Madras Literary Gazette* in 1816. According to Sherwood's account, which would later become one of the most widely read versions in the colonial era, the Phansigars were both a criminal and a religious sect, patronized by the local rulers who gave it protection and shared its profits. They were, in short, "villains as subtle, rapacious and cruel as any who are to be met with in the records of human depravity." Being "skilled in the arts of deception," the Phansigars would first send ahead scouts in order to identify wealthy travelers on the roads, and then pose in the guise of fellow travelers, walking alongside the targeted party and gaining their trust.[22] Having deceived their intended victims, the Phansigars would then suddenly break that trust by strangling their victims from behind, using their trademark handkerchief or scarf.

However, the Thuggee became infamous as a criminal organization only due to the efforts of Colonel William Sleeman, later renowned as "Thuggee Sleeman." Born to a respected Cornish family in a long line of soldiers, Sleeman arrived in India in 1809 and served in Nepal from 1814 to 1816. In 1818, Sleeman grew curious about these notorious gangs of murderous robbers and requested to be transferred to the civil service in order to investigate the Thuggee full-time. Soon Sleeman concluded that the Thuggee were far more than a small band of petty criminals, but were in fact a nationwide organization—"a numerous and highly organized fraternity operating in all parts of India."[23] "He believed that India was under attack—that the foundation of human society was in danger of being destroyed. . . . He recognized Thuggee as instruments of the ultimate evil in their day, of that which as an end in itself takes human life indiscriminately. He was inspired by the belief that Thuggee must be destroyed."[24]

The most intensive period of the Thuggee investigation began in 1831–32, as Sleeman and his men gradually widened their circle from their initial forays in Bundelkand and western Malwa to spread throughout the subcontinent: "From the foot of the Himalayas to Cape Comorin, from Cutch to Assam, there was hardly a province . . . where Thuggee had not been practiced."[25] In short, as Amal Chatterjee observes, "Thugs, once 'discovered' sprang up all across India. . . . [S]o convinced were the propagators of the fiction that it began to be recorded everywhere," as every petty criminal from highway thief to river pirate was identified with the "Thuggee menace."[26] Sleeman had meanwhile gathered a vast body of reports, rumors, and confessions regarding the activities of this group, eventually publishing them in *Ramaseeana; or, A Vocabulary of the Peculiar Language Used by the Thugs.* The most famous of these accounts is the confession of the leader known as Feringhea, "the prince of thugs," who reportedly unveiled the secrets of the cult, which were "so incredible that at first Sleeman would not believe them."[27] In Sleeman's eyes, this cult represented an ancient evil in the heart of India, possibly going as far back as the Tartar and Mogul tribes, and surviving secretly for centuries as the terrifying underbelly of India.

Perhaps the most disturbing aspect of the Thug was precisely his dissimulating, duplicitous character—that he was first and foremost a *deceiver.* While appearing to be a good citizen and loyal subject of British law, the Thug was in fact a murderous criminal of the most sinister type:

> The most astounding fact about the Thug is that . . . he was a good citizen and model husband devoted to his family and scrupulously straight when not on his expeditions, presenting a complexity of character utterly baffling to a student of psychology. It was essential to the safety of their criminal operations that they should pass as peaceful citizens. . . . Not only had they left no trace behind of their foul deed, but they concealed their trail by every art and craft, and with ill-gotten rupees bribed officials, police and villagers, in whose territory the murders had occurred. . . . It is not extraordinary that Thuggee remained a mystery; rather it is remarkable that it was ever brought to light.[28]

Thus, if it is true, as Homi Bhabha suggests, that "colonial power produces the colonized as a fixed reality which is at once an other and yet entirely knowable and visible,"[29] then the Thug is a threat precisely because he is both *unknowable and invisible.* He is a deceiver who defies the all-penetrating gaze of colonial rule.

Whether the Thuggee were a real or an imaginary cult, a rich lore quickly grew up around them, combining fact and fantasy into a vivid narrative. Through the combined influence of Sleeman's personal accounts, the vivid chronicles of Thuggee persecution by Sir Edward Thornton (1837), and the popular fictional account by Philip Meadows Taylor (1839), a kind of Thuggee mythology had emerged, much of it centering on the figure of Kālī and her Tantric cult.[30] Under the form of Bhowani, it was believed, Kālī was worshiped by the Thuggee before they went out on their sprees of killing and banditry. According to the now infamous Thuggee legend, Kālī had come in the form of Bhowani in order to kill the demon Rukt Bij-dana. Although Kālī cut the demon in two, every drop of his blood that fell to earth gave birth to new demons; therefore the goddess created two men from the sweat of her arms and commanded them to strangle the demons using a *rumal,* or handkerchief. Kālī then established the cult of Thuggee, dedicated to her, which would continue the ritual art of strangulation and robbery. Initially, the story goes, Kālī had agreed to devour the corpses herself; however, after one of her devotees looked back to watch her as she consumed a victim, she refused to eat the bodies any longer. Instead she gave the Thuggee a sacred pickax with which to bury the corpses.

Not only were they thought to engage in rampant violence in the name of Kālī, but the Thuggee were also believed to hold dark secret rituals dedicated to her. These sinister rites were described as a kind of Black Mass, consisting of blood sacrifice and sacramental consumption of wine and meat. (While reading these accounts, it is difficult for a modern reader not to be reminded of medieval Inquisitors' accounts of witchcraft, or the Christian Fathers' accounts of the perverse rituals of certain Gnostic heresies):

> A silver or brazen image of the goddess . . . together with the implements of Phansigari, such as a noose, knife and pick axe, being placed together, flowers were scattered over them and offerings of fruit, cakes, spirits, &c. are made. . . . The head of the sheep being cut off, it is placed with a burning lamp upon it . . . before the image . . . and the goddess is entreated to reveal to them whether she approves of the expedition.[31]

> A ritual feast . . . took place after every murder, sometimes upon the grave of the victim. The goor or coarse sugar took the place of the Christian communion bread and wine.[32]

In sum, in the eyes of many British officials, the Thuggee and their demonic patroness, Kālī, came to represent the most extreme example of the natural tendency toward lawlessness, perversion, and murderous instinct lying at the darkest heart of the Indian race:

> The dark night of superstition, which has long clouded the moral vision of India, has given rise to practices so horrible that without the most convincing evidence, their existence could not be credited. . . . That giant power which has held the human race in chains wherever the . . . doctrines of revelation have not penetrated, has in India reveled in prosperity. . . . Here the genius of paganism had reared a class of men who are assassins by profession, called Phansigars or Thugs.[33]

Thus, with their sinister skills in deception, their ties to indigenous political corruption, and their devotion to the cruel goddess Kālī, the Thuggee seemed to provide the clearest evidence of the need for British rule in the subcontinent. "These common enemies of mankind, under the sanction of religious rites, have made every road between the Jumna and Indus rivers . . . a dreadful scene of lonely murder," Sleeman lamented, concluding that "we must have more efficient police establishments along the high roads . . . to root out entirely this growing evil which has been . . . increasing under the sanction of religious rites."[34]

The India that the British found in the late eighteenth century seemed to them a land sunk in immorality and decay, destroying itself with criminal gangs who preyed upon its own citizens, and woefully misruled by self-serving *rāja*s. According to most colonial narratives, India suffered a profound social breakdown following the collapse of the Mughal empire; the officers of the East India Company found India "ravaged and exhausted," strewn with "sacked palaces, vanishing roads, toppled fortresses . . . and ruined towns."[35] As Sir John Malcolm comments, the widespread presence of the Thuggee was the most acute example of this general state of moral and political decay: "the native states were disorganized and society on the verge of dissolution; the people crushed by despots, the country overrun by bandits. . . . [G]overnment had ceased to exist; there remained only oppression and misery."[36] At the same time, the Thuggee cult also revealed the political corruption that was rampant throughout India. Protected by the local rulers whom they bribed, the

Thuggee were able to survive due to the greed of the petty kings and a hypocritical legal system: "In an Eastern court of those days, bribery almost always took the place of justice and this, combined with fear, was responsible . . . for the extreme leniency shown."[37]

Given a political system so corrupt, Agent to the Governor-General F. C. Smith argued, the Thuggee should never be entrusted to the indigenous authorities. Instead, they should be tried by the more competent and efficient authority of the British government: "the feeble efforts of the native Chiefs having totally failed to suppress them, no Thug should . . . be made over to a native Chieftain for punishment, experience having shown their utter incapacity to put them down and expose their corrupt practices of concealing Thugs for valuable considerations."[38] The suppression of the Thuggee therefore demanded not only the assertion of British authority over that of local rulers, but also the formation of new special courts and the spread of British legal structures over the whole of India: "Nothing but a general system, undertaken by a paramount power, strong enough to bear down all opposition by interested native chiefs, could ever eradicate such well-organized villainy."[39] Perhaps the most important of the new legal structures was Act 30 of 1836. Extending Company jurisdiction to territories outside its actual dominions, the act allowed the offense in question to be tried in any Company court; it allowed trials to be conducted without any form of Islamic law; and it allowed conviction on the sole basis of membership in a gang of Thuggee. Hence this new system provided the ideal legitimation for the persecution of the "Thug menace." For even if there was often little evidence against the alleged Thuggee cult that would hold up in a regular court of law, now the British officials had a new license to receive and use evidence however they saw fit.

Ultimately, it was believed to be due in large part to the British suppression of Thuggee that the indigenous Indian population finally learned to respect the just authority of its colonial rulers. For the British had apparently been able to contain and control a disease that had been ravaging India for hundreds of years: "Those were the days when British rule in the East was synonymous with courage, strength and justice. . . . [T]he Indian had faith in British government and learned to respect it."[40] In sum, the heroic work of Sleeman and his men to suppress the Thuggee menace was regarded as the most "fitting monument to British rule." Just as benign British rule had saved India from its own moral decay and political chaos, so the selfless labors of Sleeman had saved India from a disease that had rotted the country from within.

> If the only monument to British rule in India was the suppression of Thuggee, it is doubtful whether any other nation could show a finer one. For . . . the Englishmen themselves suffered no harmful effects from this malignant enterprise and therefore no selfish motive prompted those who were responsible for suppressing this secret . . . system of murder. What other men of any other Western nation have deliberately imperiled their lives for years on end to protect native life only?[41]

By the late nineteenth century, however, the Thuggee myth had begun to assume a much darker and more threatening form. If the early narratives used the Thuggee as an example of India's lawlessness and the need for strong British rule, the later narratives reveal a fear that the Thuggee had grown into something far more dangerous than a mere underground criminal group. Particularly in the decades after the mutiny, the Thuggee myth grew into a full-blown paranoid fantasy, now imagined as a nationwide political organization, fueled by religious fanaticism, and dedicated to the overthrow of British rule itself. As MacMunn concludes,

> Thuggism was rampant all over India, from the Himalaya to the edge of Ceylon, and east and west from Cutch on the Indian Ocean to Assam on the Burma border. . . .
>
> For many years the Department of Thuggee . . . kept watch on this movement lest it should show its head again, and also on various secret movements, subversive of both civilization and the British Raj. Eventually it was merged in the Criminal Intelligence Department, whose annals will make the most astounding reading in the world, in which crime mingles with Shiva and Vishnu in a manner unknown elsewhere.[42]

Thus it is not surprising that this criminal menace would soon be linked to more overt political agitation, as well.

"Perverted Religion and Equally Perverted Patriotism"

> In its extreme forms Shakti worship finds expression in licentious aberrations which . . . represent the most extravagant forms of delirious mysticism.
>
> Valentine Chirol, *Indian Unrest* (1910)

The fear of the subversive power of Tantra would reach its height of intensity in the early twentieth century, with the rise of overt political resistance, particularly in hotbed regions like Bengal. Beginning with the Swadeshi (*swadeshi,* "of our own country") movement, which burst into violent agitation after the partition of Bengal in 1905, the nationalist revolutionaries appeared to the British government to represent a dangerous combination of religion and politics (a confusion almost as dangerous as the perverse mingling of sex and religion). For "in India, indeed, religion enters into politics as it does into most of the activities of man which in the West are usually described as secular."[43]

This monstrous fusion of religious fanaticism and subversive activities had reached its terrifying fruition in the revolutionary nationalist groups of the twentieth century. As the Rowlatt Commission of 1918 reported, the revolutionary outrages in Bengal were "the outcome of a widespread movement of perverted religion and equally perverted patriotism."[44] Calling upon the terrible mother Kālī for power, worshiping her with orgiastic violence, and even "sacrificing the white goats" of British officials to the goddess, they threatened the moral and political fabric of the colonial state itself. In many accounts, the nationalist movement is described as nothing less than a pervasive secret organization combining mysticism and political subversion—an "underground murder cult" comprised of a "strange melange of masonic ritual and a festival of horrible furious Kali in her wilder aspects."[45]

All of this was only natural, however, since the "Indian mind" was believed to have an inherent tendency toward the fusion of sexual license and political violence. The revolutionaries exploited this natural proclivity toward eroticism and criminality, inciting the sexually volatile young men to vent their frustrations at the British: "The Hindu student, depraved . . . by too early eroticism, turns to the suggestiveness of the murder-monger and worships the nitro-glycerine bomb as the apotheosis of his goddess."[46] Many authors attributed the prevalence of revolutionary activity among Bengali students to the overstimulating sexual practices of this culture—specifically the exposure of men to "early eroticisms" and young marriage, which is "terribly reflected in its effect on erotic young students . . . with their erotic hothouse nature."

> One of the most pitiful of all the manifestations of unrest . . . is the strange underground movement . . . which has produced a secret bomb and revolver cult, an assassination society with secret initiation. . . . Behind all the cruelty and sudden death of the world lies . . . Kali, the goddess of all horror. . . . "I am hungry" is her cry. "I want blood, blood victims." . . . Not even the perverted imaginations of the Marquis de Sade could devise a more horrible nightmare than Kali. . . . To minds such as students . . . overstrained by premature eroticism . . . this deity becomes a cult in which half-mystical murder may be a dominant thought.[47]

Here are conflated in the colonial imagination all the worst aspects of Tantra. Moral corruption, religious perversion, and political unrest come together around the image of Kālī and her obscene devotion. In the colonial imagination, Tantra is not just an example of the "savagery they yearn to colonize," but the presence of a savagery that *cannot be colonized,* an irrational, violent, and sexual power that threatens to consume the white masters.

KĀLĪ RISES IN THE EAST! TANTRA AND REVOLUTIONARY NATIONALISM

> On the day on which the Mother is worshipped in every village, on that day the people of India will be inspired with a divine spirit and the crown of independence will fall into their hands.
>
> *Jugantar* (1905)

> Just when [human beings] seem engaged in revolutionizing themselves . . . in creating something that never existed before, precisely in such epochs of revolutionary crisis they conjure up spirits of the past and borrow from them names, battle slogans and costumes in order to present the new scene of the world in this time-honored disguise. . . . Thus Luther wore the mask of the Apostle Paul, the revolution of 1789 . . . draped itself alternately as the Roman Republic and Roman Empire.
>
> Karl Marx, *Die Revolution* (1852)

As in every case of colonial domination, the Indians were by no means content to remain passive and unreflective, merely accepting the imaginary representations imposed upon them by colonial authorities. On the contrary, like native peoples in all situations of colonial contact, they had the potential to engage in a variety of "strategies of appropriation and subversion," often by "taking over colonial sources and turning them to anti-colonial uses."[48] They too had the ability to engage in a fierce war of images, often by manipulating the figure of Kālī and transforming her into a source of anticolonial struggle.

Borrowing Benjamin's phrase, we could say that Kālī is an ideal example of a dialectical image—a crystallized fusion of past and present, ancient religious myth and contemporary politics. Every community, Benjamin suggests, has a kind of "cultural memory" or a "reservoir of myths and utopian symbols from a more distant Ur-past."[49] These collective images can be used by established institutions to legitimate existing ideologies and political hierarchies; but they can also be used by oppressed classes as a source of political awakening. In the form of the dialectical image, mythic narratives of past traditions, utopian visions, and nostalgic longings for lost paradise can be seized upon, "reanimated," and transformed into revolutionary visions of liberation.

> Paradoxically, collective imagination mobilizes its powers for a revolutionary break from the past by evoking a cultural memory reservoir of myths and utopian symbols from a more distant Ur-past. . . . Utopian imagination thus cuts across the continuum of . . . historical development as the possibility of revolutionary rupture.
>
> [The] shock of this recognition [can] jolt the dreaming collective into a political awakening. The presentation of the historical object within a charged force field of past and present, which produces political electricity . . . is the dialectical image.[50]

It is in precisely this sense, I will argue, that the terrifying figure of the Tantric goddess Kālī was seized by the radical nationalist movement as an image of revolutionary awakening.

During the colonial era, the image of Kālī thus became the focus of a complex play of representation and misrepresentation, a play of *mimesis,* in Benjamin's and Taussig's sense of the term. As the basic human faculty for grasping the foreign or the unknown, mimesis is our ability to represent the Other.[51] Within the colonial imagination, the native is often represented as the negative antitype of the colonizer: conceived as savage or feminine, the native embodies the irrationality and backwardness against which the colonizer imagines himself. Yet particularly in cases like the terrifying goddess Kālī, this image often becomes a frightening mirror that reflects back the colonizers' own deepest fears, fantasies, and dangerous desires.

At the same time, of course, colonized peoples also have their own powers of mimesis and their own ways of imaginally representing the colonizing Other. In some cases, this takes the form of a playful mimicry or parody that mocks the colonial ruler; in other cases, it assumes a more subversive form, as the colonized subject appropriates the representations of the colonizers themselves, often inverting them as counterhegemonic weapons of resistance. For example, Taussig points to the construction of the image of the "shaman" in colonial South America.

As a powerful dialectical image, the shaman was in large part the result of a complex play of mimesis between the Europeans and the colonized Indians. If the colonial rulers had imagined the Indian to be an inherently savage and mysterious creature—a wild man and dangerous sorcerer, with threatening magical powers—then the Indians could likewise seize upon that image. Thus they embraced and exploited it, transforming the image into the dialectical image of the shaman, a figure embodying the power of wildness and supernatural danger, so threatening to the white man: "the shaman tames savagery, not to eliminate it, but to acquire it."[52] Hence, the image of the shaman demonstrates the ever threatening power of the oppressed over the oppressor, of the colonized over the colonizer.

An even more striking example that Taussig cites is the common eighteenth-century European representation of America as a woman, typically a beautiful naked woman adorned with feathered headdress, bow, and arrows. This New World/Woman, however, could assume both benevolent and terrifying features, imagined either as an inviting maiden awaiting the European colonizers, "languidly entertaining Discoverers from her hammock," or as a horrifying demoness, "striding brazenly across the New World as castrator with her victim's bloody head in her grasp."[53] Yet, as Taussig points out, the image of America as female was not only used by the European colonizers, but it was also reappropriated by the Indians, who transformed it into a symbol of Indianness, an anti-European, revolutionary spirit (for example, in Pedro Jose Figuero's famous painting of Bolivia as a woman wearing a feathered headdress, seated next to the liberator of the nation, Simon Bolivar [1819]).

An Avatār *That Cannot Be Slain: Kālī, Tantra, and the Nationalist Movement*

Nationalism is an *avatār* that cannot be slain. Nationalism is a divinely appointed Śakti of the Eternal and must do its God-given work before it returns to the bosom of Universal Energy from which it came.

Sri Aurobindo, quoted in Iyengar, *Sri Aurobindo* (1950)

We find much the same dialectical play of imagery in the role of Kālī in colonial Bengal. Above all, in the Bengal nationalist movement, the violent image of Kālī was transformed into the supreme symbol of Mother India fighting violently against her foreign oppressors. The origins of the

Figure 7. Sri Aurobindo as a young man. Frontispiece to Haridas Choudhuri, *Sri Aurobindo and the Life Divine* (San Francisco: Cultural Integration Fellowship, 1973).

Bengal nationalist movement lie in the more moderate ideals of the Indian National Congress of the last quarter of the nineteenth century, led by more conservative figures like R. C. Dutt or G. K. Gokhale. However, its second and most volatile period began in 1904, with the Swadeshi movement's more direct challenge to the legitimacy of British rule. Finally, in 1905, it burst into open conflagration with the British partition of West Bengal (with Bihar and Orissa) from East Bengal and Assam. In the period after 1907, the Swadeshi movement began to assume a more violent and extremist form, abandoning the earlier doctrines of passive resistance or boycott in favor of the tactics of revolutionary terrorism.[54]

One of the most outspoken members of the revolutionary strain of the movement was Aurobindo Ghose (figure 7), a man who in his later years would renounce the political life in order to pursue the spiritual path, eventually becoming one of the greatest religious leaders of modern India. Born in India but educated in England, Aurobindo returned to his homeland in 1893 to work for the State Service in Baroda. With the partition of Bengal in 1905, however, Aurobindo decided to leap headlong into the political maelstrom of Bengal. Leaving his position in Baroda, he arrived in Calcutta at the very height of the Swadeshi movement. The ideal that Aurobindo came to adopt was that of *swaraj,* or complete autonomy for India, which could only be achieved by a radical overthrow of British power. Although he is credited as one of the first advocates of passive resistance, Aurobindo also did not hesitate to promote armed resistance. In a just cause, "all methods were permissible"; therefore, "he shrewdly kept in reserve the weapon of secret revolutionary activity to be brought into the open . . . when all else failed."[55] As Aurobindo later wrote of his own involvement in the national movement, "my action in giving the movement . . . its militant turn or forming the revolutionary movement is very little known."[56]

The primary medium for Bengal's early revolutionary activities was a network of secret societies and underground movements. Calcutta, Dhaka, and other cities were filled with a host of secret organizations, both religious and political, working on the margins of and often in violent opposition to the existing social and governmental structures. Decades earlier, Aurobindo's grandfather Rajnarain Bose had organized a secret society, of which Rabindranath Tagore had been a member, dedicated to revolutionary action. The two most prominent of these secret groups were the Anushilan Samiti—which was originally founded by Aurobindo and others in 1902—and a looser group later known as Jugantar (the New Age).[57] As Aurobindo put it in a letter of 1911, his aim was to instigate "a secret revolutionary propaganda and organization."[58] Although Aurobindo would later deny his involvement with the radical actions of the Jugantar group, his brother Barindra and other members clearly regarded him as its founder, chief inspiration, and *karta,* or boss.

Throughout these organizations, there were often deep connections between Śākta Tantra and revolutionary politics. Much of the impetus for the secret groups came from the well-known novel of Bankim Chandra Chatterjee, *Ānandamaṭh*—the story of a group of revolutionary *sannyāsīs* (renunciants, ascetics) and devotees of the Mother Goddess who hope to overthrow Muslim rule in Bengal. Inspired by Bankim's work, Aurobindo and others deployed a network of secret organizations in order to work behind the scenes toward an armed revolution. As Kees Bolle, Leonard Gordon, and others have observed, the revolutionaries explicitly appropriated many structures of Śākta Tantra, adapting "neo-Tantric rituals" and initiations to the service of building up an underground revolutionary organization. "Śākta religious rituals played a significant role in cementing unity and discipline. . . . The left wing extremists which organized themselves into revolutionary secret societies followed the practice of taking vows before the goddess Kālī."[59] Peter Heehs summarizes the initiatory oath, as recorded by the Government of India Home Department:

> The Sanskrit oath, probably written by Aurobindo, took the form of a Vedic sacrificial hymn. Invoking Varuna, Agni and other deities . . . bowing down to the ideal heroes of India that sacrificed their lives to save the motherland . . . the oath-takers poured their hatred and shame into the fire . . . to save the country. Renouncing all life's pleasures, they vowed to dedicate themselves to the establishment of the Dharma Rajya [Righteous Kingdom]. . . . Then bowing to a sword, crown of all weapons, the symbol of death, they lifted it up in the name of the Adya Shakti (original Energy, conceived as the Goddess Kālī).[60]

The public voice of the movement was communicated through the Calcutta newspapers *Bandemataram,* to which Aurobindo was a regular contributor, and the more radical *Jugantar,* begun by Aurobindo's brother, Barin. The latter openly preached revolution and subversion of British authority. Calling the Bengali youth to give themselves in "sacrificial death" to the nationalist cause, the newspaper gave precise directions as to how one should start a secret terrorist organization and carry out terrorist activities.[61] Not surprisingly, *Jugantar* was prosecuted for sedition six times before its final suppression in 1908.

Under Barin's direction, the revolutionaries worked underground, collecting arms and making bombs. Although Aurobindo did not carry out terrorists acts himself, it seems probable that he both knew of and helped guide the group's terrorist activities. What Aurobindo sought was not random terrorism, but "a full-scale insurrection," hoping that "successful revolutionary acts might create popular interest and at the same time intimidate the enemy."[62] Thus, a laboratory was built at the Bengal Engineering College in order to make bombs; and on April 30, 1908, members of the society at Muzaffarpur threw a bomb intended for Douglas Kingsford, who was just transferred from his post as chief presidency magistrate at Calcutta. Tragically, however, the bomb instead hit the carriage bearing Kingsford's daughter.

Despite his violent revolutionary activities, Aurobindo considered his cause to be not merely political but also profoundly religious. For him, nationalism was a divine a mission, and religion was the life-blood that flowed through the organic body of the Indian nation:

> Nationalism is not a mere political program; Nationalism is a religion that has come from God. Nationalism is a creed which you shall have to live. . . . If you are to be Nationalist . . . you must do it in the religious spirit. . . . It is not by any mere political programme . . . that this country can be saved. . . . What is the one thing needful? . . . the idea that there is a Power at work to help India, that we are doing what God bids us.[63]

India in Aurobindo's day had been offered up to "the secularity of autonomy and wealth, the pseudo-divinities upon whose altars Europe has sacrificed her soul."[64] Thus Indian youths must now be willing to sacrifice themselves—and to sacrifice their enemies—to divine cause of nationalism. Predictably, Aurobindo's political activities soon attracted government attention. The police identified his publications as "the germ of the Hindu revolutionary movement," condemning its "combination of religion and politics" as a "deliberate perversion of religious ideals to political purposes."[65] According to one official report, his project was "nothing but a gigantic scheme for establishing a central religious society, outwardly religious but in spirit, energy and work political. . . . [Aurobindo] has misinterpreted Vedantist ideas for his own purpose."[66] Finally, after the disastrous failure of the Muzaffarpur bombing, in May 1908, Aurobindo was arrested and sentenced to one year's imprisonment in Alipur jail.

The Mother Is Thirsty!

> Offer sacrifice to me. Give for I am thirsty. Seeing me, know and adore the original Power, ranging here as Kālī, who . . . hungers to enjoy the heads of bodies of mighty rulers.
>
> Sri Aurobindo, "Bhavani Bharati"

From the outset, the extremist leaders of the nationalist movement had made use of traditional religious and mythic themes to legitimate their revolutionary activity. The newspaper *Jugantar,* for example, employs the traditional model of the *avatār* or successive incarnations, of Viṣṇu sent to right the world and combat evil during each cosmic era: "the army of young men is the . . . Kalki incarnation of God, saving the good and destroying the wicked."[67] But surely the most powerful symbol employed by the revolutionaries was the Tantric goddess Śakti, particularly in her most frightening incarnation, Kālī.

Although Kālī has long appeared in Indian mythology as a goddess of military power and violence, her largely mythological figure was to assume a very concrete political role in the context of colonial Bengal. The most famous depiction of Kālī as the symbol of the motherland appears in Bankim Chandra's fictional account of the Sannyāsī rebellion, *Ānandamaṭh* (The abbey of bliss). As we will see in more detail in chapter 3, it remains unclear whether Bankim's original intention was to arouse anti-British revolutionary sentiments, or, on the contrary, to promote anti-Muslim but ultimately pro-British ideals. In any case, his novel later would be reinterpreted by the leaders of the nationalist movement as a weapon against the British and a model for revolution in the name of the Goddess.[68]

Perhaps most importantly, Bankim presented the image of the Goddess as the symbol of the Indian nation, the motherland, who is glorious in her original splendor and terrible in her present oppression: "Kālī was at once the symbol of the degradation of society under alien rule and a reservoir of unlimited power."[69] In one of the most remarkable passages in Bankim's work, the Goddess appears as a fusion of past, present, and future. Inside the temple at the Abbey of Bliss, we are successively introduced to three goddesses, representing India in three historical periods. First we meet a beautiful image of Jagaddhatri as the "Mother, what once was," as India's golden past. Then we encounter the terrible Kālī, the bloodthirsty image of India in an age of foreign oppression: "Kali, covered with the blackest gloom, despoiled of all wealth. . . . The whole of the country is a land of death and so the Mother has no better ornament than a garland of skulls." Last, we see a third image: a radiant, ten-armed goddess, who represents the future of India, the liberated nation in its original glory. "This is the Mother as she would be."[70]

During the first years of the Swadeshi movement, Bankim's novel and his image of the Goddess became favorite weapons of the revolutionaries. Newly appropriated by figures like Swami Vivekananda and Sister Nivedita (in her influential book *Kālī the Mother* [1907]), and seized upon by the extremist Bengali journals, the image of Kālī suddenly assumed a markedly political form. Aurobindo, in particular, was deeply inspired by Bankim's work and his depiction of Mother India. Aurobindo's translation of the famous song "Bande Mataram" (Hail to the Mother) became the battle cry of the nationalist movement: "It was the gospel of fearless strength and force which he preached under a veil and in images in *Ananda Math*."[71] However, Aurobindo also reinterpreted Bankim's story, transforming it into a radically anticolonial call to revolution. In an even more explicit attempt to fuse the political and the religious domains, he drew on the traditional Tantric imagery of the Goddess as power on both the spiritual and revolutionary planes. As Kumari Jayawardena suggests, Aurobindo's "emotional juxtaposing of Mother Goddess and Mother Country" was an effective image both psychologically and sociologically, which reflected at once the painful personal loss of his own mother and the traditional power of the Mother in the Indian mythic imagination: "Aurobindo's uncompromising opposition to British rule was couched in the language of the cult of the Mother. Deprived of his own mother (who was insane) while in Britain for fourteen years, Aurobindo, in the political and spiritual phases of his life, constantly invoked the divine mother who would make India strong again."[72]

The most influential work from Aurobindo's early political period is a pamphlet entitled *Bhawani Mandir,* "The Temple of the Goddess," published in 1905. Here, Aurobindo lays out his ideal of a secret religio-political organization, an order of young ascetics who would consecrate themselves to the liberation of the motherland. The ascetics would meet at a temple of the goddess Bhawani, a manifestation of Kālī, hidden in a secret place where her disciples would prepare for the armed struggle for independence. Very soon, *Bhawani Mandir* became among the most influential works in the national movement, a "handbook for revolutionary groups of Bengal."[73] As Gordon comments, "In *Bhawani Mandir,* as in the Tantras, the organ for emancipation and the urge for power go together. Aurobindo . . . syncretized religious elements and national messianism. Aurobindo gives fellow Indians a mission to 'Aryanize' the world."[74]

The central figure of *Bhawani Mandir* is the goddess Śakti, who is nothing other than "pure power." She is the world-creating divine energy, which has existed since the beginning of time, spinning creation into being; but now, in this most extreme age of crisis in the Kali yuga, she has become manifest even more openly, with the rise of new political forces and the spread of violent powers across the earth. Aurobindo even identifies Śakti as the underlying force beneath the power, wealth, expansion, and industrialization—including the growing military power of the West—that characterizes the modern world:

> Wherever we turn our gaze, huge masses of strength rise before our vision, tremendous, swift and inexorable forces, gigantic figures of energy, terrible sweeping columns of force. All is growing large and strong. The Shakti of war, the Shakti of wealth, the Shakti of science are tenfold more mighty and colossal . . . a thousand-fold more prolific in resources weapons and instruments than ever before. . . . Everywhere the Mother is at work; from

> her mighty and shaping hands enormous forces of Rakshasas, Asuras, Devas are leaping forth. . . . We have seen the . . . rise of great empires in the West. . . . Some are Mleccha Shaktis . . . blood-crimson . . . others are Arya Shaktis bathed in . . . self-sacrifice; but all of them are the Mother in Her new phase. . . . She is whirling into life the new.[75]

But although she is at work everywhere in the modern world, Śakti is first and foremost the power of the Indian nation. While the forces of Westernization and industrialization manifest the demonic form of Śakti, harnessed to destructive ends, the Indian nation reveals the true, Aryan force of Śakti, turned toward spiritual ends. For Aurobindo, this divine Śakti is nothing other than the collective power of India, the combined energy of each individual Indian soul. "What is our mother-country? It is not a piece of earth, nor a figure of speech. . . . It is a mighty Shakti, composed of the Shaktis of all the millions of units that make up the nation."[76]

But, Aurobindo continues, in these years of foreign rule the Indian had become weak and powerless, for he had become ignorant of his mother, Śakti. Like Vivekananda and other spiritual leaders of the early twentieth century, Aurobindo is painfully aware of the figure of the "effete babu" in the colonial imagination, the fawning, submissive, emasculated servant of British administration. Aurobindo, too, criticizes the passivity and weakness of Bengalis, calling them to a more virile, militant stance against their oppressors. He urges his countrymen to find a new inner strength and even "hypermasculinity"—the warrior ideal of the *kṣatriya:* "the one thing wanting . . . is strength—strength physical, strength moral, but above all strength spiritual."[77]

As I would argue, the image of hypermasculine militant Bengali was the counterpart to the image of Kālī or Śakti as the powerful, destructive goddess. If the colonial imagination had juxtaposed the two images of the effete, emasculated babu and the lustful, violent Kālī, the revolutionary nationalists *inverted and transformed* these two images, juxtaposing the virile, strong Bengali warrior and the powerful goddess. As Nandy observes, the nationalists hoped to refashion and remake the self-image of the Bengali male himself. Whereas the British had continually ridiculed the Bengali babu as weak, effeminate, morally corrupt, and sexually perverse, the nationalists created an image of the Bengali male as powerful, militant, and hypermasculine.[78] Hence the two images of the violent, militant goddess Kālī and the strong, hypermasculine Bengali revolutionary worked together as dialectical complements; and together, they

TABLE 1

	Male	Female
Imperial imagination	Effeminate, weak, morally degenerate, licentious	Overly sexual, violent, masculine
Nationalist imagination	Strong, virile, militant, morally pure, hyper-masculine *kṣatriya*-hood	Violent, strong, but not sexual

represented the dialectical inversion of the imperial imagination, which had depicted the Bengali male as effeminate and sexually depraved and the Bengali female as excessively sexual and lustful. All of this could be schematically represented as in table 1.

At the same time, however, I would also suggest that the image of Śakti as Mother India played a more powerful role as a source of revolutionary inspiration, serving as a "dialectical image," in Benjamin's sense. For Aurobindo and the other leaders of the Jugantar group drew upon precisely those elements of the Goddess that the British most feared and despised—the violent and wrathful Mother-in-arms, who drinks human blood and wears garlands of severed heads. One of the most powerful images used by the national movement was taken explicitly from a traditional Tantric image of Kālī as Chinnamastā, who stands naked on the corpse of her husband, Śiva, holding her own severed head and drinking the blood that flows from it. Bipanchandra Pal, another leader in the revolutionary movement, offered a new interpretation of this traditional image: it is a representation of the motherland herself, which has been beheaded by the British and drinks her own blood in order to survive:

> The Mother . . . became Kālī, the grim goddess, dark and naked wearing a garland of human heads—heads from which blood is dripping—and dancing on the prostrate form of Śiva. . . . This is the Mother as she is, dark because ignorant of herself, the heads with dripping blood are those of her own children destroyed by famine and pestilence; the jackals licking these drippings are . . . the decadence of social life and the prostrate form of Śiva means that she is trampling her own God under her feet.[79]

Now every Indian is called upon to serve as a "priest of Kālī" and to offer himself as a sacrificial victim to the Goddess, spilling his own blood in her defense: "The hero, the martyr . . . the grim fighter . . . the man who cannot sleep while his country is enslaved, the priest of Kali who can tear his heart out of his body and offer it as a bleeding sacrifice on the Mother's altar."[80]

However, the traditional Tantric image of Kālī was used not only to represent the humiliation of modern India, but also to arouse revolutionary fervor and violence. For since her earliest appearances in Hindu myth, Kālī has also been the symbol of destruction, bloodshed, and war, and hence an effective symbol for inciting political violence. As Aurobindo described the Dark Mother in his "Bhavani Bharati, Mother of India":

> Garlanded with the bones of men and girdled with human skulls, with belly and eye like a wolf's hungry and poor, scarred on her back by the Titan's lashes, roaring like a lioness who lusts for kill . . . filling the world with bestial sounds and licking her terrible jaws, fierce and naked, like eyes of a savage beast, thus did I see the Mother.
>
> Thou naked art Kālī and utterly ruthless thou art. . . . I bow to Thee as the violent One, O Ender of worlds. . . . The mighty Mother of creatures has vanquished the age of Strife . . . in East and West, I hear the cry of the whole world hastening with the praise on its tongue to this country, the ancient Mother of the Vedas . . . firmly established in the Aryan country. Abide forever gracious in this land, O mighty One.[81]

Nothing now can satisfy this terrible Mother but the spilling of blood. The rage of Mother India in her violent form has been unleashed, and it cannot be pacified until it tastes the severed heads of her oppressors. As the radical newspaper *Jugantar* exhorts its readers,

> The Mother is thirsty and is pointing out to her sons the only thing that can quench that thirst. Nothing less than human blood and decapitated heads will satisfy her. Let her sons worship her with these offerings and let them not shrink even from sacrificing their lives to procure them. On the day on which the Mother is worshipped in every village, on that day the people of India will be inspired with a divine spirit and the crown of independence will fall into their hands.[82]

Today, Aurobindo tells us, Bengalis are like Arjuna on the battlefield of Kurukṣetra, on the verge of a holy struggle in which they "must not shrink from bloodshed" but be willing to give their own lives as sacrificial victims to the Goddess. Like Kurukṣetra, the field of the great bloody "sacrifice of battle," the soil of contemporary Bengal becomes the "cremation ground" upon which the violent Kālī unleashes her terrible power. But it is also the cremation ground of the great cosmic sacrifice at the end of time, the conflagration of worlds that signals the end of the old yuga and the violent dawn of the new.[83]

Submitting to the Mother: The Failure of Revolutionary Śāktism

There is one force only, the Mother's force—or, if you like to put it that way, the Mother is Sri Aurobindo's Force.

Sri Aurobindo,
Sri Aurobindo on Himself and the Mother (1953)

Ironically, despite its powerful shock effect, the nationalists' use of the image of Kālī does not appear to have been successful. For in many ways it could be said to have played back into the colonial view of India as morally depraved, a land of barbarous violence and perverse irrationality. As Nandy argues, the self-image created by the revolutionaries also backfired and worked against them: the "hypermasculine" *kṣatriya* ideal of the revolutionaries still played by the rules of the colonial views of sexuality and manhood, replicating the European ideal of the virile, active male and the passive, submissive female. It could not succeed in overthrowing colonial ideology, but ultimately reinforced it.[84] Likewise, the use of Kālī as a symbol of the nation in many ways only reaffirmed the Western view of Indians as morally degenerate, violent, and subversive. The solution that would win out, ultimately, was not the radical program of the extremists, but the ideal of passive resistance promoted by Mahatma Gandhi. By 1910, Aurobindo himself would abandon the revolutionary project and turn inward to the life of the spirit.

During his period of confinement in Alipur jail, Aurobindo claimed to have received an inner message from God, informing him that he had a worldwide purpose; he had been chosen "to uplift this nation" and "give the Indian people freedom for service of the world."[85] Upon his release from prison in 1910, Aurobindo left the active political realm and retired to Pondicherry, a small former French colonial town on the west coast. His own account of this change of heart was that he had received information that the government intended to search his office and arrest him; he then received a sudden command from above to go to Chandernagore in French India, where he lived in secrecy and solitary meditation. Immersed in the study of yoga and Indian philosophy, a small group of disciples eventually gathered around his ashram. Henceforth he began to write a vast body of works on various aspects of spirituality, along with poems, plays, and even epics. Despite urgings from many members of the nationalist movement, Aurobindo never reentered the political arena, claiming instead that he was having a greater impact on the course of world history through his spiritual teachings. When he was invited to preside over 1920 Indian Congress, he declined, saying, "I am no longer first and foremost a politician, but have commenced another kind of work with a spiritual basis."[86]

After his withdrawal from the political life, Aurobindo began to envision a new ideal for the Indian nation and also to imagine a new role for the Divine Mother. Whereas, in his youth, Aurobindo had conceived of the Mother in Tantric terms, as Śakti, the terrible power of the nation in revolt, he now began to reimagine the Goddess in a far more benevolent and seemingly "un-Tantric" form. She was now the ideal of pure Spirit, the embodiment of India as the land of literature, culture, art, and above all religion. Here I would like to borrow some insights from Partha Chatterjee and his analysis of the changing construction of the Bengali *bhadralok* ("respectable classes") identity in nineteenth-century Bengal. Many middle-class Bengalis, Chatterjee argues, withdrew from the outward political sphere, dominated as it was by foreign colonial power. Instead, they turned inward to the private sphere of religion and domesticity—"an inner domain of sovereignty far removed from the area of political context with the colonial state"—as the stronghold of traditional Indian values. For "the strategy of survival in a world that is dominated by the rich and powerful is withdrawal. Do not attempt to intervene in the world, do not engage in futile conflict."[87]

A critical part of the construction of Indian national identity, as an inner private sphere in opposition to the colonially dominated public sphere, was the dichotomy of the "material West and the spiritual East." Even as early as 1902, Aurobindo had drawn a sharp distinction between the materialism or "morbid animalism" of the West and the eternal religion of India.

> Science had freed Europe from the shackles of Christianity but it had not provided a new system of values to replace the one it had rendered obsolete. The result . . . was an upsurge of "morbid animalism" demonstrating Europe's "neurotic tendency to abandon itself to its own desires." . . . Hinduism alone among the great embodiments of the old religious and moral spirit did not . . . stand naked to the assaults of Science. Hinduism therefore could serve as the framework for a new world outlook.[88]

Later in life, Aurobindo would make this dichotomy even more explicit, identifying "the two principal ways of regarding existence—the spirituality preserved in the religious traditions of the East and the practicality represented by the political and economic systems of the West."[89] As Halbfass points out, Aurobindo may have withdrawn from the political arena into the spiritual realm in the second half of his life, yet there is a deep continuity between the two phases. Both are attempts at Indian *self-assertion,* attempts to identify a domain of national and religion identity, a uniquely *Eastern* cultural sphere, set apart from that of the West: "Hindu nationalism and spiritualistic universalism dominate the two major phases in Aurobindo's Neo-Hindu life. They are . . . complementary means of self-assertion."[90]

Yet Aurobindo's new nonpolitical, spiritual ideals would continue to center on the overarching figure of the Great Goddess, the Mother. The striking irony, however, is that Aurobindo would later come to identify the Mother, not with the violent, bloodthirsty, and militant Tantric goddesses Kālī, Durgā, or Chinnamastā, but instead with one particular woman, and most remarkably, a Western woman—Mira Alfassa (later Mira Richards, 1878–1973). Born in Paris of a Sephardic Jewish family, Richards had been a student at the École des Beaux Arts and part of the artistic avant-garde scene in Paris. She had also begun from an early age to dabble in occultism and Eastern religions, and was soon attracted by Aurobindo's unique blend of Western philosophy and Indian mysticism. Leaving behind home and children, she joined Aurobindo and became his disciple in 1914. As his new religious community began to gather around him, Aurobindo eventually elevated Mira to a divine status nearly equal to his own. After his own wife's death in 1918, Aurobindo would grow increasingly closer to Mira. When her husband left her in 1920, Mira was moved into the master's house, occupying the quarters adjacent to his apartment, where she would remain until his death. Not only did Mira progressively take over all the details of running the growing ashram, but, by 1926, she came to be revered as none other than the Mother herself, the manifestation of the supreme Śakti in human form.[91] As Aurobindo described her,

> There is one divine Force which acts in the universe and in the individual. . . . The Mother stands for all these but she is working here in the body to bring down something not yet expressed in this material world so as to transform life here. . . . [Y]ou should regard her as the Divine Shakti. . . . She is that in the body, but in her whole consciousness she is also identified with all other aspects of the Divine.[92]

As Aurobindo explained in a letter of 1926, Mira was none other than his own counterpart and complement in the spiritual realm: "Mother and I are one but in two bodies."[93] While he himself was the embodiment of the masculine, spiritual Puruṣa—which, rather strikingly, he now interprets as *passive and unacting*—the Mother represents the feminine, practical element of Prakṛti or Śakti—which is inherently *active and dynamic.* As Heehs comments, "His personal force, representing the Purusha element, acted in the realm of spiritual knowledge, while Mira's representing the Shakti element, was practical. . . . Without the Mother . . . his conception of a divine life on earth could never have been embodied."[94] Together, he and the Mother had been working as the primordial male and female principles moving through all history, guiding the evolution of humankind. Not only did their divine interaction lie at the font of creation and within all the world's great events, but it even determined the course of contemporary history, including the onset and final end of World War II. "The War ended in 1945, with the victory of the Allies, as Sri Aurobindo had willed."[95]

This mother is no longer the violent Kālī of the *tantra*s or the bloodthirsty Śakti of the nationalist movement, to be worshiped by strong *kṣatriya* warriors with offerings of severed heads; rather, it is a loving mother to whom the soul must surrender itself like a child at her breast: "when you are completely identified with the Divine Mother and feel yourself to be no longer another separate being . . . but truly a child and eternal portion of her force."[96] As Nandy comments on this striking paradox, Aurobindo's choice of a Western woman as his Śakti was his final attempt to resolve the profound oppositions in his life, his long struggle between East and West, between his English education and his search for an Indian identity: "For him the freed East had at last met the nonoppressive West symbolized by the Mother."[97] Hence, we might add to our schema of contrasting sexual-symbolic images a third pair, the new Male and Female archetypes of Aurobindo's postpolitical, spiritual phase (see table 2).

Following the lead of Partha Chatterjee, I would suggest that the rather curious union of Aurobindo and Mira Richards is a profound symbol of the deeper ambivalence underlying Indian nationalism as a whole. Aurobindo, like many members of the nationalist movement, struggled to create a uniquely Indian, Hindu identity—an inner, spiritual, and cultural private sphere—set in opposition to the political and material public sphere of the West.[98] Yet at the same time, he clearly absorbed many of the basic structures and oppositions of the West, including the opposition between the inner, private sphere and the outer, politically active, public sphere. The choice of a Western woman as Śakti—a spiritual mother who replaces the violent, destructive Śakti of

TABLE 2

	Male	Female
Colonial imagination	Effeminate, weak, morally degenerate, licentious	Overly sexual, violent, masculine
Nationalist imagination	Strong, virile, militant, morally pure, hyper-masculine *kṣatriya*-hood	Violent, strong, but not sexual
Aurobindo's postrevolutionary imagination	Spirit (Puruṣa), passive, inward, inactive, the Spiritual East	Power, Nature (Prakṛti), outward, active, the material West

his revolutionary nationalist period—is a profound symbol of the deeper conflicts at work the hearts of Aurobindo and other intellectuals of the early twentieth century. It is a clear embodiment of his own attempt to identify a uniquely Indian or Eastern identity, in opposition to the material West. And yet this identity is itself constructed with Western categories and terms. As Halbfass comments, "Even in their rejection of . . . European ideas and orientations, modern Indian thinkers are not free from such ideas. Explicit or implicit reference to the West, and membership in a Westernized world, is an irreversible premise of modern Indian thought."[99]

In the face of his failure as a revolutionary opponent of Western domination in the name of the Tantric mother Kālī, Aurobindo seems to have turned instead to a more complex, ambivalent, though perhaps more tolerable solution. He has now tried to accommodate the power of the West—the power of European technology, science, and material advancement—while at the same time asserting the ultimate spiritual superiority, and seeming political impotence, of the East. While the dangerous, violent Śakti of the Tantras has failed, a new hope lies in the attempt to incorporate the Śakti of the West.

TANTRA AND THE POLITICS OF COLONIAL INDIA

The pride of prosperity throws man's mind outwards
and the misery . . . of destitution draws men's hunger-
ing desires likewise outwards. These two conditions

> alike leave man unashamed to place above all other gods, Shakti the Deity of Power—the Cruel One, whose right hand wields the weapon of guile. In the politics of Europe drunk with Power we see the worship of Shakti.
>
> Rabindranath Tagore, "Letters from an On-Looker" (1919)

In sum, the shifting representations of Tantra and the Tantric goddess might be seen as a metaphor for the changing image of the Indian nation itself in the nineteenth and twentieth centuries. A powerful dialectical category, Tantra passed back and forth between colonial and anti-colonial imaginations, used by some to attack the criminality of the Indian subject and by others to instigate revolution against the imperial master. If the colonizers projected onto Tantra the "savagery they yearned to colonize," in the form of criminal Thuggee and subversive agitators, the leaders of the radical nationalist movement appropriated Tantra as the awesome power of the Indian people *that could not be controlled.* The heart of this play of representations was the Tantric goddess of power—a goddess who embodied all the darkest fears of subversion within the colonial imagination and all the hopes for violent revolt among the extremists. She is thus a fitting symbol for the birth, hope, and failure of the revolutionary nationalist movement.

Ironically, the use of violence and power did not prove to be a viable solution for either colonizer or colonized. The radical ideal of the Tantric Śakti gave way to passive resistance of Gandhian nationalism and the relatively peaceful withdrawal of the British from India in 1947. Thus, like many Western-educated Indians of his day, Aurobindo ultimately seems to have sought a kind of compromise, a reconciliation between the passive spirituality of the East and the active power of the West, now embodied in his seemingly "un-Tantric" consort, Mira Richards. Hence, we might be tempted to follow the lead of the members of the Subaltern Studies collective, such as Ranajit Guha, by regarding Aurobindo's retreat from active politics as yet another example of "the historic failure of the nation to come to its own."[100] That is, it could be seen as the failure of genuine resistance, a disappointing compromise with the West. I would argue, however, that Aurobindo's solution is better understood as another example of a *strategy for dealing with a situation.* Like Rāmmohun Roy's paradoxical use of the *Mahānirvāṇa Tantra* in the service of his own cultural reforms, Aurobindo's turn from the dark Tantric Śakti to the more benign Western Śakti was an ingenious, through perhaps not entirely successful, attempt to resolve the "situational incongruities" of India under late colonial rule.

I would like also to point out some larger comparative implications of this discussion of Tantra and colonial politics. The shifting role of Tantra in the British and Indian imaginations sheds some important light on the role of religious symbolism in the formation of political identities, particularly during periods of colonial rule. As Ranajit Guha, Partha Chatterjee, and others have acknowledged, the power of religious symbolism has long been one of the least understood and most neglected problems in the literature on subaltern studies.[101] Commonly reduced to a mask of political ideology or an instrument of domination, religious symbols have seldom been discussed as weapons of insurgency or tools for revolutionary struggle. As I hope to have shown in the case of Tantra and the goddess Śakti, religious symbols can indeed be used as masks of ideology, to reinforce a given political arrangement; but they can also be manipulated as profound dialectical images, appropriated by dissident factions to subvert the status quo and even instigate revolutionary struggle. Like all symbols, however, the image of the Goddess is an ambivalent, even contradictory one, which leads her devotees to both heroic victories and tragic failures in their fight for independence.

CHAPTER 3

India's Darkest Heart

Tantra in the Literary Imagination

The follower of the Tantric cult professes no austerities. He seeks to kill desire by an unlimited indulgence which brings satiety and extinction of emotion. The indulgence is enjoined by his so-called religion; and his depravity is commended as a great virtue.

F. E. F. Penny, *The Swami's Curse* (1929)

Flee even now—don't you know that the *tāntrika*'s worship consists of human flesh?

Bankimcandra Caṭṭopādhyāy, *Kapālakuṇḍalā* (1866)

Much of our richest and most colorful material for the imagining of Tantra comes not from scholarly sources, but from the realm of drama and the novel. In both India and Europe, the morbid, sexual tales of Tantra quickly sparked the imaginations of many creative authors, serving as the vehicle for the expression of intense fears, fantasies, and repressed desires. In a wide array of Victorian British and Indian fiction, we find virtually all the themes discussed so far in this book, brought together in the most vivid and entertaining way: the fears of social degeneracy, the threat of sexual pollution, the paranoia of criminal or subversive activity. Yet the novelists not only adapted these images of Tantra from Orientalist literature; they also contributed a new imaginary layer of their own—an often hyperexaggerated layer of fantasy—that in turn fed back into the Orientalist imagination even as it disseminated the image of Tantra to a popular audience. As Pratt argues in her analysis of colonial travel narratives, "The fruits of empire . . . were pervasive in shaping

European domestic society, culture and history"; yet at the same time, "Europe's constructions of subordinated others [were] shaped by those others, by the constructions of themselves . . . that they presented to the Europeans."[1] What we find in these novels is a complex feedback loop between "serious" scholarship and popular culture, between the "hard facts" of Orientalist research and the vivid play of literary creations. And it is also a dynamic interplay between Indian and English narrative imaginations.

This sort of fictional portrayal of Tantra is not, of course, entirely a byproduct of the colonial era. As we have already seen in examples like Bāṇabhaṭṭa's *Kādambarī* (see the introduction), many early Sanskrit works do contain colorful, often quite funny, descriptions of various yogis and ascetics who later came to be identified as *tāntrikas*. The most notorious of these are the Kāpālikas, or skull-bearers—wandering ascetics who take a vow to imitate Lord Śiva in his terrible form of Bhairava, as he travels the earth smeared in ashes and carrying a skull for a begging bowl. Feared for their awesome occult powers, the Kāpālikas were also ridiculed for their alleged practice of the most transgressive rituals, such as intercourse with lower-class women and offerings of human sacrifice.

Although they seemed to have disappeared by the thirteenth century, the Kāpālikas survived as buffoons and favorite targets of satire in Sanskrit fiction. We have already encountered the drunken Kāpālika Satyasoma, the main character in Mahendra-varman's comic farce (see the introduction). For Satyasoma, enjoyment of wine and women is the surest road to divine bliss: "The infinite incomparable bliss that wise sages first discovered, is now as close as one could wish, for we have added a special measure. No need to abandon the life of a lover. This bliss includes all sensual pleasure."[2] Indeed, consumption of alcohol becomes for Satyasoma the true elixir of Soma that is consumed at the highest sacrificial rite: "This liquor shop equals the majesty of the sacrificial enclosure. Here the flag pole equals the sacrificial post; the liquor cup equals the soma; the drinkers the priests. . . . The thirst of the drinker is the sacrificial fire."[3]

Later in the eleventh century, Kṛṣṇamiśra includes an amusing satire of a Kāpālika in his drama *Prabodhacandrodaya*. Inhabiting cremation grounds, drinking wine from skulls, and offering human sacrifices, the Kāpālika is portrayed here as the epitome of all impurity and transgression. Amid a theological argument between a Buddhist mendicant and a Jain monk, the Kāpālika appears and describes himself in rather awe-inspiring terms: an inhabitant of cremation grounds and a lover of human flesh, he sees nothing as impure and all as divine:

> I, who am adorned with a garland of human bones, who live in the cremation ground and who eat out of a human skull, with an eye purified by the instrument of Yoga, see the world having differences within itself but being non-different from God. . . .
>
> We who offer oblations in the fire in the form of human flesh, brains, entrails and marrow break our fast with alcohol kept in the skull of a Brāhmaṇa. Mahābhairava has to be worshipped with human offerings, lustrous with streams of blood flowing from the stiff throat which is freshly cut.[4]

Above all, the Kāpālika is the one who seeks the dangerous wedding of sensual pleasure and transcendental bliss, the paradoxical synthesis of physical indulgence and spiritual liberation: "Nowhere is happiness seen without objects of pleasure. . . . [T]he liberated one having a body (equal to Śiva . . .) . . . enjoys the pleasant embrace of his beloved who is an image of Parvatī."[5]

Yet although such accounts of licentious, corrupt, and frightening characters had long appeared in Indian literature, we don't begin to see Tantra appearing as a major literary subject until the nineteenth century. Incorporating, playing upon, and exaggerating the fears of Tantra in the colonial imagination, many British authors began to portray the hideous obscenities of Tantra in ever more fantastic forms—not only as licentious or criminal, but as threatening to all rationality and moral order. Similarly, in a growing body of Bengali, Hindi, and other vernacular novels of the colonial era, Tantra emerges as a powerful, but deeply troubling presence lurking in the forbidden margins of Indian society. As such, I will argue, the representations of Tantra in these novels was a key part of the national imagining of both England and India in the late colonial period. As Homi Bhabha, Timothy Brennan, and others have shown, the novel was a key part of the creation of the modern nation-state as a unified, bounded, and yet complex "imagined community," both in Europe and in the colonies.[6] This was especially true of the novels of empire, through which Europe imagined itself against the mirror of its colonized Others. But it was no less true of the novels written by Indians during the colonial era, in which they reimagined themselves as subjects of foreign power. However, as I hope to show, the disturbing presence of Tantra was a continuous, haunting threat to that very imagined community; it was a frightening reminder that the nation is always a fragile, tenuous thing, vulnerable to subversion from within and from without its imaginary borders.

"THE MINGLED PERFUME OF LOVE AND WORSHIP, SEX AND RELIGION": TANTRA IN THE BRITISH LITERARY IMAGINATION

> So here they were in a new world without post or telegraphs, laws or order; time itself turned back hundreds of years. . . . Even the learned and most loyal lingered on the steps to whisper and call obscure prophecies and admit that it was wondrous and strange that the numerical values of the year should yield the anagram, "*ungrez tubbah shood ba hur soorut,*" briefly, "the British shall be annihilated." For the Oriental mind loves such trivialities.
>
> Flora Annie Steel, *On the Face of the Waters* (1896)

The India of the British literary imagination appears to be a land of dark, mysterious Otherness, a realm of passion and violence, at once seductive and terrifying. A world where "time itself [was] turned back hundreds of years," the India portrayed in late-nineteenth-century British fiction is a place of frightening extremes, where awesome natural beauty and cultural splendor are pervaded by ignorance, fanatical superstition, and sexual depravity. It is "a country of unfathomable people, 'those natives constantly moving in the dark,' whose . . . proclivities can be glimpsed by the white man only if . . . he goes amongst them in secret."[7]

And Tantra might be said to lie at the deepest core of this world, as "India's darkest heart." Much like the mysterious temple dancer *(devadāsī),* who combined "spiritual and sexual love," Tantra was a source simultaneously of moral horror and erotic allure.[8] This fascination with Tantra and with the dark goddess Kālī was already apparent in Philip Meadows Taylor's widely read narrative of the Thuggee cult, *Confessions of a Thug,* but it would become a central preoccupation by the end of the nineteenth century. As Benita Parry and Lewis Wurgaft have argued in their studies of British fiction between 1880 and 1930, many novelists were fascinated by what they had heard about the erotic, violent practices of the Tantras. They filled their works with lurid tales of the horrible, yet strangely seductive Tantric yogis and their lascivious goddess, the naked, cruel Kālī. As Flora Annie Steel put it, they perceived a dark underworld that reeked heavily of "the mingled perfume of love and worship, sex and religion."[9]

Vampires, Villains, and Tantris: *Sir Richard Burton and Tantra*

> Whereas holy men, holding that subjugation of the passions is essential to final beatitude, accomplish this by bodily austerities, he proceeded to blunt the passions with excessive indulgence.
>
> Sir Richard Francis Burton, trans., *Vikram and the Vampire* (1870)

One of the most important figures in the construction of Tantra in the literary imagination—and in the modern imagining of Tantra in Western popular culture as a whole—was Sir Richard Francis Burton. Today most famous as a bold world traveler, adventurer, and the first translator of the *Kāma Sūtra,*[10] Burton was also one of the first British authors to take a serious interest in Tantra. As Edward Rice argues, it is likely that Burton had some contact with the Tantric practices of a group known as the Nagar Brahmans during his stay in Baroda in the 1840s, and that he worked this experience into his writings and translations. He first studied, then entered into, "one of the most extreme and underground of all Hindu practices, that of Tantric Yoga. . . . He sought arcane, subterranean knowledge, hoping to find some key to the mysteries of life in the worship of . . . the phallic king Shiva and the . . . female power, Shakti."[11]

One of the most popular of Burton's works is *Vikram and the Vampire; or, Tales of Hindu Devilry,* a loosely translated edition of the Sanskrit collection of folk tales called *Vetālapañcaviṃśatikā.* Burton himself admits that he felt an obligation to expand upon the Sanskrit text with some of his own personal material and his own experiences in India: "I have ventured to remedy the conciseness of their language and to clothe the skeleton with flesh and blood."[12] As Edward Rice argues, Burton actually inserted a number of "Tantric practices that were not in the original text but which he had learned from personal experience."[13]

Thus, Burton's translation includes the story of a villainous hunchbacked character, who is driven primarily by greed, lust, and malice. A gambler, womanizer, and ruthless thief, the hunchback abandons the prohibitions of orthodox society and religion in order to become a nefarious "Tantri." Engaging in the most obscene rituals with wine, women, and corpses, he hopes to conquer the senses through such indulgence:

> The hunchback became a Tantri, so as to complete his villainies. He was initiated by an apostate Brahmin, made a declaration that he renounced all the ceremonies of his old religion . . . and proceeded to perform an abominable rite. In company with eight men and eight women—a Brahman female, a dancing girl, a weaver's daughter, a woman of ill fame, a washerwoman, a barber's wife and the daughter of a landowner, choosing the darkest time of night and the most secret part of the house, he drank with them . . . and went through many ignoble ceremonies, such as sitting nude upon a dead body. The teacher told him that he was not to indulge shame or aversion to anything . . . but freely enjoy all the pleasures of sense. . . . Whereas holy men, holding that subjugation of the passions is essential to final beatitude, accomplish this by bodily austerities, he proceeded to blunt the passions with excessive indulgence.[14]

Here we find the quintessential Tantric ritual, as it had become standardized in the colonial imagination by the late nineteenth century: blasphemous black ceremonies, sex with low-caste women, and complete indulgence of all the senses. Rather remarkably, while the original Sanskrit text does include the story of the villainous hunchback, it says *absolutely nothing at all* about his turn to the dark rites of the Tantras or his participation in the terrible *cakra pūjā* (circle worship);[15] all of this appears to the be fabrication of Burton's own fertile imagination, inspired by the widespread fantasies of Tantra current in nineteenth-century England. In any case, however, it is not so surprising that Burton's version of Tantra would later come to be confused with his version of the *Kāma Sūtra*—or indeed, that the two would eventually become more or less synonymous in the contemporary Western imagination.

Debauchery in the Search for God: Tantra and British Women Writers

> Some debauch themselves for wealth, some for lust,
> I debauched myself in a search for God.
>
> Elizabeth Sharpe, *Secrets of the Kaula Circle* (1936)

Some of the most colorful descriptions of Tantra in British fiction would come from the many women romantic novelists of the late colonial era. Tantra would seem to represent the most terrifying and yet seductive antipode to the conventional image of femininity in the British imagination. As Benita Parry has shown, the dual theme of sensuality and religious fanaticism is one of the most recurrent tropes in women's writing of the nineteenth and early twentieth centuries. As we read in I. A. R. Wylie's novel *The Daughter of Brahma* (1912), "here in this hell" the

Englishman feels that he is assaulted by some "diabolical force directed against his race and against civilization. The dreaming woman amongst the lotus-flowers was the personification of a bloodthirsty heathenism—a religion replete with hideous cruelty."[16] As the most perverse union of sexuality with mystical ecstasy, Tantra was thus the epitome of this dark seductive world. Far from the model of chaste moderation within the bounds of legal marriage, Tantra presents a vision of unbridled feminine sexuality and transgressive antisocial relations. Thus, F. E. F. Penny—an evangelical Christian and wife of a famous missionary—recounts these hideous rites in her novel *The Swami's Curse:* the Tantric "seeks to kill desire by an unlimited indulgence which brings satiety. . . . The indulgence is enjoined by his so-called religion; and his depravity is commended as a great virtue."[17]

One of the most vivid descriptions of the depraved rites of the Tantras appears in Elizabeth Sharpe's novel *The Secrets of the Kaula Circle*. Narrated by a French woman, Mary de la Mont—"who now [has] naught of shame"—it is the story of a young woman seduced by a Tibetan Tantric lama and driven to the depths of corruption by his insidious rituals. The narrator begins her tale by lamenting that the rites of the Tantras have already become widespread in the West and that it is her moral obligation to reveal their terrible secrets: "The cult of the Circle is already in vogue in Europe in secret places; and I must tell the world of it all."[18] Married to her lama at age twenty-six, she is just one "among the many thousands of deluded women who prostrate before Lamas." Like so many naive Western women, she was seduced by the mystery, power, and erotic allure of the Tantric master:

> I saw the Lama's eyes flash with interest the first time he caught sight of me, a white woman so different to the others. From that day onwards I saw him daily; he deprived me of much: beauty, ideals and money. . . . I gave him all I had to give. . . . I shuddered often at his ugliness, his crudity, and his strength, but I submitted to his wishes all the same. . . . He placed me under a spell, bewildered me with the glamour of power. . . . Indian and Tibetan alike spoke of my husband with hushed breath: a Mahatma, a man of superhuman power. I too thought that through him I might reach godhood. . . . He said that I was the greatest Yogini of any world. . . . He said that my beauty had driven him mad. He assured me I would gain superhuman powers by the union. . . . Something weak in me made me yield my body unresistingly to this man of an alien land.[19]

The core of Sharpe's novel, and the darkest depth of her narrator's descent into iniquity, is the secret ritual of the Kaula circle or *cakra pūjā*.

The most secret and sinister ritual of the left-hand Tantrics, the Kaula circle is the ultimate excuse for the unrestrained gratification of all desires: incest, drunkenness, gluttony, and every imaginable sexual perversion here become the holiest sacraments:

> The Kaula circle is the circle of the worshipers of the left-hand path, whose secrets none but they of the circle have known till now. In this circle the woman is the mother—but all desires are fulfilled—that is the vow. Few woman come through the ordeal unstained. . . . The outer circle of the temple of the goddess was heaped with raw flesh, fish and these with wine, were given to those of the outer circle. Man after man . . . passed by me singing, reeling and dead drunk. Later on they would be forced to drink the forty-two bottles of wine prescribed by the rules of the ceremony: eat, drink and be merry and die: for their doom—poor fools—was already on them. . . . [S]tark naked men and women, who . . . with excruciating yells, leapt to their feet, shaking their heads. . . . A voice would then cry out . . . "Let their desires be satisfied," and there would be a perfect orgy of bestiality.[20]

One of the most fascinating characters in Sharpe's novel, however, is not an Indian devotee of the *tantra*s, but an Englishman who has turned to Tantric worship in order to satisfy his own dark desires. Like many Europeans, he is drawn to the secrets of Tantra in the hope of acquiring some dark awesome power; indeed, "It is for secrets like these we of Europe come to seek wisdom." It seems almost certain that this strangely handsome but frightening individual is modeled after a real person, the infamous "Great Beast 666," Aleister Crowley, who did in fact travel in India and appears to have learned something of the secrets of Tantra.[21] Sharpe tells us that he "calls himself by a number," the satanic number 666, and that he engages in magical ceremonies that sound a great deal like those of Crowley's esoteric order, the Ordo Templi Orientis:

> I met a European who was one of X.Y.Z.'s pupils. He called himself by a number. In the beginning he was extremely handsome, afterwards he grew gross. . . . He had many women at his disposal. . . . He learnt many magical processes by which he drew into his circle great phantoms. . . . He had with him a pupil, a thin, long-nosed boy. . . . I wondered why he had followed the man whose number was 666. . . . 666 wore a ceremonial robe, had a pentacle, a wand a sword and a cup. . . . I watched that day the spirits he evoked with the help of the Lamas. . . . I saw 666 fall to the ground frothing at the mouth.[22]

Such, it would seem, is the inevitable fate of any Westerner who is seduced into the black rites of Tantra: he can only end in utter self-destruction. After her descent into debauchery and sin, however, Sharpe's heroine does have some hope of redemption. She is finally saved, not by the obscene rites of the Tantras, but by her eventual return to Christianity. Having washed her Tantric sins in the blood of the Lamb, she finds the light of salvation back in the pure faith of the Christian church: "Hope came to me again. I knew then that God lives in the sweet, tender simple things of life—and He is the resurrected man, the Christ."[23]

The Law of the Threshold: Mindless Violence and Mysterious Sexuality in the Works of Flora Annie Steel

> Kali-Ma . . . symbolises the ultimate mystery in life—the mystery of Sex.
>
> That Mai Kali will get the blood for which She asks unless quick action be taken . . . this is certain. Who governs India as a whole must govern by power.
>
> Flora Annie Steel, *The Law of the Threshold* (1924)

Perhaps the most imaginative of these fictional accounts appears in the work of the widely read Victorian novelist Flora Annie Steel (1847–1929). Born near London, Flora was a pious Christian, raised Presbyterian, who later converted to the Church of England. After marrying a civil engineer who was called to serve in the subcontinent, she arrived in Calcutta in 1868 and lived in India until 1889. Unlike many Victorian novelists, she seems to have genuinely tried to immerse herself in the Indian world and to learn as much as possible about its culture and religion; yet she still held fast to the belief in the moral superiority of the British and the need to rule this potentially dangerous people with a firm hand. For India is "a land stubbornly immutable, the peoples are slaves of custom . . . in a frozen social structure, in terror of their gods . . . but these same cowed people have as a crowd a terrifying propensity to savagery and can be aroused to violence through their superstitious religious beliefs."[24]

Steel's ambivalence toward India is mirrored by her equally ambivalent attitudes toward sexuality and the role of women. On the one hand, she was an outspoken suffragette who participated in the British campaign for women's rights; remarkably bold, she enjoyed camp life in India and found great satisfaction in riding with her husband; she cut her hair short, wore knickerbockers, and generally shunned "the formalities that structured colonial life."[25] Yet, Steel's brand of feminism was markedly austere, imitating the ideal of dispassion and strict control of desire that was the ideal of a strong male Englishman in India. As Nancy

Paxton comments in her study of Steel and other colonial women writers, "Steel's individualist understanding of feminism encouraged her to recommend that English women in India adopt the same masochistic stoicism valorized by upper class men. . . . Steel unsexes herself and identifies female sexuality as the force that has the power to destroy civilization."[26] Indeed, Paxton suggests that Steel's works reveal a kind of "gynophobia and fear of female sexuality." This sexual ambivalence becomes particularly clear in many of her Indian-based novels.

Steel is best known today as a novelist of the India Mutiny, whose *On the Face of the Waters* was a huge commercial success. However, she is also the author of an array of other popular novels and stories, many of which contain vivid accounts of the insidious rituals of the Tantras. For example, her short story "A Maiden's Prayer" centers around a young Indian woman named Parbutti, the daughter of a Kulin Brahman family who is soon to be married to a young student of suitable caste. Each day, Parbutti goes to the shrine of Mother Kālī, where she bows and recites a devotional and patriotic prayer, "In Thy Heaven Kali Mai!—Thou who lovest the flesh of man—By this blood I pray thee ban—Aliens in Hindustan."[27]

In the course of her devotions, however, Parbutti accidentally discovers that her husband-to-be is actually a member of a secret revolutionary group, dedicated to the making of bombs for terrorist acts against the British. She secretly witnesses them conceal explosives inside an image of the Goddess. As Steel describes this dangerous mixture of Tantric occultism and political agitation, "it was a sad farrago of nonsense; Western individualism dished up by professional agitators in a garb of Eastern mysticism."[28] Tragically, on the very day of the wedding, her husband is arrested and soon after commits suicide. Beside herself with grief and despair, Parbutti goes to Kālī's shrine dressed in her bridal clothes, ignites the explosives, and so offers herself as the supreme sacrificial victim to the Mother.

However, the most influential, and at times wildly imaginative, of Steel's portrayals of Tantra appears in *The Law of the Threshold.* The opening scene of the book is a graphic description of a chilling blood sacrifice to the goddess Kālī, as a wild crowd of devotees writhe and scream in a temple splattered with congealed gore:

> The vast crowd . . . ankle-deep in fast-clotting blood, was shouting itself hoarse in praise of the Dread Mother, Kali-Ma, who . . . symbolises the ultimate mystery in life—the mystery of Sex. The blood of Birth, the Blood of death! These two pivots of the Great Wheel, blended, had brought men, women and children in their thousands, to kill some miserable lambling . . .

> on the temple steps in honour of the Goddess Kali, in Atonement for their sins. . . . For Kali as the feminine principle of life is pre-eminent in Hindu mythology. . . . Her worship, full of horrors, is all but universal.[29]

The story centers around an American convert to Tantra named Nigel Blennerhasset and his companion, Maya Day, a lovely Indian girl who has been brought up and educated in the United States. Interestingly enough, the character of Nigel appear to be loosely modeled on the notorious Dr. Pierre Arnold Bernard (a.k.a. "the Omnipotent Oom"), who traveled to India to study the secrets of Tantra and then returned to the United States to found the first Tantrik order in America, in San Francisco and New York, in 1906. Nigel, in fact, proudly claims to be an initiated member of the "Third Tantrik Order in America," the headquarters of which is in San Francisco. During a conversation with a skeptical Englishman, who has heard only of the horrible licentiousness of Tantra, Nigel feels obliged to defend his Tantric faith. As his critic cynically remarks, "the old faith [the Hindus] taught wasn't so bad, so long as it stayed pure nature worship . . . but nowadays, Tantra-ism is horribly degrading! . . . I should very much like to know what teaching underlies the farrago of black magic and immorality called the Tantras." In response, Blennerhasset angrily bursts out in defense of the Tantric tradition: "The fifth Veda, called the Tantras . . . is the key to the others. It is the life and soul of modern Hinduism, for it holds the Dogma of the whole World."[30]

Other scenes, however, portray Nigel in rather ridiculous terms, as he parades about in his Tantric robes, adorned with cryptic symbols, like a bogus black magician: "There was Nigel Blennerhasset attired in the white robes of a kaula rite preceptor of the Third Tantrik Order in San Francisco. White robes covered with occult symbols in black and wanting only a stuffed cat on the shoulder to be the fancy dress of a witch!"[31] The principle message of the Tantrik order is also a rather silly doctrine of universal love, centered around the Great Mother though mingled with deeper sexual undertones:

> Love, Eternal, Creative as manifested in the one great Mother whose earthly emblem was Woman divine, immortal, was the one power in the world. The love of good, of country, of mother, of wife, the Love of which poets sang . . . the Love which gave the tie of kindred thought to the great Brotherhood of those who sought the highest.[32]

Unknown to Blennerhasset, however, his Tantric cult is secretly being manipulated: in fact, it has been subverted and exploited by two Jewish Bolshevist agents who are working with Indian nationalists, using the secret network of the Tantrik order to overthrow British rule. As the Bolshevist exclaims, "The Tantrik cult is the finest *nidus* [source] in the world for our purpose—a secret society ready-made."[33] By appealing to the Indian people's natural proclivity toward religious fanaticism, perversion, and superstition, they hope to use the Tantric cult in order to arouse widespread violence and thereby achieve (using Bakunin's anarchist phrase) "the destruction of law and Order and the unchaining of evil passions." According to their nefarious plot, "If it only enables us to touch the fifty-five millions of Tantriks in Bengal, that will be something; but if it is properly engineered it may touch all India; and then—the deluge."[34]

In sum, Steel and her fellow British novelists continue many of the Orientalist tendencies we have explored in the previous chapters. As Benita Parry argues, most of the romantic-era women writers had little actual knowledge of India, but simply elaborated upon the fragments of Orientalist accounts, projecting their own fears and fantasies into the narrative. Steel, however, had a deeper knowledge of the world of India. She believed that a thorough understanding of the darkest, most disturbing aspects of the Indian mind is crucial to maintain British rule over this inherently passionate and potentially dangerous land: "The British are chided for their ignorance about India, and India is unveiled to show the odd, the grotesque and gruesome. . . . Knowing India is redefined as essential and useful knowledge to facilitate permanent British rule."[35] Yet the presence of Tantra also represents something that remains fundamentally *unknowable,* unfathomable, and uncontrollable in the Indian world, something that continually subverts the desire for permanent rule or rational control. If the great novels of the empire typically reinforce the ideal of the nation and its just rule over the colonies, these novels that deal with the violence and scandal of Tantra reveal a frightening element of subversion that undermines and undoes the ideal of a coherent, tightly controlled nation or colony.

As such, these literary descriptions of the terrifying but seductive Tantras reflect as much the British subconscious as they do the "Indian mind." As Wurgaft argues, they are an example of the "mechanism that psychologists call projection: the displacement of one's own deep-seated wishes and fears onto some external object."[36] For British novelists writing in India, the image of Tantra was often a powerful projection of their own repressed desires and anxieties, objectified in the mirror of an exotic Other. Parry observes, "The repressed thoughts of these irreproachable matrons were brought to the surface by India and were projected onto Indians as proof of their depravity. . . . They were repelled because they saw their society's taboos violated and were involved in the betrayal, they were allured by the forbidden on shameless display."[37]

As the characters Mary de la Mont, the mysterious 666, and Nigel Blennerhassett discovered, this Tantric world reeks with the mingled perfume of sex and religion. These novelists reveal not only a loathing for the violent licentiousness of Tantra, but also a secret longing and repressed desire for it. Through their vivid accounts of the sexual goddess Kālī and the unrestrained worship of her Tantric devotees, these authors express a shameful desire for the carnal, passionate underworld of India, a land that threatens to seduce and corrupt the colonizers themselves.

THE LURE OF THE FORBIDDEN: TANTRA IN THE INDIAN LITERARY IMAGINATION

On this path of *maithuna,* there is firm restraint at the beginning—but in the end, the desire for *maithuna* is aimed at gratification.

Pramod Kumār Caṭṭopādhyāy,
Tantrābhilāṣīr Sādhusaṅga (1963)

Surely the British novelists were not the only ones to imagine vivid, terrifying narratives of lascivious *tāntrika*s and bloody worship of the dark mother Kālī. At the same time, there was a growing body of Indian vernacular literature, which continued many of the themes already present in traditional Sanskrit literature—such as the horrific tales of Kāpālikas in Sanskrit drama—and combined them with the new fears and fantasies about Tantra that emerged during the colonial era. And if the English fiction of the nineteenth century was a crucial part of the imagining of the British as a colonizing power, so too the Indian literature of this period was a crucial element in the reimagining of Indian identity.

For example, one popular genre that emerged in Bengali literature is the semifictional travel narrative, often with a religious theme. Among the more widely read and colorful of these is Pramod Kumār Caṭṭopādhyāy's *Tantrābhilāṣīr Sādhusaṅga,* which recounts the spiritual wanderings of a young man between 1911 and 1918. After leaving his home in Calcutta, the narrator goes in search of *tāntrika*s and other *sādhu*s throughout north India, delving as far as possible into these mysterious cults. In Caṭṭopādhyāy's fertile imagination, Tantra was a dark, frightening tradition, comprised mainly of "depraved licentious women, fallen from society." Thus he recounts his conversation with another Bengali regarding the Tantric ritual of *cakra-pūjā,* held in utmost secrecy in a cremation ground late at night:

> I asked: "Why is the gathering held in such darkness?"
> Pundārik said, "You know that the preferred place of the *tāntrikas* is in darkness; everything they do is very secret."
> I asked further: "So have you ever been present at their *cakra?*"
> Pundārik: "No. I've heard these things from outside; I've never entered the *cakra.* I don't like all these things. I don't care for their trickery or their reckless behavior. All the things they do, righteous people say, cannot be understood as dharma. They're all wicked. And spiritual practice involving women—Oh!"[38]

Overcome with curiosity about this tantalizing Tantric world, the narrator pays a secret visit to the *cakra-pūjā,* sneaking up and hiding in the bushes around the lonely cremation ground in the dead of night. Presided over by a frightening Aghorī ("one without fear") and his Bhairavī (female Tantric) consort, the *cakra* consists of a circle of naked men and women drawn from all castes, from Brahmans to untouchables, where all the normal restraints of class and status are ignored.[39] As the wind howls and lightning flashes all around him, the narrator secretly witnesses the most awesome rites of the *cakra:* the infamous five M's. The narrator sees the first four of the awesome five M's; but mysteriously, just before he witnesses the performance of the fifth and final rite—the most transgressive act of *maithuna,* or sexual intercourse in violation of caste—a strange darkness comes over his mind, and he falls unconscious: "suddenly with the sharp light of a powerful lightning bolt, my memory and consciousness were lost."[40]

In sum, within the Indian popular imagination, Tantra seems to be something frightening, dangerous, and yet strangely alluring. On the forbidden margins of society, far beyond the regulated boundaries of the imperial center in Calcutta, Tantra is an awesome power, tied to the forces of sexuality, death, and ecstasy, which continues to escape the rational control of both the British government and the Hindu reformers.

Skull-Bearers and Sannyāsī Rebels: Kāpālikas, Tāntrikas, and Other Nefarious Characters in the Works of Bankim Chandra Chatterjee

> Whose magic is this? or am I under a delusion. These words indicate danger, but danger of what? Tantriks can accomplish everything. . . . Where am I to flee to?
>
> Caṭṭopādhyāy, *Kapālakuṇḍalā*

The colonial era gave birth not only to a new genre of British fiction, but also to the Indian novel as a literary form in its own right. Expressed through vernacular languages like Bengali and Hindi, the novel emerged as one of the most popular literary forms of the nineteenth century, a medium for the expression of both aesthetic values and political ideals. Like British novels of this period, the Indian novel became a crucial literary space for reflection on India's own cultural identity under colonial rule, and also for the imagining of its emerging national identity. This is particularly true in the case of Bengal, where language, literature, and national identity became increasingly intertwined during the colonial and postcolonial eras. As Firdous Azim comments in *The Colonial Rise of the Novel,* "The nation's commitment to Bengali manifests itself as a search for authenticity, for the motherland created by the mother tongue."[41] And like British novels, Indian novels often used the tropes of Tantra and the terrible goddess Kālī as ways of thinking through this complex, shifting identity.

One of the most influential figures in the modern Indian imagining of Tantra was also the first major novelist in the Bengali language, Bankim Chandra Chatterjee (or Bankimcandra Caṭṭopādhyāy, 1838–94). Bankim was surely one of the most conflicted and ambivalent characters in nineteenth-century Bengal, who held extremely complex attitudes toward India, nationalism, British colonial rule, and the nature of Hinduism, including the *tantras*.[42] Born to a Kulin Brahman family that had lost its pure status, Bankim was one of the first graduates of the newly founded Calcutta University; upon his graduation in 1858, he held the office of deputy collector for the British government until his retirement.

Given his complex background—a fallen Brahman working for the British government—it is not surprising that Bankim held many conflicting attitudes toward his country, his culture, and his British masters. On the one hand, as Tapan Raychaudhuri observes, Bankim was deeply patriotic man, whose passionate nationalism "informed the bulk of his creative writing and social effort and was the mainspring of emotive life"; on the other, Bankim was a believer in the beneficence of British rule. He seems to have resigned himself to the fact that the British would be there for a long time to come and that independence could only be achieved by sustained effort at national integration over a long time.[43] Even in his powerful assertion of Hindu nationalism, Bankim internalized many Western ideals of national identity and independence, based on the British model of physical and worldly attainment. "India must look to its foreign lords, the British, in order to obtain . . . proficiency in this domain which is indispensable for the . . . securing of India's own national strength and autonomy."[44] In short, Bankim seems to have believed that India could Westernize without losing her soul.

Like many other Westernized elites of his day, Bankim inherited Orientalist attitudes toward Indian religion and culture, including views of Tantra. Like Rāmmohun before him, Bankim basically accepted the Orientalist critique of modern popular Hinduism, which was seen as idolatrous, irrational, and degenerate. "It is no exaggeration to say," he lamented, "that there is greater affinity between Muhammadism and Christianity than between the Shaktism of the Tantras and the Vaishnavism of Caitanya."[45] Thus he imagined the rebirth of a noble, purified Hinduism that would strip away all the polytheistic superstition and center instead around a single deity like the "incarnate deity," God made flesh, Śrī Kṛṣṇa. "The 'truly' religious elements of Hinduism had to be . . . separated from the multifarious forms of superstition, from local and popular cults. Such a purified Hinduism . . . could be placed above Islam and Christianity."[46]

Perhaps Bankim's greatest romance is *Kapālakuṇḍalā,* a love story about a woman named Kapālakuṇḍalā, after the mendicant in Bhavabhūti's *Mālatī-Mādhava.* The story begins with the hero, Nabakumār, lost at sea and washing up on the shore of an unknown land. There he encounters both the ravishing young beauty Kapālakuṇḍalā and the terrible *tāntrika,* a Kāpālika ascetic, who has raised Kapālakuṇḍalā from infancy for the carnal demands of his dark religion. Nabakumār's first meeting with the Kāpālika is described in particularly vivid and gruesome imagery: building on the imagery of the Kāpālikas in earlier Sanskrit drama and combining it with colonial fantasies of the horrors of Tantra, Bankim portrays the cruel *tāntrika* seated in a cremation ground, surrounded by human bones, and performing the secret rite of *śava-sādhana,* meditation on a human corpse:

> From his waist to his knees he was covered with a tiger skin. Around his throat was a necklace of *rudrākṣa* seeds, and the broad circle of his face with surrounded with matted hair and beard. . . . Nabakumār could smell a terrible stench. . . . The form with matted hair was seated on a headless putrid corpse. With even greater fear he saw that a human skull lay before him, and inside it was some red liquid. On all sides bones were strewn. . . . He knew that this person must be a terrible Kāpālika.[47]

When the naive Nabakumār strays into the dense forest that is the *tāntrika*'s lair, the Kāpālika takes him as a godsend that will allow him to complete the requisite number of sacrifices according to the black rites of the *tantras*:

> The Kāpālika seated Nabakumār and Kapālakuṇḍalā in a fitting place on a bed of kusa grass and began his worship according to the rites of the *tantras*. Holding Kapālakuṇḍalā by the hand, Nabakumār led her across the burning ground to bathe her. Bones began sticking to their feet. . . . Wild animals were roaming in all directions eating the corpses.[48]

Out of her intense devotion and self-sacrificing nature, however, Kapālakuṇḍalā decides to offer herself as the victim in Nabakumār's place: "Kapālakuṇḍalā was at heart a *tāntrika*'s child. Just as a *tāntrika* is not afraid to take another's life out of desire for Kālikā's grace, so Kapālakuṇḍalā was ready to sacrifice her own life out of the same desire."[49] Yet in the dramatic end to the scene, a great wave suddenly rises up and washes the cruel Kāpālika away.

In sum, the terrible, ghoulish Kāpālika in this tale not only reflects the fantastic image of Tantra that had emerged in both the Indian and British imaginations of the nineteenth century; it also reflects that dark, degenerate, idolatrous, and superstitious side of the Hindu tradition that Bankim, as a nationalist and reformer strongly influenced by Western science and morality, saw as the greatest obstacle to India's self-assertion and independence.

But the most important of Bankim's novels for modern imagining of Tantra—particularly in its violent, politicized forms—is *Ānandamaṭh* (The abbey of bliss), which we have already encountered in chapter 2. Originally published in serial form in the journal *Baṅgadarśan* (the last installment was on May 1882), the story was first published in book form in December 1882.[50] As we saw earlier, *Ānandamaṭh* was to become the single most important text for the radical nationalist movement in Bengal in the early twentieth century. For revolutionaries like Aurobindo, this text was a manifesto for anticolonial insurgency and its author the prophet of Indian nationalism. Yet Bankim's original intention in writing this book is by no means clear. With his own dedication to nationalism and his ambivalent attitude toward British rule, Bankim leaves us with the lingering question of whether this book should be read as an anticolonial, revolutionary text, or as a procolonial defense of benign British rule.

The novel centers around the historically actual Sannyāsī rebellion of 1772, when a group of renunciants led a major revolt against the Muslim ruler in north Bengal. Afflicted by the severe famine that swept Bengal in 1770 and the oppressive taxation of their rapacious landlords, the Sannyāsīs in this novel gather in a secret temple dedicated to the Mother—the Great Mother, who is at once the divine Śakti and the physical land of Bengal. Hence Bankim's Sannyāsīs are a very odd sort of religious sect: for they are said to be Vaiṣṇavas, devotees of the generally non-Tantric god Viṣṇu; yet at the same time, Bankim has transformed them into disciples of the Goddess in her most awesome, seemingly "Tantric" form. As the Sannyāsī Bhavānanda declares, "Motherland is superior to heaven. . . . We have only one Mother—richly watered, richly fruited . . . with green fields"; and the Sannyāsīs are devoted to the liberation of the Mother from her bondage under oppressive rule. Making a secret oath in the name of the Goddess, the Sannyāsīs vow to forsake all worldly pleasures, to forget caste distinctions, and never to retreat from the battlefield. (As Sisir Kumar Das observes, it is likely that this oath draws not only on Tantric traditions, but also on European secret societies like the Carbonari, which influenced Aurobindo and Tagore.)[51]

Inside the Sannyāsīs' secret temple in Bankim's novel, as we saw in chapter 2, the Goddess is manifest in three forms, each embodying one of three historical periods in Bengal: first, as the goddess Jagaddhatri, as she was in her glory during the pre-Muslim age of Hindu sovereignty; second, her terrible bloodthirsty form during the dark age of foreign misrule as the black Tantric Mother, Kālī; and finally, the radiant Mother of an independent nation, where we see "on all sides . . . the enemy trampled under her feet and the lion engaged in killing her foes."[52] In each of these three forms, however, the Goddess is a powerful embodiment of the Indian nation as Bankim imagines it, and as he immortalized it in his classic song "Bande Mataram":

> Who hath said thou art weak in thy lands
> When the sword flashes out in the seventy million hands
> And seventy million voices roar
> Thy dreadful name from shore to shore?
> With many strengths who art mighty and stored,
> To thee I call Mother and Lord!
> Thou who savest, arise and save!
> To her I cry who ever her foeman drove
> Back from plain and sea
> And shook herself free.[53]

Yet, strangely, despite the volatile context in which the novel was published—in 1882, in the lingering aftermath of the Indian Mutiny and just three years before the founding of the Indian National Congress—

Ānandamaṭh reflects an extremely ambivalent attitude toward British rule and Indian nationalism. Bankim himself appears to have been insecure about the reception of the novel. In the serialized version of the novel, Bankim's rebels call for an attack upon *both* the English and the Muslims; yet in the first published edition, this was modified to exclude the British and to portray instead a primarily anti-Muslim uprising.[54] This ambivalence becomes all the more striking in the final chapter of the book, when Bankim expresses what seems to be a powerful pro-British sentiment. A mysterious healer appears in the final pages and argues that the British are the real saviors of India, without whom the nation cannot overcome its own ignorance or regain its true strength. For though India may possess spiritual knowledge, it still needs the superior physical knowledge and scientific advances of the West:

> There is no hope of a revival of the True Faith if the English be not our rulers. . . . The True Faith does not consist in the worship of 330 million deities; that is only a base religion of the masses. Under its influence, the True Faith . . . disappeared. . . . The True Hinduism is based on knowledge and not on action. . . . [O]bjective knowledge has disappeared for our country. . . . [O]bjective knowledge must be imported from elsewhere. The English are great in objective sciences. . . . Therefore the English must be made our sovereign. Imbued with a knowledge of objective sciences by English education our people will be able to comprehend subjective truths . . . till the Hindus are great again in knowledge virtue and power, then English rule will remain undisturbed. . . . Desist from fighting with the English. . . .
>
> The rebellion was raised only that the English might be initiated into sovereignty. . . . Where is the enemy now? There is none. The English are a friendly power, and no one had the power to come off victorious in a fight with the English.[55]

Bankim's forword to the first edition states this pro-British and antirebellion attitude even more clearly: "Social revolution is often suicidal," Bankim concludes, "but the rebels defeat themselves. . . . The English have redeemed Bengal from anarchy."[56]

Thus it is not surprising that since the novel was first published there have been a wide array of conflicting interpretations of its political implications. On one side, many argue that Bankim was a realist who also admired many aspects of European culture and accepted British rule as a necessary transitional stage until India was strong enough to rule herself. Some critics go even further, arguing that Bankim was an "antirevolutionary" and a loyal subject, who used this book as a way of condemning violent insurgency, particularly when mixed with religion: "[The revolutionaries] are half-baked monks who play with the idea of revolution and are defeated in the end. Their revolution is bogged up in love and . . . mysticism."[57] A few even see him as an ardent champion of just British law, which has at last brought order to this violent, chaotic land: "He hails British rule with enthusiasm . . . for having put an end to Muslim oppression and anarchy."[58]

Yet on the other end of the spectrum, many recent authors see Bankim as a man with markedly anticolonial sentiments, which he expressed covertly throughout *Ānandamaṭh* but which he was forced to conceal in actual life. As Das observes, Bankim's portrayal of the Sannyāsīs is generally quite positive, as they appear to be noble, patriotic heroes struggling to redeem the motherland; meanwhile, apart from the odd concluding chapter of the book, the British are often portrayed negatively, and in many cases "subjected to mortification, insults and unsavory jokes."[59] Bankim also edited numerous parts of the original text—replacing, for example, "English" with *yavana* (Muslim) and eliminating the sexual exploits of the English Captain Thomas among the Santal girls. Moreover, the book was published just five years after another Bengali author, Upendranāth Dās, had been prosecuted for the apparently anti-British sentiments in his play *Surendra Binodinī.* As Raychaudhuri suggests, it is likely that Bankim censored his originally revolutionary opinions for pragmatic reasons of self-protection:

> As a government servant he was forced to modify his initial statements into which an anti-British . . . sentiment was quite correctly read. Bankim's pragmatism in trying to retain his job . . . illustrates the predicament of a colonial intelligentsia and suggests that his positive assessment of British should not always be taken at face value. There is plentiful evidence that he saw that rule as painful bondage.[60]

Bankim himself later cryptically remarked that the meaning of the revolutionary anthem "Bande Mataram" would only be understood by a future generation. As Raychaudhuri observes, "'Bande Mataram' became the slogan of Indian nationalism and *Anandamath* the bible of armed revolutionaries. One has the feeling that their creator had almost expected such a result."[61]

We may never know with certainty what Bankim's original intention was in writing *Ānandamaṭh;* nor, probably, will we ever know whether he changed his views from anti-British revolutionary to pro-British loyalist, or whether he simply censored his real opinions for reasons of political expedience. In any case, I would argue, Bankim's work and the different interpretations of its political significance are acute examples of the changing attitudes toward both Tantra and Indian nationalism during the colonial era. The question that Bankim's work raises is one that faced many Indian elites of his day: should the transgressive power of Tantra and the irrational terror of the Goddess be unleashed in order to inspire revolution? Or should it be contained and suppressed in submission to the stable rule of the British? This is a question that runs throughout the late colonial era, haunting both the Indian literary imagination and the larger Indian political unconscious, finally bursting into the violence of the revolutionary nationalist movement.

The Mother's Day Is Past: The Failure of Revolutionary Nationalism in Tagore's Fiction

The mother's day is past. . . . All duties have become as shadows: all rules and restraints have snapped their bonds.

Rabindranath Tagore, *The Home and the World* (1926)

Another important figure in the literary imagining of Tantra is also among the most chief figures in modern Indian literature: the Bengali poet, novelist, and Nobel Prize winner Rabindranath Tagore (1861–1941). Tagore's work dramatically portrays the intense violence and despair that followed the politicization of Śākta Tantra in Bengal, in the aftermath of the revolutionary nationalist movement.

Born to an affluent Calcutta family, Tagore turned from his youthful concentration in the arts to an increasing concern with public affairs and the political life of Bengal. As Kopf argues, Tagore has so often been subject to hagiography and aesthetic idealization that it is often forgotten that he was also deeply involved in nationalist politics.[62] Indeed, Tagore played an important role in the history of the revolutionary politics of Bengal in the early years of struggle against the British. In the years up to 1907, Tagore was an active participant in the nationalist movement and helped to form the Swadeshi Samāj, for which he wrote fiery pamphlets and composed patriotic songs that swept Bengal. Yet he later grew disillusioned with the movement, which proved to be both fundamentally elitist, run by the educated landowning classes, and increasingly violent. Disturbed by the schisms and violence within the movement, he withdrew from the center of action and began to turn increasingly toward his more private spiritual and poetic life, spending most of his time at his school in Shantiniketan and at his country home. As he wrote to

C. F. Andrews, "I do not belong to the present age, the age of conflicting parties. . . . I must share in the life of the present world, though I do not believe in its cry. . . . I try to listen . . . to the murmur of the stream carrying its limpid waters to the sea."[63]

Retreating from the active world of nationalism to the inner realm of spirituality, art, and culture, Tagore shifted his ideal for society from an explicitly political one to a vision of a new humanism and universalism, rooted in a nonsectarian religion of man. This was in part the reason for his ambivalent involvement in the Brāhmo Samāj, which he had hoped might realize his humanist and universalist ideals. Although he was critical of the more narrow-minded and reactionary tendencies within the movement, he believed that the true spirit of the Brāhmo Samāj represented the revival of the most noble elements of the Hindu tradition. Tagore also hoped that this new humanism might help undo the dehumanization of man that was the result of industrialization and materialism in the West. Against the fragmented impersonal character of the West, with its rampant nationalism and intolerance, he sought a vision of the simplicity and freedom of all human beings: "the world—especially the West—urgently needed the universal humanism of the Brahmo faith. . . . It was the key role of the Brahmo Samaj to help in saving the world from the 'madness of Nationalism.'"[64]

This profound disillusionment with the violence of the nationalist movement and the retreat into a more passive, private sphere of art and spirituality is poignantly expressed in his novel *The Home and the World* (Ghare bāire). One of Tagore's darkest works, it is a story set during and after the terrorist violence of 1907, concluding with scenes of Hindu-Muslim riots and armed robbery. However, it actually was written during Tagore's own personal crisis and descent into severe depression in 1914. Condemned by Western critics like Georg Lukacs as "a petit bourgeois yarn of the shoddiest kind," and by E. M. Forster as "a boarding house flirtation that masks itself in patriotic talk," the novel has also been attacked by Indian readers who thought it betrayed Tagore's insincerity in fighting colonial rule.[65] Recent critics, however, have praised it as one of Tagore's greatest works, a profound reflection of a man torn by conflicting forces during the tumultuous years of the nationalist movement: "The 'home' and the 'world' referred to his own mind divided against itself, to himself versus his school . . . to Bengal versus India, to India versus Britain, to the East versus the West."[66]

The novel features a triad of characters, symbolically charged with the various conflicting forces of Bengal in the early twentieth century.

The primary protagonist is Nikhil, a wealthy landowner who is altruistic, benevolent, rational, and Westernized in his ideas. A humanist, Nikhil faces isolation and ridicule because of his opposition to the violent means employed by the charismatic but unscrupulous revolutionaries. In stark opposition to Nikhil's conservative figure is Sandip, a revolutionary dedicated to independence, who stops at nothing, neither robbery nor murder, to achieve his ends. Like the Śakti-worshiping, Tantric-influenced revolutionaries of the Jugantar movement, Sandip is fanatically dedicated to the liberation of the Mother in her most terrible and bloody form. The novel is in many ways the dramatization of the tension between these two, the clash between conservative and revolutionary.

Bimala, Nikhil's wife, is especially torn between these two powerful forces. In a sense, Bimala is an icon of Bengal, the motherland, which is caught between tradition and change, rational adherence to colonial law and bloody revolution. As Anita Desai observes, "She is referred to frequently as Mother . . . suggesting that she is Durgā, the mother goddess and favorite deity of Bengal. Her husband offers her gold and tender love; Sandip offers her worship, and revolutionaries . . . touch her feet in obeisance."[67] Seduced by Sandip's fanatical charisma, Bimala betrays her husband and throws herself into the Swadeshi movement. Nikhil, however, refuses to banish Sandip but insists that Bimala must freely choose between the two of them herself. The novel finally ends in horrific violence, as Bimala at last realizes that Sandip's path is evil and withdraws from it; but she does so too late to avert the inevitable violence that comes with fanatical nationalism.

Tagore's narrative is thus a fictional representation of the drama that had unfolded in colonial Bengal—namely, the rise of the extremist wing of the nationalist movement and its use of religious imagery drawn from Śākta Tantra and the Tantric goddess. As Kopf comments, Tagore's narrative "blasted the justification for extremism and terrorism in the Swadeshi period," and particularly the use of Śākta Tantra in the service of revolution: "The book is revealing not merely as a critique of nationalism in fictional form, but . . . as condemnation of a concrete revolutionary tradition in twentieth century Bengal. Terrorism inspired by neo-Śaktism was the target. It came at the very time of the 'Tantric revival.'"[68]

The character of Sandip is a clear embodiment of the radical Bengali youth, cleaving to the ideal of the self-sacrificing warrior who lays down his life as he takes the life of a white goat in an offering to the Goddess. In Sandip's eyes, the gods of India are tired and outdated; India now needs to modernize and refashion its gods to meet the challenge of the West: "Evolution is at work amongst the gods as well. . . . The grandson has to remodel the gods created by the grandfather to suit his own taste, or else he is left an atheist. It is my mission to modernize the ancient deities. I am born the savior of the gods, to emancipate them from the thraldom of the past."[69]

Sandip sees the image of the Goddess—particularly in her most violent forms—as the ideal means to move the spirits of the ordinary people, to awaken them from their submissive slumber into revolutionary action. For it is precisely this kind of mythic image, deeply rooted in the popular imagination, that can be used as a political tool to arouse a nationalist spirit:

> True patriotism will never be roused in our countrymen unless they can visualize the motherland. We must make a goddess of her. . . . We must get one of the current images accepted as representing the country—the worship of the people must flow toward it along the deep-cut grooves of custom. . . .
>
> Illusions are necessary for lesser minds . . . and to this class the greater portion of the world belongs. This is why divinities are set up in every country to keep up the illusion of their weakness. . . . For them who can truly believe . . . her image will do duty for the truth. With our nature and our traditions we are unable to realize our country as she is, but we can easily bring ourselves to believe in her image.[70]

For even though she is an illusion created for the ignorant masses, this goddess is the very embodiment of the power that can rouse men to political action—above all, when she appears in her terrible Tantric forms as Kālī and Durgā, as she is worshiped in Bengal:

> Just look at the worship of Durga which Bengal has carried to such heights. . . . Durga is a political Goddess and was conceived as the image of the Shakti of patriotism in the days when Bengal was praying to be delivered from the Mussulman domination. What other province of India has succeeded in giving such wonderful visual expression to the ideal of its quest?[71]

For Sandip, India is now in an urgent situation, which means that all traditional morality and humanitarian values must be sacrificed to liberate the oppressed nation. Extreme situations call for extreme measures, including what seem to be utterly ruthless, violent, and brutal acts, so long as they are carried out in the just name of the Goddess:

> This is not the time for nice scruples. We must be unswervingly, unreasoningly brutal. We must give our women red sandal paste with which to anoint our sin. . . . Down with righteousness which cannot smilingly bring rack

> and ruin. . . . Give to us indomitable courage to go to the bottom of Ruin itself. Impart grace to all that is baneful.[72]

This means that the Indian must learn to use the dangerous, often immoral power of the West—to employ Western nationalist ideals, science, and military strength in the service of the higher spiritual cause of Indian liberation. "We must have our religion and also our nationalism. . . . I want the Western military style to prevail, not the Indian. We shall then not be ashamed of the flag of our passion, which mother nature has sent with us . . . into the battlefield of life."[73]

Yet, by the end of the novel, Sandip's ideal of revolutionary nationalism, steeped as it is in the violence of Tantra and the goddess Śakti, has ended in disastrous failure. Much like Aurobindo and the members of the secret Jugantar movement, Sandip ultimately discovers that even this powerful image of the Goddess cannot succeed in bringing about genuine political liberation; for this projection of the Goddess as the spirit of the nation, and this quasi-magical attempt to draw upon her power through Tantric rites and blood sacrifices, is after all only an illusion. As Nikhil cynically remarks, the Marathas and the Sikhs took up real arms and fought with real strength against their oppressors during the Muslim era; but the Bengali, instead of taking real action, retreats into mystical superstition: "Maratha and Sikh turned revolutionary and got statehood, but the Bengali contented himself with placing weapons in the hands of his goddess, and muttering incantations to her . . . and as his country did not really happen to be a goddess, the only fruit he got was the lopped off heads of the goats of the sacrifice."[74]

Sandip has abandoned his once firm belief in the power of the goddess of "Bande Mataram," turning instead to a kind of nihilistic despair, in which all previous values are meaningless, and descending into an emptiness without hope for redemption:

> My watchword . . . is no longer *Bande Mataram*. . . . The mother's day is past. . . . All duties have become as shadows: all rules and restraints have snapped their bonds. . . . I could set fire to all the world outside this land on which you have set your feet and dance in mad revel over them. . . . My devotion to you has made me cruel; my worship of you has lighted the raging flame of destruction within me. . . . I have no beliefs.[75]

Tagore eloquently narrates here the sudden rise and tragic failure of revolutionary nationalism, along with its attempt to use the violent power of Tantra in the service of political ends. Like Aurobindo, Tagore's characters realized that the dangerous power unleashed by Tantra can indeed arouse intense revolutionary hopes; yet the violence and bloodshed it brings can lead only to despair and a loss of hope in overt political action. As both Aurobindo and Tagore ultimately concluded, the only solution would be to abandon the terrible power represented by the bloody Tantric goddess, to withdraw from the political realm, and to retreat into thc inner domain of spirituality and the arts.

THE "PRECARIOUSNESS OF POWER": IMAGINING AND SUBVERTING THE NATION

> Kill for the love of killing! Kill lest ye be killed yourselves! Kill for the love of Kali! Kill, Kill, Kill!
>
> Priest of Kālī (Eduardo Cianelli), in the film version of *Gunga Din* (1939)

> Narration occurs to confirm the precariousness of power.
>
> Sara Suleri, *The Rhetoric of English India* (1992)

In sum, the image of Tantra in British and Indian fiction played a critical role in the decades of the late nineteenth and early twentieth centuries. For it was a key element in the reimagining of the Indian nation during the confusing, often violent decline of colonial rule. As Bhabha and others suggest, the genre of the novel played a crucial role in the rise of nationalism, both in Europe and in the colonies, throughout the modern period. Just as the novel emerged as a complex, composite, yet unified and bounded narrative, so too, the modern nation emerged as a complex, unified, imagined community, with a coherent narrative of its inception and development: "The rise of the modern nation-state . . . is inseparable from the forms and subjects of imaginative literature. . . . It was especially the novel as a composite but clearly bordered work of art that was crucial in defining the nation as an 'imagined community.'"[76]

And yet, the "nation" can surely never be the seamless, bounded, coherent, and unified entity imagined by literary narratives. On the contrary, as Bhabha observes, the nation will always be in a profound sense fragmented, splintered, and hopelessly plural: "Dissemination, ambivalence, hybridity and heterogeneity constantly disrupt the narratives of social, cohesion, holism and homogeneity."[77] Hence, the narratives of nationalism must always in some sense be fabricated illusions of unity, created in the desperate attempt to cover this ambivalent hybridity: "Nationalism is not what it seems, and above all not what it seems to itself. . . . The cultural shreds and patches used by nationalism are often arbitrary historical inventions."[78] As Sara Suleri put it in her study of British colonial literature, the narratives created by the colonizers always in some way betray their own deep insecurity, their own fears of disorder and subversion. They reveal the fundamental "precariousness of power." But this could be said equally of the colonized peoples themselves, as they attempt to imagine narratives for their own emerging national identities—narratives that also reveal their own precariousness and insecurity. Thus, the fiction of the colonial era does not reflect a static, unchanging, imaginal representation of the exotic Orient, but rather a complex and dynamic "vision of India which is . . . nuanced, contradictory, and subject to changing historical and political circumstances."[79]

As we have seen throughout the British and Indian fiction of the colonial era, Tantra emerges as one of the most frightening symbols of this very precariousness and a subversive threat to the nation. Embodied in the terrible goddess Kālī, Tantra continually rises up as a dangerous "otherness"—not just the otherness lurking in the Indian underworld, but also the even more disturbing otherness that has begun to appear within Western culture itself. "It is for secrets like these we of Europe come to seek wisdom," as Sharpe put it in her *Secrets of the Kaula Circle*. In the form of Nigel Blennerhasset, the Great Beast 666, Mary de la Mont, and other white devotees of the Goddess, Tantra is a seductive power that threatens to infiltrate and pervert the colonial world. For "the other is never outside or beyond us; it emerges forcefully within cultural discourse, when we think we speak most intimately . . . 'between ourselves.'"[80] Yet at the same time, Tantra is a terrible power within the Indian community, threatening to undermine India's own emerging hopes for national identity. As both Bankim and Tagore remind us, the Śakti of Tantra is an awesome force that promises transgressive liberation, sensual gratification, and material power, but also often leads to self-destruction, explosive violence, and the ultimate shattering of the very idea of a unified nation.

Of course, these fictional imaginings of Tantra—so colorful and vivid, at times humorous, at times terrible—were by no means limited to the genre of novel or even to the colonial era. Later in the twentieth century they would be taken up by a number of British novelists, such as John Masters in his tale of the Thuggee, *The Deceivers*.[81] And they were used as well in American Hollywood films, such as *Gunga Din*, a remarkable, double-order, doubly-distorted representation: an American imagining of the British imagining of India, centering around a Kālī-worshiping Thuggee cult (whose priest is played by an Italian American) and a faithful Indian water-bearer (played by a Jewish American). Even those of us in the ostensibly politically correct, postcolonial world still enjoy old-fashioned Orientalist films, like Stephen Spielberg's *Indiana Jones and the Temple of Doom*—a reworking of the *Gunga Din* motif, featuring one of the most horrific (and strikingly un-Indian) Kālī images ever conceived. And, of course, such popular imagining of Tantra has long since been taken up by Bollywood, as well. One of my own favorite Indian pop films, mentioned in the introduction, is *Shaitan Tantrik,* a movie clearly influenced by *Temple of Doom,* which features a diabolical mad Tantric priest who bears a suspicious resemblance to the priest of Kālī in Spielberg's film.

The fictional representation of Tantra continues to be a key part of the imagining of both Indian and Western identity in the postcolonial era. As the frightening, insidious Other within, it forms a crucial element in remembering the dark side of India's colonial past and in representations of its conflicted, contested present.

CHAPTER 4

Deodorized Tantra

Sex, Scandal, Secrecy, and Censorship in the Works of John Woodroffe and Swami Vivekananda

I protest and have always protested against unjust aspersions upon the civilization of India. . . . The Tantra Śāstra is not, as some seem to suppose, a petty Śāstra of no account. . . . It is on the contrary, with Veda, Smṛti and Purāṇa, one of the foremost important Śāstras in India, governing in various degrees . . . the temple and household ritual of the whole of India . . . for centuries past.

Sir John Woodroffe, *Shakti and Shākta* (1918)

This form of practice must never even be mentioned in the Math. Ruin shall seize the wicked man, both here and hereafter, who would introduce vile Vamachara into His fold.

Swami Vivekananda to members of Alambazar Math (27 April 1896)

By the dawn of the twentieth century, Tantra had come to represent a troubling, sometimes threatening, and often quite embarrassing problem for Indian and Western authors. Already widely regarded as representing the most primitive, idolatrous, and immoral side of the Indian mind, it had also become increasingly associated with religious fanaticism, terrorist violence, and the failure of the revolutionary nationalist movement. It is not surprising therefore to see various efforts on both the Indian and colonial sides to suppress, control, or eliminate the dangerous practices of the *tantra*s. What is more surprising, however, is that we also find an attempt on the part of more sympathetic figures to defend, revalorize, and purify the Tantric tradition, cleansing it of the taint of licentious immorality and redefining it as a noble philosophical tradition. As Sumit Sarkar observes, "Tantric traditions were being made more respectable through excisions, and at times . . . suppressed altogether . . . as stricter ideas about gentility developed in the shadow of 'Victorian' norms."[1]

We have already seen at least one major attempt to purify or sanitize the Tantras, in the strange case of the *Mahānirvāṇa Tantra* and its complex relations to the reforms of the Brāhmo Samāj. But this process of sanitization would only intensify in the early decades of the twentieth century, in the face of rising nationalism, political agitation, and a new desire to reimagine Hinduism in response to the Western world. If Hinduism and the Indian nation were to be defended as strong, autonomous, and independent of Western control, then the foul stench of Tantra would have to be "deodorized," as it were—either by rationalization and purification, or by concealment and denial.

Two of the most important figures in this process were Sir John Woodroffe (1865–1936), otherwise known as Arthur Avalon, the father of modern Tantric studies in the West; and Swami Vivekananda (1863–1902), born Narendra Nath Datta, one of the greatest spiritual leaders of modern India.[2] A High Court judge in Calcutta, Woodroffe surely stands out as one of the most remarkable and enigmatic figures in the entire history of British India. While maintaining his public profile as a judge and scholar of British Indian law, Woodroffe was also a private student of the *tantra*s, who published a huge body of texts and translations and thus pioneered the modern academic study of Tantra in the West. Yet Woodroffe was also an apologist, seeming to have bent over backward to defend the Tantras against their many critics and to prove that they represent a noble, pure, and ethical philosophical system in basic accord with the Vedas and Vedānta.

Vivekananda, conversely, was the chief disciple of the great modern Bengali saint Sri Ramakrishna Paramahaṃsa—a man who was deeply influenced by the teachings and practices of the *śākta tantra*s. Yet Vivekananda would reinterpret, transform, and adapt Ramakrishna's teachings to his own neo-Hindu and nationalist agendas, turning this ecstatic devotee of the violent Tantric goddess Kālī into an *avatār* of highly abstract, philosophical Advaita Vedānta and Hindu nationalism.[3] For Vivekananda and his followers, the Tantric practices of Ramakrishna would become a source of scandal and embarrassment, a dark secret that remained a disturbing presence throughout the later tradition.

Yet both Woodroffe and Vivekananda shared several common agendas: first, they each sought to redefine and reinterpret Tantra from a modern perspective informed by the encounter between India and the West during the colonial era. And they each re-presented Tantra in a form that was—like so much of twentieth-century neo-Hinduism, as Halbfass argues[4]—heavily influenced by modern Western paradigms of morality, science, and rationality. Second and more important, however, they both subjected Tantra to a profound form of *censorship;* that is, they each in different ways suppressed, edited, and covered over those aspects of Tantra that were considered most offensive to both Western and Indian audiences. As Sue Curry Jansen argues, censorship is in many ways one of the key "knots" in the social fabric, a knot that "binds knowledge and power." For if knowledge is power—the power to define, categorize, and control our perception of the "way things are"—then those who hold or seek power must be able to silence views that threaten their ideal of the way things ought to be.[5] For both Woodroffe and Vivekananda, Tantra was something that was very much in need of censorship and reform—either (for the former) a moralizing sanitization, or else (for the latter) a form of suppression and denial.

THE "REFORM" OF TANTRA: SIR JOHN WOODROFFE AND THE DEFENSE, RATIONALIZATION, AND SANITIZATION OF TANTRA

> Tāntrikism in its real sense is nothing but the Vedic religion struggling with wonderful success to reassert itself amidst all those new problems of religious life . . . which historical events have thrust upon it.
>
> Woodroffe, *Shakti and Shākta*

> See some Lama and understand from him what your beliefs are. It is so extraordinary to us Europeans that you Buddhists and Hindus or everyone of you do not understand your own religions. . . . I speak particularly of the Tantric doctrines.
>
> Woodroffe to Lama Kazi Dawasamdup (15 June 1917)

Although his scholarship is now considered rather biased and flawed, Sir John Woodroffe (figure 8) must be acknowledged as a remarkable pioneer and even as the father of the modern study of the Tantras. Ironically, Woodroffe himself did not care to use the term "Tantrism," argu-

Figure 8. Sir John Woodroffe, at the Konark temple in Orissa. From Woodroffe, *Introduction to Tantra Śāstra* (1913; reprint, Madras: Ganesh, 1973).

ing that it was a mistaken Western imposition; yet today, Woodroffe more than any other scholar has become identified with the term.

Woodroffe appears to have led a kind of dual life, working publicly as a respected British judge and studying privately as a scholar of the *tantras*. After serving as a barrister at the High Court of Calcutta beginning in 1890, Woodroffe was a judge from 1904 to 1922. When he returned to England from India, he became the All Souls Reader in Indian Law at Oxford University until 1930, and then retired to France where he died in Beausoleil. A well-known author of many texts on British-Indian law, Woodroffe was an Indophile and art connoisseur who belonged to the circle around the Tagores. Yet in his private life as a scholar of the *tantras*, Woodroffe would publish a vast corpus of writings, translations, and commentaries. As Kathleen Taylor summarizes Woodroffe's remarkable, somewhat schizoid persona, he seems to have maintained two separate identities: "One identity is public, British and official: the Judge, the scholarly Orientalist. . . . The other is secret, Indian and Tantric."[6]

As Taylor has argued, it seems fairly clear Woodroffe was involved with a circle of disciples who had gathered around a popular Tantric teacher named Śiva Candra Vidyārṇarva Bhaṭṭācārya. Originally from East Bengal, Śiva Candra attracted a number of educated *bhadraloks* in Calcutta, along with a few interested Westerners, one of whom was John Woodroffe. Although Woodroffe never acknowledged any direct participation in Tantra, many believe that he was initiated by Śiva Candra; in fact, an account of this initiation was later published by another disciple in the 1960s.[7]

Whatever may have been his personal involvement in Tantric practice, Woodroffe was a key member of a small group called the Āgamānusandhana Samiti (Agama Research Society), an organization created to publish Tantric texts.[8] Yet the editor of this society was identified, not as John Woodroffe, but as a mysterious character named Arthur Avalon (taken from an idyllic island of British mythology, the last resting place of King Arthur). While most scholars have long assumed that Avalon was a simple pseudonym for Woodroffe himself, Taylor has argued persuasively that Avalon is a much more complicated figure. Rather than Woodroffe alone, "Avalon" was more likely a composite identity, a dual being, comprised of both Woodroffe and the unnamed Bengali who actually did most of the translations. Based on his correspondence with his collaborators, Lama Kazi Dawasamdup and Atal Behari Ghose, it seems fairly clear that Woodroffe was not particularly competent at Sanskrit. In fact, some Indian linguists have asserted that Woodroffe could not even read the script accurately.[9] As Taylor argues, Woodroffe relied heavily on the aid of his Bengali friend Atal Behari Ghose, the secret other half of his Avalon-self.[10] Woodroffe more or less admits this in the preface to *Shakti and Shākta,* the first of his Tantric works published under his own name: the earlier work, he notes, had appeared under the name of Avalon "to denote that they have been written with the direct cooperation of others and in particular with the assistance of one of my friends who will not permit his name to be mentioned."[11]

In any case, Woodroffe seems to have taken it upon himself to defend the tradition of the *tantras*, fighting valiantly to rescue them from the attacks of the European Orientalists and colonial administrators. While his fellow Englishmen denounced Tantra as a "weltering chaos of terror, darkness and uncertainty . . . the most childishly superstitious animism . . . a pit of abomination as far set from God as the mind can go," Woodroffe set out to show that this tradition is "so reasonable" that it cannot be misconstrued as the "absurd and altogether immoral thing which some have supposed it to be."[12] As Woodroffe points out, most of the authors who so fiercely attack the *tantra*s actually have very little idea what "Tantrism" is or how it should be defined. Thus he cites one amusing legal case in which an Indian author was prosecuted for having published one of these allegedly immoral and indecent *tantra*s. Yet the deputy magistrate himself was quite incapable of defining precisely what a *tantra* is or why exactly it should be such a criminal offense to publish its contents: "An Indian Deputy Magistrate who had advised the prosecution and who claimed to be an orthodox Hindu stated . . . in the witness box that he could not define what the Tantraśāstra was or state whether it was a Hindu scripture of the Kali age or whether a well-known particular *śāstra* shown to him was one of the *tantras*."[13] It was precisely to combat this absurd ignorance that Woodroffe set out to defend the tradition of the *tantra*s. Unfortunately, as many authors have pointed out, Woodroffe often went far in the opposite direction.

Woodroffe seems to have inherited much of this reformist attitude from his master, the Bengali Tantric pundit Śiva Candra, whose massive *Tantratattva* was published (by "Arthur Avalon") under the title *The Principles of Tantra*. As Avalon explains in the preface to the book, Śiva Candra's work is in many ways a highly conservative defense of Hindu orthodoxy against the onslaughts of modernism and secularization. Far from a radical or transgressive teaching, *The Principles of Tantra* presents a reactionary defense of authentic Hindu tradition in the face of a rapidly changing, increasingly desacralized modern world. Avalon even compares it to the defense of traditional Catholicism against the threat of modernism in the early twentieth century:

> The present work is a defense of the Tantra . . . undertaken in the interests of Hindu orthodoxy in its Tāntrika form against Secularism . . . and various reforming movements. . . . The book reads like an orthodox Catholic protest against "modernism" and is interesting as showing how many principles are common to all orthodox belief, East or West.[14]

According to Woodroffe's reformed version of Tantra, which he adapts in part from Śiva Candra, this tradition is by no means opposed to the teachings of the Veda and the Upaniṣads; on the contrary, it contains "doctrines of a lofty speculation" that form the innermost essence and continuation of the orthodox tradition.[15] The religion of India, he believes, is not the chaotic plurality of beliefs that it is often imagined to be. Rather, it forms a coherent, unified, systematic whole, a single *bhārata dharma*, or Aryan religion:

> To the Western, Indian Religion seems a jungle of contradictory beliefs amidst which he is lost. . . . It has been asserted that there is no such thing as Indian religion, though there are many Religions in India. This is not so. . . . There is a common Indian Religion . . . Bhārata Dharma, an Aryan Religion held by all Aryas.[16]

The Tantras form an integral part of this greater "Aryan religion," in direct continuity with the teachings of the Vedas and Vedānta. "The Vedānta is the final authority and basis for the doctrines set forth in the Tantras," Woodroffe concludes; for "the Tantra Śāstra . . . has been for centuries past one of the recognized scriptures of Hinduism, and every form of Hinduism is based on Veda and Vedānta."[17] The Tantras are nothing other than the practical application of the teachings of the Vedānta (which, for Woodroffe, is the essence of Indian philosophy):

> The Śākta Tantra simply present the Vedāntik teachings in a symbolic form for the worshipper, to whom it prescribes the means whereby they may be realized in fact.
>
> Vedānta in its various forms has for centuries constituted the religious notions of India, and the Āgamas . . . are its practical expression in worship.[18]

Here we find a profound reversal of the typical Orientalist and reformed Hindu rhetoric: far from being the worst degeneration from the Golden Age of the Veda, Tantra is now the true fulfillment of the noble philosophy revealed in the Vedas and cultivated in the Vedānta.

Science for a New Age: Reuniting Spirit and Matter, East and West

> Tantra is scientific discovery not revelation.
>
> Sir John Woodroffe, *Bharata Shakti* (1921)

Not only are the Tantras in continuity with the most noble traditions of the Vedas, Woodroffe suggests, but they are also in basic agreement with the latest discoveries in modern European science, and "in conformity with the most advanced scientific and philosophic thought of the West."[19] Like modern science, Tantra is also an eminently *practical and experimental* form of knowledge, "a philosophy one not merely argues but experiments."[20] As such, many of Woodroffe's interpretations involve an odd mixture of Western scientific terminology (evolution, matter, energy, etc.) and Sanskrit philosophical language. With the findings of modern science, the *tantras* agree that all matter and all energy is essentially one, and that there is ultimately no duality between the physical and the supraphysical worlds:

> This oneness of origin that underlies all forms in creation is a fact of spiritual experience which is being increasingly corroborated by the results of . . . Science. The Cartesian dualism of mind and matter no longer holds. . . . The missing links pertain only to the superfices of the process of Evolution and, probed deeper, the universe reveals an unbroken Continuum over all the tiers of existence.[21]

The *tantras*, moreover, describe the "evolution" of the world by means of the goddess Śakti, who is the driving power of energy and matter. The aim of this cosmic evolution is the birth of the highest man, the self-realized yogi, who has discovered his own unity with all things: "In the highest man evolution on the material plane ends. Evolution takes place through the Power of God which is always transforming itself into higher forms in order that Spirit may be freed of the bonds of Mind and Matter. . . . This is the Eternal Rhythm of the Divine Mother as Substance-Energy."[22]

Ultimately, as a religious path that weds spirit and matter, body and mind, Tantra forms the ideal bridge between modern Western science and ancient Indian metaphysics. As the power that is the foundation of both matter and spirit, body and consciousness, the Śakti of the *tantras* would seem to offer the ideal solution to the apparent dichotomy of East and West. Rather ironically, Woodroffe asserts the ultimate superiority of the spiritual East over the material West, while using the larger (seemingly Western) paradigm of *science* as the most authoritative source of knowledge about reality.

Deodorizing Tantra: Eliminating the "Foul Stench" of Tantric Practice

> There is nothing "foul" in them except for people to whom all erotic phenomena are foul.
>
> Woodroffe, *Shakti and Shākta*

However, in order to prove that the *tantras* contained noble philosophical teachings, in line with both Vedānta and with Western science, Woodroffe was forced to go to great lengths to rationalize, explain, or excise the more offensive aspects of this tradition. Above all, Woodroffe had to rationalize the Tantric use of substances that are normally forbidden in Hindu society—especially the *pañcatattva*, or "five M's," meat *(māṃsa)*, fish *(matsya)*, wine *(madya)*, parched grain *(mudrā)*, and sexual intercourse *(maithuna)*, which were seen as the defining features of Tantra in most Orientalist discourse. The secret rites of the Tantra, he explains, are strictly closed to the ordinary *paśu*, or bestial man; they can only be revealed to the true *vīra*, the hero or spiritually evolved man, who can fathom their deeper spiritual meaning. In their highest understanding, the meaning of these practices is not literal or physical, but rather "of a purely mental and spiritual character." Thus *madya* represents the "intoxicating knowledge acquired by yoga; meat is not any fleshy thing but the act whereby the *sādhaka* consigns all his acts to [God]; *matsya* is that knowledge by which the worshipper sympathizes with the pleasure and pain of all beings. *Mudrā* is the act of relinquishing all association with evil . . . and *Maithuna* is the union of Śakti Kuṇḍalinī with Śiva in the body of the worshipper."[23] In fact, Woodroffe goes so far as to argue that the Tantras may be considered in many respects even more "ethical" in their sexual attitudes than many of his own, often hypocritical, countrymen:

> There is nothing "foul" in them except for people to whom all erotic phenomena are foul. . . . [T]he ancient East was purer in these matters than the modern West, where, under cover of a pruriently modest exterior . . . extraordinarily varied psychopathic filth may flow. This was not so in earlier days . . . when a spade was called a spade and not a horticultural instrument.[24]

It is no accident that Woodroffe believed the most noble of all *tantras* to be the curious and suspicious text of the *Mahānirvāṇa Tantra*. As we saw in chapter 1, the *Mahānirvāṇa* is an extremely unusual work, one that many suspect was composed in the late eighteenth century as part of an attempt to bring the *tantras* into harmony with the new system of British Indian law. Not only does this text present a highly Vedāntic vision of the supreme Brahman; and not only does it contain an enormous amount of material on orthodox laws of caste, marriage, inheritance, and other legal concerns; but it also strongly downplays the more objectionable erotic aspects of Tantric practice, mentioning them only by means of "great euphemisms." As Woodroffe himself acknowledged, this "woman's Tantra" was generally less popular among many *tāntrika*s than it was among Hindu reformers and Western scholars, precisely because "certain of its provisions appear to display unnecessary timidity" and even a "puritanical" outlook.[25] Nonetheless, in Woodroffe's mind, this idiosyncratic and probably intentionally "deodorized" text is the most noble exemplar of the Tantric tradition.

Far from being depraved licentious rituals, the practices of the *tantras* are, for Woodroffe, no different in essence from the rituals of the Christian tradition. Not only does Woodroffe wish to find parallels between the *tantras* and modern science, but he also seems to have a persistent desire to find parallels with the traditions of the Catholic Church. Like the ancient and carefully guarded liturgy of the Church, he suggests, the *tantras* have preserved throughout the ages an elaborate ritual tradition, whose true aim is not to incite the physical senses, but rather to awaken higher spiritual ideals. In the following, rather remarkable passage, Woodroffe goes so far as to compare the Catholic liturgy, point for point, with a Tantric ritual, identifying specific ritual elements with corresponding Sanskrit terms:

> So, as the Council of Trent declared, the Catholic Church, rich with the experiences of ages and clothed with their splendor, has introduced mystic benediction *(mantra)*, incense *(dhūpa)*, water *(ācamana)*, lights *(dīpa)*, bells *(ghaṇṭā)*, flowers *(puṣpa)*, vestments and all the magnificence of ceremonies in order to excite the spirit of religion to the contemplation of the profound mysteries which they reveal. As are its faithful, the Church is composed of both body *(deha)* and soul *(ātma)*. It renders to the lord *(īśvara)* a double worship, external *(bāhyapūjā)* and interior *(mānasapūjā)*, the latter being the prayer *(vandana)* of the faithful.[26]

Here, in Woodroffe's reformulation, Tantra has become the precise opposite of the scandalous cult of perverse ritual and black magic described by the early Orientalists; on the contrary, Tantra is now a rich spiritual tradition comparable to the highest ceremonial of Tridentine Catholicism. Ironically, whereas earlier scholars like Waddell had attacked and ridiculed Tantra because of its "popish" ritualism and seemingly "Catholized" idolatry, Woodroffe has turned these features into a supreme virtue.

The Religion of Power: Tantra as Spiritual and Political Power

> What India wanted at present was the *Religion of Power.*
>
> Woodroffe, *Bharata Shakti*

Writing in the early decades of the twentieth century, surrounded by the violence of the nationalist movement and the increasing association of Tantra with political dissidence in the popular imagination, Woodroffe could not help but be aware of the political dimension of Tantra. Yet this political dimension remains one of the most complex and ambivalent aspects of his life and work.

As a High Court judge serving in Calcutta, Woodroffe was confronted with a number of cases directly related to the political violence and revolutionary unrest of the radical nationalist movement in Bengal. As Taylor notes, he was serving in the midst of the bloody violence and controversy generated by secret groups like the Jugantar movement, with their explicit use of Tantra and the goddess Kālī in the service of political subversion: "The whole of Woodroffe's career on the bench was governed by what was called 'the Indian unrest.' Soon after he became a judge a period of revolutionary ferment began."[27] At least in his capacity as a judge in the service of the empire, Woodroffe appears to have been quite unsympathetic to the revolutionaries. In 1912, he created a furor among the nationalists throughout Bengal when he passed a controversial ruling against the radicals and in favor of the British authorities:

> Woodroffe as a British judge drawn to Tantrism might seem then to have been in a particularly ambiguous position. Yet, paradoxically—perhaps—Woodroffe was not a judge who was . . . sympathetic to those accused of "extremism" in court—on the contrary, the opposite was the case; and most of the time Woodroffe supported the British authorities rather more enthusiastically than did some other British judges.[28]

Yet, in his private life as a scholar of the *tantra*s and an exponent of Indian culture, Woodroffe was often severely critical of Western values and defensive of India's spiritual and national identity. Like Bankim Chandra and Aurobindo, Woodroffe clearly had inherited the rhetoric of the "spiritual East and the material West," praising India as the land of philosophical wisdom and ancient religious tradition, while identifying the West as a land of material strength and technological superiority but also of spiritual emptiness and moral decay. "The East and particularly India possesses that which is of the highest value. I wish to see this possessed for the mutual benefit of East and West"; for "India possesses a wonderful solvent—a solvent of irreligion and materialism."[29] Woodroffe is often severely critical of the West, which he sees as a civilization based on greed and consumption, seeking material prosperity alone without any higher spiritual concerns: "some of the grossest urges are to be found in what we call advanced civilization."[30] "Our Western civilization is a great eater. We consume. What is called a 'higher standard of life' has meant that we consume more and more. Industrialization instead of satisfying has increased our Western needs. We want more wants."[31]

The all-consuming materialism of the West now threatens to destroy the ancient spiritual civilization of India. Ironically, whereas so many Orientalists had used the metaphor of the "disease" of Tantra—that invasive illness that had weakened and corrupted Hinduism in modern times—Woodroffe uses the same metaphor to describe the potentially destructive invasion of modern materialism, which now threatens to corrupt both East and West alike: "Is Indian civilization about to be renewed or broken up in another instance of that disintegration which has followed the introduction of Western civilization amongst Eastern peoples? Its poison does not harm the snake but it is death to others. . . . [T]he coming assault on Hindu civilization will be the greatest it has ever had to endure."[32]

In the face of this threat of Western materialism and the social ills that it bears in its wake, India now more than ever needs *śakti*—power, in both its spiritual and material forms. For now, in the early decades of the twentieth century, this ancient civilization is being thrust into the maelstrom of global politics, suddenly confronted with economic and cultural forces that it has never seen before.

> India is now approaching the most momentous epoch in its history. . . . The country will be subject to the play of monster economic forces. . . . For the first time in her history she will be thrown into the world-vortex, political, economic, cultural and social, from which her past form of Government has (I believe providentially) preserved her. Will she have the strength to keep her feet in it? I hope she may.[33]

> The world of India should be strong, enduring, massive, adamant to wrongful assault, but beneficent—the kind of massive power suggested by the figure of Kapila carved on the rock of Ceylon.[34]

It is in this sense that Tantraśāstra—the way of power in all its manifestations—is the religion most suited to this most dangerous era in Indian history. For it is the Tantric path alone that weds material power with spiritual power, physical force with intellectual and moral might: "What India wanted at present was the *Religion of Power*. . . . By power I do not mean only physical force. Material force was necessary and serviceable in its way, but it must be backed by mental and spiritual force."[35]

What, then, are we to make of statements like these in light of Woodroffe's far more conservative, antirevolutionary official stance as a High

Court judge? Was he simply inconsistent and contradictory? Or was he maintaining some kind of delicate "double life," with an outward facade of conformity to British rule, while holding to more subversive ideals in his inner secret life as a *tāntrika*? The answer to these questions may never really be known, but what seems most likely is that all of this is only another illustration of Woodroffe's own complex, multifaceted, and in many ways conflicted personality.[36] Above all, it illustrates his own inner conflicts over the problem of Tantra—a tradition long associated in the European imagination with sex, violence, and subversion, but which Woodroffe struggled so much to defend. Tantra, for Woodroffe, could not be associated with violence and revolutionary dissent, any more than it could be associated with black magic or hedonistic excess. In Woodroffe's eyes, those radicals who invoked the Tantric goddess in the service of revolutionary dissent had misunderstood the true essence of Tantra every bit as much as had the Orientalists who attacked it as idolatrous and immoral. And yet, as we see from the above quotation, this "religion of power" remained a troubling problem for Woodroffe; for it is a power that can lift India to its deserved place beside the West but that potentially can foster real unrest, bloodshed, and violence.

In sum, the works of Woodroffe present us with a complex and ambivalent attempt to reimagine Tantra for a new era. While defending the philosophical and intellectual side of the tradition, Woodroffe also submits it to a significant form of deodorization, censoring those practices that might be offensive to a Western audience. Yet at the same time, it is clear that Woodroffe was responding to a particular historical situation; the political context had much to do with how he approached his subject. In Woodroffe's hands, Tantra became a double-edged weapon, defending the purity of Hindu culture against its Western critics and against the destructive materialism of the modern West. Despite the many flaws and contradictions running throughout his work, Woodroffe's reformed version of Tantra continues to have a profound impact on the modern imagining of Tantra in both India and the West.

Woodroffe himself seems to have anticipated the profound impact that Tantra would have on the modern West: above all, he believed that the Tantric reverence for the feminine principle had the potential to meld with and transform the Western world, serving as the inspiration for a more egalitarian, democratic, and gender-equal social order:

> The full inclusion of the feminine element in public life will be the great fight of the immediate future, together with the uprising of a complete democracy . . . based on the equal rights . . . of men and women. . . . These circums-

> tances, and the manner in which they are capable of being met by the Tantra Śāstra, give another ground for the belief that some of the . . . principles of this ancient scripture will become one of the religious influences in modern life, not . . . superseding Christianity, but in an interaction through which the Śākta Śāstra will help as an irritant . . . in the great oyster of Western . . . religion, to produce the Mother-pearl of a complete and true religious exegesis.[37]

As we will see in chapter 6, when we explore contemporary American appropriations of Tantra, Woodroffe's prediction would perhaps be realized in a form he might never have imagined.

SHAME, DISGUST, AND FEAR: TANTRA IN THE RAMAKRISHNA-VIVEKANANDA TRADITION

> Shame, disgust, fear—these three must not remain.
>
> Mahendranāth Gupta,
> *Śrīśrīrāmakṛṣṇakathāmṛta* (1902)

> The path of the Vedas is not meant for the Kali yuga. The path of Tantra is efficacious. . . . Do you mean to say that one cannot follow the path of Tantra? That which is Brahman is also Śakti, Kālī.
>
> "Knowing the secret that Kālī is one with the highest Brahman, I have discarded once and for all, both righteousness and sin."
>
> Swami Nikhilananda, trans.,
> *The Gospel of Sri Ramakrishna* (1942)

In Woodroffe's strategy to censor and cover up the more scandalous, immoral aspects of the *tantra*s, while emphasizing their loftier philosophical dimensions, we find a rather different kind of censorship at work in the teachings of neo-Hindu authors like Swami Vivekananda. As a disciple of the enigmatic Śākta mystic and mad "child of Kālī," Sri Ramakrishna, yet also embarrassed by much of his master's erratic behavior, Vivekananda held a far more ambivalent attitude toward the *tantra*s. Like Woodroffe, Vivekananda was a defender of Hindu culture against the West's criticisms as well as a severe critic of the West. And he too developed a strategy of "censorship," which he applied above all to the often scandalous, embarrassing teachings of the *tantra*s. Yet his censoring strategy was not aimed so much at trying to purify Tantra, but instead at glossing over the Tantric elements within his own tradition.

The Secret Back-Door or Latrine Entrance of the Tantric Path: Ramakrishna's Ambivalent Relation to the Tantras

> That very thing about which it has been said in the Vedas and Purāṇas, "don't do this, that would be bad behavior," in the *tantras* has been called good.
>
> Gupta, *Śrīśrīrāmakṛṣṇakathāmṛta*

> Sakti-sadhana is no joke. There are very strenuous and dangerous practices in it. I passed two years as the Mother's "hand-maid" and "friend." Mine, however, is the mood of the "child," and to me the breasts of any women are like unto my mother's.
>
> Sri Ramakrishna, *Sayings of Sri Ramakrishna* (1949)

Hailed today as a national hero and as an *avatār* for the modern age, revered worldwide by disciples of virtually every nationality, Sri Ramakrishna (figure 9) is surely one of the most important holy men of the modern world and one of the most enigmatic figures in modern Indian history. Born Gadādhara Caṭṭopādhyāy to a poor Brahman family in 1836, Ramakrishna spent most of his life as a priest of Kālī at the temple of Daksineswar, north of Calcutta. An intense visionary mystic, who reported a series of remarkable spiritual encounters with the dark mother Kālī and with a host of other divine beings, Ramakrishna came to be regarded by his disciples not merely as a charismatic holy man; rather, he was progressively identified as an *avatār,* a divine incarnation for this most dangerous of eras in the Kali yuga of India under colonial rule.

Today, Ramakrishna is most widely regarded as a spokesman of religious universalism and tolerance. All religious traditions, according to the usual interpretation of Ramakrishna's teachings, are so many paths leading to the same summit, to one supreme truth embracing all human beings, cultures, and religious views. Ramakrishna has thus been revered by both Indian and European authors as a prophet of religious harmony, who was as comfortable worshiping Jesus or Muhammad as he was praising Kṛṣṇa, and who saw the inner unity of all religions in the encompassing vision of Hindu Vedānta.[38] However, as a variety of recent scholars have argued, this usual interpretation of Ramakrishna is at best simplistic and at worst deeply colored by the views of Vivekananda and other disciples. Kripal, for example, argues that Ramakrishna's teachings are much less

Figure 9. Sri Ramakrishna. From Swami Nikhilananda, trans., *The Gospel of Sri Ramakrishna* (New York: Ramakrishna-Vivekananda Center, 1942).

about the highly abstract and intellectual system of Advaita Vedānta than about a profoundly sensual, mystical encounter with the terrible Mother Kālī, in her most frighteningly sexual and violent forms.[39]

One of the most troubling and controversial aspects of Ramakrishna's personality is his relation to Tantra. "Everything about a *tāntrika* is secret," the master warned, "that's why not everyone understands a *tāntrika [tāntriker sab gopan. tāi tāntrikke sab bojhā jāy nāi]*."[40] Ramakrishna was from the beginning a devotee of Kālī in her most terrifying forms; his rich visionary life was filled with often violent and erotic images of the Dark Mother. He was, moreover, introduced to many of the most esoteric Tantric rites, particularly during his period of study with the mysterious female guru Bhairavī Brāhmaṇī. Under Bhairavī's guidance, from 1861 to 1863, Ramakrishna was initiated into at least the first four of the five M's, engaging in such transgressive acts as eating fish cooked in a human skull and tasting rotten human flesh. "Having heard that the Divine Mother sometimes assumes the form of Śiva, and that dogs are the bearers of Bhairava, he ate the leftovers of dogs as if they were pure" (LP 1.206). Elsewhere he declared, "I saw with my own eyes [God] dwelling in the vagina. I saw [God] in the sexual intercourse of a dog and a bitch."[41] Many of Ramakrishna's intense visions were colored by his Tantric experience:

> Sri Ramakrishna set himself to the task of practicing the disciplines of Tantra; and at the bidding of the Divine Mother he accepted Brahmani as his Guru. . . . He practiced all the disciplines of the sixty-four principal Tantra books. . . . After the observance of a few preliminary rites, he would be overwhelmed with a strange divine fervor and would go into *samādhi*. . . . Evil ceased to exist for him. The word "carnal" lost its meaning. The whole world and everything in it appeared as the *līlā*, the sport of Śiva and Śakti. He beheld everywhere manifest the power and beauty of the Mother.[42]

Initially, Ramakrishna was very suspicious of the dark powerful rites of the *tantras*; yet he gradually came to accept them as one possible—albeit dangerous and potentially destructive—path to the divine. Hence he compares the Tantric path to entering a house through the "latrine door," instead of through the front door: it is a way to reach God, but a path by which one "gets very filthy":

> This too is a path for reaching God—
> But this path is a very filthy *[noṅgrā]* one.
> Just as there are various doors for entering a house,
> by some doors one enters the front room;
> and by some doors one can enter the inner chambers,
> but there is a separate door for the Sweeper *[methar,* i.e., the latrine door].[43]

In any case, this period of practicing the "filthy path" of the Tantras represented a pivotal moment in the saint's spiritual life, a moment in which he realized the all-pervasive power of the Goddess in all things, pure or impure—what he described as a "fundamental transformation of his entire nature *(pūrva svabhāver āmūla parivartana)*" (LP 1.212).

Indeed, Kripal has gone so far as to argue that Ramakrishna's life and teachings not only are influenced by, but are fundamentally rooted in and shaped by, the powerful, frightening world of Tantra: "Ramakrishna was a Tāntrika," with his feet planted firmly in Tantric soil, Kripal concludes; yet at the same time, the saint himself felt intense ambivalence, shame, and embarrassment about his Tantric background and denied his own Tantric tendencies: "Tantra for Ramakrishna was . . . a grave and ominous tradition of teachings and techniques that haunted him, that horrified him, and yet somehow formed who he was. Tantra was Ramakrishna's secret."[44] Above all, Ramakrishna was particularly ambivalent about the infamous fifth M, *maithuna,* or sexual union, in which he ultimately refused to engage and which he always seems to have regarded as a particularly dangerous practice.

> *Narendra:* "Isn't it true that the Tantra prescribes spiritual discipline in the company of women?"
>
> *Master:* "That is not desirable. It is a very difficult path and often causes the aspirant's downfall."[45]

Even in his intimate practice with Bhairavī, the saint remained ever chaste and unsullied by the taint of sexual contact. He seems to have been quite terrified by the idea of actual sexual relations with a woman, choosing instead the attitude of a "child toward its mother": "Just as my attitude towards all women, that of a child towards its mother, remained unshaken during the long period of practice according to the *tantra*s" (LP 1.206).[46]

Yet even the chaste and pure Ramakrishna seems to have felt powerfully conflicted, attracted by sensual lust and yet terrified of union with a female body: "it should not be supposed that his self control was an easy matter. . . . Ramakrishna frankly admitted that he was attacked by lust."[47] As Kripal argues, this profound ambivalence about the transgressive power of Tantric sexuality is embedded in the saint's psyche and lies at the heart of much of his visionary life:

> There are good historical reasons why Tantra has been overlooked for so long, not the least of which is Ramakrishna's own profound ambivalence toward the tradition. If he consistently associated Tantra with the latrine, it was because he himself . . . was disgusted with the dark abusive side of the tradition. All these emotional reactions . . . made Tantra for Ramakrishna a thing of almost limitless and so terrifying power.[48]

Going still further, however, Kripal makes the more daring argument that much of the root of the saint's intense ambivalence about Tantric sexuality was his conflicted feeling about his own sexual orientation—specifically, the homoerotic impulses and desires which, Kripal suggests, recurred throughout the saint's life and manifested themselves vividly in his intense mystical experiences. For while Tantric practice requires that the *sādhaka* become a masculine hero and engage in ritual sexual intercourse, "for a homoerotic saint like Ramakrishna, such a . . . ritual necessity led to serious conflict and emotional pain."[49]

Kripal's rereading of Ramakrishna's life from a Tantric perspective has not, however, gone unchallenged. On the contrary, at the same time that it has been praised by the academic community and granted a major award from the American Academy of Religion, it has also generated intense controversy and furor within the Indian community. In a full-page review in Calcutta's major English paper, *The Statesman,* Narasingha Sil decried Kripal as a sloppy, sensationalist, and scandal-mongering scholar with a perverse imagination, who has ransacked another culture and produced a work that is, in short, "plain shit" (this review has since generated more reader mail, against Kripal's book, than any printed in the two-hundred-year history of the paper).

> Kripal's enterprise is a classic example of what happens when an author's clever use of dictionary, index card and intelligence without an understanding of the . . . culture of people other than his ethnic group but with a pretension to insider's knowledge . . . produces a psychoanalysis of the . . . experience of a saint from another religion.[50]

The book has thus been attacked by some Indian intellectuals as an insidious form of neocolonialism and the exploitation of exoticized Indian religious traditions in the form of slickly produced paperbacks. Much of this controversy, it would seem, has arisen precisely because Kripal pointed to the deeply embarrassing problem of Ramakrishna's Tantric past and his ties to the troubling world of transgressive sexuality. And as a consequence, Kripal's own book—not unlike the Tantric life of Ramakrishna itself—has now been subjected to a powerful form of *censorship and silencing,* ironically now itself "becoming a secret."[51]

If Tantra was a matter of ambivalence and discomfort for Ramakrishna, then it seems to have been an even more embarrassing problem for his disciples. Indeed, it appears that the dominant tradition within the Ramakrishna Mission has made a consistent effort to censor, cover up, and conceal much of the saint's troubling Tantric past. As Kripal and others have pointed out, the Bengali text of the *Śrīśrīrāmakṛṣṇakathāmṛta* was in many ways profoundly bowdlerized, edited, and sanitized in its English translation, *The Gospel of Sri Ramakrishna,* by Swami Nikhilananda; most of the objectionable sexual references either were concealed with innocuous euphemisms or deleted altogether. "A highly cultivated individual in charge of one of the largest Rāmakṛṣṇa missions in the United States . . . Nikhilānanda frequently excised Rāmakṛṣṇa's vulgar expressions with explicitly sexual connotations."[52] In the process, Ramakrishna—this intense, ecstatic, devotee of Kālī—was progressively transformed into a prophet of philosophical monism, religious universalism, and Hindu nationalism.

Still more striking, however, is the fact that there are *other* early biographies of the saint, which were later ignored, marginalized, and suppressed by the mainstream tradition. The oldest known biography of the saint is Ramācandra Datta's *Śrīśrīrāmakṛṣṇa Paramahaṃsadever Jīvan-avṛttānta* (1890)—a text that offers a more explicitly Śākta Tantric view of the saint's life, largely ignoring Vivekananda's neo-Vedāntic interpretation (it does not mention Vivekananda at all).[53] Not surprisingly, this text was severely criticized and angrily dismissed by Vivekananda and his followers: "I am simply ashamed of the Bengali book," the Swami declared, dubbing it *"bosh and rot."*[54] As Kripal concludes, there has been intense debate within the movement from the outset, much of it centering around Ramakrishna's troubling sexual life: *"From the very first biography,* attempts to represent the historical Ramakrishna have been contested, argued over and rejected. . . . [O]ne of the central themes of this debate has been . . . the nature and religious importance of Ramakrishna's secret sexuality."[55] So too, the intense furor and scandal over Kripal's own book only proves that the saint's Tantric past remains a painful source of embarrassment for the later tradition. Regardless of the ultimate truth or falsehood of Kripal's thesis, it is obvious that the very suggestion that Ramakrishna—this national hero and *avatār* for the age of darkness—might have had a sordid Tantric past has touched a deep, unhealed wound that lies buried at the innermost heart of the tradition.

Swami Vivekananda and the Transformation of Tantric Madness into Neo-Hindu Religious Nationalism

> It is not only that we must revive our own country. . . . [M]y idea is the conquest of the whole world by the Hindu race. . . .
>
> [W]e must conquer the world through our spirituality . . . we must do it or die. The only condition of . . . awakened and vigorous national life is the conquest of the world by Indian thought.

As our country is poor in social virtues, this country [America] is lacking in spirituality. I give them spirituality, and they give me money.
Swami Vivekananda to Ramakrishnananda (19 March 1894)

Surely the most influential of Ramakrishna's disciples, and also the one most deeply troubled by his master's Tantric past, was the great neo-Hindu leader and religious nationalist Swami Vivekananda.[56] Born Narendra Nath Datta to a comfortable middle-class family, Vivekananda is today best known as the first great missionary of Hinduism to the West. With his famous address at the World Parliament of Religions at Chicago in 1893, Vivekananda began to spread his version of Vedānta throughout America and England. The most aggressive of Ramakrishna's early devotees, Vivekananda would emerge as the man whom Paul Hacker calls "the most influential shaper and propagandist of the Neo-Hindu spirit," and the most powerful exponent of Hindu self-representation vis-à-vis the West.[57] Yet Vivekananda was also an instrumental figure in the transformation of Ramakrishna from a detached visionary mystic and devotee of the Goddess into a national hero and divine *avatār* for this dark age of India under foreign rule. For Vivekananda, Ramakrishna was the culmination of all Hindu scriptures and revelations, embodying all the inherited wisdom of the Vedas, Upaniṣads, Śāstras, and newly revealing them for this darkest moment in history; "with his birth the golden Age, the Age of truth had dawned once again."[58] As Vivekananda proclaimed, "The time was ripe, it was necessary that such a man should be born. . . . Sri Ramakrishna [is] the fulfillment of the India sages, the sage for the time, one whose teaching is just now . . . most beneficial."[59] And Vivekananda would be the one to receive this *avatār*'s divine message and transform it into a source of national awakening. In the words of his British disciple Sister Nivedita, "Just as Sri Ramakrishna . . . without knowing any books, had been a living exemplar of the Vedanta, so was Vivekananda of the national life."[60]

Yet Vivekananda's ideal seems to have been a very different one from that of his master. In striking contrast to Ramakrishna's Tantric tendencies, erotic visionary experiences, and childlike devotion to the Dark Mother, Vivekananda promoted a strong, virile, and masculine ideal of a reformed Hinduism that could meet the challenge of the West. "Rejecting such feminine states, Narendra the Lion begins to preach the virtues of spiritual manliness and renunciation. . . . Narendra's songs of manly renunciation, of Śiva and Śaṅkara, begin to replace those of

Kālī . . . so dear to Ramakrishna."[61] Embarrassed by the image of the effete babu so ridiculed by the British, Vivekananda advocated an aggressive model of Hindu identity, ready to meet the challenge of the West. "What our country now wants are muscles of iron and nerves of steel, gigantic wills which nothing can resist," the swami admonished his disciples.[62] If India is to realize a new national awakening and take pride in itself as an independent power, it must overcome its debilitating passivity and assume a more muscular stance toward the West. "Say brother, this soil of India is my highest heaven, the good of India is my good. . . . O thou Mother of the universe, vouchsafe manliness unto me, O thou Mother of strength, take away my weakness, take away my unmanliness and make me a Man!"[63]

Vivekananda's goal seems to have been nothing less than a spiritual conquest of the West—what we might call a form of "reverse colonialism" or "spiritual imperialism." For just as England has conquered and colonized India through its military might, so now India will conquer the West through its superior morality: "Vivekananda described the worldwide propagation of spirituality in militant terms—propagation as a form of conquest. . . . Armed with the spirituality of Advaita Vedanta, young Hindu men are given the mission of conquering the world and reestablishing the power of their own nation."[64] As Narasingha Sil observes, Vivekananda could thus be described as an "ambitious, idealistic militant monk," who envisioned a "global spiritual conquest in the manner of Napoleonic imperialism."[65]

Perhaps even more fiercely than Sri Aurobindo or any other twentieth-century neo-Hindu reformers, Vivekananda constructed a sharp duality between the cultural worlds of the Occident and Orient—between the "material West" and "the spiritual East."[66] Throughout his writings, the West is portrayed as a fundamentally materialistic and shallow world, a civilization based on wealth and death-dealing weapons, spiritual emptiness and the oppression of other countries. With their one-sided materialism, secularism, and rationalism, the Western nations are ruled by the pursuit of profit, the desire to control, and the "ideal of eating and drinking." They are "degraded by political ambitions and social scheming. . . . [I]n spite of the sparkle and glitter of Western civilization, in spite of all its . . . marvelous manifestation of power . . . I tell them to their face that it is all vain."[67] "You Americans worship what? The dollar. In the mad rush for gold, you forget the spiritual until you have become a nation of materialists."[68] India, conversely, is a culture founded on eternal tradition and religion. The timeless Hindu tradition is not only anterior and superior to all other religions of the world, but even the foundation of every other major spiritual tradition. With its supreme philosophy of Advaita Vedānta, Hinduism is also the culmination of all the world's religions, which encompasses them all in its universal vision.[69]

Appropriating the Aryan narrative of the Orientalists—*but turning it completely on its head*—Vivekananda even claims that the Hindus are the purest form of the Aryan race, the most noble, beautiful, and civilized of all the Indo-European peoples. The modern Europeans, conversely, represent a kind of degeneration from this pristine Aryan stalk:

> To the great tablelands of the high Himalaya mountains first came the Aryans and there to this day abides the pure type of Brahman, a people which [the Westerners] can but dream of. Pure in thought, deed and action. . . . Their features are regular, their eyes dark and the skin the color which would be produced by the drops which fell from a pricked finger into a glass of milk.[70]

In contrast to this pure Aryan spirit, the English of today are addicted to alcohol, money, and violence, using their savage strength to bully and conquer more peaceful, spiritual peoples: "You look about India, what has the Hindoo left? Wonderful temples everywhere. . . . What has the Englishman left? Nothing but mounds of broken brandy bottles!"[71] "Ah, the English only just a little while ago were savages, the vermin crawled on the ladies' bodices . . . and they scented themselves to disguise the abominable odor of their persons. . . . They are quite savage. . . . They only think to kill."[72] Indeed, Vivekananda even goes so far as to suggest that the Europeans are themselves left-hand *tāntrika*s of a sort—for they too worship power *(śakti)* in its grossest, most physical form, the religion of force and strength as a brutal end in itself: "Their religion is Sakti Puja: it is a form of Vamacara—except for the last elements of the five Ma-karas."[73]

Thus Ramakrishna was for Vivekananda the divine incarnation for this dark age of Western domination, when the evils of materialism had overrun the earth. Heralding the rebirth of the Golden Age, Ramakrishna embodied the culmination of the whole long history of Hindu tradition, now bursting forth to meet the threat of Western domination: this divine *avatār* "came to save the Indians from the spell of the worldly glamour of Western culture."[74]

Yet at the same time, as Halbfass argues, Vivekananda's thought was itself very much informed by Western values, ideals, and modes of reasoning. He denounced the West largely by using the tools and lenses of modern Western criticism: "He adopts Western motifs of self-criticism . . . and transforms them into aspects of Hindu self-assertion. . . . [H]e demonstrates the extent to which the Neo-Hindu dialogue with the West employs or presupposes Western means of self-reflection and self-critique."[75] As King points out, Vivekananda assimilated many Western stereotypes of India—above all, the image of India as land of mysticism, spirituality, and otherworldliness, in contrast to the science, technology, and material wealth of West.[76] However, the swami also actively attempted to incorporate and adapt certain key Western values. This is particularly evident in Vivekananda's ideal of a kind of "practical Vedānta"—that is, a form of Vedānta that would also incorporate the positive Western values of social action, work ethics, charity, and social mobility: "The Hindu should make the organizational abilities, the pragmatic orientation, the work ethic, the social virtues and the scientific power of Europe . . . their own. They should overcome their lethargy and advance to new vigor and self-confidence."[77]

At the same time, Vivekananda adopted many of the structures and strategies of one of his foremost rivals in the spiritual marketplace—the Christian missionaries. Armed with his "gospel of Ramakrishna," Vivekananda established his own Ramakrishna Mission and aggressively proselytized his message using many tactics appropriated from the Baptist Missionary Society and other Christian groups working in Bengal: "What I want is a band of fiery missionaries," the swami declared; for "the monk . . . is the soldier of God."[78] In sum, it would seem that even as he attacked the evils of the West and asserted the superiority of Advaita Vedānta, Vivekananda already had assimilated a largely Western ideology, which informs much of his construction of Hinduism and Indian culture: "He is not willing or able to see how far he has removed himself from the position of Śaṅkara and how much he has yielded to those Western means of orientation against which he desires to assert Hinduism."[79]

"Sex-Love and Creation": The Ambivalence and Embarrassment of Tantra

> Sex-love and creation! These are at the root of most religions. . . . How few have dared to worship Death or Kali! Let us embrace the Terrible, because it is terrible, not asking that it be toned down.
>
> Swami Vivekananda, "Sayings and Utterances" (1926)

Given his commitment to the defense of Hinduism and the strength of the Indian nation, it is not surprising that Vivekananda should have been particularly embarrassed by the transgressive practices of the *tantras*. Vivekananda was even more ambivalent than his master had been about the dark power of Tantra and Mother Kālī. The swami clearly inherited many of the biases of the European Orientalists, often identifying Tantra as the worst example of everything that was wrong with Indian religion and everything most in need of reform if India were to achieve this new self-definition and this spiritual conquest of the Western world. Like Rāmmohun before him, he laments that the pristine vision of the Vedas and Upaniṣads gradually has been perverted, corrupted, and displaced by the vulgar superstition of the *tantras*: "Vivekananda deplores that the truly authoritative Veda is eclipsed . . . by the Puranas and Tantras, documents of an increasing historical degeneration."[80] And like many other Hindu authors of his day, he located the origins of this crippling Tantric disease, not within the Hindu tradition or India itself, but in the barbarous foreign lands of central Asia and in the licentious rites of the Buddhists of Tibet.

> From central Asia the cruel barbarians came, having established their terrible practices in their own land; in order to attract the ignorant barbarians the true path took on the form of the Tantras and Mantras; and that is why when they became misunderstood, weakened and corrupt . . . they resulted in the terrible abominations of Vamacara and barbaric practices.[81]

> The Tantrick practices of Tibet . . . came to India during the final stages of the Buddhist religion . . . the Buddhists were the origin and essence of all the Tantras which are now current among us. . . . And when Buddhism became impotent because of this kind of immorality, they were driven out by Kumarila Bhatta.[82]

Hence the swami makes it clear that left-hand Tantra is absolutely forbidden for the monks of the Ramakrishna mission; indeed, they are explicitly warned *not even to speak of such horrible rites*, on threat of expulsion from the order:

> The Vamachara form of practice . . . should on no account be practised at the Math. Anyone demuring to this must step out of this Order. This form of practice must never even be mentioned in the Math. Ruin shall seize the wicked man, both here and hereafter, who would introduce vile Vamachara into His fold.[83]

As Agehananda Bharati comments, Vivekananda was thus at the vanguard of the reformist attempt to purify Hinduism of its unsavory erotic elements. In doing so, however, he also imbibed many of the puritanical values of the Christian missionaries whom he so reviled: "Vivekananda was the first who, fighting the Christian missionary, adopted the latter's denigration of Eros, and began to unsex the Hindu pantheon."[84]

Religious Nationalism, Anticolonialism, and the Problem of Tantra

Give up this filthy Vamachara that is killing your country.

Swami Vivekananda,
"The Vedanta in All Its Phases" (1926)

Much of Vivekananda's ambivalent attitude toward Tantra seems to be closely tied to his unique form of religious nationalism and his attempts to rebuild India's self-respect as a strong, powerful nation. For "his was a message of national awakening. The message was one of activity and strength, as well as of conscious action for the masses."[85] As Partha Chatterjee suggests, a key part of this nationalism was the creation of a new narrative of Indian history that retold the story of India's past and asserted the strength and autonomy of the Indian people as shapers of their own destiny: "the call sent out by Bankimchandra—We have no history, We must have a history!—implied an exhortation to launch the struggle of power, because in this mode of recalling the past, the power to represent oneself is nothing other than political power itself."[86] However, much of this narrative was borrowed from the European Orientalists—namely, the Orientalist narrative of a pristine Golden Age, a period of medieval decline, and finally a rejuvenation or renaissance in the modern era: "For Indian nationalists . . . the pattern of classical glory, medieval decline and modern renaissance appeared as one that was . . . approved for India. What was needed was to claim for the Indian nation the historical agency for completing the project of modernity."[87]

At the same time, this imagining of the Indian nation—the construction of a singular, unified, imagined community out of the bewildering diversity of ethnicities, cultures, and languages that comprise the peoples of the subcontinent—went hand-in-hand with the imagining of Hinduism—the construction of singular, unified, "imagined religion" out of the bewildering diversity of rituals, beliefs, deities, and traditions that comprise the living practice of India. As King points out, the Hindu nationalists, who fought so valiantly against European political domination, ironically adapted the European model of both the nation-state and the "world religion" in their constructions of Hinduism and the Indian nation:

> The invention of Hinduism as a single world religion was accompanied by the rise of a nationalist consciousness in India. . . . The modern nation-state . . . is a product of European socio-political and economic developments . . . and the introduction of the nationalist model into Asia is a further legacy of European imperialism. . . . It is somewhat ironic to find that the very Hindu nationalists who fought so vehemently against British imperialist rule themselves accepted the homogenizing concepts of nationhood and Hinduism which ultimately derived from their imperial rulers.[88]

For Hindu reformers like Vivekananda, the *tantra*s became an important part of this new imagining of both the Indian nation and the Hindu tradition as a singular great "world religion." For the *tantra*s were precisely the debilitating disease that had weakened the noble Hindu spirit, leading to its medieval decline and opening the door for the Muslim invasion. It is the lingering illness of left-hand Tantra that has allowed the British to penetrate and dominate this weakened country; and therefore, it is only by eradicating this insidious Tantric influence that the nation can regain her original strength and be restored to her rightful autonomy. To this day, degenerate Vāmācāra Tantra pervades the very "marrow" of the body politic, emasculating the nation and sapping its vital strength. Only by purging this demoralizing parasite can India recover its virile, masculine power:

> Just look to your own province and see how this Vamachara (immoral practices) of the Tantras has entered into your very marrow. Even modern Vaishnavism . . . is saturated with Vamachara! We must stem the tide of this Vamachara which is contrary to the spirit of the Vedas.[89]

> Give up this filthy Vamachara that is killing your country. . . . When I see how much the Vamachara has entered into our society, I find it a most disgraceful place with all its boast of culture. These Vamachara secrets are honeycombing our society in Bengal. . . . The Bengali Shastras are the Vamachara shastras. They are published by the cartload and you poison the minds of your children with them. . . . Fathers of Calcutta, do you not feel ashamed that such horrible stuff as these Vamachara Tantras . . . should be put into the hands of your boys and girls, and their minds poisoned, and that they should be brought up with the idea that these are the Shastras of the Hindus? If you are ashamed, take them away from your children and let them read the true Shastras, the Vedas, the Gita and the Upanishads.[90]

The category of Tantra might thus be said to have functioned in relation to the imagining of the Indian nation in much the same way that it functioned in relation to the imagining of Hinduism as a whole: it represented the dark underbelly, the corrupt, degenerate side of the tradition, and the antithesis or parodic inversion against which the nation defined itself.

The Embarrassment of Tantra and the Problem of Ramakrishna

For fear of the Tantras, for fear of the mob, in his attempt to cure a boil, he amputated the very arm itself!

Swami Vivekananda to Akhandananda (1890)

Despite his fierce criticisms of Tantra, Vivekananda's attitude toward it was in fact quite ambivalent. After all, he was born into a Bengali world that was saturated with traditions commonly identified as "Tantric," such as bloody worship of the violent goddesses Kālī and Durgā, and he was the disciple of the enigmatic Ramakrishna, a man whose visions were filled with highly erotic Śākta imagery. "There are . . . symptomatic changes and ambiguities in his attitude towards Tantrism which he often condemned publicly and yet accepted . . . as an essential ingredient of his . . . Bengali identity."[91] Hence, he often speaks more sympathetically of the Tantras, acknowledging that they too are rooted in the Vedas, as a kind of practical adaptation of Vedic ritual, which is the common form of practice for most Hindus today:

> Barring some of the abominable things in the Tantras . . . they are not so bad as people are inclined to think. There are many high and sublime Vedantic thoughts in them. . . . All the forms of our worship and the ceremonials of the present day, comprising the Karma Kanda, are observed in accordance with the Tantras.[92]

At times, the swami speaks quite apologetically for the *tantra*s, suggesting that they are in their original spirit essentially valid Hindu scriptures that were only later corrupted by degenerate Buddhism and the obscene rites of the left-hand (Vāmācāra) path:

> I denounced only the present corrupted form of Vamachara of the Tantras. I did not denounce the Mother worship of the Tantras. . . . The purport of the Tantras is to worship women in a spirit of Divinity. During the downfall of Buddhism, the Vamachara became very much corrupted, and that corrupted form obtains to the present. . . . I denounced only these corrupt . . . practices.[93]

Vivekananda's ambivalence toward Tantra is particularly obvious when it comes to the mysterious life of his master, Ramakrishna. Even upon his first meetings with the master, when he was a college student, Narendra was "scandalized by the bizarre behavior of the 'madman' of Dakṣineśvar."[94] Throughout his life, Vivekananda seemed disturbed by the saint's odd, at times openly erotic, behavior, and he went to some lengths to assert that his master was not in fact one of these scandalous, transgressive *tāntrikas*: "Some are saying that Ramakrishna was a Tantrika and a Kaula . . . but do not listen to such one-sided estimates."[95] Instead, the swami constructed an image of his master as a living icon of Advaita Vedānta, an embodiment of lofty speculations and the universal ideal of Śaṅkara's absolute nondualism. Written as they were within a particular social context (colonial Bengal at the turn of the century) for a specific audience (middle-class Bengalis strongly influenced by the West), Vivekananda's comments on Ramakrishna might be said to "fail miserably to meet the standards of historical accuracy and scholarly objectivity." For "like so many of the photographs we have of the saint, Ramakrishna's image has been 'touched up' in their writings, even painted over, in order to cover up some of his more troubling wrinkles and undesirable features."[96]

In fact, it seems that Vivekananda tried in various ways to conceal his master's strange sexual visions and involvement in the dark realm of Tantra. He decided that it was best not to speak much about his master before Western audiences during his trips to England and America, for fear that they would only misunderstand Ramakrishna's more disturbing Tantric side. As Thomas Bryson observes, "Vivekananda was hesitant to present the life of his Guru . . . to Westerners because Ramakrishna's life was so extraordinary and alien to Western understanding"; and when he did speak of him, it was surely not as a *tāntrika* but as a "great teacher, saint and prophet," and as a spokesman for Advaita Vedānta.[97] Thus he explicitly instructed his disciples to be circumspect in their portrayal of the master, making sure not to reveal any of the more embarrassing aspects of his (at times scandalous) life: "he warned his followers that in writing Ramakrishna's life for a Western audience, they must 'avoid all irregular indecent expositions about sex.'"[98] They were not to speak of anything that touched too closely upon the sexual content of the master's teachings, which would be misunderstood easily and were "quite unsuitable for young minds."[99]

Vivekananda seems to be aware that there was some discrepancy between the master's own life and his representation of it—for even Ramakrishna had not understood himself, and it was left to his disciples to interpret the meaning of his intense life and experiences: "He did not understand himself. He knew nothing of England or the English. . . . But he lived a great life and I read the meaning. He knew nothing of Vedānta, nothing of theories! He was contented to live that great life, and let others explain!"[100]

Thus it would seem that Vivekananda subjected his own master to a form of censorship, covering over those troubling Tantric elements that lingered in the saint's complex personality. One might well impute to Vivekananda the sort of behavior that he himself once identified in the Vedānta sage Śaṅkara: that he attacked and rejected a darker religious practice, Buddhism, for fear its degenerate Tantric element would infect the Hindu tradition: "For fear of the Tantras . . . in his attempt to cure a boil, he amputated the very arm itself!"

In sum, Tantra was for Vivekananda—and for many reformers of the early twentieth century—a crucial element in the reimagining of both the Hindu religion and the Indian nation. It was a shameful reminder of all that was most embarrassing about India's past and that stood in the way of her strength, autonomy, and independence. As we can see in the case of Sri Ramakrishna, the *avatār* for a new age of Hindu renaissance, the *tantra*s would remain a dark secret at the very heart of the tradition. Never fully suppressed or censored, the *tantra*s continue to plague the dominant tradition as its embarrassing secret, a troubling reminder of the sensuality, violence, and scandal that lies beneath the surface of the most rational philosophical abstractions and the noblest political aspirations.

"MEN MISUNDERSTAND ONE ANOTHER EVERYWHERE"

> Unfortunately . . . [the Tantras'] intentions have been so grossly misrepresented in our days that the very name of Tantra shocks our nerves; yet two thirds of our religious rites are Tantrik, and almost half our medicine is Tantrik.
>
> K. C. Chakravarti, *Lectures on the Hindu Religion* (1893)

> I think it is possible that Hindus may have misunderstood Buddhists and Buddhists Hindus. Men misunderstand one another everywhere.
>
> Woodroffe to Lama Kazi Dawasamdup (26 May 1919)

Together, the works of Woodroffe and Vivekananda represent two simultaneous, highly influential, yet ultimately unsuccessful attempts to reform the depiction of Tantra in the modern imagination. Each in his own way subjected Tantra to a kind of censorship—in Woodroffe's case, by covering over its more transgressive and immoral aspects, and in Vivekananda's case, by attacking the left-hand side of the tradition and trying to conceal the embarrassing aspects of his own master's Tantric practice.

For both authors, moreover, this sanitization of Tantra was tied to a specific political agenda: namely, the construction of a new Indian national and cultural identity in the face of two centuries of British colonialism. In their dichotomy of the spiritual East and material West, Tantra was a troubling presence—a part of the spiritual East that seemed disturbingly "material" and frighteningly sensual. It had to be sanitized and spiritualized, therefore, or else suppressed.

Yet neither of these attempts at censorship and sanitization would prove very successful in the end. As Kripal's controversial work has made clear, the dark side of Ramakrishna's Tantric past remains a source of embarrassment for the Ramakrishna Mission and for the Hindu tradition as whole. Neither Woodroffe nor Vivekananda succeeded in purifying Tantra or in excising it from the Hindu tradition; if anything, their work has only fanned the fires, piquing the interests of later generations in a tradition that was a source of such titillating scandal and agonizing debate.

CHAPTER 5

Religion for the Age of Darkness

Tantra and the History of Religions in the Twentieth Century

The Tantra may be regarded as the religious experience most appropriate to the present condition of man—to life in the kali yuga, the age of darkness. . . . Humanity is fallen: it is now a case of swimming against the stream. . . . The *tāntrika* does not renounce the world; he tries to overcome it while enjoying perfect freedom.

Mircea Eliade,
Myths, Dreams, and Mysteries (1960)

Following in the wake of John Woodroffe's heroic defense of Tantra, a new wave of scholars began to take an active interest in, and often a strange preoccupation with, the teachings of the Tantras. Many of the greatest European Indologists and scholars of comparative religion, such as Mircea Eliade, Agehananda Bharati, and even C. G. Jung, were extremely interested in Tantra and in some cases saw it as the very essence of Eastern spirituality.[1] At the same time, a new generation of Indian scholars also began to take an interest in Tantra, which they saw as one of the most primordial forms of Indian religions. Thus D. N. Bose and Hiralal Haldar praise Tantra as a tradition deeply rooted in the Vedas and as the "standard bearer of Aryan culture."[2] Thus, whereas some authors have lamented the neglect of Tantra in modern discourse, I would argue, on the contrary, that we might even speak of a "Tantrocentrism" at the heart of the history of religions. This is a trend that runs parallel to what Steven Wasserstrom calls the "esocentrism" of the modern study of religion, or the preoccupation with the mystical, interior side of religion, to the neglect of its more mundane, practical, and social dimensions. Similarly, the modern study of Eastern religions has often been characterized by a central preoccupation with Tantra, as the most erotic and alluring aspect of the exotic Orient itself.[3]

For both Indian and European authors, moreover, the scholarly imagining of Tantra has had profound political implications, tied to the cultural, economic, and nationalist interests of those who studied it. Indeed, the history of scholarship on Tantra is in many ways a political history of the history of religions as an academic discipline; for it has been tied from its inception to larger questions, not just of colonialism and nationalism, but also to the re-formation of political identities in the aftermath of imperialism and in the decades of the Cold War.[4]

In what follows, I will examine five exemplary figures, three Europeans and two Indians. On the European side, surely among the three most influential modern scholars of religion were also among the most widely read authors on the subject of Tantra: Heinrich Zimmer, Julius Evola, and Mircea Eliade. These three have had a formative impact on the fields of Indology (in the case of Zimmer), esotericism and right-wing politics (Evola), and comparative religions (Eliade). And all three felt a strong attraction to Tantra, a tradition that they defined as the culmination of all Indian thought: the most radical form of spirituality and the archaic heart of aboriginal India. There are, of course, other important scholars who could be mentioned here, such as the Italian Buddhologist Giuseppe Tucci and the Austrian convert to Hinduism Agehananda Bharati, both of whom played important roles in the study of Tantra. However, because these two have been discussed by others (most notably by Gustavo Benevides and Jeffrey Kripal), I only mention them in passing in this chapter.[5]

But why this special preoccupation with the sexy, steamy world of Tantra among the most influential modern scholars of religions? As I will argue, each of these three regarded Tantra as the ideal religion for the modern era. In what they described as this modern "age of darkness," they felt an intense sense of dislocation and a longing for an idyllic traditional past. As Benevides has argued in his study of Giuseppe Tucci, this feeling of loss and nostalgia was true of many European intellectuals in the early decades of this century, who shared a profound disillusionment with the rapid changes of modernity and the "dislocations that took place in Europe as a result of industrialization and urbanization." As Europe shifted from a stable, traditional agrarian world to the changing, uprooted world of the modern city, many felt a longing for "a world not touched by the icy winds of modernity."[6] Some would try to return to a more traditional religious spirit; some would turn to right-wing political movements; and some would turn to the still fixed, unmodernized, "Traditional" world of the Orient.

Long imagined to be the most exotic of all forms of Eastern religions, and the one most opposed to the modern West, Tantra seemed to provide an ideal solution to modern man's spiritual crises. It appeared to offer a means of *affirming* this material world, in all its sensuality and passion, while at the same time *transforming* this world into a means to spiritual liberation. Still more strikingly, Zimmer, Eliade, and Evola all saw Tantra as the most *transgressive* and *violent* path to the sacred—beyond good and evil, in violation of conventional law. This fact is all the more noteworthy when we recall that each of these authors underwent intense personal transformation during the violent years of the two world wars. Having encountered the horror, violence, and amorality of war, they each turned to Tantra as the most appropriate—perhaps unavoidable—religion for this darkest, most violent of epochs.

Simultaneously, Tantra began to play a central role in modern Indian scholarship. In India, too, the imagining of Tantra was intimately tied to the shifting political landscape in the decades after independence. For some, like Gopinath Kaviraj, Tantra was not only the culminating synthesis of Indian philosophy, but even the most needed solution to the crises of the modern age; indeed, it is the means to achieve a kind of collective liberation for all humanity. For others, like Narendra Nath Bhattacharyya, Tantra could be interpreted from a more explicitly political perspective, through the lens of Marxist theory. Thus Tantra becomes for Bhattacharyya the religion of the oppressed masses, rooted in a kind of primitive socialism and the precapitalist ideals of agrarian labor and matriarchy. The "age of darkness" in this case is a world dominated by economic exploitation and the alienation of the masses. Tantra thus emerges as an ideological weapon and instrument of critique, as evidence of a primitive communal mode of life that is more basic to human existence than class divisions or private property.

THE PATH OF POWER AND THE DARK AGE OF MODERNITY: TWENTIETH-CENTURY EUROPEAN SCHOLARSHIP ON TANTRA

> Tantrism, like yoga and Vedānta . . . could be respectable even in the Western world, provided that the tradition of solid scholarship, of learning and of intellectual effort . . . did accompany their migration into the

occidental world. Without these, I regard them as fraudulent.

Agehananda Bharati, *The Tantric Tradition* (1970)

The modern imagining of Tantra was born in large part out of the dialectical interplay between two very different ways of conceptualizing it—at one extreme, the denigration of Tantra by the European Orientalists, and at the other, the rationalization and purification of Tantra by John Woodroffe. It is this dual inheritance that informs the work of many historians of religions of the twentieth century, particularly Zimmer, Evola, and Eliade. As Bharati predicted, Tantra first entered the West, not through spiritual proselytizers, but through scholars and intellectuals, who saw in Tantra an alternative worldview to that of the modern West. Each of these three scholars in some sense accepted the Orientalist assumption that Tantra embodies, in all its Otherness, the most extreme aspect of the Indian mind. But at the same time, they also turned the Orientalist model on its head, praising Tantra as a much-needed affirmation of the human body and sexuality. "In the Tantra," as Zimmer put it, "the manner of approach is not that of Nay but of Yea . . . the world attitude is affirmative. . . . [M]an must approach through and by means of nature, not by rejection of nature."[7]

Tantra was a central element, not only in the academic writings of Zimmer, Evola, and Eliade, but also in the personal lives and the *scholarly method* of each of these authors. Yet despite their agreement as to the centrality of Tantra, each would offer very different interpretations in light of their own personal and political interests: Zimmer, as a liberal fleeing Nazi Germany with his Jewish wife; Evola, as an unrepentant fascist; and Eliade, as a complex and conflicted figure who fled his own fascist history in order to profess an allegedly "apolitical" (though perhaps not untainted) ideal.

Imagining India: Heinrich Zimmer and the Tantric Imagination

The world no longer possesses a sheltering womb where one could be perfectly safe. . . . In Europe everywhere, a new breed of man has been concocted. . . . Now man will tear to pieces the body of his mother, Nature, and will quarry her for new and different forms of power.

Heinrich Zimmer, "Indische Mythen als Symbole: Zwei Vorträge" (1934)

An irrepressible romantic and dreamy idealist, Heinrich Zimmer remains to this day one of the widely read, even if not always the most reliable, Indologists of the twentieth century. His vision of Tantra—which he conceived as both the most profound aspect of Indian thought and the most sophisticated aesthetic tradition—has been formative in contemporary Indology. Born in Greifswald in 1890, the son of a respected scholar of Vedic culture, Zimmer studied German and comparative philology in Berlin. During the First World War, Zimmer fought in the trenches of the front lines, an event that appears to have left a deep mark on his psyche and played a formative role in his later life and work. From 1924 to 1938, Zimmer held the chair of Indian philology in Heidelberg, a post he then lost with the rise of fascist government because of his marriage to Christine von Hofmannsthal, a woman of partial Jewish descent. At the invitation of the British government, Zimmer emigrated to Oxford, and then later to the United States, where he would die in 1943.[8]

Throughout his career, Zimmer's life and scholarship were intimately related: as his daughter recalls, his spiritual vision and his object of study were inseparable, fueling one another in a prolific search for meaning: "life and learning for him were never separated. All his work was part of his life and his life part of his work. The answers he found in dealing with religion were valid for himself."[9] For Zimmer, the study of myths and sacred images is far more than an academic exercise; it is a personal and transformative experience, in which the scholar realizes the "mythic heart of his own being" and sees the world through the lens of the sacred image. "Only after myth is . . . comprehended as a timeless way of relating to the world, only when the mythic heart of our own being is stirred, do we begin to start experiencing its meaning."[10]

Zimmer's interest in India was intimately tied to his own sense of disenchantment and disgust with the Christian tradition in which he had been raised. Tired of the stale, lifeless world that surrounded him, he turned to the exotic, erotic mysterious land of India:

> What made me abandon Western studies . . . and set forth on the quest for the East? I could not stand the stale . . . atmosphere of pseudo-romantic Western medievalism: this rotten and degenerated mixture of Old and New Testament, classic humanism, German folklore, degraded and diluted for high school teacher consumption. . . .
>
> Imagining India, its dense deep fragrance in my nostrils, the jungle before me, unknown, perhaps unknowable, I thought of this southern sky . . . studded with strange stars and bewildering asterisms. . . . [Y]et many civilizations steered their boats . . . orienting themselves from this totally different pattern.[11]

Ironically, although he tried to do so three times, Zimmer would never actually travel to India. Despite his love of its culture and religion, "Ewiges Indien," would remain for him always a land of idealization—"a country Zimmer never visited except in his imagination."[12]

As Zimmer recounts, one of the definitive events in his early life was his experience in World War I. It was the violence of the war that shocked him out of his "academic straitjacket" and thrust him into the terrifying realities of death and suffering. War was for Zimmer nothing short of an intense *"initiatory ordeal."* "I went into war: four years of human, sub- and super-human experience, initiation in the trenches . . . the initiation of Life (including death) playing its symphony with the fullest possible orchestration."[13] It was this "initiation by violence" that liberated him from the oppression of his elders, freeing him to search for truth within himself:

> The only benefit which I derived from my participation in the war was a complete liberation from the authority of the older generation who had managed the war. . . . I said to myself, " . . . henceforth I shall decide what I take seriously. . . . I offered my life for the ideals . . . of the community and did it naively, willingly. With this life I brought back, I am free to do what I decide to do. . . . They have no claim upon me anymore."[14]

It was the war, moreover, that made Zimmer realize that modern Western civilization had reached a terrible spiritual crisis: modern man had destroyed his religious faith, slain all his gods, and was now waiting for a new source of faith to fill his spiritual void. "People in our day and age have just come to the edge of the shore of the sea of tears and suffering they have yet to cross. . . . A fate we cannot transform into meaning will crush us." Since we have slain all the external gods, Zimmer continues, we must search for the divine within us: we each bear our gods within ourselves, in the depths of our consciousness, in the creative powers of our imaginations: "We are ourselves the meaning that gives life; our breath, our vision . . . creates patterns of meaning. . . . If our imagination . . . our most profound faculty, is crippled—then we are lost and will plunge like Icarus as he soared toward the sun."[15] It was for this reason that Zimmer was drawn to the works of Jung and the new science of depth psychology. If modern man can no longer find the gods outside himself in the heavens, he must turn inward to recover them within his own soul. "In this dark age, we cannot grasp the great symbols that have lived in other times. We must accept what is available to us: depth psychology, which transforms cosmology into psychology."[16]

The Hero's Path: The Godlike Power of the Tantric Imagination

The Tantric hero goes directly through the sphere of greatest danger . . . and rises through and by means of nature, not by the rejection of nature.

Heinrich Zimmer, *Philosophies of India* (1956)

But it was in the religions of India, and specifically in the meditative disciplines of Tantric yoga, that Zimmer found the most sophisticated science of the human psyche and the most developed techniques of creative imagination. In the Tantric tradition, as Zimmer describes it, the creative imagination is the most effective instrument of liberation: the Godhead lies within us, not without, and it is through techniques of meditative vision that we can project it outward. This, for Zimmer, is the essence of both Indian yogic practice and artistic traditions, which use the powers of creative vision to awaken the divine forces within us. Through the use of *yantras* and *maṇḍalas,* the Tantric initiate draws forth the gods and demons, heavens and hells, all from the depths of his own imagination. Thus he realizes his own godlike creative power, his ability to conceive, destroy, and reabsorb the cosmos: "The adept in possession of super-sensual vision can experience in the mundane apparatus the divine energy itself. . . . The worshipper projects within himself a vision of the divine reality; to project the worship of the divine is to become oneself divine."[17] Here we find the meeting point of Zimmer's personal and scholarly pursuits: the power of creative imagining is both his object of study and his means for recovering the sacred within the secularized world of the modern West.

Yet the most compelling aspect of Tantra, for Zimmer, lies not solely in the power of creative imagination, but in its this-worldly, life-affirming attitude. In the *tantras,* with their "vigorous affirmation of the world of flux and time," man can discover the gods not only in his imagination, but also in his own body and sexual powers. If the modern West had become sterile, cerebral, bloodless, and cold, then the solution to the maladies of our age lay in the sensuous religion of Tantra. Derived from the most archaic stratum of human civilization—the ancient matriarchal culture of goddess worship—Tantra is the antidote to the patriarchal, life-denying Christian tradition. Whereas Christianity has repressed the power of the body and sex, Tantra represents the greatest affirmation of embodied existence: "The tidal flood of Tantric literature reflects the last commanding vision of the world in which the very spirit of India . . .

magnificently manifested before the Western world which, in following its Christian positivist bias . . . destroyed the fiber of its being."[18] "The ideal of Tantrism is to achieve illumination precisely by means of those objects which earlier sages sought to banish from their consciousness. . . . [T]he world attitude is affirmative, as in the Veda, but the gods are now addressed as dwelling in the microcosm."[19]

In the final pages of his *Philosophies of India,* Zimmer makes it clear that Tantra is at once the most archaic substratum of aboriginal India and also the final fruition of the entire history of Indian thought. Characteristically Hegelian, Zimmer depicts the history of India as a dialectical unfolding, proceeding from the largely unconscious strata of pre-Aryan India, to the world-denying asceticism of Brahmanical culture, to the unifying synthesis of Tantra, which achieves the final integration of these two opposing forces.

> Brahman philosophy produced a last synthesizing statement in the courageous esotericism of the Tantras . . . where the old Aryan frenzy for non-dualism . . . fruitfully combined with the archaic matrilineal world-feeling of the aboriginal civilization of India. What the Vedic sages had recognized in the heavens . . . the Tantric adept felt dwelling bodily within him.[20]

With its ideal of self-divinization, realizing the gods within one's own body and imagination, Tantra provides the needed antidote to the life-denying, hyperintellectualized world of the Judeo-Christian West. Thus, in the final paragraph of *The Philosophies of India,* we find Zimmer's self-realized, godlike Tantric hero starkly contrasted with the weak, self-effacing, humble, and all-too-human figure of Job in the Hebrew Bible: "In contrast to the attitude of Job who cried out to Yahweh, 'what is man that thou shouldst magnify him?' the Indian . . . equates himself with God, transcends God and is at peace in the knowledge of himself as Brahman."[21] Here we find the final culmination of Zimmer's unusual life and works. Having passed through the violent initiatory ordeal of war-torn Europe, Zimmer left behind the sterile world of the modern West, to discover the gods within his own heart, revealed through the power of the creative imagination and the sensual body itself.

Riding the Tiger: Julius Evola and the Fascist Uses of Tantra

> We have now reached the last era, the dark age or Kali
> Yuga, which is a period of dissolution. . . . According

> to Tantra, the path most suitable for such circumstances is one characterized in the directive "Ride the Tiger." . . . Rather than avoid . . . a dangerous force one should grasp and hold it tight with the idea of getting the better of it. The arrival of the Kali Yuga cancels the bond which at other times imposed secrecy regarding the doctrines and practices of the way of the Left Hand because of their perilous nature. . . . The fundamental principle of the secret teaching . . . is the transformation of poison into nectar, of the very forces that have led . . . to man's fall and perdition.
>
> Julius Evola, *The Metaphysics of Sex* (1969)

If Zimmer shows us the close interaction between personal experience and scholarly method in the study of Tantra, Julius Evola reveals the most extreme appropriation of Tantra in the service of a full-blown ideological stance and political agenda. And if Zimmer—a man who married a Jewish woman and fled Nazi Germany—shows a more "liberal" interpretation of Tantra as an alternative to the violence of the modern West, then Evola—an outspoken fascist—shows the manipulation of Tantra in the service of right-wing violence. To this day, Evola remains one of the most enigmatic, poorly understood, and yet influential figures in the scholarship and politics of modern Europe. Not only has he been described as "arguably the most important thinker of the right radical Neo-Fascist revisionists," and even the "guru of the counterculture right," but he has also been very influential in the development of the history of religions. Along with many other enigmatic aspects of Evola's life, his role in shaping the modern image of Tantra remains largely unexplored.[22]

Born in Rome in 1898 to a noble Sicilian family, Baron Giulio Alessandro Evola (later to take the name Julius, or Julius Cesare) was from his youth drawn to the heroic, aristocratic, and dramatic side of life. After joining the army at age nineteen and fighting as a mountain artillery officer, Evola began a spiritual quest for absolute transcendence and liberation. With a Nietzschean contempt for what is "all too human," he went in search of a higher value, "beyond the ethical limitations of bourgeois prejudices" that he felt ruled modern Judeo-Christian Europe.[23] This quest led him to experiment in a variety of avant-garde practices, such as hallucinogenic drugs and the art of Dada and

Surrealism. While studying engineering from 1923 to 1927, Evola read widely in philosophy, particularly the works of Schopenhauer and Nietzsche, and developed an interest in the occult traditions of Hermeticism and alchemy. Advocating a Nietzschean will to power, Evola's foremost imperative was *tu diventare Dio,* "you must become God."[24] In a world where God is dead, the true superman must take his rightful place as God-maker and as God himself. At the same time, as an anti-Christian, pagan fascist, Evola idealized the martial glory of ancient Rome in opposition to the effete Catholic virtues of humility and compassion. Calling for a return to a true "aristocracy of spirit," Evola imagined the birth of an elite spiritual nobility—and perhaps even a secret military brotherhood—who could regenerate the decaying world of modern Europe.[25]

Not surprisingly Evola found welcome company among the most extreme movements in Italy in the years before and after World War II, soon becoming one of Europe's most influential proponents of fascism. Although he never joined the Fascist Party, he was a strong supporter of Mussolini and was honored by Il Duce's endorsement of his *Synthesis of the Doctrine of Race* (1941). Evola's fascism, however, was different from the Nazi ideology in Hitler's Germany: in contrast to the biological racism of the Nazis—what Evola called a "Romantic telluric Dionysianism"—Evola's was a "spiritual" and Apollonian fascism.[26] During the Second World War, however, Evola had a falling out with Mussolini, and in 1943 joined a group of dissident intellectuals to meet with Hitler to discuss the formation of the Fascist Republic of Salò. After narrowly escaping arrest by the Americans in 1944, Evola fled to Vienna, where he was hit by a shell and left permanently crippled. His fascist work continued, however, and he was arrested in 1951 on charges of attempting to revive fascism. Today, Evola is regarded as one of the most influential figures in the various neofascist movements of Europe, praised as the "spiritual master of the new Right" and the leading thinker of groups like the terrorist Nuova Destra.[27]

Revolt against the Modern World: Tantra and the Age of Darkness

> Tantrism may lead the way for a Western elite which does not want to become the victim of these experiences whereby an entire civilization is on the verge of being submerged.
>
> The main characteristics of Tantric deities must be

considered as symbols of destroying forces, nude and
free, superior to all laws.

Julius Evola, "What Tantrism Means
to Modern Western Civilization" (1950)

While Zimmer and other European intellectuals had been generally pessimistic in their attitudes toward the modern West, with its secularism and loss of tradition, Evola is surely one of its most scathing and merciless critics. His agenda is nothing less than a wholesale "revolt against the modern world." For the modern West marks the lowest point in the downward spiral of the Kali yuga, the darkest moment in this darkest of cosmic eras. "The modern point of view . . . [is] typical of the most advanced phase of the dark age."[28] Not only has it lost its traditional spirit, but the modern West has been corrupted by the deluded ideals of democracy (in contrast to the aristocratic, hierarchical society of traditional man), the unhealthy, life-denying ideals of Christianity (with its rejection of the body and sex), and the twisted psycho-babble of Freudian psychoanalysis (with its gross misunderstanding and "turbid repression" of sexuality).[29]

One of the most conspicuous themes in Evola's works is his radically antidemocratic, aristocratic, and elitist vision of society. In strict opposition to modern ideals of democracy, Evola's model of civilization is one of strong hierarchy, in which the nobility or truly "spiritual" elites would rule the ordinary, unskilled, "somatic," or "physical" masses of ordinary humankind. "Evola always harbored an aristocratic contempt for the hoi polloi," Guido Stucco comments, "racism was for Evola an opportunity to proclaim his anti-egalitarian and anti-rationalist views."[30] Thus Evola predicts the coming of a new "counter-revolution," a revolt against the flaccid democracy of the modern West, and a return to the "traditional" ethics of spiritual nobility. He foresees "an authentic counter-revolution" that will be "radically opposed to democracy and socialism" and will provide the "foundation necessary to begin . . . a work endowed with a metaphysical, transcendent, ethical and social character."[31]

Given that we live in the darkest, antitraditional age, the only solution for us is to turn to the most extreme and violent spiritual means. There can be no going back, no retreat from the modern world into the premodern past. Rather, our only hope is to "ride the tiger," as it were—to accept, embrace, and harness the most destructive impulses in human nature as they have now been unleashed by modernity, turning them to the service of liberation. This, for Evola, is the essence of the Tantric path: to grab the snake by the throat and to transform his poison into ambrosia, to embrace the forces of violence and lust and transmute them into forces of freedom and transcendence:

> The teachings . . . that would have been viable in the first age . . . are no longer fit for people living in the following ages, especially in the last age, the dark age. . . . Mankind in these later ages may find knowledge . . . not in the Vedas, but rather in the Tantras. . . . Only Tantric practices based on shakti . . . are efficacious in our contemporary age.
>
> During the Kali Yuga . . . the traditional law is wavering, reduced to a shadow of its former self . . . during the last age, elementary, infernal and abyssal forces are untrammeled. The immediate task consists in facing and absorbing these forces, in taking the risk of riding the tiger . . . or to transforming the poison into medicine.[32]

This is the age of sex and the body, the age in which nothing can motivate man apart from sensual pleasure: thus it is to the bodily, sexual, path of Tantra that we must turn in order to liberate degenerate modern man: "mankind living in this age is strictly connected to the body. . . . Therefore the only way open is not that of pure detachment . . . but rather that of knowledge, awakening and mastery over secret energies trapped in the body."[33] Because sex is the most powerful and "violent" force in human nature, it is also the most potent impetus to spiritual liberation. Even in its most degraded modern forms, sex retains a distant vestige of its original spiritual power: "Sex is the greatest magical force in nature; an impulse acts in it which suggests the Mystery of the One. . . . The metaphysics of sex survives in those very cases where, in looking at wretched mankind . . . it is hard to overcome a feeling of disgust and revolt."[34]

Thus Tantra represents the most effective antidote to the "womanly," passive, and emasculated character that has come to dominate modern Western man. The modern West may be perversely preoccupied with sex—but it is sex of the most "womanly," effeminate kind, not the truly "masculine" virile sexuality of "traditional" man: "Now we are degraded people, weak, woman comes before all else—a universal and feverish interest in sex and woman is a mark of every twilight period. . . . [W]e are living in a civilization whose predominant interest is neither intellectual, spiritual nor heroic. . . . Rather the subpersonal—sex and the belly—are idolized."[35] In contrast to the weak and womanly attitude of the modern world, Evola found in Tantra a virile, masculine path of action and strength. This is the way of the *vīra,* "a term with the same Latin root *vir* which does not describe an ordinary man but rather an eminent man . . . a manly and heroic nature."[36] Such a heroic, *active* path is the only means of effecting real change in this present age of passivity: "In this age of decadence the only way open . . . is one of action."[37]

The Destructive Power of the Absolute: Tantra, Heroism, and Violence

> This Absolute is a power that on the plane of finite beings acts in a destructive fashion, almost as Dionysius Zagreus brings havoc to all things.
>
> Julius Evola, *The Yoga of Power* (1968)

As the most extreme and dangerous path, the Tantric way steps outside the ethical boundaries that confine ordinary human beings to the conventional world. Passing through an intense "destruction of human limitations," the *tāntrika* experiences "forms of anomia, beyond good and evil which are so extreme that they make the Western supporters of the idea of the superman look like innocuous amateurs." Because this Kali yuga is the darkest era, in which existing laws have become either oppressive or irrelevant, the true initiate is often compelled to violate even the most sacred laws in the service of liberation and empowerment.

> All ethics of a merely human nature, however elevated, cease to have any validity. . . .
>
> If a spiritual catastrophe is to be averted man must make himself capable of developing his own being in a higher dimension—and it is in this connection that Jünger had announced the . . . watchword of "heroic realism" and . . . the "absolute person" capable of . . . seizing the highest meaning of existence in the most destructive experiences, in those actions wherein the human individual no longer counts: of a man acclimatized to the most extreme temperature and having behind him the "zero point of every value."[38]

This, in Evola's reading, is the essence of the Tantric path, the path of the virile hero who dares to transgress the laws that bind other human beings. To the *tāntrika,* there is no good or evil, for he has realized *"the relativity of all moral precepts."* To him, all "passions lose their impure character once they become absolute"; and henceforth, "the siddha can do as he pleases, while remaining spiritually invulnerable."[39] For Evola's *tāntrika* hero, even hedonistic excess is by no means an obstacle on the path to spiritual transformation, but is its necessary condition: "A siddha is one who . . . can do anything he wants . . . he is beyond both dharma and karma."[40]

As such, Tantra is for Evola not a radically "Eastern," Other form of spirituality. Rather, in contrast to the effeminate Christian religion—which has been infected by Eastern dualism and quietism—Tantra represents the most authentically *Occidental* form of spirituality, in the original, pre-Christian, pagan sense of that term. For it unites the Western mastery of material nature and power with the Eastern sense of spirit and transcendence: "Tantrism in its spirit . . . should be considered distinctly Western. It is more conspicuously Western than Christian soteriology, which proclaims an ideal of salvation from a world that is looked upon as a vale of tears. . . . The password of Tantrism is . . . the unity of spiritual discipline and enjoyment of the world."[41] Thus Tantra is the most needed path to reinvigorate the decaying post-Christian West—a world in which former morality has disintegrated and the majority of mankind is ruled by the law of the belly and the genitals. As the most authentically "Occidental" form of spirituality, in the original heroic sense, Tantra is the "existential attitude proper to a differentiated human type who lives in an era of dissolution and in a world in which God is dead. . . . [T]here are no longer any values left standing, and all the surviving traditional structures are . . . empty shells."[42]

Ultimately, the radical path of Tantra, which transcends all finite conceptions of good and evil, is also the path of the warrior. Like the Tantric *vīra,* the warrior must overstep the moral boundaries that confine ordinary bestial men. He must act like the hero Arjuna upon the battlefield of Kurukṣetra in the *Mahābhārata.* Even though he risks violating dharma, the warrior must still, at the command of God, plunge into the bloodbath; he must transcend and transgress dharma in the service of the often destructive and amoral Absolute Godhead:

> Krishna incites Arjuna to fight and to kill even those friends and relatives militating on the enemy side, declaring that his actions would not generate karma so long as they were performed in a detached, impersonal way. . . . Dharma appears to be limiting the warrior's way of life. . . . In the end this limitation is not absolute, especially after Krishna . . . reveals the nature of the Absolute. This Absolute is a power that . . . acts in a destructive fashion, almost as Dionysius Zagreus brings havoc to all things. The teaching transmitted to Arjuna culminates with a vision that . . . corresponds to the destructive and horrifying attributes of Shiva and the Tantric Kali.[43]

It is not difficult to understand how Evola's version of Tantra would have helped him to rationalize a political agenda of fascism, racism, and violence; or why Evola's extremist right-wing politics and interpretation of Tantra have continued to exert influence among European neofascist movements and certain branches of contemporary esotericism.[44] As a path of transgression, amorality, and power, Tantra is for Evola and his followers the most fitting corrective to this dark era, in which impurity and violence already run rampant.

The Sacred as the Profane: Mircea Eliade, Tantra, and the Terror of History

> The irresistible Tantric advance implies a new victory for the pre-Aryan popular strata. It is through this channel that the great underground current of autochthonous . . . spirituality made its way into Hinduism.
>
> Mircea Eliade, *Yoga: Immortality and Freedom* (1971)

While Zimmer may have been the most poetic of Tantric scholars in the twentieth century, and while Evola may have been the most radical political spokesman, Mircea Eliade was surely among the most influential. We might say that Tantra—with its radical identification of the sacred with the profane, its call for the most extreme measures in this most extreme historical era—provided both the ideal object and the hermeneutic *method* for Eliade's "history of religion" as a whole. However, Eliade is also complex and ambiguous; his work is strewn with contradictions and aporias: influenced by both Zimmer and Evola, Eliade seems to embody the *coincidentia oppositorum* of their interpretations of Tantra, liberal and fascist.[45]

Born in Romania in 1907, Eliade was always a voracious reader with a lively imagination. An author of creative fiction and scholarly works from an early age, Eliade read extensively in Romanian, French, and German, and later learned Italian and English in order to read Raffaele Pettazzoni and James George Frazer in the original. In 1925, Eliade enrolled at the University of Bucharest, where he studied philosophy under Nae Ionescu, a man bound up with the extreme right in Romania, who was to have a lasting influence on Eliade's thought. From 1928 to 1931, Eliade fled the growing violence of interwar Romania to travel to India, where he studied Indian philosophy and yoga, an experience that "left an indelible mark on him" and "persuaded [him] of the viability of . . . Oriental spirituality in the Western world."[46] His doctoral thesis, "Yoga: Essay on the Origins of Indian Mysticism," was completed in 1932 and later published as his classic *Yoga: Immortality and Freedom.*

When Eliade returned to Romania in 1932, he found his homeland immersed in political upheaval. Dominated by the rise of fascism to the west and Soviet communism to the east, Romanian nationalism gave birth to the Legion of the Archangel Michael, headed by Corneliu Zelea Codreanu. With a fierce nationalist spirit, often leaning toward racism and xenophobia, the Legionaries posed a radical challenge to the forces of democracy and modernization, calling for a restoration of Romania's folk and religious roots.[47] It was to this more radical side of the Romanian right that Eliade was drawn upon his return from India, as he began to forge his own unique scholarly and literary styles.

The Terrors of History and the Search for the Archaic

> Today the master of us all is the war. . . . It has confiscated the whole of contemporary history, the time in which we are fated to live. . . .
>
> Against the terrors of history there are only two possibilities of defense: action or contemplation. . . . Our only solution is to contemplate, that is to escape from historic Time to find another Time.
>
> Stefan, in Mircea Eliade, *The Forbidden Forest* (1954)

Surely the most troubling and controversial period of Eliade's life was the period before and during World War II, a violent, chaotic period in Romanian history. Eliade himself would later remark that "the most terrible historical crisis of the modern world" was "the Second World War and all that has followed from it."[48] Its events haunt Eliade's fiction, forming the dark backdrop for novels such as *Huliganii* (1935) and *The Forbidden Forest* (1954).

I will not attempt here to resolve the many conflicted arguments surrounding Eliade's politics—that is, his troubling involvement in the extreme fascist movements of this period and its possible impact on his later scholarship. These questions have been treated in great detail, by his critics and by his supporters.[49] Here, let it suffice to say that—as even his most ardent defenders acknowledge—Eliade was a vocal supporter of the most extreme right-wing, ultraconservative, and traditionalist movements in Romania of the 1930s. Fiercely nationalistic in his politics, he ardently opposed any ceding of Romanian autonomy to non-Romanian factions such as the Hungarians, Bulgarians, or Jews, and he contributed frequently to a number of right-wing publications, such as *Vremea, Cuvantul,* and *Credinta.* During these years, he maintained close ties with many leading figures of the radical Romanian right, most notably Nae

Ionescu, under whose influence he advocated an antimodernist form of traditionalism, rejecting democracy and calling for a return to the Romanian peasant spirit. Still more striking, however, is his support for the most active fascist groups in prewar Romania, such as the Legion of the Archangel Michael and their paramilitary order, the Iron Guard—"a movement of the extreme right whose members were guilty of violence, murder and anti-Semitic atrocities."[50] In 1938 Eliade was imprisoned for four months because of his Iron Guard sympathies. At the start of the war, he was appointed to the Romanian Legation under the fascist royalist dictatorship of Carol II, serving for nine months in London as attaché in the department of press and propaganda. Then from 1941 to 1945, after Carol's abdication and the rise of Antonescu's National Legionary State, Eliade was employed as press secretary at the Romanian legation in Portugal. After the war, Eliade was unable to return to the newly communist Romania largely because of his connection with the right-wing Ionescu.[51]

Whatever the precise nature of Eliade's political involvement in the years before and during World War II, there is no doubt that this era had a critical impact on Eliade's personal and scholarly life. It appears, for example, in the apocalyptic anarchism of his novel *Huliganii,* which centers around the violent youth groups of interwar Romania. Engaged in "cruelties and excesses of all sorts," Eliade's hooligans turn to the most radical extremes of destruction and eros in order to burst the bonds of the world and experience a fleeting kind of transcendence: "these furious negateurs seek a paradise recovered by the paradoxical weapons of violence and eroticism."[52] However, following the violence that swept Romania during the years before World War II and the devastation during it, Eliade retreated from the "terrifying" realm of modern history, turning inward to the timeless world of myth. In place of revolutionary upheaval and political change, Eliade now sought the transcendent world of symbolism and the ahistorical life of *homo religiosus.* His disillusionment with the forces of modern history can be glimpsed in his protagonist Stefan in *The Forbidden Forest,* who seems to reflect Eliade's own character during these painful years: "He suffered a nervous shock. . . . History has taken revenge on him. He has a phobia against history. He has a horror of events. He'd like things to stand still the way they seemed in the paradise of his childhood."[53]

However, as Strenski suggests, Eliade's early involvement in the traditionalist movements of the Romanian right wing would provide the foundation for much of his later scholarship: it profoundly colored his vision of "traditional" man, or *homo religiosus,* his rejection of modern civilization, and his quest for the primordial Origin beyond the terrifying vicissitudes of history. "The radical traditionalism of the Romanian right becomes for Eliade not a mere political programme, but a sweeping ontological judgment upon the material secular modern world, asserting the value of nostalgia for the archaic, cosmic and telluric."[54]

So it is that Eliade—perhaps the most influential spokesman for the "history of religion" in the United States—is arguably also the "leading anti-historian of religions."[55] His scholarly method is rarely one of specific historical analysis, but rather a search for the suprahistorical, transcendent element concealed within material forms. This is his "creative hermeneutics," a method that, using the creative imagination, is as much a work of art as a scholarly endeavor. As Strenski suggests, Eliade's turn to the ahistorical method of creative hermeneutics was part of his own attempt to deal with the real terrors of history in his past, to flee the violence of time in the timeless realm of myth: "Eliade has chosen to deal with the disaster of his Romanian past by . . . transvaluing it through the method of creative hermeneutics."[56]

For Eliade, creative hermeneutics is not just a scholarly method that parallels his method as an author of fantastic fiction: it is a personal mode of being in the world. In order to encounter the myths and symbols of other cultures, the scholar must embark on an imaginal journey outside his own cultural world: he must journey from his known familiar condition "to relive" through his imagination the suprahistorical world of *homo religiosus:* "creative hermeneutics *changes* man; it is more than instruction, it also a spiritual technique susceptible of modifying the quality of existence. . . . A good history of religions book ought to produce in the reader an action of awakening."[57]

However, as Strenksi and others have pointed out, this ideal of a self-transformation and the birth of a new man sounds disturbingly like certain ideas championed by the Iron Guard and other extremist groups of Eliade's youth. Above all, it resembles the ideal of violent initiation and the birth of a new being, embodying "traditional" national and religious values: "The new man as envisaged by Codreanu and others on the radical right emerges . . . as the new humanism of Eliade's creative hermeneutic vision. Like the Romanian traditionalist image of the new man, Eliade's vision of a new humanism embraces the image of man as *homo religiosus,* archaic and integrated into personal wholeness."[58] And one of the most powerful ways of realizing this new man would be the disciplines of Indian yoga, and above all, the radical path of Tantra.

The Camouflage of the Sacred

We must . . . rediscover the technique of camouflaging ourselves, the art of lying and deceiving. . . . [I]t's difficult and dangerous . . . to preserve the soul . . . hibernating under a mask. . . . [W]e are faced with the problem of how to accomplish the preservation of our soul in the New Dark Age that's beginning.

Stefan, in *The Forbidden Forest*

At the heart of Eliade's creative hermeneutics lies the dialectic between the sacred and the profane. For Eliade, the human being is first and foremost a *homo religiosus*—an inherently religious creature with an innate thirst for the sacred as the source of all being, meaning, power, and reality, beyond transience and change. The sacred, however, is continually masked within, concealed behind and yet partially manifesting itself within this profane world of history and death. The profane provides the symbols and disguises through which the sacred reveals itself. And the task of the historian of religions is to decipher the presence of the sacred hidden within the masks of history; for the history of religions is itself nothing less than "a series of messages waiting to be deciphered and understood."[59]

However, if the sacred is always partially veiled to man of "traditional" or premodern societies, then it has become ever more deeply buried, almost entirely opaque to modern Western man. Like Evola, Eliade was from his earliest publications a severe critic of the modern world. The modern West is characterized above all by radical secularization, loss of faith in the traditional myths that form the timeless heritage of *homo religiosus,* and the subsequent reduction of man to an historical creature of meaninglessness and death.

> It is only in modern societies of the West that non-religious man has developed fully. Modern non-religious man . . . regards himself solely as the subject of history and refuses all appeal to transcendence. . . . Man makes himself and only makes himself completely in proportion as he desacralizes himself and the world. The sacred is the prime obstacle to his freedom. . . . He will not be truly free until he has killed the last god.[60]

Yet, despite modern man's efforts to slay all his gods, the sacred can never be wholly eradicated from human existence. The sacred continues to survive in the most seemingly profane forms, hidden beneath the disguises of half-forgotten myths and symbols. Because man is *homo reli-*

giosus, he always retains the vestiges of the sacred lying secretly within his dreams and fantasies, in his novels and works of art. Herein lies the last hope of reawakening the sacred in the context of a secular society. For "it is the historian of religion who is capable of recognizing and deciphering the religious structures of these . . . imaginary Universes."[61] This attempt to decipher the presence of the sacred concealed in the profane world is perhaps the essence of Eliade's whole hermeneutic endeavor, his lifelong search for the sacred hidden behind the historical form: "His fascination with the theme of the camouflage of the fantastic in the daily event frames his whole epistemology. . . . The point is to see how the sacred is symbolized in the world. This, like uncovering a disguise, is a matter of hermeneutics."[62]

Religion for the Age of Darkness: Tantra and the Sacrality of the Profane

> Most of the excesses, cruelties and aberrations referred to as "Tantric orgies" spring, in the last analysis, from the same traditional metaphysics.
>
> Eliade, *Yoga: Immortality and Freedom*

Given Eliade's antimodernist stance, his ideal of an ahistorical primordial Origin set in opposition to the contemporary ideal of progress, and his lifelong search for the sacred hidden within the masks of the profane material world, we can now begin to appreciate his fascination with the Indian tradition of Tantra. Tantra seemed an ideal solution to all the evils of the modern Western world. In Eliade's eyes, Tantra is the most archaic, primal, and "autochthynous heart of aboriginal India," the most ancient layer of the timeless Orient itself. A kind of living remnant of the deepest stratum of Indian consciousness, Tantra dates back to pre-Aryan days when popular religion and worship of the Mother Goddess had not yet been overtaken by the priestly, androcentric Aryans: "Tantrism is the expression of the indigenous spirituality, the reaction of the not-fully Hinduized popular strata."[63] Embodying the "great underground current of autochthonous spirituality," the "irresistible Tantric advance in the medieval period implies a new victory of the pre-Aryan popular strata."[64]

Like Evola and Zimmer, Eliade praises Tantra as a much-needed affirmation of the powers of the human body and sexuality, and thus as a corrective to the repressive world of the modern West. Indeed, for Eliade, Tantra "reveals an experience that is no longer accessible in a desacralized society—the experience of a sanctified sexual life."[65] With its radically "anti-ascetic and anti-speculative attitude," and its affirmation of the powers of nature, fertility, and sexuality, Tantra marks a return to the feminine, material side of life: it is thus a "religious rediscovery of the mystery of woman, for . . . every woman becomes the incarnation of the Śakti. . . . Woman incarnates the mystery of creation and the mystery of Being, of everything that *is,* that incomprehensibly becomes and dies and is reborn."[66]

But most importantly, Tantra is for Eliade the clearest instance of the central dialectic of the religious imagination—the sacred and the profane. In Tantra, the sacred and the profane are not simply bound in a dialectical relationship, the former both concealed and revealed by the latter; rather, in Tantra we find the ultimate *identification* of them. For the Tantric initiate, the profane forms of physical pleasure, meat, wine, and sexual intercourse become the most rapid, expedient (and dangerous) path to the sacred. By violating all social laws, he achieves the fullest experience of freedom, unleashing the "terrifying emotion one feels before the revelation of the cosmic mystery."[67] As such, Tantra is the most relevant spiritual path for our own age of darkness—it enacts a radically desacralized world where the sacred is not simply camouflaged behind the profane, but is actually *identified* with it: "The ultimate stage of desacralization . . . illustrates the complete camouflage of the sacred, more precisely, its identification with the profane."[68] The *tāntrika* is the one who dares to confront the profane, who can turn the profane to his advantage, to master and transform it. But to confront this dangerous power demands the most "heroic" character, who has undergone the most difficult initiatory ordeal and transcended the bestial level of the profane masses:

> The courage and intelligence needed to confront, defeat and transform this incandescent irruption of telluric forces into an experience of paroxystic vitality amounts to a true initiation of a heroic type. While by hundreds of thousands the profane (. . . the naive, the immature) let themselves be . . . consumed by sensual pleasures . . . a minute number of others reach that level of existence that traditions call heroic.[69]

In Tantra, the sacred is no longer merely hidden within the profane: it *is* the profane—or rather, the two are perfectly merged in Eliade's favorite image of the *coincidentia oppositorum,* the union of contrary principles. The problem of *coincidentia oppositorum,* Eliade admits, "will fascinate me till the end of my life,"[70] and it remains the key to his entire complex life and his scholarly method. Embodied in classic symbols like the androgyne, the golem, or the philosopher's stone of the alchemists, the *coincidentia oppositorum* represents the ideal wedding of male and female, spirit and matter, and ultimately, sacred and profane. And Tantra above all—with its explicit use of *maithuna* or sexual intercourse—is perhaps the most explicitly "biological" and physical expression of this central mystery.

> This conception, in which all contraries are reconciled . . . constitutes what is the most basic definition of divinity and shows us how utterly different it is from humanity. . . . The *coincidentia oppositorum* . . . can be achieved by man in all sorts of ways. . . . [T]he orgy . . . symbolizes a return to the amorphous and indistinct where all attributes disappear and contraries are merged.[71]

Here is the key to much of Eliade's complex character, both personal and scholarly—the relentless search for that mysterious unity existing beyond or outside of time, transcending the contradictions of history. It is a unity, however, that can only be achieved by first passing through the most dangerous acts of violence and transgression.

In any discussion of Eliade's view of Tantra, we must face the difficult and troubling question of whether Eliade's vision was a kind of cryptofascism, tainted with the same sorts of repugnant right-wing political interests as Evola's. I believe that Eliade's vision of Tantra, like the figure of Eliade himself, is too ambiguous to be reduced either to a simple "new humanist" purity or to a malicious fascist agenda. It is true that Eliade retreated from active political engagement, fleeing the horrors of fascist Romania and twentieth-century history into the ostensibly "apolitical" world of myth and scholarship. Yet as Wasserstrom, Strenski, and others have argued, Eliade's reactionary, antimodernist ideals were in many ways carried over into his later scholarship as a troubling shadow that haunts his entire oeuvre. Nowhere is this more apparent than in Eliade's conception of Tantra, which inherits both Zimmer's romantic vision of Tantric sensuality and Evola's fascist notion of Tantric violence. But for this very reason, Eliade offers us a valuable insight into the image of Tantra in the history of religions as a whole—an image that contains the promise of liberation and power, and yet that is also haunted by the specters of violence, immorality, cruelty, and terror.

THE RELIGION OF LIBERATION: REIMAGINING TANTRA IN TWENTIETH-CENTURY INDIAN SCHOLARSHIP

> Throughout the ages, the Female Principle stood for the oppressed peoples, symbolizing all the liberating potentialities in the class divided, patriarchal and authoritarian social set up of India, and this alone explains why attempts were made . . . to blacken Śākta-Tantric ideals.
>
> Narendra Nath Bhattacharyya, *History of the Śākta Religion* (1974)

If Tantra played a crucial role in the political history of the history of religions in the West, it played no less a role in the political history of India scholarship in this century. In the aftermath of colonial rule, amid a new proliferation of competing political, religious, and cultural factions, Tantra became one of the key elements in the reimagining of Indian identity. Thus S. B. Dasgupta made the "obscure religious cults" like the Sahajiyās, Nāths, and other Tantric sects the necessary "background of Bengali literature."[72] And more recent authors, like Ajit Mookerjee, praise Tantra as the innermost heart of Indian religion, the integration of sensuality and spirituality, and thus a path desperately needed in the modern world.[73]

Two of the most important figures in the reimagining of Tantra were Bengali, Gopinath Kaviraj and Narendra Nath Bhattacharyya—though, as we will see, they arrived at very different interpretations of Tantra and its significance. While for Kaviraj, Tantra is both the culmination of Indian philosophy and the means to a kind of collective salvation for all humanity, for Bhattacharyya, Tantra provides evidence of an archaic communism and thus a prefiguration of the egalitarian society envisaged by Marxism. Yet for both, Tantra represents in a sense a religion of "liberation" amid a dark age of suffering and oppression.

The Collective Liberation of Humanity: Gopinath Kaviraj's Supreme Integral Yoga

> So much of the disharmony and opposition in the world today, engendering bitterness and strife, is due to our lack of sympathy and sense of oneness. . . . There is but one Self which is love and Wisdom eternal, and we shall share it if we but know it in a proper way. Discord

> and hatred are bound to disappear like mists before the light of the sun. It will herald the advent of a New Life in the world, when the central principle of Unity and Love will reign.
>
> Gopinath Kaviraj, "Mother" (1990)

Although his work is still not widely known in the West, Gopinath Kaviraj (1887–1976) must surely be recognized as one of the single most important figures in the study of Tantra in the twentieth century. Not only was Kaviraj one of the first to try to synthesize all of the known Tantric texts and traditions into one integrated Tantric system; but he also developed a highly original interpretation of Tantric yoga that aimed at collective liberation for all humankind.[74]

Born to a Brahman family in Dhamrai, East Bengal, Kaviraj received his early education first in Dhaka and then in Jaipur. Because the nationalist movement had exploded into violence in Bengal and he had lived his early years in the midst of it, Kaviraj was initially influenced by the ideas of Aurobindo and the other radicals fighting for independence:

> Gopinath could not be left untouched by the strong wave of nationalism which was then moving in the country. Bengal . . . was agitated by the partition and a revolutionary movement took birth there. Gopinath was a regular reader of Sri Aurobindo's *Vande Mataram* and engaged in political discussions. . . . [T]he search for India's past came to occupy a prime place in the intellectual adventure of young Gopinath.[75]

Yet Kaviraj chose, not the life of the political activist, but rather that of the scholar and spiritual seeker. After receiving his master's degree in Sanskrit in Varanasi, he worked as a research scholar placed in charge of the Saraswati Bhavan Library at the Government Sanskrit College, Varanasi. By 1917, however, Kaviraj had also come into contact with a number of sādhus and was later initiated by a Bengali guru named Śrī Śrī Viśuddhānanda, a master well known for his supernatural powers. Eventually, Kaviraj would abandon the worldly life altogether, retiring in 1937 to live as a saint and teacher. So highly regarded was his scholarship that the government conferred upon him the title of Mahāmahopadhyāya (Great Teacher) in 1934, followed by the Coronation Medal in 1937 and the title of Padmavibhūṣaṇa (Lotus-Adorned) in 1964. As G. C. Pande suggests, Kaviraj should be understood as an important figure in the larger cultural, spiritual, and national awakening of India in the twentieth century. Although he retreated from direct political involvement, Kaviraj was one of the most important agents in the cultural and religious renaissance of India:

> Bengal . . . took the lead in the Indian Renaissance of the nineteenth century and produced a memorable galaxy of saints . . . statesmen and revolutionaries. In the midst of colonial rule . . . they helped to revive India's sense of pride in her own past. . . . It is through them that her new national consciousness was fashioned. . . . It meant not only the emergence of a political movement aiming at the liberation of the country but also a revolution in its thought and creativity. Gopinath Kaviraj was one of the towering figures in this revolution.[76]

Like Woodroffe before him, Kaviraj took it upon himself to defend and relegitimize the tradition of the *tantra*s, which had so long been denigrated by Indian and European scholars. Whereas most modern Indians regarded the *tantra*s as "an abomination . . . because ill-educated charlatans duped their adherents by obscene matters," Kaviraj showed that they are "so stupendous and colossal . . . that it is not possible in one's life span to study them, not to speak about their esoteric interpretation."[77] And like Woodroffe, Kaviraj saw Tantra not in opposition to the traditions of the Veda and Vedānta, but as their complement, and ultimately as the culmination of the history of Indian philosophy.[78]

Profoundly influenced by the Kashmir Śaivite schools, Kaviraj undertook a synthesis of the various Tantric traditions. Not unlike Abhinavagupta in his *Tantrāloka,* Kaviraj sought to create an overarching ontological system, a hierarchical gradation of teachings that would find a place for all the many Hindu perspectives: "These relative or fragmentary truths, or aspects of the Absolute Truth . . . represent varying stages in the ascending order of the Sadhaka's journey in quest of self-realization. When pieced together, and studied in light of the resultant whole, they will present a sublime picture of synthesis."[79] Kaviraj's synthesis could be compared to a vast temple whose foundations are the six systems of Indian philosophy and whose walls are the traditions of Śāktism, Śaivism, and Vaiṣṇavism. Kaviraj's own philosophy is thus the *śikhara* of the temple, and his practice of *akhaṇḍa mahāyoga* is the deity installed in the shrine.[80]

Surely the most fascinating and original aspect of Kaviraj's system is his new vision of Tantra, which is now conceived as something far more than a quest for individual liberation. For Kaviraj, Tantra has the potential to achieve a collective salvation or universal liberation for humankind. Through his new ideal of *akhaṇḍa mahāyoga,* or supreme integral yoga, Kaviraj imagined Tantra to be a spiritual method of universal dimensions, one that could realize the liberation of all beings within his own lifetime. Seeking a perfect, metaphysical solution to the human suffering he saw around him, Kaviraj might be said to have "sacrificed his life to find out a solution of that mysterious riddle called *Suffering Humanity.*"[81] This seems to have been Kaviraj's own spiritual and metaphysical solution to the severe crises facing India in the modern era—this world torn by "disharmony and opposition." Rather than a social or political response to collective crisis in the Kali yuga, Kaviraj conceived a spiritual answer that could, in theory, offer perfect liberation for all:

> His concern is for the rest of he world, which he characterizes as humanity sunk in its ignorance. . . . Considering the far reaching crises of contemporary times, he wonders if there could be any true individual welfare without collective welfare. . . . While others might choose to work socially or politically for this welfare, Kaviraj dedicated himself to . . . a metaphysical solution.[82]

Through the practice of *akhaṇḍa mahāyoga,* the yogin may not only realize his own personal self-realization, but then return with full compassion and bring this realization back into this world of suffering. Much like the Mahāyāna Buddhist ideal of the compassionate bodhisattva, who renounces his own personal *nirvāṇa* in order to help all beings achieve liberation, the integral guru vows to return out of selfless love in order to bring the liberating knowledge of the supreme Brahman into this world. He thus becomes the conduit through which universal grace floods into and permeates the universe. The supreme yogin aims to realize his own nature as Śiva—the supreme Self who lies within us all, who is imagined in mythological terms as the deity sleeping blissfully upon the cosmic ocean. But rather than simply enjoying the bliss of his identity with Paramaśiva, the yogin must then strive to awaken the supreme consciousness of the Self, thereby cutting the very root of cosmic delusion and causing all beings to wake up from the dream of the phenomenal universe:

> The *mahāyogin* who has attained his own integral Self-realization must look back compassionately upon all people sunk in their collective ignorance and dedicate himself to winning the integral Self-realization of the entire world. . . . One *mahāyogin,* working prodigiously within one lifetime, could eventually become identified with *paramaśiva* as the imperishable *puruṣa* sleeping on the supercausal ocean. If this *mahāyogin* could then awaken from the world-dream while still holding the physical body, the root-ignorance in absolute subjectivity would disappear and the new

> kingdom of dynamic consciousness (*caitanya*) would be created. . . . The realm of rebirth would disappear.[83]

Kaviraj's system therefore embodies a kind of "eschatological vision"—an ideal of universal salvation that would, in effect, bring about the dissolution of the entire cosmos. For the yogin is seeking to "make *mahāpralaya* [the cosmic dissolution at the end of the age] to happen quicker through the control of the perennial source of creation."[84] Once the integral yogin has brought this supreme consciousness back into this world, the boundaries between Brahman and *saṃsāra,* absolute reality and the ignorance of *māyā* would disappear, and all beings would be free to enter the single boundless kingdom of divine consciousness: "As world-redeemer the integral guru must effect a complete ontological reconstruction, replacing the old Tantric cosmology with its complexity of ontic domains with the boundlessness of a single *maṇḍala* as the radiant kingdom of dynamic consciousness where all may attain their integral self-realization."[85]

Kaviraj's disciples appear to have believed that he had nearly reached this sublime state of realization and was in the process of completing the final stages of supreme integral yoga. He had, it is said, been embraced by Mahāśakti, the supreme Mother and the power of the universe herself, who was now working through him to begin "the action of total transformation of the world."[86] Yet, "although Kaviraj believed he was approaching the realization of his ultimate goal, he was unable to achieve it in his lifetime."[87] Nonetheless, he left us with a remarkable vision of a universalized Tantra that seeks the liberation of all. Although he seems to have given up the possibility of a concrete political solution to the crises of the modern world, Kaviraj conceived of a radically innovative form of Tantra as the ideal solution to this age of chaos and suffering, in which "discord and hatred are bound to disappear like mists before the light of the sun. It will herald the advent of a New Life in the world, when the central principle of Unity and Love will reign."[88]

The Religion of the Oppressed Masses: Narendra Nath Bhattacharyya and the Marxist Reading of Tantra

> This parallel Tantric tradition . . . was evolving since time immemorial as the philosophy of the masses.
>
> Narendra Nath Bhattacharyya, *History of the Tantric Religion* (1982)

While for Kaviraj Tantra is interpreted in a fairly apolitical sense, as a means of a spiritual collective liberation, for many other Indian authors, Tantra could be used as an explicitly political weapon and as part of a larger socioeconomic agenda. What is most interesting, however, is that Tantra in India was taken up most forcefully as a political tool, not by the more right-wing movements, as it often was in Europe, but rather by a number of Marxist-influenced scholars. Two of the most important scholars of Tantra in modern India—Debiprasad Chattopadhyaya and Narendra Nath Bhattacharrya—both lived and wrote in West Bengal, one of the major hotbeds of Marxist activity in this century, during the height of the communists' rise to power; and both approached the *tantra*s, and indeed all of Indian history, from a decidedly materialist and socialist perspective. Thus, Chattopadhyaya begins his seminal work, *Lokāyata,* by quoting Marx and Engels: "the simple fact, hitherto concealed by an overgrowth of ideology [is] that mankind must first of all eat and drink, have shelter and clothing, before it can pursue politics, science, art, religion, etc." And he describes his own work as a "systematic effort to study ancient Indian philosophy from the materialistic point of view," adopting an explicitly Marxist perspective that looks first and foremost "at the material roots of each phenomenon."[89]

The origin of the Communist Party in India (CPI) is usually dated to 1925. However, its roots go back as far as the early 1920s, when Bengali intellectuals like M. N. Roy (1887–1954) began to forge ties with the Third Communist International (Comintern). Disappointed by the failure of the communist revolts in Europe, Lenin and his colleagues began to turn their attention to revolutionary possibilities in Asia, choosing Roy as their premier organizer for India. In contrast to Lenin, however, Roy was critical of the mainstream Indian nationalist movement and opposed Gandhi's conservative social ideals. Rejecting the dominant nationalist movement as the expression of petty-bourgeois interests, Roy saw India's hope in the proletariat masses, who were moved primarily by economic forces and material needs.[90] Having broken with the Congress Party in 1929, the CPI would reject India's independence as a chimera that benefited primarily the bourgeoisie and neglected the poor; instead they called for the more radical goal of a people's democracy, a form of politics that combined socialism and democracy.

By the 1950s, however, a split had emerged within the party. The contending factions differed largely over the question of how the party should view the national bourgeoisie (and by extension the dominant Congress Party) and how far it should work within the existing Indian constitution. Finally, in 1964, there was a formal split between the official CPI, centered in Bombay, and the more radical group in Calcutta, later known as the CPI (M), which rooted itself in Marxist-Leninism and a more militant view of the economic and political milieu.[91]

From the beginning, West Bengal has been one of the primary centers of communist activity—particularly in its more extreme forms. Because West Bengal opposed the Congress Party's apparent acquiescence to the partition of Bengal after independence and its neglect of state problems, West Bengal gave strong support to the CPI. Then, dismayed by the official CPI's apparent accommodation to the Congress, the overwhelming majority of the party's members sided with the CPI (M) after the party's split. After the partition of Bengal in 1947, the state was faced with mounting economic and social deprivation, compounded by a dramatic increase in population, particularly in the rapidly expanding urban center of Calcutta. Voicing the Bengali people's resentment at the seeming chronic neglect of the state's difficulties, the CPI (M) drew new support from the impoverished rural peasantry and laborers in urban areas, and so finally assumed power in 1977. Since the 1980s, however, a growing number of Bengalis have grown disaffected with the party, disillusioned by its apparent failure to offer a viable solution to the staggering social and economic problems in urban areas like Calcutta.[92]

Born in Chinsurah (Hooghly district, West Bengal) in 1934, Narendra Nath Bhattacharyya was raised in the midst of the often violent political turmoil of Bengal in the aftermath of partition and independence. Born to a Brahman family, Bhattacharyya received his undergraduate degree from Hooghly College and then studied ancient Indian history at Calcutta University. His father was descended from a Śākta lineage. Though he had no personal involvement in any religious movement, Bhattacharyya was drawn from an early age to the study of Śākta Tantra. Having read Frazer's *Golden Bough* and Robert Briffault's *The Mothers* as a college student, Bhattacharyya later worked as the research assistant to Debiprasad Chattopadhyaya (whom he considered his guru).[93] Inspired by Chattopadhyaya's Marxist interpretation of Indian history and Tantra, Bhattacharyya went on to write his doctoral thesis on the Indian Mother Goddess (1965, later published in 1971).

In marked contrast to Kaviraj, Bhattacharyya was never personally drawn to Tantra; he was suspicious of religion throughout his life. Nonetheless, like the European scholars, Bhattacharyya's work was closely tied to his life experience and political commitments. Like many Bengali intellectuals of his time, Bhattacharyya was strongly influenced by Marxist theory. During the mid-1950s, after the events of Poland and Hungary, Bhattacharyya discovered the work of M. N. Roy and was particularly drawn to Roy's critical version of Marxism. Significantly, however, Bhattacharyya was not a supporter of the communist parties; on the contrary, he appears to have felt a "tremendous hatred for the Indian Communists for their anti-national activities and denunciation of Indian culture." Instead, he describes himself as a "keen student of classical Marxism and not its distorted version as propagated by Lenin."[94] Most of Bhattacharyya's early work, we will see, bears the distinct imprint of fundamental Marxist ideas—for example, a dialectical, materialist view of history; the belief that social changes are caused by economic changes; and the assumption that religious ideas have socioeconomic background. Yet in his later work, Bhattacharyya would grow increasingly disillusioned with the role of Marxism in India—particularly in its political forms in the CPI and CPI (M)—and would eventually tone down his stronger Marxist rhetoric.

Throughout his work, Bhattacharyya makes it clear that he sees the kinds of deities worshiped in a given society, its various symbols and rituals, as closely tied to the society's material circumstances and economic structure. Although Bhattacharyya is not nearly as explicit as his predecessor Chattopadhyaya in invoking the work of Marx and Engels, it is clear that he is working out of a basically Marxist model: "The material mode of life of a people ordinarily provides the rationale for the type of deity and the manner of worship prevalent in a given society."[95]

Bhattacharyya also assumes that there is a common evolutionary development among most civilizations of the ancient world. And here he seems to draw both on a Marxist dialectical model of history and on nineteenth-century European scholarship on the "Great Mother" and "mother right" in primitive cultures (J. J. Bachofen, E. O. James, etc.). Like Eliade, Bhattacharyya traces the origins of Tantra to an archaic matriarchal society based on agriculture and fertility cults. The primitive peoples of India, like those of the ancient Near East, Egypt, and other parts of the ancient world, are thus imagined to have been a goddess-centered culture, focused on the reproductive powers of nature: "The primitive . . . belief in the equation of earth and woman, of natural and human fertility, forming the infrastructure of numerous agricultural rites . . . connects the mystery of nature with that of the human body."[96] This, Bhattacharyya thinks, is the basis of Tantra: a primitive worship of the reproductive power of the Earth, imagined in a female form, which is tied to the powers of sexuality. Like Eliade, he identifies this matriarchal sex-based religion with the earliest known inhabitants of India—the Indus Valley civilization—which he in turn associates with the Dravidian cultures of south India and with the tribal groups that survive throughout India today. Yet he also believes that this sex-based religion was associated with sexual rituals throughout the ancient world, such as the cult of Cybele or the worship of Isis, both of which referred to the vegetative cycle of the Great Goddess.[97]

In the course of history, this archaic, goddess-centered culture was progressively overtaken by a masculine, patriarchal civilization. In the Western world, this was marked by the rise of the patriarchal traditions of Judaism and Christianity; and in India, it was marked by the Aryan invasion and conquest of the Indus Valley:

> Historically . . . Tantric ideas and practices are rooted in primitive sex rites based on the magical association of natural and human fertility. . . . Such primitive sex rites contributed everywhere to the evolution of human thought as a whole. . . . [T]he Tantric . . . rites associated with earlier existing religious system sank into oblivion.[98]

In India, the matriarchal traditions of the Indus Valley were supplanted by the patriarchal Aryan Vedic culture, with its hierarchical, class-divided social structure. With the triumph of the Aryans, India witnessed a "stupendous social transformation, the growth of class society with all its ugliness, the rise of state power as an organization of plundering and oppressing the people and . . . the ruthless extermination of the ancient moral values."[99]

Yet the archaic belief in the powers of woman and sexuality could never fully be eradicated. On the contrary, it would persist throughout India in the many, never fully-Hinduized tribal cultures that still survive; and it would also evolve into the more elaborate traditions of Śākta Tantra. Thus Tantra represents a parallel secret tradition that can never be fully "hushed up" by the repressive patriarchal and class-based Vedic culture:

> Even [in the Vedic period] the evidences relating to the sexual rituals and their connection with the cult of the mother Goddess could not completely be hushed up. . . . Many rituals of the other traditions . . . became the visible portion of the Tantric iceberg, the significance of which were denied . . . by subsequent generations.[100]

Śākta Tantra is thus a continuation of the most archaic traditions of the ancient world—above all, the worship of the female body and the feminized earth as incarnations of divine creative power, *śakti.* Perhaps it is the clearest single vestige of the originally female-dominated worldview held by most peoples of the ancient world: "Śāktism . . . is a direct offshoot of the primitive Mother Goddess cult which was so prominent a feature of the religion of the agricultural peoples who based their social system on the principle of mother right."[101]

Not only does Tantra reflect a social order in which women have equal power to men, but it also embodies a social vision that is classless and egalitarian, in which *śūdra*s have status equal to the twice-born. Tantra is for Bhattacharyya a working man's religion, a religion of the laborers, and this explains its popularity among the masses. It thus embodies a kind of primitive communism, which runs counter to the dominant social order expressed in the orthodox Hindu tradition: "Its intimate association with the practical aspects of life is proven by the emphasis it attached to the arts of agriculture, metallurgy, manual and technical labor. . . . The sociological viewpoints expressed in the Tantras were in opposition to those upheld by the Smarta-Purāṇic tradition."[102] In contrast to the abstract, philosophical vision expressed in the Upaniṣads, Tantra represents a far more practical, concrete, and material worldview. Its primary concern is not with otherworldly speculation, but with the more pragmatic matters of labor, fertility, and agricultural production. This explains the central focus on sexuality and the female body in Tantra—all of which, Bhattacharyya argues, is rooted in primitive fertility rites aimed at the enhancement of human and natural reproduction:

> Because of its original association with the simpler peoples, popular cults . . . became an integral part of the Tantric way of life. This brought the cult of the Mother Goddess and the fertility rites . . . into close relationship with Tantra. The magical rites performed to obtain greater fertility of land . . . really underlay elaborate Tantric rituals. . . .
>
> To the working people Tantra meant more than a religious system . . . knowledge meant worldly knowledge, which guided them in their . . . productive works.[103]

In sum, Bhattacharyya finds in Tantra evidence for the existence of an archaic class-free society, based on matriarchy and the power of the laboring classes—a system that would eventually be displaced by Brahminical Hinduism and its patriarchal, class-based social order.

Rather ingeniously, then, Bhattacharyya has turned the usual Orientalist narrative on its head. No longer is Tantra a corrupting disease that has crippled the once noble Hindu tradition; instead, the patriarchal, class-based Vedic culture is what has destroyed the originally egalitarian worldview embodied in Śākta Tantra. And over the course of history, Tantra itself would become infected by the class divisions and hierarchies of patriarchal Aryan culture. Eventually, its once noble egalitarian vision as a religion of the masses would be corrupted by socioeconomic divisions and the power of the wealthy elites:

> Tantra . . . has nothing to do with the caste system but in the later Tantras caste elements are pronounced. . . . [A]lthough most of our known Tantric teachers were non-Brahmans . . . belonging to the lower and despised classes, almost all of the known authors of Tantric treatises were Brahmans who could not give up their caste prejudices.[104]

Finally, the materialist, practical view of Tantra would be polluted by the elitist, otherworldly speculations of schools like Advaita Vedānta: "Although Tantra in its earlier stage opposed the Vedāntic philosophy of illusion and admitted the reality of the world and its evolution out of a material principle . . . the superimposed elements brought it into line with Vedānta."[105]

Though most critical readers today would probably find it problematic, Bhattacharyya's version of Indian history is a remarkably bold attempt to invert the conventional narrative constructed by the Orientalists and Hindu reformers. Rather than being the worst example of the degeneration of modern Hinduism, Tantra in Bhattacharyya's view is the embodiment of the most archaic, pure substratum of Indian culture, which has been progressively corrupted by classical Hinduism.

Tantric Radicalism and the Failure of Modern Hindu Nationalism

> The success of Śāktism could not be checked because it
> had its root among the masses.
>
> Bhattacharyya, *History of the Śākta Religion*

As the "religion of the oppressed," as Bhattacharyys calls it, Tantra has always contained a pronounced streak of radicalism and revolutionary potential. Despite its later corruptions, Tantra always preserved some vision of a classless, matriarchal society rooted in the material strength of the masses. As the mythic image of power, the goddess Śakti embodies the oppressed masses' dream of rising up against their unjust rulers:

> From the beginning of the Christian era the priestly and ruling classes, the landlords and big traders, enjoyed surplus of social production and those on whose labour rested this social structure were mostly *śūdra*s . . . leading

> miserable lives marked by endless oppression . . . and agonizing humiliation. The Devī's fight against the demons served as a cathartic dream to which the toiling masses, struggling against the intolerable conditions of life, eagerly responded but which remained out of reach.[106]

But the role of Tantra was not simply a wish-fulfillment. Throughout Indian history, Bhattacharyya suggests, Tantra also had the potential to play a more active role in the attempt to fight economic oppression, reform the social order, and regain the rights of the lower orders: "In the medieval age many . . . Tantric sects launched religious reform movements. They fought for the religious rights of the *śūdra*s and women, preached their doctrines among the hill tribes and tried to bring back the converted Muslims."[107]

The role of Śākta Tantra would become especially crucial in the nineteenth and twentieth centuries, in the face of colonial rule and the Hindu reform movements. While the Hindu reforms were geared primarily to the educated upper and middle classes, the masses needed a much more concrete and material source of liberation:

> Since all these reform movements were confined only among the English-educated intelligentsia, they had very little access among the greater section of the people. . . . The followers of the reformist sects . . . kept themselves aloof from the masses while the orthodox section lived in the world of exaggerated notions. But the common people needed an ideology in their struggle for existence, an ideology that would serve the practical purposes of life and . . . overcome the . . . spiritual crisis of the age.[108]

Hence, the toiling classes would find a more persuasive symbol of empowerment and liberation in the image of the Great Mother—particularly in her most awesome, powerful, and terrible forms as Durgā and Kālī: "The conception of the country in the form of the Divine Mother was of a general character acceptable to all irrespective of caste and creed, and it . . . enhanced the patriotic feeling of the Indians. . . . Secret societies were started in order to propagate revolutionary ideas, collect arms and rise in rebellion."[109] Yet despite the failure of the revolutionary nationalist movement, the power of the Goddess could never be fully suppressed. She remains an eternal symbol of the oppressed masses, the power of the land, and the common laborers, which continually returns to fight the injustice of class and economic exploitation:

> Throughout the ages, the Female Principle stood for the oppressed peoples, symbolising all the liberating potentialities in the class divided, patriarchal and authoritarian social set up of India. . . . Chronic insistence upon

> the authoritarian . . . values by the writers of the *smṛtis* and their violent enforcement in social life by the ruling class contributed to the development of another set of values quite opposite in character . . . but the success of Śāktism could not be checked because it had its root among the masses.[110]

Yet, ironically, Bhattacharyya eventually lost faith in Tantra and in the power of an overt political movement in Bengal.

The Hopes and the Failures of the "Religion of the Oppressed"

> The recognition of this proto-materialism has its importance . . . for the modern materialist and this importance can be compared to that of the recognition of primitive communism by the scientific socialist. He lays stress on it not because he dreams of returning to it; his purpose rather is to show that human relations based on private ownership and class-exploitation are not without a beginning and end.
>
> Debiprasad Cattopadhyaya, *Lokāyata* (1959)

Given his early Marxist commitments and his assumption of a material basis of all culture and religion, the question remains: why would a scholar like Bhattacharyya have been so interested in Tantra and in portraying it as a form of primitive socialism and a "religion of the oppressed"? Surely he is not holding Tantra up as an exemplar of a future, ideal society or as a viable prototype of an egalitarian society. If he was essentially critical of religion throughout his career, why would Bhattacharyya have gone to such trouble to describe and often champion the religion of the Tantras?

Bhattacharyya himself does not appear to give us an answer to this. However, if we look to the work of his Marxist predecessor, Cattopadhyaya, we do perhaps find a compelling reason. The "proto-materialism" that he sees in Tantra is by no means held up as an ideal to be emulated; rather, it functions in much the same way that "primitive communism" did for Marx and Engels. The existence of a form of primitive communism is, for Marx and Engels, proof that the present system of class hierarchy is neither natural nor inevitable: it had a specific historical beginning and it will have a specific end. This primitive communism is proof that human beings could live in ways other than bourgeois capitalism, even as it bears the seeds of a future, truly egalitarian, and communist society. In much the same way, Chattopadhyaya argues, primitive materialist traditions like Tantra give us evidence that private property and class divisions are not permanent or immutable, but that they had their origin in a particular historical formation and will one day be overturned.

> But what is the significance of the recognition of the primitive proto-materialism . . . ? Its value is comparable to the recognition of primitive communism in Marxism. The Marxists emphasise the importance of primitive communism not because they dream of a return to it. The purpose is rather to show that private property and the state machinery are not eternal adjuncts to human existence. . . . Similarly the primitive proto-materialism is discussed not for the purpose of a glorification of it. . . . [I]t has its value by way of showing that the spiritualistic outlook is not innate in man. It, too, will be washed away as inevitably as it arose at an earlier stage.[111]

Though Bhattacharyya never articulated it quite this way himself, it would seem that he was drawn to Tantra for similar reasons.

Like many Indian intellectuals, however, Bhattacharyya would grow increasingly disillusioned with the political role of Marxism in Bengal and the party politics of the CPI (M). Confronted with the Communist Party's chronic failure to improve the real material situation, along with its increasing fragmentation, internal dissent, and concessions to interests of the political right, many Bengali intellectuals would distance themselves from the CPI (M) and Marxism. Though he remained sympathetic to Marxism throughout his life, Bhattacharrya was drawn to the later work of M. N. Roy, who adopted a more critical Marxist stance, rejecting the communists' devaluation of the individual and advocating instead a kind of radical humanism.[112] In his later work, Bhattacharyya would tone down much of his early Marxist rhetoric. For example, his *Religious Culture of North-Eastern India* (1995) contains little materialist rhetoric or Marxist historical narrative. And if we compare the later editions of his early books, we can see that he backed away from many of his materialist interpretations of Indian history. In the 1999 edition of *History of the Tantric Religion,* sections like "Class-Orientation of Tantra" are renamed or replaced; and, significantly, the 1996 edition of *History of the Śākta Religion* simply deletes the entire final paragraph of the 1974 edition, which had praised Śāktism as the religion of "the oppressed peoples, symbolising all the liberating potentialities in the class divided . . . social set up of India."[113] Now modern Śāktism appears simply as the failure of yet another ideology.

In sum, Bhattacharyya seems to have seen in Śākta Tantra the hope, however vain and futile, for some kind of liberation from the age of darkness—from the class-divided, exploitative system that characterizes both premodern and modern India. A kind of primitive communism, Tantra offered a vision of a class-free, gender-equal social order rooted in material needs and the interests of the oppressed masses. Yet Bhattacharyya seems to have held fundamental reservations about both Tantra and Marxism as real political solutions. For all its emphasis on egalitarianism and the power of the lower classes, Tantra remained bound to a mystifying religious system; and Marxism, for all its utopian aspirations, was all too easily co-opted by the interests of party factions and political corruption. Though both offered a hope for liberation from the age of darkness, both seemed to Bhattacharyya ultimately doomed by their own internal contradictions.

AN EXTREME RELIGION FOR AN AGE OF EXTREMES

> The historical study of Tantrism has been handicapped, complicated and conditioned by the preoccupation of those working in the field.
>
> Bhattacharyya, *History of the Tantric Religion*

The history of discourse about "Tantra," it turns out, is also a political history of the academic study of religions in the twentieth century: a history arising out of the most racist and exploitative era of colonial rule and bursting into the most violent debates of twentieth-century European and Indian politics. By no means neglected or ignored in modern scholarship, Tantra has been central to modern discourse on Indian culture and a key part of the reimagining of both European and Indian identity in the modern era. I have only scratched the surface of modern scholarship on Tantra here, as I also could have explored the work of art historians such as Philip Rawson and Ajit Mookerjee, Jungians such as Erich Neumann (and Jung himself), and other important scholars such as Bharati, Tucci, and Guenther.[114] Not only has Tantra been taken up by depth psychologists and art historians, but it has also been transmitted to a wider public through the work of neo-Jungian mythographers like Joseph Campbell. As Campbell suggests, it is the dark presence of the Tantric Mother, Kālī, that runs throughout the whole long history of Indian religion itself: "In the end (and in fact secretly throughout) the enduring power has always been the same old dark goddess of the long red tongue who turns everything into her own everlasting awesome, yet finally somewhat tedious, self."[115]

Yet Tantra has by no means been a singular or static category in modern scholarship: rather, its history is one of contradictions, transformations, and inversions. Whereas more liberal scholars like Zimmer saw Tantra as an alternative to the violence of the war-torn modern West, fascists like Evola saw it as the inevitable, violent solution to a degenerate civilization. Finally, the more complex and contradictory Eliade saw Tantra as both the primordial heart of the ancient Orient and the religious form most appropriate to the modern West. As the spiritual path that explicitly identifies the sacred with the profane, using the secular forms of history to experience the transcendent truths of the sacred, Tantra is one of the few paths still accessible to fallen modern man. Yet for each of these scholars, Tantra seemed the ideal solution to an age of darkness in which the reassuring structures and traditional hierarchies of the old regime were rapidly crumbling.

In marked contrast to the more individualistic interpretations suggested by the European scholars, both Kaviraj and Bhattacharyya found in Tantra an ideal of collective liberation. For Kaviraj, this was largely a spiritual ideal, a liberation that will bring about a universal, even eschatological transformation. For Bhattacharyya, the roots of Tantra have always been much more material and socioeconomic. As a primitive form of egalitarian, communal society, grounded in the power of the laboring classes, Śākta Tantra has always carried with it the hope of genuine political liberation. Though he would later back away from his early Marxist enthusiasm, Bhattacharyya seems to have seen in Tantra the utopian hope for a more egalitarian, nonhierarchal community, and as a kind of primitive, albeit now inadequate and illusory, alternative to a class-based, exploitative socioeconomic order.

Yet despite their wide diversity of interpretations, all of these scholars found in Tantra a potent response to the age of darkness that seemed to be reigning in the war-torn, politically and socially divided modern world.

CHAPTER 6

The Cult of Ecstasy

Meldings of East and West in a New Age of Tantra

What I tell you must be kept with great secrecy. This must not be given to just anyone. It must only be given to a devoted disciple. It will be death to any others.

If liberation could be attained simply by having intercourse with a *śakti* [female partner], then all living beings in the world would be liberated just by having intercourse with women.

Kulārṇava Tantra (KT 2.4, 2.117)

Because the science of Tantra was developed thousands of years ago . . . many of the techniques are not relevant to the needs of the contemporary Western lover. . . . I see no need for repetition of long Sanskrit mantras . . . or the strict ritualization of lovemaking. . . . So while I have retained the Tantric goal of sexual ecstasy, I've developed new approaches to make this experience accessible to people today. High Sex weaves together the disciplines of sexology and humanistic psychology to give the Western lover the experience of sexual ecstasy taught by Tantra but using contemporary tools.

Margo Anand, *The Art of Sexual Ecstasy* (1989)

Inspired by the new valorizations of Tantra by Eliade, Zimmer, and more popular authors like Joseph Campbell, Tantra began to enter in full force into the Western popular imagination of the twentieth century. Already in the early 1900s we find the foundation of the first "Tantrik Order in America"—an extremely scandalous, controversial affair, much sensationalized by the American media—and by the 1960s and 1970s, Tantra had become a chic fashion for Western pop stars, as Jimi Hendrix began

Figure 10. American Tantra, "New Millennium Flag Bearer," from the Third Millennium Magic web site (http://www.3mmagic.com/at_main.html). Courtesy of Third Millennium Magic, Inc. © www.3mmagic.com 1999.

displaying *yantras* on his guitar and Mick Jagger produced a psychedelic film, *Tantra,* depicting the five M's. Taking Eliade's positive reinterpretation a step further, Tantra is now celebrated as a "cult of ecstasy": an ideal wedding of sexuality and spirituality that provides a much needed corrective to the prudish, repressive, modern West. In the process, it has also spawned a variety of new spiritual forms, such as American Tantra, neo-Tantra, and even the Church of Tantra (figure 10). At the same time, these transformed versions of Tantra have been reappropriated by Indian authors. In a complex cross-cultural exchange or "curry effect" between India and the West, we not only find neo-Tantric gurus like Osho-Rajneesh, but even a heavy-metal band in Calcutta called "Tantra." Amid the ever increasing circulation of material and spiritual capital throughout the global marketplace, it seems that Tantra has been exported to the West, where it has been processed, commodified, and reimported by the East in a new form.

An examination of the history of Tantra and its contemporary manifestations shows that it has undergone profound transformations in the course of its long, convoluted "journey to the West" and back. For most contemporary American readers, Tantra is basically "spiritual sex," the "exotic art of prolonging your passion play" to achieve "nooky nirvana."[1] This would seem to be an image of Tantra that is very different from that in most Indian traditions, where sex often plays a fairly minor, "unsexy" role and there is typically far more emphasis on guarded initiation, esoteric knowledge, and elaborate ritual detail. At present there is a profound shift in the imagining of Tantra—a shift from Tantra conceived as *dangerous power and secrecy* to Tantra conceived as *healthy pleasure and liberated openness.* This shift is exemplified by the two epigraphs for this chapter. The first, the quote from the *Kulārṇava Tantra,* warns of the perils of revealing secrets to the uninitiated masses. *Kula* practice, it is true, involves rites of sexual intercourse and consumption of wine, but these must occur only in strictly guarded esoteric contexts; in the hands of the uninitiated masses, they would lead to moral ruin and depravity. The contemporary neo-*tāntrika,* however, takes the opposite position. Jettisoning the old ritual trappings as outdated and irrelevant, the neo-*tāntrika* takes only the most expedient elements of these age-old techniques, mixes them with contemporary self-help advice, and adapts them to a uniquely late-capitalist consumer audience.

Since at least the time of Agehananda Bharati, most Western scholars have been severely critical of these new forms of pop Tantra or neo-Tantra. This "California Tantra," as Georg Feuerstein calls it, is "based on a profound misunderstanding of the Tantric path. Their main error is to confuse Tantric bliss . . . with ordinary orgasmic pleasure."[2] My own view, however, is that "neo" or "California" Tantra is not "wrong" or "false," any more than the Tantra of the *Mahānirvāṇa* or other traditions; it is simply a different interpretation for a specific historical situation. As such, the historian of religions must take it very seriously as an example of a new adaptation of a religious form to a new social and political context.

Above all, the popular fascination with Tantra as "spiritual sex" is closely related to the larger preoccupation with sexuality in contemporary culture as a whole, which is now filled with sexual discourse, imagery, and advertising. As Angus McLaren comments, "Today's media, while claiming to be shocked by the subversiveness of carnal desires, deluge the public with explicit sexual imagery to sell everything from Calvin Klein jeans to Black and Decker power drills. Sexuality . . . has invaded every aspect of public life. Sexual identity has become a key defining category in the twentieth century."[3] Yet, as Foucault argues, it is a common misconception to suppose that the history of sex in the West is a progressive narrative of liberation from Victorian prudery. Just as the Victorian age was not simply an era of repression and silence, our own age is perhaps not the age of sexual revolution that we commonly imagine it to be. Our sexual liberation has been accompanied by new forms of regulation, backlash, and conservatism. What *has* happened, however, is that we have produced an incredible body of discourse on the subject, a kind of "over-knowledge" or "hyper-development of discourse about sexuality."[4] Thus it is more useful to think of sexuality as a constructed and contested category, whose boundaries have been renegotiated in each generation. The category of "sexuality" is itself a recent invention, a product of the late nineteenth century, by no means static—ever imagined anew in the changing political contexts of the past one hundred years.[5]

As I will argue in this chapter, the contemporary preoccupation with Tantra has been part and parcel of our larger preoccupation with and anxieties about sexuality, a source of both titillating fascination and moralizing censorship. I will examine three transformations in the transmission of Tantra to the United States: the founding of the scandalous Tantrik Order in America by Pierre Bernard; the "sex magick" of Aleister Crowley and his followers; and the equation of Tantra with sexual liberation during the countercultural revolution of the 1960s and 1970s. But this preoccupation with Tantric sex has also been *reimported* by India via a complex feedback loop, through such figures as Osho-Rajneesh, Chogyam Trungpa, and Swami Muktananda. Finally, as we can see in the rapidly proliferating web sites, Tantra appears to have shattered the boundaries between the "spiritual East and the material West." Today, anyone with a fast modem and Internet access may attend the Church of Tantra, sample the Sensual Spiritual Software System, and discover Ecstasy Online.

These new forms of Tantra are in many ways well suited to our unique socioeconomic context. With its apparent union of spirituality and sexuality, sacred transcendence and material enjoyment, Tantra might well be said to be the ideal religion for contemporary consumer culture—what I would call, adapting Fredric Jameson's phrase, "the spiritual logic of late capitalism." Using some insights of Jameson and others, I will argue that there is an intimate relationship between the recent fascination with Tantra and the current socioeconomic situation, which has been variously described as late capitalism, postindustrial capitalism, or disorganized capitalism. It is precisely this kind of "fit" with late-capitalist society—a fit not unlike that of Weber's Protestant ethic and early capitalism—that characterizes many new appropriations of Tantra. Indeed, Tantra might be said to represent the quintessential religion for consumer capitalist society at the turn of the millennium.

TANTRA, AMERICAN-STYLE: FROM THE PATH OF POWER TO THE YOGA OF SEX

> Where can tantra happen? It can only happen in American and Western Europe. . . . Tantrism may happen here and maybe it has started right here in Boulder, Colorado, 80302.
>
> Agehananda Bharati, "The Future (if Any) of Tantrism" (1975)

In 1975, at the peak of the New Age movement and when the Naropa Institute was a burgeoning Mecca for Tantric spirituality, Agehananda Bharati made the qualified prediction that the United States might become the new center for the revival of Tantra. India, he believed, had become so morally repressive that it could no longer provide any space for Tantra; the affluent West alone had the openness and freedom to accommodate Tantra in the modern world. Yet he also warned of the real dangers of this transmission of Tantra to the United States, where it could be (and in his day already was being) all too easily misinterpreted as a simple excuse for self-gratification and hedonism:

> It is conceivable that the more affluent . . . of the West, particularly Western Europe and north America, might espouse some form of tantrism. . . . Some steps have been made, but probably in the wrong direc-

> tions: the frustrated middle aged North American lusting for the mysterious has opened a door for tantrism to enter. However, I feel that this entry is dangerous and . . . that it would have havoc out of tantrism.[6]

It would seem that both Bharati's prediction and his warning have been realized. The West, particularly America, has indeed become a fertile new land for the spread of Tantra, yet it has also offered new opportunities for its gross misinterpretation and reckless abuse.

The Western appropriation of Tantra had already begun in the late nineteenth century, with the Theosophical Society and Madame Blavatsky's descriptions of the mysterious "masters" who dwell in forbidden Tibet, the heartland of Vajrayāna Buddhism. The massive text of her *Secret Doctrine* is alleged to be based on a mysterious Tibetan text discovered by Blavatsky. What is most striking, however, is that Blavatsky did not identify Tibetan Buddhism as "Tantra"; on the contrary, influenced by Orientalist attitudes, she went to some pains to distinguish it from the disreputable tradition of black magic and hedonism known as Tantra. While Tantra could be understood in a spiritual sense as a form of "white magic," most of its modern forms are degenerate "necromancy" and "invocations to the demon," comparable to Western black magic: "The *Tantras* . . . are the embodiment of ceremonial *black magic* of the darkest dye. A Tantrika . . . is synonymous with 'Sorcerer.' . . . [T]hose Kabalists who dabble in the ceremonial magic described . . . by Eliphas Levi are as full blown Tantrikas as those of Bengal."[7]

It was not until the beginning of this century, and particularly in the United States, that Tantra was newly appropriated in a positive form in the Western popular imagination. No longer conceived as a religion of black magic and occult power, Tantra began to be identified more and more with the pursuit of sensual pleasure and erotic bliss. This was above all the case following Richard Burton's scandalous translation of the classic Indian erotic manual, the *Kāma Sūtra,* a text that was originally published in 1883 only for private circulation but that was soon pirated and sold widely throughout Europe. The *Kāma Sūtra* itself, of course, really has nothing to do with "Tantra." In the Victorian imagination, however, the dark secrets of the Tantras and the tantalizing secrets of the *Kāma Sūtra* would soon blend together and take on a variety of new forms.[8] And three of the most interesting of these new forms were perhaps the founding of the first Tantrik Order in America, the spread of Crowleyian "sex magick," and the "yoga of sex" that emerged with the counterculture of the 1960s and 1970s.

The Omnipotent Oom: Pierre Arnold Bernard and the Tantrik Order in America

> Wily con man, yogi, athlete, bank president, founder of the Tantrik Order in America . . . the remarkable "Doctor" Bernard was all of these. He was also the Omnipotent Oom, whose devoted followers included some of the most famous names in America.
>
> Charles Boswell,
> "The Great Fuss and Fume over the Omnipotent Oom"

> I'm a curious combination of the businessman and the religious scholar.
>
> Pierre Arnold Bernard

Not only was he the first man to bring Tantra to America, but Pierre Bernard was also surely one of the most colorful and controversial figures in early-twentieth-century American history. Described as "both a prophet and showman," Bernard was a man "who could lecture on religion with singular penetration and with equal facility stage a big circus, manage a winning ball team or put on an exhibition of magic which rivaled Houdini."[9] Infamous in the press as "the Omnipotent Oom," Bernard claimed to have traveled to the mystic Orient in order to bring the secret teachings of Tantra to this country and to found the first "Tantrik Order in America," in 1906. Surrounded by controversy and slander regarding the sexual freedom he and his largely female followers were said to enjoy, Bernard is in many ways an epitome of Tantra in its uniquely American incarnations.

Virtually nothing is known about Bernard's early life; in fact, he seems to have gone to some lengths to conceal his real background behind a veil of fictitious identities and false biography, often using the persona of "Peter Coons" from Iowa.[10] Probably born in 1875 to a middle-class family from California, Bernard left home in his teens to work his way to India in order to study the "ancient Sanskrit writings and age old methods of curing diseases of mind and body." After studying in Kashmir and Bengal, he won the title "Shastri" and was supposedly initiated into the mysteries of Tantric practice. Returning to America, and now introducing himself with the title of "Doctor," he worked at various odd jobs in California and began to study hypnotism. By 1900, he had become moderately famous as a master of self-hypnosis who could use yogic tech-

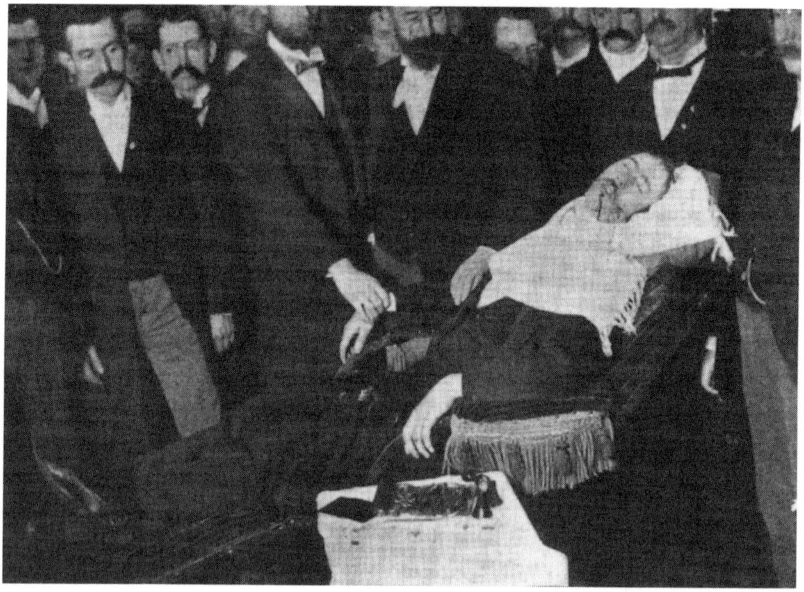

Figure 11. Pierre Bernard, demonstrating the Kālī *mudrā,* or simulation of death. From *International Journal of the Tantrik Order* 5, no. 1 (1906).

niques to place himself in a state simulating death (figure 11). It is also likely that Bernard received instruction in Tantric practice from one Swami Ram Tirath, an Indian yogi who had come to California in the early 1900s, who praised Bernard as a man of "profound learning," comparable to "the Tantrik High Priests of India."[11]

In 1904, Bernard established a clinic in San Francisco where he taught his own versions of self-hypnosis and yoga; the clinic eventually became known as the Bacchante Academy. Even by then, Bernard had become something of a scandal in the California press, who charged that the academy "catered to young women interested in learning hypnotism and soul charming—by which they meant the mysteries of the relations between the sexes."[12] Sometime in the years 1906–7, Bernard founded the first Tantrik Order in America, with an accompanying journal—the *International Journal of the Tantrik Order*—whose charter document for initiation reads as follows:

> As a tear from heaven he has been dropped into the Ocean of the TANTRIK BROTHERHOOD upon earth and is moored forevermore in the harbor of contentment, at the door to the temple of wisdom wherein are experienced all things; and to him will be unveiled the knowledge of the Most High. . . .

> Armed with the key to the sanctuary of divine symbolism wherein are stored the secrets of wisdom and power, he . . . has proven himself worthy to be entrusted with the knowledge . . . to soar above the world and look down upon it; to exalt the passions and quicken the imagination . . . to treat all things with indifference; to know that religion is the worship of man's invisible power . . . to enjoy well-being, generosity, and popularity. . . . He has learned to love life and know death.[13]

After the San Francisco earthquake in 1906, Bernard left California and relocated in New York City, where he opened his "Oriental Sanctum" in 1910. Teaching *haṭha* yoga downstairs and offering secret Tantric initiation upstairs, the Oriental Sanctum quickly became an object of scandal in the New York press: the notorious "Omnipotent Oom" was charged with kidnapping and was briefly imprisoned, though the charges were later dropped. "I cannot tell you how Bernard got control over me," said one of the alleged kidnappees, Zella Hopp. "He is the most wonderful man in the world. No women seem able to resist him."[14] Similar controversy surrounded the "New York Sanskrit College," which Bernard founded a few years later. The press reported "wild Oriental music and women's cries, but not those of distress."[15]

By 1918 Bernard and his followers had moved out to a seventy-two-acre estate in Upper Nyack, New York—a former girls' academy that he renamed the Clarkstown Country Club, making it the site of his own "utopian Tantric community." A sumptuous property with a thirty-room Georgian mansion, the club was designed to be "a place where the philosopher may dance, and the fool be provided with a thinking cap!"[16] Eventually, he would also purchase a huge property known as the Mooring and then later open a chain of Tantric clinics, including centers in Cleveland, Philadelphia, Chicago, and New York City, as well as a Tantric summer camp for men in Long Island. His clinics were well known for attracting the most affluent clients—"mostly professional and business men and women from New York," including Ann Vanderbilt, Sir Paul Dukes, composer Cyril Scott, and conductor Leopold Stokowski, among others.[17] According to *Town and Country* magazine of 1941, "Every hour of the day limousines and taxies drove up to the entrance of the Doctor's New York clinic. In the marble foyer behind the wrought-iron portal of 16 East 53rd Street, a pretty secretary handled appointments."[18] Hence, it is not surprising that Bernard quickly achieved a remarkable degree of wealth, fame, and status: "Almost overnight, Oom found himself showered with more money than he had ever dreamed of and chieftain of a tribe of both male and female followers. . . . This tribe . . . would number well over 200, and would carry on its roster some of the best-known names in America."[19] And much of the appeal of Bernard's teachings, as well as the scandal they generated, centered around his views of sexuality.

Sex, Secrecy, Slander, and Censorship: Bernard's Tantric Teachings and Their Reception in the American Popular Imagination

Love, a manifestation of sexual instinct, is the animating spirit of the world.

Pierre Bernard,
"Tantrik Worship: The Basis of Religion" (1906)

Many of Bernard's Tantric teachings appear to have been surrounded with an aura of secrecy, considered so profound and potentially dangerous that they had to be reserved for the initiated few. Thus the *International Journal of the Tantrik Order* warns that "whoever has been initiated, no matter what may be the degree to which he may belong, and shall reveal the sacred formulae, shall be put to death."[20] According to the police reports from a raid on Bernard's clinic, entry involved a secret signal and complex series of taps on the bell. There also seems to have been a certain hierarchy of disciples, with the lower-level initiates performing physical exercises downstairs, while the "inner circle"—the "Secret Order of Tantriks"—engaged in the more esoteric rituals upstairs:

> Downstairs, they found a bare room where Oom's physical culture clients, paying $100 bite, toiled through exercises designed to produce the body beautiful. Upstairs . . . on canvas-covered mattresses, Oom's inner-circle clients participated in secret rites. . . . [T]he upstairs customers, following physical examinations, had to pay large sums and then sign their names in blood before they could be initiated into the cult.[21]

The popular press offered some vivid and probably somewhat fictional accounts of Bernard's secret Tantric rituals, occult initiations, and arcane esoteric techniques.

> During Tantrik ceremonies, Oom sat on his throne wearing a turban, a silken robe and baggy Turkish pants, and flourished a scepter. While so engaged, he invariably smoked one of the long black cigars to which he was addicted. . . .
>
> A frequent Tantrik ceremony involved the initiation of new members. "To join the order," an Oomite later disclosed, "the novitiate must first have confessed all sins, all secret desires, all inner thoughts; must then promise to abide by Doctor Bernard's orders and . . . take the Tantrik vow."

> The novitiate looks upon Doctor Bernard as a high priest—indeed, as a sort of man-god. He kneels before Doctor Bernard and recites: "Be to me a living guru; be a loving Tantrik guru." Then all present bow their heads as though in church and repeat in unison: "Oom man na padma Oom." It is sung over and over in a chanting monotone, like the beating of drums in a forest, and is supposed . . . to induce a state of ecstasy.[22]

There does appear to have been some real need for the secrecy in Bernard's Tantric practice—particularly in the moral environs of early-twentieth-century America. According to the accounts that came out of Bernard's Nyack Country Club, much of the spiritual practice there centered around full enjoyment of the physical body and complete liberation of sexual pleasure. As we read in the *International Journal of the Tantrik Order,* the human body is the supreme creation in this universe and the most perfect place of worship—a truly embodied, sensual worship that requires no priesthood or churches of stone: "The trained imagination no longer worships before the shrines of churches, pagodas and mosques or there would be blaspheming of the greatest, grandest and most sublime temple in the universe, the miracle of miracles, the human body."[23]

Like dance and yoga, sex is thus a spiritual discipline, a means of experiencing the divine within the physical body. "The secret of Bernard's powers," one observer comments, was "to give his followers a new conception of love. . . . Bernard's aims are . . . to teach men and women to love, and make women feel like queens."[24] (Thus, in his Tantrik journal, Bernard even spells the word *tantra* in *devanāgarī* characters comprised of tiny hearts.) As we read in his article "Tantrik Worship," the sex drive is in fact "the animating spirit of the world."

> The animating impulse of all organic life is the sexual instinct. It is that which underlies the struggle for existence in the animal world and is the source of all human endeavor. . . . That affinity which draws the two sexes together for the . . . production of a new being, that overmastering universal impulse, is the most powerful factor in the human race and has ever been the cause of man's most exalted thought.[25]

Yet in modern Western culture, the mysteries of sexual love have been stupidly repressed, relegated by self-righteous prudes to the realm of depravity. Today, "matters pertaining to the sexes are generally avoided, and we are taught that the sexual appetite is an animal craving that should be concealed," such that most Americans now "are blind to the vast importance of the sexual nature" and fail to realize that it is in fact the "wellspring of human life and happiness."[26] According to one disciple's account, Bernard was one of the only teachers of that time who recognized the natural beauty and power of sex, which is nothing other than an expression of our union with the divine: "He teaches the Oriental view of love as opposed to the restrained Western idea. Love . . . is akin to music and poetry. It unites men and women with the infinite."[27]

Bernard's wife, Blanche de Vries, also became a teacher of Oriental dance and *haṭha* yoga. She would eventually develop her own sort of "Tantric health system," which she marketed very profitably to the wealthy New York upper-class society, who were increasingly obsessed by matters of physical health and beauty. Among her more affluent patrons, for example, was Mrs. Ogden L. Mills, a stepdaughter of the Vanderbilt family. As Mrs. Bernard commented, the Tantric teaching of love is the most-needed remedy to modern America's social ills, most of which derive from repression, prudery, and self-denial: "Half the domestic tragedies . . . and not a few suicides and murders in America are due to the inherent stupidity of the average Anglo-Saxon man or woman on the subject of love. We will teach them, and make our adventure a great success."[28] Apparently, Bernard also believed that for certain individuals (particularly overly repressed women of the Victorian era) more drastic, surgical measures might be needed to liberate their sexual potential. Sexually unresponsive or "desensitized women" could be helped by a form of partial circumcision, in which the clitoral hood was surgically removed—an operation believed to improve female receptivity by exposing the clitoral gland to direct stimulation.[29]

Not surprisingly, the popular press of the day took no end of delight in sensationalizing Bernard's scandalous Tantric practices and soon dubbed him the "Loving Guru." Bernard's clinics represented something terribly shocking yet also tantalizing in the American imagination—something deliciously transgressive, in a world where sex for the sake of procreation within heterosexual marriage was the unassailable pillar of decent society: "The rites are grossly licentious and . . . a couple skilled in the rites . . . are supposedly able to make love hour after hour without diminution of male potency and female desire."[30]

It seems inevitable that Bernard's Tantric clinics would have elicited some complaints from his neighbors and attracted the attention of the authorities. One F. H. Gans, who occupied an apartment across the way, summed up the neighborhood grievance: "What my wife and I have seen through the windows of that place is scandalous. We saw men and women in various stages of dishabille. Women's screams mingled with wild Oriental music."[31] In Nyack, where Bernard was a respected citizen, the authorities received a host of complaints about this scandalous Tantric clinic; reluctantly, the state police investigated, and riding into the estate on horseback:

> Nyack concluded Oom was running a love cult. The local prudes clucked and gasped their alarm. Oom, obviously, was a danger to the young of the community and would have to be run out of town.
>
> But the Nyack police refused to act. Oom was a big taxpayer. So the prudes complained to the New York State Police, then a recently formed, eager-beaver organization. . . . The night they received the complaint, a squad of troopers galloped to Oom's estate and swung down from their saddles near the main building.[32]

After his rise to celebrity, soon followed by his rapid descent into scandal, Bernard seems to have retired into a relatively quiet later life. Enjoying an affluent lifestyle, Bernard was known for his lavish wedding celebrations, his generous patronage of professional baseball and boxing, and his investment in sporting venues like baseball stadiums and dog tracks. Eventually he assumed a more respectable position in Nyack society, becoming president of the State Bank of Pearl River in 1931. With a fondness for collecting fine automobiles, such as Rolls-Royces, Stutzes, and Lincolns, Bernard is said to have been worth over twelve million dollars at his peak. Remembered as a "curious combination of the businessman and the religious scholar," he died in New York City in 1955, at the age of 80.

In sum, we might say that the enigmatic and colorful character of Pierre Bernard is important to the history of Tantra for three reasons. First, he was a bold pioneer in the transmission of Tantra to America, where it quickly took root and flourished; second, he was one of the first figures in the larger reinterpretation of Tantra as something primarily concerned with sex and physical pleasure; and finally, like so many later American Tantric gurus, he generated intense scandal and slander from the surrounding society, foreshadowing Tantra's role in the American imagination as something wonderfully tantalizing and transgressive. As such, Oom's popular brand of Tantra would help lay the foundation for the new synthesis of Tantra and Western sex magic that later emerged.

"Do What Thou Wilt!" Sex Magick, Tantra, and Modern Western Esotericism

True Sex-power is God-power.

Paschal Beverly Randolph,
The Ansairetic Mystery (ca. 1873)

> Mankind must learn that the sexual instinct is . . . ennobling. The shocking evils which we all deplore are due to perversions produced by suppressions. The feeling that it is shameful and the sense of sin cause concealment . . . creates neurosis and ends in explosion. We produce an abscess and wonder . . . why it bursts in stench and corruption. . . . The Book of the Law solves the sexual problem completely. Each individual has an absolute right to satisfy his sexual instinct.
>
> Aleister Crowley, *The Confessions of Aleister Crowley* (1968)

Once the seeds of Tantra had been sown in this country, they soon began to proliferate wildly in the fertile soil of the American imagination, mingling with a number of existing Western esoteric traditions. Most modern forms of sexual magic, I would argue, are largely the fusion of Indian Tantric techniques, as reinterpreted by figures like Bernard and by Western occult movements emerging from the Masonic, Rosicrucian, and Kabbalistic traditions.

Sex, magic, and secrecy had long been associated in the Western imagination. From the early Gnostics to the Knights Templar and the Cathars of late medieval Europe, esoteric orders had been accused of using sexual rituals as part of their secret magical arts.[33] However, perhaps the first evidence of a sophisticated use of sexual magical techniques appears in the mid-nineteenth century, with the mysterious figure of Paschal Beverly Randolph (1825–75). Born to a wealthy Virginian father and a slave from Madagascar, Randolph was raised a poor, self-taught, free black in New York City. After running away from home at age sixteen, he traveled the world, wandering through Europe, the Middle East, and Asia. In the course of his travels, Randolph encountered a wide variety of esoteric traditions—not just European Spiritualist and Rosicrucian orders, but also a number of Sufi lineages. He claims to have derived much of his knowledge from a group of fakirs in the area of Jerusalem, which may have been a branch of the Muslim order of the Nusa'iri—a group long persecuted by orthodox Islam because of its alleged Gnostic sexual rituals.[34] Eventually Randolph would emerge as one of the leading figures in nineteenth-century Spiritualism and the most famous scryer of his time.

However, Randolph is most famous as an exponent of spiritual eroticism, or Affectional Alchemy, a form of sexual magic that would have a profound impact on later Western esotericism. In sexual love, "he saw the greatest hope for the regeneration of the world, the key to personal fulfillment as well as social transformation and the basis of a non-repressive civilization."[35] For Randolph, orgasm is the critical moment in human consciousness and the key to magical power. It is the instant when life is infused from the divine realm into the material realm, as the soul is suddenly opened to the spiritual energies of the cosmos: "at the instant of intense mutual orgasm the souls of the partners are opened to the powers of the cosmos and anything then truly willed is accomplished."[36] As such, the experience of sexual climax has the potential to lead the soul either upward or downward, to higher states of transcendence or to depraved states of corruption: "The moment when a man discharges his seed—his essential self—into a . . . womb is the most solemn, energetic and powerful moment he can ever know on earth; if under the influence of mere lust it be done, the discharge is suicidal."[37] If one can harness the creative energy of orgasm, he or she can deploy it for a wide range of uses, to realize virtually any worldly or otherworldly goal. Not only can we achieve the spiritual aims of divine insight, but we can also attain physical health, financial success, or regain the passions of a straying lover.[38]

One of the most striking features of Randolph's sexual magic, however, is his insistence that both male and female partners must have an active role in the process; in fact, both must achieve orgasm—ideally a simultaneous orgasm—for the magical operation to successful: "The woman's orgasms should coincide with man's emission, for only in this way will the magic be fulfilled."[39] The resulting pleasure that both partners feel in this union is nothing less than the overflowing joy of the divine emanating from above: "The joy . . . is diffused over both beings and each is based in the celestial and divine aura—the breath of God, suffusing both bodies, refreshing both souls!"[40]

Although Randolph seems to have no direct connection to Indian sexual practices, his teachings were to have a formative impact on later Western occult traditions, "releasing the genie" of sexual magic.[41] And they would soon become mingled with the sexual traditions now being imported form the Orient, including the titillating erotica of the *Kāma Sūtra* and the esoteric mysteries of Tantra.

While it seems unlikely that Randolph had any knowledge of Tantra, it is more plausible that several later Western occultists did—in particular, the organizers of the highly esoteric movement of the Ordo Templi Orientis. Founded in the late nineteenth century by Karl Kellner (1861–

1905) and Theodor Reuss (1855–1923), the OTO became the main conduit through which Western sexual magic began to merge with a (somewhat deformed) version of Indian Tantra. A wealthy Austrian chemist and industrialist, Kellner claims to have been initiated into Indian sexual techniques in the course of his Oriental travels, citing three masters—one Sufi and two yogis, one of whom may have been a Bengali *tāntrika*. Reuss, too, seems to have had some knowledge of left-hand Tantra, which he cites in his work.[42] However, others suggest that Kellner's inspiration may have been Randolph, whose sexual magic had been spread to Europe by a group of disciples in the late nineteenth century.[43]

Whatever their origins, much of the OTO ritual appears to have centered around the "inner kernel" of sexual magic—a quite different one from the more conservative system of Randolph. As the OTO proclaimed in 1912 in the Masonic journal *Oriflamme:*

> One of the secrets which our order possesses in its highest grades is that it gives members the means to re-erect the temple of Solomon in men, to refind the lost Word. . . . Our Order possesses the Key which unlocks all Masonic and Hermetic secrets, it is the teaching of sexual magic and this teaching explains all the riddles of nature, all Masonic symbolism and all religious systems.[44]

The OTO developed a system of nine degrees (later expanded to eleven), the first six of which were more conventional Masonic initiations. The seventh, eight, and ninth, however, focused respectively upon the theory of sex magic and on the techniques of auto- and heterosexual magic. Homosexual intercourse also appears to have played a central role in the rituals.[45] Through the magical act of intercourse, by focusing all of one's will on a desired goal at the moment of orgasm, one can accomplish any occult operation, from the invocation of a god to the finding of hidden treasure. One may, for example, use these techniques to empower a talisman or another magical object: by focusing one's will on the desired object during auto- or heterosexual orgasm, and afterward anointing that object with the semen, one can use the empowered object to achieve virtually any desired end. Similarly, the power of sex can be used to incarnate a god within one's own consciousness, by concentrating on the deity at the moment of orgasm and so "blending their [man's and god's] personalities into one."[46]

Surely the most infamous member of the OTO was the notorious magician and self-proclaimed "Great Beast 666," Aleister Crowley (1875–1947; figure 12). Crowley's practice is the clearest example of Western

Figure 12. Aleister Crowley, costumed as an Eastern sage for a publicity photo to attract students (ca. 1936). Courtesy of Ordo Templi Orientis, Berlin.

sexual magic combined (and perhaps hopelessly confused) with Indian Tantra. The son of a preacher in the puritanical Plymouth Brethren sect, Crowley is in many ways an exemplar of the Victorian age—raised in a prudishly repressive environment and turning later to extremes of sexual excess. Following Nietszche in his fierce rejection of Christianity as emasculated and weak, he "declared that all orthodox religions are rubbish and that the sole true gods are the sun and his vice-regent, the penis."[47] A poet, novelist, and accomplished mountain climber, Crowley would also become one of the most reviled characters of the twentieth century. Known in the press as "the wickedest man on earth," Crowley was vilified as a "vicious Satanist who employed illicit drugs and perverted sex to enliven the weary charade of his blasphemous 'magick.'"[48] Much like Bernard's infamy and scandals, Crowley's were mostly about his sexual practices.

His most recent biographer, Lawrence Sutin, suggests that Crowley may have first learned Tantric practices in Ceylon as early as 1901, while studying Buddhism; yet he seems to have been initially quite repulsed by them, dismissing them as "follies of Vamacharya (debauchery)."[49] His attitudes toward such rituals appear to have changed in the next few years, however, when he began to experiment in his own sexual magic. Already in 1902, Crowley and his partner Rose had begun to engage in a series of "secret rites, of a sexual nature (and related to Tantric practices, such as the emulation of the passive Shiva in cosmic coupling with the mounted energetic Shakti)."[50] Other authors think Crowley may have been even more deeply involved in left-hand Tantric rites during his travels in India. We have already considered Elizabeth Sharpe's semifictional account *Secrets of the Kaula Circle,* which describes a mysterious Englishman calling himself by the number 666. Once handsome, but later gross, 666 uses various magical processes, pentangles, and swords to draw phantoms into his circles with the help of Tantric lamas; yet he later falls to the ground frothing at the mouth, the victim of his own decadent black magic. Nik Douglas concludes that this is clearly a reference to Crowley and provides evidence that he had extensive knowledge of Tantra (though it seems equally likely that Sharpe has worked the infamous Beast 666 as a fictional character into her narrative).[51]

Yet whatever their origin, sexual practices clearly formed an integral part of Crowley's magical repertoire. "Sex is a sacrament," as the Great Beast put it in his *Book of Lies.* These practices became particularly central during the years of his involvement with the OTO. After reading his *Book of Lies* in 1912, Theodor Reuss allegedly contacted Crowley and accused him of revealing the innermost secret of the OTO: the secret of sexual magic. Though Crowley had done so unintentionally, the story goes, he was named the Sovereign Grand Master General of Ireland, Ioana, and all the Britains. In his *Confessions,* Crowley discusses the nine degrees of the OTO's initiations, together with the two he later added, and also points to the kernel of sexual magic at the center of the higher degrees:

> If this secret [of sexual magic] which is a scientific secret were perfectly understood, as it is not by me after more than twelve years' almost constant study and experiment, there would be nothing which the human imagination can conceive that could not be realized in practice. . . . If it were desired to have an element of atomic weight six times that of uranium that element could be produced.[52]

Thus in his magical rites, Crowley calls not for any ascetic withdrawal or denial of the flesh, but rather for the fullest celebration of the body, with all its desires, in the ceremony of love:

> Then comes the call of the Great Goddess, Nuit, Lady of the Starry Heaven. . . . "Come forth, O children under the stars and take your fill

> of love! I am above you and in you. My ecstasy is in yours. . . . Is ours the gloomy asceticism of the Christian . . . ? Are we walking in eternal fear lest some 'sin' should cut us off from 'grace'? By no means. . . . Dress ye all in fine apparel, eat rich foods and drink sweet wines that foam! Also take your fill of and will of love as ye will when, where and with whom ye will!"[53]

Crowley's most intense period of experimentation in sexual magic appears to have begun in 1914, during his "Paris workings." Together with his homosexual lover, the poet Victor Neuberg, Crowley engaged in a variety of sexual rites intended to achieve both spiritual and material ends—both the primary goal of "invoking the gods Jupiter and Mercury and the secondary one of getting these gods to supply Crowley and Neuberg with money."[54] As Julius Evola suggests, Crowley saw in orgasm (as in drug experience) a means to create "openings or breakages of consciousness" that give the soul access to supersensual and ecstatic states.[55] However, as others point out, Crowley was perhaps more often concerned with the efficacy of sexual techniques for "obtaining wealth or anything else the magician might desire."[56] For example, Crowley suggests that one might use sexual magic to "perform an operation to have $20,000." By totally focusing one's will upon an object at the moment of orgasm, one can powerfully influence the course of events and achieve the desired goal: "The purpose of these operations of High Magick Art was to obtain priestly power and, on a lower plane, money."[57]

However, the ultimate goal that Crowley sought through his sexual magical practices seems to have gone far beyond the mundane desire for material wealth; in his most exalted moments, Crowley believed that he could achieve the birth of a divine child—a spiritual, immortal, godlike being, who would transcend the moral failings of the body born of mere woman. This goal of creating an inner immortal fetus, Crowley suggests, lies at the heart of many esoteric traditions, from ancient Mesopotamia to India to the Arab world:

> This is the great idea of magicians in all times—To obtain a Messiah by some adaptation of the sexual process. In Assyria they tried incest . . . Greeks and Syrians mostly bestiality. This idea came from India. . . . The Mohammedans tried homosexuality; medieval philosophers tried to produce homunculi by making chemical experiments with semen. But the root idea is that any form of procreation other than normal is likely to produce results of a magical character.[58]

Now, if it is possible that Crowley had some contact with Indian Tantra and drew some of his sexual practice from Eastern sources, it would seem that he also creatively reinterpreted them through his own occult system. Much of Crowley's magic, for example, involved homosexual intercourse—something almost never found in Tantric rituals. More importantly, Crowley was not content simply to achieve a spiritual union of the divine male and female principles; rather, he sought nothing less than the conception of a magical fetus or spiritual child—a kind of golem like that of the Kabbalistic and alchemical tradition:

> The principal difference between Crowley's sexual magic and traditional Tantric techniques now becomes clear. For Crowley, the object of the ritual was not limited to mystic union with the goddess . . . but could further involve the creation of a new spiritual form—a magical child. . . . This magical child could be . . . any form of concentrated inspiration, or it could manifest physically as a talisman or even within a human being—as in a newborn baby or a newly spiritually transformed adult man.[59]

Thus, we might say that the magical and sexual career of Aleister Crowley was in many ways parallel to that of Pierre Arnold Bernard. In fact, the two briefly met. Not only do many of Crowley's teachings seem to bear some resemblance to those of Bernard's American Tantra, but it would seem that Crowley also had direct contact with the members of the Tantrik Order in the 1920s. Crowley was first introduced to his infamous "Scarlet woman," Leah Hirsig, in New York in 1918 by her sister Alma, who was an ardent disciple of Bernard in his Tantrik Order in New York. Alma would later publish her expose of Bernard's group, under the pseudonym of Marion Dockerill, entitled *My Life in a Love Cult: A Warning to All Young Girls* (1928). As Sutin observes, "There are . . . obvious parallels in the paths of Alma as High Priestess and Leah as Scarlet Woman."[60] This parallel between the sister-consorts of Crowley and Bernard is quite fitting: after all, both Crowley and Bernard were to become notorious in the American popular imagination as high priests of secret Tantric rituals; and both would soon face intense scandal and media attack, largely because of their illicit sexual practices.

Crowley and Bernard were instrumental in three ways in the transmission and transformation of Tantra in the West. First, they were both key figures in the *sensationalization* of Tantra in the popular imagination, as it became an increasing object of scandal and media exploitation during the early twentieth century. Second, both were key figures in the *reinterpretation* of Tantra, as it was transformed from a tradition concerned primarily with secrecy and power to one focused on the optimization of sexual orgasm. Finally, the combined influence of Crowley and Bernard led to the increasing fusion of Western esoteric traditions with Indian Tantra. Today, one need only browse the shelves of any New Age bookstore to find a range of magazines, videos, and texts bearing titles like *Tantra without Tears; Sex, Magic, Tantra, and Tarot;* and *Secrets of Western Tantra*—most of which are based on the fundamental equation of Indian Tantric techniques and Crowleyian-style sexual magic.[61]

The Yoga of Sex: Tantra, Counterculture, and "Sexual Liberation"

> Tantra is . . . not withdrawal from life but the fullest possible acceptance of one's desires, feelings and situations as a human being. . . . Explore the fascination of desire, love and lust to its limit. . . . Thus the follower of the Tantric way plunges himself into just those things which the ascetic renounces: sexuality, food and drink, and all the involvements of worldly life.
>
> Alan Watts, "Tantra" (1976)

Although Tantra had begun to emerge in the early twentieth century as something scandalous, shocking, and yet also terribly interesting, it didn't burst into popular culture as a full-blown "cult of ecstasy" or "yoga of sex" until the 1960s. Now mingled with the erotica of the *Kāma Sūtra,* Pierre Bernard's sex scandals, and the magick of the Great Beast 666, Tantra fit in nicely with the American counterculture and the so-called sexual revolution. As critics like Jeffrey Weeks and others argue, the period of the 1960s and 1970s represent something more complex than a simple liberation of the Western libido from its prudish Victorian shackles; for the freedom of sex in the age of promiscuity also came with all sorts of new oppressions and bonds. Nonetheless, it seems clear that this period witnessed an unprecedented proliferation of discussion and debate about sex, along with new fears about the growing promiscuity among young people. "Violence, drugs and sex, three major preoccupations of the 1960s and 70s blended symbolically in the image of youth in revolt."[62]

The literature on Tantra was a key element in this new proliferation of discourse about sexual freedom. Thus, in 1964, we see the publication of Omar Garrison's widely read *Tantra: The Yoga of Sex,* which advocates Tantric techniques as the surest means to achieve extended orgasm and optimal sexual pleasure: "Through . . . the principles of Tantra Yoga, man can achieve the sexual potency which enables him to extend the ecstasy crowning sexual union for an hour or more, rather than the brief seconds he now knows." Fighting against the repressive prudery of

Christianity, which has for centuries "equated sex with sin," Garrison sees in Tantra a much needed cure for the Western world, bearing with it "the discovery that sexual union . . . can open the way to a new dimension in life."[63] As one contemporary Tantric teacher observes, "The radical no-nonsense nature of Tantric teachings made them very attractive to the sixties generation. Psychedelic mind-expanding drugs, uninhibited sex, and the quest for spiritual experiences took on new meaning. . . . Tantra helped legitimize the sixties experience, helped give it spiritual *and* political meaning."[64]

At the same time, Tantra began to enter into the Western popular imagination in a huge way, as entertainers, musicians, and poets began to take an active interest in this exotic brand of Eastern spirituality. This process had already begun with the Beat poets like Allen Ginsberg, who saw Tantra as a means of breaking through the repressive morality of middle-class American society. One of the first hippies to journey to India in search of enlightenment, intense spiritual experiences, and/or cheap drugs, Ginsberg would later become a disciple of Chogyam Trungpa's radical brand of Tantric Buddhism. Tantra is for Ginsberg categorized with other methods of "organized experiment in consciousness," such as "jazz ecstasy" and drugs as a means of altering mental states and achieving "increased depth of perception on the nonverbal-nonconceptual level."[65] For Ginsberg, India represents the complete opposite of modern America: whereas America is sexually repressed, uptight, and overly rational, India is the land of unrepressed, spontaneous sexuality. And Tantric sexuality, embodied in the violent, terrifying goddess Kālī, is a liberating alternative to the oppressive prudery of Cold War America:

> Fuck Kali
> Fuck all Hindu Goddesses
> Because they are all prostitutes
> [I like to fuck]
> . . . .
> Fuck Ma Kali
> Mary is not a prostitute because
> She was a virgin
> Christians don't
> Worship prostitutes
> Like the Hindus.[66]

Not only is Kālī an intense image of sexual liberation, but she also serves as a powerful political symbol. In a wonderfully ironic use of images, Ginsberg superimposes the terrible mother Kālī onto the figure of the Statue of Liberty, combining the violently sexual Tantric goddess with the icon of American identity. In the Beat poet's inverted vision, the skulls around Kālī's neck become the world's great leaders—American presidents, fascist dictators, and Soviet leaders alike—while the Terrible Mother stands atop the prostrate corpse of Uncle Sam:

> The skulls that hang on Kali's neck, Geo Washington with eyes rolled up & tongue hanging out of his mouth like a fish, N. Lenin upside down, Einstein's hairy white cranium. Hitler with his mustache . . . Roosevelt with grey eyeballs; Stalin grinning; Mussolini with a broken jaw . . . Mao Tze Tung & Chang Kai Shek shaking at the bottom of the chain, balls with eyes and noses jiggled in the Cosmic Dance. . . . A huge bottomless throat and a great roar of machinery chewing on these Hydrogen Bombs like bubble gums & bursting all over its mouth as big as the Lincoln Memorial. . . . The Vajra Hand balancing a high Rolls Royce on end, fenders sticking up into the empty night heavens—battleships dangling from an arm. . . .
>
> Her foot is standing on the godlike corpse of Uncle Sam who's crushing down John Bull, bloated himself over the Holy Roman Emperor & Mohammed's illiterate belly.[67]

In sum, for Ginsberg and other voices of the American counterculture, Tantric imagery is turned into a powerful weapon to criticize the dominant sociopolitical order, which is perceived as repressive, bankrupt, and corrupt. With its emphasis on the terrible, erotic Mother Kālī, Tantra seemed to offer a much needed antidote to a hypercerebral Western world that had lost touch with the powers of sex, femininity, and darkness. In the words of Alan Watts, an ex-Anglican priest who became a Zen master and a psychedelic guru of the Beat generation,

> Tantra is therefore a marvelous and welcome corrective to certain excesses of Western civilization. We over-accentuate the positive, think of the negative as "bad" and thus live in a frantic terror . . . which renders us incapable of "playing" life with an air of . . . joyous detachment. . . . But through understanding the creative power of the female, the negative . . . we may at last become completely alive in the present.[68]

qenwd

Religion for the Age of Aquarius: Tantra and the New Age

To all those Tantra souls of the New Age who are leading the world into a Kingdom of perfect love.

Dedication in Howard Zitko, *New Age Tantra Yoga* (1974)

By the 1970s, this American version of Tantra would become one of the most important elements in the proliferation of a new wave of alternative religious movements, collectively known, ratherly vaguely, as New Age—a category that is, of course, every bit as amorphous and polyvalent as "Tantra" itself. Most often, "New Age" refers to an enormous heterogeneity of different spiritual movements, lifestyles, and consumer products—"a blend of pagan religions, Eastern philosophies and occult-psychic phenomena," drawn from "the Euro-American metaphysical tradition and the counterculture of the 1960s."[69] Yet as Paul Heelas has recently argued, beneath the tremendous diversity, there are some basic unifying themes that pervade the many phenomena we label New Age. Above all, he suggests, the dominant tropes include "the celebration of the Self and the sacralization of Modernity"—that is, the fundamental belief in the inherent divinity of the individual self and an affirmation of many basic values of Western modernity, such as "freedom, authenticity, self-responsibility, self-reliance, self determinism, equality, and above all the self as a value in and of itself."[70]

In more recent years, there has been a growing movement within the New Age toward a sanctification, not only of the self and modernity, but also of material prosperity, financial success, and capitalism. In contrast to the 1960s countercultural rejection of materialism, more recent New Agers have shifted to an affirmation of material wealth, searching for a harmonious union of spirituality and prosperity, religious transcendence and success in capitalist business: "God is unlimited. Shopping can be unlimited," according to Sondra Ray, best selling author of *How to Be Chic, Fabulous, and Live Forever.*[71] Since at least the early 1970s, this "world-affirming" side of the New Age had begun to emerge in movements like EST, Scientology, and the Human Potential Movement; and it came into full bloom during the power generation of the 1980s, with Shirley MacLaine, Bhagwan Shree Rajneesh, and a wide array of gurus promoting the union of spirituality and financial success through books and videos such as *Money Is My Friend* or *Prosperity Consciousness.* For this more worldly side of the New Age, "the more spiritual you are the more you deserve prosperity," for "being wealthy is a function of enlightenment."[72] The "New Age" has itself become a highly marketable phenomenon, a catch-all label with which to sell a vast array of consumer products: books, videos, health foods, diet supplements, crystals, incense, clothing, ritual implements, workshops, classes, seminars, and so on. As Heelas comments, "Today . . . we have New Age leaders praising capitalism and teaching that it is fine to work and succeed within the system . . . teaching that there is nothing wrong with materialistic consumption . . . and providing training to engage managerial efficacy."[73]

It is hardly surprising that many New Age practitioners have turned to Tantra—a form of spirituality that seemingly affirms the essential divinity of the human self and seeks the union of sensuality with spirituality, material enjoyment with otherworldly bliss. No longer imagined as the religion for the age of darkness, Tantra has reemerged as one of the most powerful "religions for the Age of Aquarius." For it seems to embody both the countercultural revolt against prevailing Christian values and the celebration of the body and sensual ecstasy. Now mingled with various occult movements like Crowleyian sex magic and traced back to ancient Egypt and the lost city of Atlantis, Tantra has entered fully into the Western imagination:

> Tantra, the dual yoga of sexual rejuvenation by spiritual ritual . . . has been suppressed, censored and ridiculed. . . . This is the period of history wherein . . . nothing shall be hidden; all shall be known. It is in this spirit of revelation that this work is added to that growing number which is opening the New Age to whosoever will contemplate the future of Mankind Two, the inheritors of the New World . . . of the 21st century.[74]

For many of this generation, the Tantric wedding of spirituality with sensuality, otherworldly transcendence with this-worldly ecstasy, seemed to represent the very essence of the dawning Age of Aquarius. But Tantra would also undergo some changes in the course of its rebirth: no longer a dangerous esoteric cult centered on transgressive power, Tantra has reemerged as a life-affirming, celebratory, "pop religion," a sensual spirituality for the masses:

> As the New Age manifested, traditional Tantra was transformed into a Tantra for the masses, a neo-Tantric cult of sensual pleasure with a spiritual flavor. . . . In the 21st century Tantra will . . . bless those prepared to deal with the new spiritual reality . . . in the flowering of the Age of Aquarius which commenced in 1962.[75]

One of the most interesting developments in the rise of this "New Age Tantra" has been Nik Douglas's revival of Pierre Bernard's Tantrik Order. Now promoting the "New Tantric Order in America," Douglas has created a revised version of the Omnipotent Oom's Westernized spiritual sex, reconstituted for a new millennium. Offering online initiations into the "secret" teachings of his New Tantric Order, Douglas has drafted an "Updated New Tantric Order Document" (1996), which brings Bernard's own 1906 document more in line with contemporary American concerns: "TantraWorks (tm) offers membership in the 'New Tantric Order,' which will offer participants the opportunity to advance through personalized Tantra initiations and allow access to all the Tantra databases on this Web Site."[76] For Douglas, Tantra is now a movement of truly revolutionary potential, one that will reunite the realms of sex and spirit, so long dichotomized by the Western mind:

> It's wondrous, exhilarating and true; you can use sexual pleasure as a guide to spiritual fulfillment. Not only is the sensual path enriching and joyful, but it's delightfully accessible with Tantra. . . . A revolutionary movement sure to be a watershed . . . in the coming millennium, spiritual sex celebrates the mystical aspects of sexuality while revealing the secrets that allow men and women to reach a zenith of ecstasy.[77]

Rather significantly, Douglas's New Tantric Order does not seem to have generated any of the scandal or moral outrage that surrounded Bernard's original Tantrik Order; on the contrary, its brand of sacred sexuality seems to be remarkably at home in American consumer culture at the start of the millennium.

We Neo-Victorians: Tantra and the Narrative of Sexual Liberation

> People are suffering from a wound. Sex has become a wound; it needs to be healed.
>
> Osho,
> *Autobiography of a Spiritually Incorrect Mystic* (2000)

> Tantra has thus far been glimpsed in the West only in its most vulgar and debased forms, promulgated by unscrupulous scoundrels who equate sex with superconsciousness.
>
> Robert E. Svoboda,
> *Aghora: At the Left Hand of God* (1986)

Tantra, it would seem, has undergone a series of transformations in the course of its tangled journey to the West. Most importantly, we can see two phenomena at play in the transmission of Tantra to America and its embrace by the New Age. The first is the more or less complete identification of Tantra with "sacred sex." Tantra has increasingly been associated and often hopelessly confused, not only with the Indian erotic arts like those of the *Kāma Sūtra,* but also with Western erotic-occult practices like those of Crowley and the OTO. In the process, the focus has shifted more and more to the power of sexual orgasm as the essence of Tantric magic. As we read, for example, in Christopher Hyatt's *Secrets of*

Western Tantra, "Unlike most forms of Tantric practice, orgasm is not only allowed but *essential* to create the desired results. . . . Many forms of Tantra are restricting . . . focusing on holding back. . . . Western Tantra is completely different. . . . [C]omplete Orgasm is freeing and energizing."[78]

The second phenomenon is the appropriation of Tantra in this larger narrative of "liberation." By the end of the twentieth century, Tantra had come to be synonymous with freedom on every level—sexual, spiritual, social, and political. According to a common narrative, repeated throughout New Age and alternative spiritual literature, our natural sexual instincts have long been repressed by the distorted morality of Western society and Christianity. "For centuries organized religions have used guilt about sex as a subtle way of exploiting people and the recent liberalization of sexuality has not yet succeeded in erasing this cruel legacy."[79] Thus, Tantra is the most needed spiritual path for our age, the means to liberate our repressed sexuality and reintegrate our physical and spiritual selves: "Sexual liberation implies the liberation of the whole being: body, mind and spirit."[80]

Not surprisingly, Tantra has been taken up in the service of a variety of calls for social and sexual liberation. Since at least the 1970s, the aggressive Tantric goddesses Śakti and Kālī have been appropriated by a number of feminists in search of a radical symbol of empowerment. Thus we find the rise of the "Shakti woman," with her "new female shamanism," along with the birth of the "Erotic Champion," holding a power that "far exceeds the claims of any woman's liberation movement."[81] More recently, the seemingly quite heterosexual practices of Tantra also have been adapted in the service of gay and lesbian calls to liberation. Like the sexual secrets of Tantra, many gay-rights advocates claim, homosexuality has been suppressed by Western religion for two millennia, and Tantra can be employed as a tool for their liberation as well.[82]

Yet both of these imaginings of Tantra—as sex magic and as liberation—would seem to have much less to do with any particular Indian tradition than they do with the peculiar obsessions, fantasies, and repressed desires of the modern West. It is, I would argue, an extreme example of the larger role of sexuality in contemporary Western culture. As Foucault observes, it may not be entirely true that we in the modern West have "liberated" sexuality in some radical way; but it does seem that our generation has taken sex to the furthest possible extremes—to extremes of transgression and excess, not resting until we have shattered every law, violated every taboo: "We have not in the least liberated sexuality, though we have . . . carried it to its limits: the limit of consciousness, because it ultimately dictates the only possible reading of our unconscious; the limit of the law, since it seems the sole substance of universal taboos."[83] It is precisely this relentless search for the limit that seems to drive the characteristically American style of Tantra.

GURUS, GOD-MEN, AND GLOBALIZATION: TANTRIC MASTERS, FROM EAST TO WEST AND BACK AGAIN

> Of all emotions man suffers from, . . . sex and sex-oriented emotions demand the most vital sacrifice. It is the most demanding . . . of emotions; it is also the most self-centered. . . . It adores the self most and hates to share its joy and consummation. It is wanted the most; it is regretted the most. It is creative, it is destructive. It is joy; it is sorrow. Bow to sex, the *hlādinī* [the power of delight].
>
> Brajamadhava Bhattacharya, *The World of Tantra* (1988)

> The sex act has more names in America than anything else. . . . The problem is that not only are they obsessed with sex, they're making the rest of the world equally crazy.
>
> Anurag Mathur, *The Inscrutable Americans* (1999)

If Swami Vivekananda worked hard to cover over the Tantric nature of his master's teachings, and even wholly to censor this dimension of the Hindu tradition, a variety of new gurus arrived in America in the 1970s who would do just the opposite. Beginning with the notorious neo-Tantric masters Osho-Rajneesh and Chogyam Trungpa, a number of Hindu and Buddhist teachers would make the journey to the West, openly proclaiming Tantra as the most powerful means to liberation. At the same time, these Tantric masters have been influenced by Western ideas and obsessions—perhaps above all, the preoccupation with sex and its liberation. "Sex has become an obsession, a disease, a perversion," as Rajneesh observed in 1971.[84] Indian gurus, too, seem to have accepted the identification of Tantra with sex and to have taught a largely "sexo-centric" brand of Tantra marketed as the most exciting path to enlightenment. As such, they are powerful examples of the feedback loop between East and West, as Tantra has been exported, imported, and reexported for a new age of consumers.

The Danger, Power, and Madness of Tantric Wisdom: Chogyam Trungpa and the Lightning Bolt of Tantra

> Many people in America have heard about Tantra as the "sudden path"—the quick way to enlightenment. . . . Exotic ideas about Tantra are not just misconceptions; they could be destructive. It is dangerous . . . to practice Tantra without establishing a firm ground in Buddhist teachings.
>
> Chogyam Trungpa, *Journey without Goal* (1985)

> All the monsters of the Tibetan Book of the Dead might come out and get everybody to take LSD! . . . The Pandora's Box of the Bardo Thodol has been opened by the arrival in America of one of the masters of the secrets of the Tibetan Book of the Dead.
>
> Allen Ginsberg, quoted in Barry Miles, *Allen Ginsberg* (1989)

Born in Tibet in 1939 and dying in the United States fifty years later, Chogyam Trungpa stands out as one of the most controversial Tantric gurus in the late twentieth century. As he recounts in his autobiography, Trungpa led an amazing life of adventure, tragedy, fame, and scandal.[85] Born in a small tent village in the Tibetan mountains, he was identified by Buddhist monks at eighteen months as the reincarnation of the abbot of Surmang monastery. Thus named the eleventh Trungpa of the Karma Kargyupa tradition, he took monastic vows at age eight and led a rigorous life of study, meditative discipline, and ritual practice. In 1959, he fled the new communist regime, leading three hundred Tibetans through the mountains to refuge in India. Having taught himself English, he traveled to Oxford in 1963. Finally, after being injured in a car accident and paralyzed on his left side, he came to the United States in 1970, at the height of the countercultural revolution's search for alternative realities through drugs, Eastern mysticism, and other intense psychic or physical experiences.

When he arrived, however, Trungpa was far from what most Americans expected in a Tibetan lama. Caring little for asceticism, Trungpa dressed and lived lavishly, freely partaking of food, alcohol, drugs, and the pleasures of a wealthy life. He was known for wearing expensive suits, riding in a chauffeured Mercedes, retaining servants, and living in the finest suites of expensive hotels. "He ate what he liked, consumed any quantity of alcohol, smoked and freely joined . . . ingesting psychedelics. . . . He understood his own crazy-wise conduct as a counter-point to the widespread disease of spiritual materialism."[86]

Nonetheless, this behavior did not prevent Trungpa from establishing a large and powerful following of eager American adepts in Boulder, Colorado, where he founded the Naropa Institute in the 1970s.[87] A Mecca for alternative spirituality and new meldings of Eastern and Western thought, Naropa quickly attracted a wide array of dropouts, hippies, and students, and a number well-known poets, musicians, and countercultural leaders, like Alan Watts, W. S. Merwin, Gregory Bateson, and Agehananda Bharati. Trungpa's American disciples appear not to have been repulsed by, but rather to have relished his bizarre and erratic behavior, worshiping Trungpa as the ideal crazy-wisdom guru who could shock them out of their comfort and complacency in the bourgeois capitalist West. Acting in a consistently unpredictable and incorrigible manner, Trungpa was regularly late for his own lectures, often arriving inebriated and sometimes downing a few beers in the course of his teachings. "During meditation he was occasionally seen to nod off, but on other occasions he would sneak up on unsuspecting meditators to squirt water at them with a toy pistol."[88] In order to shock his disciples out of their "spiritual materialism"—that is, the overattachment to religion, which the ego tends to turn into yet another object of pride—Trungpa would break up his meditations with raucous parties, bouts of drunken abandon, or orgies. "Trungpa had disciples carry him around naked at a party, broke antennas off cars . . . spent days speaking in spoonerisms. Assuming that the ego . . . will subvert any material it is given . . . these masters attempt to wake people through extreme behavior which challenges their everyday behavior."[89]

All this seeming hedonism and madness, Trungpa explained, was only part of his radical and direct spiritual method. His was the way of the Tiger—a quick, direct, but also dangerous and potentially deadly path to liberation:

> Here comes Chogyam disguised as a hailstorm
> no one can confront him
> . . . .
> He cannot be defeated
> Chogyam is a tiger with whiskers and a confident smile
> . . . .
> He escaped from the jaws of the lion.[90]

This tiger-guru was therefore not afraid of using the most violent and shocking tactics to liberate his disciples. Anything is permissible for the guru, as long as it is for the ultimate good of his devotee: "What if you feel the necessity for a violent act in order ultimately to do good for a person? You just do it."[91]

This, for Trungpa, is the very essence of Tantra. As the lightning-bolt path, Tantra is both the quickest and the deadliest, the easiest and the most easily abused of spiritual means: it is a path that attempts, not to repress the lower impulses of passion, sensuality, and violence, but to harness these darker energies as the most potent fuel propelling us to liberation: "Passion, aggression and ignorance, the source of human suffering, are also the wellspring of enlightenment. . . . They can be transformed into Buddha-mind."[92] On the Vajrayāna path, one must attempt to drink the poison of desire and to transform it into divinizing ambrosia. And perhaps most potent of all is the energy of sexual desire:

> In Trungpa's teaching style, sexual passion was accepted as a reflection of our basic goodness and could be a way of experiencing enlightenment. His favorite metaphor for giving in to the dharma was having an orgasm. "You just do it . . . all at once." He referred to arousing *bodhicitta* as tickling the clitoris of the heart. . . . Trungpa and Tendzin were both notorious for the number of their sexual partners or consorts.[93]

Not surprisingly the Tantric path is also a potentially deadly one—a path demanding that the disciple surrender his entire self to the power of the guru, who alone can guide him through this dangerous ordeal: "working with the energy of Vajrayāna is like working with a live electric wire," he warns. "It is better not to get into Tantra, but if we must get into it, we had better surrender. . . . We surrender to the fact that we cannot hold on to our ego."[94] The guru must be accepted as the absolute, unquestioned authority, and in fact as the supreme deity who will shatter the false ego of the disciple and lead him or her to liberation. As Trungpa put it in one lecture to his students, "Thank you for accepting me as your friend, teacher, DICTATOR." And as Butterfield reflects on his own experience,

> Trungpa . . . seemed bent on stoking the agony by acting so bizarre that I wondered if he was capable of ordering us all to commit suicide. On the night of the Vajrayana transmission he rambled from subject to subject in a series of blazing non sequiturs . . . waited until we were dozing off and then shouted "Fat!" or "Fuck You!" into the microphone loud enough to burst our eardrums.[95]

When we look more closely at the complex history of Trungpa's following in Boulder, however, we might begin to wonder whether he heeded his own advice as to the danger of his Tantric teachings. For the history of his life and community is a disturbing story of turmoil, emotional violence, and scandal. Trungpa's socially objectionable behavior had begun to be made public as early as 1975, when a poet, W. S. Merwin, and his wife attended an intensive three-month seminar with Trungpa. At the beginning of the course on Vajrayāna Buddhism, Trungpa suddenly interrupted the seminar with a raucous Halloween party. Arriving quite late and intoxicated, Trungpa began to ask people to undress, then took off his own clothes and had himself carried around naked on the shoulders of his students. Merwin and his wife soon decided that the party had gotten out of control and went to their rooms to pack their bags. When the couple repeatedly refused Trungpa's order that they join the party, locking themselves inside their room, a band of drunken disciples kicked in their windows and dragged them forcibly before the master. Trungpa then proceeded to insult Merwin's Oriental wife with racist remarks, threw a glass of sake in the poet's face, and had the pair stripped in front of everyone. One student was apparently courageous enough to oppose the mob mentality, but his pleading was rewarded only by a punch in the face from Trungpa.[96]

Even more disturbing events surrounded Trungpa's American disciple Thomas Rich, renamed Osel Tendzin, who was appointed his successor in 1976. An alcoholic like Trungpa, Tendzin was also known to have had sexual relations with female students—even after he was diagnosed with AIDS, and so infected at least one of his many disciple-lovers with the virus. As such, Butterfield suggests, he is a striking embodiment of the very real danger of the spiritual "poison" of the Tantric path: "The Tantric Buddhist way of handling passion may lead to disaster . . . no matter how great a master we become the danger never disappears."[97]

Most of this shocking and outrageous behavior, however, was not mentioned by Trungpa's disciples. In accordance with the Tantric injunction to keep such powerful, dangerous, potentially misunderstood teachings hidden from the eyes of the masses, such events were kept strictly secret among the inner circle of closest initiates.

> To be part of Trungpa's inner circle you had to take a vow never to reveal . . . some of the things he did. This co-personal secrecy is common with gurus. . . . It is also common in the dysfunctional family systems of alcoholics and sexual abusers. The inner circle puts up an almost insurmountable barrier to a healthily skeptical mind.[98]

As Butterfield reflects on his own experience with Trungpa's radical brand of Tantra, it was indeed, as the master had often said, much like the experience of sexual intercourse—an intense, shocking, yet also potentially damaging and emotionally crippling encounter: "It was like jumping from a cliff into a quarry pool. . . . You just do it, he said, 'like having an orgasm'—an image that had uncomfortable associations with getting screwed."[99]

Rather remarkably, in the years since his death, Trungpa's scandalous crazy-wisdom tactics appear to have been forgiven and largely forgotten by most of his disciples. Many see his radical behavior and controversial teachings as a part of his "skillful means" *(upāya)*. Thus Allen Ginsberg defended Trungpa as one of those great spiritual masters, who, like the radical poets of the 1960s and 1970s, had the "right to shit on anybody they wanted to. . . . Burroughs commits murder, Gregory Corso . . . shoots up drugs for twenty years . . . but poor old Trungpa, who has been suffering since he was two years old to teach the dharma, isn't allowed to wave *his* frankfurter." Trungpa's crazy-wisdom tactics, even his alcoholism and sexual misconduct, were but so many skillful "tricks" designed to jolt his deluded, brain-dead disciples into awakening.[100] Today, Trungpa is still venerated as one of the greatest pioneers in the transmission of Buddhism to America and one of the most innovative masters of Tantra in the last century.

From Sex Guru to Guru of the Rich: The Neo-Tantrism of Osho-Rajneesh

> Tantra is a dangerous philosophy, it is a dangerous religion. It has not yet been tried on a larger scale, man has not yet been courageous enough to try it on a larger scale because the society does not allow it. . . . [T]he society thinks this is absolute sin. . . . Tantra believes in joy because joy is God.
>
> Bhagwan Shree Rajneesh, *The Tantric Transformation* (1978)

> I *sell* happiness. I *sell* enlightenment.
>
> Rajneesh, interview with Mike Wallace on *60 Minutes* (1985)

The second American Tantric guru I want to examine here is one who represents a good complement, comparative contrast, and striking juxtaposition to Dr. Pierre Bernard—namely, the infamous sex guru and guru of the rich known in his early years as Bhagwan Shree Rajneesh and in his later life simply as Osho (figure 13). If Bernard was among the first

Figure 13. Osho in Poona, 1988. Copyright © Osho International Foundation, www.osho.com.

Americans to travel to India and bring Tantra to this country, Osho-Rajneesh was one of the first Indians to travel to America and import his own brand of "neo-Tantrism," marketed to late-twentieth-century American consumer culture. Whereas Bernard's version of Tantra represents a kind of sexualization and scandalization of Tantra, Osho-Rajneesh's version is a commodification and commercialization of the tradition.

In this sense Osho-Rajneesh is an embodiment of a larger shift in Western attitudes toward sexuality in the latter half of the twentieth century. As Weeks argues, the late twentieth century was characterized not so much by a radical sexual revolution or liberation of sex, but by a "commodification of sex" as part of the larger socioeconomic process of the expansion of capitalism to all domains of modern culture: "Sex had long been something you were. By the 1950s it was also something you could buy, not just in the traditional form of prostitution, but in the form of glossily marketed fantasy. . . . Not only was sex an area that could be colonized by capitalism, it was also one that could expand ever more exotically."[101] This is much the same kind of commodification of ecstasy that we see in the case of Osho-Rajneesh, the most notorious sex guru of the twentieth century. "Rajneesh offered everything Westerners imagined Tantra to be: a free love cult promising enlightenment, an exciting radical community. . . . Rajneesh slipped comfortably into the role of 'Tantra Messiah.' . . . Largely because of Rajneesh, Tantra reemerged as a New Age Cult in the 1970s and 80s."[102]

Born in 1931 in the village of Kuchwada, Madhya Pradesh, to a family of twelve, Rajneesh Chandra Mohan's parents died when he was small, and he was raised by his grandparents, a wealthy Jain couple. From an early age, Rajneesh reports having had various ecstatic experiences, finally achieving "full enlightenment" at age twenty-one. While at college at Jabalpur, Rajneesh suffered a traumatic period of depression and anorexia, and he attempted suicide; yet he emerged from his crisis with an intense spiritual breakthrough to self-realization—"an inner explosion," as he put it, in which he left his body and realized his true inner nature.[103]

After receiving his master's degree in 1957, Rajneesh taught philosophy for nine years at the University of Jabalpur. In 1967, however, he decided he could no longer keep his enlightened knowledge to himself, and so left the academic world to gather disciples and teach the spiritual life. His rather radical teachings quickly aroused enormous controversy in the Indian community, as he urged his disciples to indulge all their physical desires, even as he viciously attacked national heroes like Mahatma Gandhi (whom he ridiculed as a masochistic chauvinist pervert).[104] By 1971, Rajneesh had begun to call himself "Bhagwan"—Blessed One, or God—and had built himself an ashram in Poona, where he hoped to begin a new utopian community as the seed of a new civilization. Bhagwan's highly lucrative new civilization, however, soon ran into financial and legal problems with the Indian government. In 1981, Bhagwan and his devotees were forced to flee the country, trailed by some five million dollars in debts and a host of police and tax collectors.

Announcing himself as "the Messiah America has been waiting for," Rajneesh took refuge in the United States—the land, as he described it, of freedom, opportunity, and unfettered capitalism.[105] After a brief stay in a New Jersey mansion, he and his now large following bought a sixty-four-thousand-acre ranch in Antelope, Oregon, which they dubbed their own new city and ideal society, "Rajneeshpuram." Quickly growing into a remarkably lucrative financial complex, Rajneeshpuram amassed some 120 million dollars in revenues in its four-year existence. Meanwhile, Rajneesh's following had spread throughout the United States, Europe, and India, having over twenty-five thousand members at its peak and growing into an enormously diverse, multifaceted, international business complex.[106]

The group soon, however, came into conflict with its American neighbors. They clashed first with the local residents of Antelope's peaceful retirement community, whom they attempted to displace and push out, using terrorist tactics like dumping animal parts on the lawns of local officials and reportedly distributing salmonella bacteria in local restaurants and grocery stores. By 1985, however, the community had also come under serious investigation by the U.S. government, specifically around the issue of the interlock of the Rajneesh Church and the city of Rajneeshpuram, and its claim to tax-exempt status. Finally, in 1986, the state attorney general decided that Rajneeshpuram violated the church-state separation clause of the Constitution. Rajneesh and his disciples, meanwhile, had also come under investigation for their various criminal activities—which included, among other charges, counts of electronic eavesdropping, immigration conspiracy, lying to federal officials, harboring fugitives, criminal conspiracy, first-degree assault, attempted murder, burglary, racketeering, and arson. The movement, the state attorney general concluded, had become "sociopathic."[107] Deported from the United States and refused entry into virtually every country to which he applied, Rajneesh finally returned to his Poona ashram in 1987.

Neo-Tantrism and Religionless Religion: Rajneesh's Early Teachings

> Yoga is suppression with awareness; Tantra is indulgence with awareness.
>
> Bhagwan Shree Rajneesh, *Tantra Spirituality and Sex* (1983)

> Tantra is not revolutionary; it is rebellious. Rebellion means individual . . . it is just going beyond society. . . . It is for freedom—freedom to be
>
> Rajneesh, *The Tantric Transformation*

In itself, Rajneesh's early philosophy was not terribly original; rather, it was an ingenious synthesis of philosophical and religious ideas drawn from an enormous array of sources. Bhagwan's vast body of writings is itself a kind of postmodern pastiche: a wild hodgepodge of ideas drawn from a remarkable range of sources, from Plato to Śaṅkara to Lao Tzu to Sartre—though he had a special fondness for the more radical figures like Nietzsche, Gurdjieff, and Crowley. His teachings are, as one observer put it, an eclectic "potpourri of counter-culturalist ideas: strive for love and freedom, live for the moment, self is important, you are okay . . . the fun ethic, God is within."[108] An explicitly self-parodying, self-deconstructing guru, Rajneesh claimed that his entire teaching was itself nothing more than a joke, farce, or game—the ultimate game: "Nothing is serious. Even your disappointments are laughable. To become a Sannyasin is to enter the ultimate game. . . . [I]t is a play . . . it is the ultimate game. . . . You have played at being a husband, wife, mother, being rich, poor. . . . This is the last game. Only you are left."[109]

Rather than promoting a religion in the conventional sense, Rajneesh taught a radically iconoclastic brand of spirituality—"an antinomian philosophy and moral anarchism."[110] As a "religionless" religion, or antireligion, his was a path beyond conventional morality, beyond good and evil, and founded on the explicit rejection of all traditions, doctrines, and values. "Morality is a false coin, it deceives people," he warns. "A man of real understanding is neither good nor bad. He transcends both."[111] For Rajneesh, the cause of all our suffering is the distorting socialization or "programming" of cultural institutions, such as family, school, religion, and government. All metanarratives or overarching theories about the universe are only so many fictions, imaginary creations used by those in power to dominate the masses. True freedom can be achieved only by *deconstructing* all such narratives, liberating oneself from the confining structures of the past. One must be deprogrammed and dehypnotized: "You are programmed by family, acquaintances, institutions. Your mind is like a blackboard on which rules are written. Bhagwan writes new rules on the blackboard. He tells you one thing is true and next the opposite is true. He writes and writes on the blackboard of your mind until it is a whiteboard. Then you have no programming left."[112]

In order to help his disciples achieve this state of deprogramming and liberation, Rajneesh advocated a variety of yogic, meditative, and other psycho-physical disciplines. Most of these, we might note, came at a significant cost; at the Oregon ranch, prices ranged from fifty dollars for a one-day introduction to Rajneesh meditation, to seventy-five hundred dollars for a complete three-month rebalancing program. But perhaps the most important of these techniques was Rajneesh's unique brand of "neo-Tantrism." As he defines it, Tantra is the ultimate nonreligion or antireligion, a spiritual practice that does not demand rigorous ritual or morality but instead frees the individual from all such constraints. "Tantra is freedom—freedom from all mind-constructs, from all mind-games. . . . Tantra is liberation. Tantra is not a religion. . . . Religion is a mind-game. . . . Tantra takes all disciplines away."[113] In this sense, Tantra is the ideal form of rebellion for an age in which political revolution is no longer practical or relevant; it is not the rebellion of the masses against the state, but rather of the individual against modern society:

> Tantra is a rebellion. I don't call it revolutionary because it has no politics in it. . . . It is individual rebellion. It is one individual slipping out of the structures and slavery. . . . The future is very hopeful. Tantra will become more and more important. . . . [N]o political revolution has proved revolutionary. All political revolutions finally turn into anti-revolutions. . . . Rebellion means individual. . . . It is for freedom—freedom to be.[114]

In strongest contrast to established social institutions, Tantra does not deny life or the body; rather, it is the ultimate affirmation of passion, physicality, and pleasure. It is the supreme "Just do it!" religion, celebrating life in all its transience and contingency: "Tantra accepts everything, *lives* everything," Rajneesh declares. "This is what Tantra says: the Royal Way—behave like a king, not like a soldier. . . . Why bother about tomorrow? This moment is enough. Live it!"[115] Even the sinful and perverse side of life, even the most selfish and immoral sides of the human ego must be accepted as innately divine. Far from imposing moral restraints, Tantra celebrates human nature in all its most flawed, weak, even seemingly "evil" dimensions: "Tantra says—If you are greedy, be greedy; don't bother about greed."

> Tantric acceptance is total, it doesn't split you. All the religions of the world except Tantra have created split personalities, have create schizophrenia. . . . They say the good has to be achieved and the bad denied, the devil has to be denied and God accepted. . . . Tantra says a transformation is possible. . . . Transformation comes when you accept your total being. The anger is absorbed, the greed is absorbed.[116]

Above all, Tantra centers around the power of sex—a power that is at once the most intense force in human nature and also the one most severely distorted by Western society. Because the traditional Christian West has suppressed sexuality, Rajneesh argues, it is sexuality that must be liberated if modern students are to fully actualize their innermost self:

> Christian repression has made many locks in man where energy has become coiled up within itself, has become stagnant, is no longer flowing.
>
> The society is against sex: it has created a block, just near the sex center.

> Whenever sex arises you feel restless, you feel guilty, you feel afraid. . . . That's why I teach dynamic methods: they will melt your blocks.[117]

In opposition to this life-denying Western attitude, Tantra is the path that accepts everything, above all, the sexual impulse. As the strongest power in human nature, sex also becomes the strongest spiritual force when it is fully integrated and absorbed. "Tantra says everything has to be absorbed, *everything!* . . . Sex has to be absorbed, then it becomes a tremendous force in you. A Buddha . . . a Jesus, they have such a magnetic force around—what is that? Sex absorbed."[118] Thus many of Rajneesh's practices involved group sex—"therapy intensives," as he called them—which were "designed to bring about a catharsis followed by transformation of consciousness."[119]

The ultimate aim of Tantric practice is precisely to achieve this full self-acceptance, to love ourselves wholly and completely, with all our sin, vice, greed, and sensual desires, and to realize that we already are "perfect." Once we accept our sensual, desiring nature, once we release the pent-up sexual side of ourselves, we discover that we are already divine. We already possess truth, freedom, and infinite power within ourselves. We already are "God." "This is the most fundamental thing in Tantra, that it says you are already perfect. . . . Perfection does not have to be achieved. It simply has to be realized that it is there. Tantra offers you enlightenment right here and now—no time, no postponement."[120] "Ecstasy is your very nature. You are truth. You are love. You are freedom. . . . You are already there. . . . If you can stop all doing for a single moment the energy converges and explodes. . . . Then *you become a god.*"[121] It is not difficult to see why Rajneesh's version of Tantra was so appealing to a large American following. Promising absolute freedom and instant deification, even while allowing physical indulgence and sensual pleasure, neo-Tantra seemed to be a spiritual expression of the "Me generation" of the 1970s and the "Power generation" of the 1980s.

Osho: The Apotheosis of a Fallen Tantric Guru

> Why do I contradict myself? I am not teaching a philosophy here. The philosopher has to be very consistent—flawless, logical, rational. . . . I am not a philosopher. I am not here giving you a consistent dogma to which you can cling. My whole effort is to give you a no-mind.
>
> Osho, quoted on the osho.com web site (2001)

Perhaps the most surprising aspect of the Rajneesh phenomenon lies not so much in his scandalous career in America, but in his remarkable apotheosis and rebirth upon his return to India. A truly global Tantric guru, Rajneesh made the journey from India to America and back to India again, finally achieving even more success in his homeland, perhaps in large part because of his status as a figure who had a massive U.S. and European following. Rather incredibly, his followers were not only able to rationalize the disastrous scandal in the United States, but even to make Rajneesh a heroic martyr who had been unjustly persecuted by the oppressive imperialist U.S. government: "[The Ranch] was crushed from without by the Attorney General's office . . . like the marines in Lebanon, the Ranch was hit by hardball opposition and driven out."[122]

As part of his transfiguration in India, he would also reject his former Hindu title, Bhagwan, which had asserted his divine, god-man status. "Enough is enough! The joke is over," he declared.[123] Instead he adopted the more universal title Osho—a term which, according to some, derives from the Japanese term for master, and according to others, from the "oceanic experience" described by William James in his writings on mysticism. His message, too, became increasingly universal and marketed to a global consumer audience. "My message is too new. India is too old, ancient, traditional. . . . In fact, I am not an Indian. . . . I belong to no nation. My message is universal."[124] Osho also downplayed the more objectionable sexual elements, transforming his radical brand of neo-Tantrism into a kind of universal global religion of love. Thus his *Autobiography of a Spiritually Incorrect Mystic* makes only brief reference to Tantra or sexual practices, and even then only in the most defensive terms: "I have never taught 'free sex.' What I have been teaching is the sacredness of sex. . . . This is the idiotic Indian yellow journalism that has confined my whole philosophy to two words. . . . What they have been doing all along is misinforming people."[125]

Osho died in 1990, after just a few years back in Poona. According to many devotees, he had actually been "poisoned in Ronald Reagan's America" (given thallium during his period of incarceration in the American prisons) because of his radical and subversive teachings.[126] Rather remarkably, however, Osho seems to have become only more popular since his death. Indeed, he has published perhaps more books and received more acclaim as a disembodied photograph or video image than he ever did while still incarnate. The Poona center, meanwhile, has grown into a surprisingly successful and globalized spiritual organization, the Osho Commune International. Linked through its Global Connections

Department, the commune runs an intricate network of centers and activities worldwide, including Osho International in New York, which administers the rights to Osho's works. Describing itself as the "Esalen of the East," the Osho Multiversity in Poona teaches a dizzying array of spiritual techniques drawn from a smorgasbord of traditions: astrology training, Feldenkrais body work, crystal energy, acupuncture, neo-Zen, and other New Age activities. With an explicitly universal religious vision, the new Osho commune has combined Rajneesh's neo-Tantric "religionless religion" with a host of more generic New Age ideals, and marketed it to a global audience of spiritual consumers. As we read in an advertisement for the commune:

> Osho Commune International . . . continues to attract thousands of visitors per year from more than one hundred different countries around the world. . . . The resort meditation programs are based in Osho's vision of a qualitatively new kind of human being who is able to participate joyously in everyday life and to relax into silence. Most programs take place in modern air-conditioned facilities and include everything from short to extended meditation courses, creative art, holistic health treatments, personal growth and the "Zen" approach to sports and recreation.[127]

In sum, the character of Rajneesh has undergone an incredible transmutation, particularly since his death: from a shocking, scandalous Tantric sex guru into an international icon for a high-tech global movement and business enterprise.

A Tantric Guru among the Scholars: Muktananda and the Scandal of Siddha Yoga

> The purity of a guru should always uplift his disciples. Some people become gurus . . . and lead a completely wanton life, without self-control or discipline. A seeker should evaluate such teachers. . . . An incomplete teacher who is pure and ethical and who puts his knowledge into practice is far better than an undisciplined person who poses as a perfect Guru.
>
> Swami Muktananda, *Secret of the Siddhas* (1994)

Swami Muktananda (1908–82) is a guru who offers an even more explicit example of the complex dialectical exchange between India and the West in the late twentieth century. As the most important and most controversial leader of the widespread Siddha Yoga Dham of America (SYDA),

Muktananda has surely been one of the key figures in the transmission of both Tantric ideas and Tantric sexual scandals to America. Above all, the case of Muktananda is a poignant illustration of the ways in which scholars often become intertwined with the Tantric traditions they study. Not unlike Ramakrishna, Muktananda has become a tremendous source of embarrassment, largely because of his alleged sexual practices, which, many claim, drew naive young women into esoteric Tantric rituals. And not unlike Ramakrishna, Muktananda has a host of disciples who have attempted to use scholarship in order to justify, validate—or, as some have charged, *cover over and conceal*—his life and teachings.[128]

Born to a wealthy family near Mangalore, Karnataka, Muktananda began his spiritual searching at the age of fifteen. However, he did not find his true guru until 1947, at thirty-nine, when he met his master, Nityananda, in Ganeshpuri near Bombay. An ecstatic, mostly silent renunciant, Nityananda claimed to have been born a *siddha* and to have had no physical guru of his own. When Nityananda died in 1960, he passed the Siddha mantle on to Muktananda. Yet Muktananda's true rise to fame occurred in 1970, when he arrived in the United States teaching the message of Siddha Yoga. His mission was, as he put it, nothing less than to create a "meditation revolution," based not on nationalist politics but on widespread realization of the universal self. "This meditation revolution does not violate the laws of any government. . . . It is not against any caste or social class. . . . It does not argue with either the good or bad qualities of any country."[129] Enormously popular in the United States, Siddha Yoga has attracted at various times Jerry Brown, Werner Erhard, John Denver, James Taylor, Carly Simon, and even former Black Panther leader Erika Huggins. Today, SYDA has become a vast and remarkably successful spiritual organization, maintaining some 550 meditation centers and ten ashrams around the world and generating enormous revenues through its various spiritual services.

Although the roots of Siddha Yoga lie in a wide range of traditional Indian philosophies and practices—from classical yoga to Kashmir Śaivism to Advaita Vedānta—it is most accurately described, according to Douglas Brooks, as a kind of "right-handed Tantra." While it uses sexual and transgressive imagery, it does so only symbolically to describe the relationship between the self and the Absolute; and while it asserts the ability of the Siddha to transcend all social laws, it insists on strict ethical purity in the everyday world: "the Right Current gurus may still baffle or amaze disciples . . . but they do not intend to use concealment or defiance from social norms as a mode of teaching freedom."[130] In fact, its advocates claim, the Siddha Yoga path is *hyperethical,* for it insists on the absolute purity of the guru as the exemplar of the highest morality. In Muktananda's words, a true guru "does not indulge in sense pleasures. He neither keeps bad company nor becomes ensnared in addictions. He is free of conflicts, desires and thoughts. He is disciplined and possesses self-control, and he also makes his disciples observe discipline."[131] Above all, the Siddha guru was supposed to be restrained with regard to sexual desire, sublimating all his physical lust into spiritual energy: "I don't have sex for the same reason you do: because it feels so good," Muktananda declared.[132] According to Brooks, this moral purity is what distinguishes Siddha Yoga from the more radical, antimonian left-hand Tantric sects like the Kaulas. On the Siddha path, "there is no compromise when it comes to ethical ideals."

> The Siddha Yoga gurus are unambiguous in their affirmation of ethically pure practice and in this way set themselves apart from . . . Tantrics of the "Left-Current" *(vāmācārin),* that is, siddhas who indulge in explicitly antinomian rituals that might include the use of intoxicants, non-vegetarian foods or illicit sexual pleasures. Swami Muktananda rejects these behaviors whether they are performed inside or outside the ritual context.[133]

In his autobiography, Muktananda describes in some detail his own struggle with sensual desire and the sexual maladies that plague most of us in the modern age. Most people today, he suggests, suffer from a kind of sexual sickness, squandering their spiritual energy through the vain pursuit of sensual pleasure and physical enjoyment:

> I would look closely at them—pallid, restless, sick,—rich but still not satisfied. There was no strength and energy in them, only more and more new sicknesses. I realized that the cause of it all was waste of sexual fluid, sensuality. . . . Man thinks he is fortunate if he can experience sensual enjoyments. He deludes himself by thinking that he is going to enjoy pleasures. . . . In the end he becomes the victim of all sorts of sickness.[134]

And Muktananda himself appears to have undergone an intense period of sexual conflict, torn by the lusts of the body and overwhelmed by sensual desires. Overcome by sexual urges, his own spiritual practice was for a time totally eclipsed by carnal desire:

> My Guru worship and the mantra Guru Om, Guru Om disappeared. Instead in their place came a powerful sexual desire. . . . It completely possessed me. I was amazed at the uncontrollable strength in my sex organ. . . . Now everything was directed toward, toward sex, sex, sex. I could think of nothing but sex! My whole body boiled with lust and I cannot describe the agony of my sexual organ.[135]

Yet it was through his spiritual practice, Muktananda claims, that he was able to redirect and transform his sexual urges into spiritual power. His period of intense sexual conflict would culminate in a vision of the naked goddess, Śakti Kuṇḍalinī, the spiritual transformation of his own sexual desire. In fact, his intense sexual drives seem to have been the raw material or fuel that gave birth to his spiritual energy as a guru and a wielder of *śakti:* "I understood that the onset of sexual desire was connected with the process of becoming an *urdhareta,* from which one gets the power to give Shaktipat."[136] As the naked *siddha* Zipruanna explained to the young Muktananda, his carnal lust had been alchemically transformed into divine love:

> Don't underestimate the generative organ. It is the organ that generates all beings. . . . When it digs into the navel and remains there . . . all the seminal fluid in the testicles starts to flow upward toward the heart. It is heated in the gastric fire and passes right up to the brain. . . .
>
> All your agonies of lust were in fact the great Shakti Kundalini expelling your previous sexual appetites from you. Now instead of lust, love will surge within you.[137]

Thus the Siddha guru is the very embodiment of sexual power that has been alchemically transmuted into pure, spiritual love. Perfectly "free of sense pleasure . . . desires and thoughts," absolutely "disciplined self-controlled," he transmits these same high ideals to his disciples.[138]

Given this insistence on the ethical standards and purity of the Siddha Yoga gurus, it is particularly ironic that Muktananda and his successors have been accused of a host of shocking sexual scandals and moral violations. Despite his insistence on chastity, Muktananda has been criticized by many ex-devotees for having engaged in a variety of clandestine sexual activities. Already in 1981, an ex-devotee named Stan Trout had distributed a letter in which he accused the then 73-year-old guru of betraying the trust of young women of the ashram by extracting sexual favors from them in the name of spiritual enlightenment.[139] Shortly afterward, in 1983, an article appeared in the "CoEvolution Quarterly" that included interviews with some twenty-five members of SYDA and offered detailed discussions of Muktananada's alleged sexual escapades. As William Rodarmor charged:

> In his teachings Muktananda put a lot of emphasis on sex—most of it negative. Curbing the sex drive released the kundalini energy. . . . The swami himself claimed to be completely celibate. Members of the guru's inner circle, however, say Muktananda regularly had sex with his female devotees. . . . [T]he guru's sexual exploits were common knowledge in

> the ashram. "It was supposed to be Muktananda's big secret," said [an ex-disciple], "but since many of the girls were in their early to middle teens, it was hard to keep it secret."[140]

Rodarmar cited one female devotee, "Mary," who was told that she was being initiated into the inner secrets of Tantric practice—though she later found that these secrets were primarily about simple sex, in its most physical form: "On the first night, Muktananda tried to convince Mary she was being initiated into tantric yoga. . . . The next night, he didn't bother. It was like 'Okay, you're here, take off your clothes. Get on the table and let's do it.' Just very straight, hard, cold sex."[141]

In her eye-opening article published in *The New Yorker* in 1994, journalist Lis Harris included a number of interviews with former Siddha Yoga devotees that provide fairly graphic details about Muktananda's sexual practices. According to one female ex-devotee, Muktananda regularly engaged in acts that involved inserting his penis into a virgin partner's vagina for hours at a time, yet without either erection or ejaculation:

> He asked me to lie down on a table. He stood close to me and placed himself inside of me. We stayed for about one and a half hours in that position. During the whole period he never had an erection or ejaculation. He never even moved. . . . He joked a lot and told me stories about his childhood. At a certain moment he said: "whatever happens now cannot be understood with the mind. Don't think about it a lot. . . . Just know that this is the greatest day of your life." It was a very extraordinary experience. . . . I was in a state of total ecstasy, and whatever happened it had nothing to do with sex.[142]

Many speculate that these quasi-sexual encounters, involving long periods of penetration without ejaculation, may have been a form of Tantric practice, specifically *vajrolī mudrā.* A very old technique described in the *Haṭha Yoga Pradīpikā,* the *vajrolī mudrā* is a way to suck the vaginal fluids out of the female body through the penis. Through this "fountain pen technique," the fluids are drawn back into the male body, where they are transformed into a powerful source of spiritual energy. As Sarah Caldwell suggests, "It was for extracting power from these young virgin girls so that he could live. He was living off their energy, sucking them dry."[143]

Years after Muktananda's death, the scandals surrounding Siddha Yoga have by no means abated; on the contrary, they seem to have intensified in manifold ways. There appears to have been a violent split within the movement, caused by a dispute between the two successors of Muktananda, the brother-sister pair Nityananda and Gurumayi (Sri

Chidvilasananda). Although Nityananda was originally named by Muktananda as his successor, a brief six months later Gurumayi was named his cosuccessor. Shortly after that, Nityananda was embroiled in a series of scandals of his own. Having admitted that he had broken his vows of celibacy and had sexual encounters with several disciples, Nityananda stepped down from leadership in 1985. However, he claims that he was not only pressured into leaving by his sister's faction, but had been beaten and assaulted by Siddha Yoga disciples throughout the years that followed.[144]

The controversy surrounding Siddha Yoga has by no means been an affair solely of the media or American pop culture; in the past few years, it also has become a central issue in the academic study of religion. Already in 1994, Dr. Robert Thurman, a specialist in Tibetan Buddhism at Columbia University, had spoken critically of the movement and its sexual scandals: "This kind of behavior should not be legitimized by calling it Tantra."[145]

At the same time, however, a number of respected South Asianists and historians of religions have become devoted members of the Siddha Yoga movement. In 1997, several of them collaborated to publish a major volume on Siddha theology and practice, entitled *Meditation Revolution.* Yet any reader of this text is immediately struck by its rather incredible omissions and silences. In light of the intense scandal and controversy surrounding Siddha Yoga, it seems quite astonishing that a group of highly trained, respected scholars should have completely ignored the serious charges leveled at this tradition. This absence is all the more striking, given that several of the articles (such as the Brooks articles cited above) go to great lengths to assert the ethical, pure chastity and strict morality of the Siddha gurus.

As Jeffrey Kripal remarks in his review of *Meditation Revolution,* it is disappointing that these scholars, who have such intimate personal involvement with the tradition, should produce a work pervaded by these haunting silences, without any open discussion of the troubling questions surrounding Siddha Yoga. This is above all the case with regard to Muktananda's alleged sexual activities: "I am sure that Brooks is right about reading the *published* and *official literature* of the lineage as 'right-handed' in its orientation . . . but what about the *unpublished* and *unofficial* traditions, both written and oral?"[146] In sum, these scholar/disciples of Siddha Yoga are an acute example of both the potential and the pitfalls of the "insider" approach to the study of Tantra; they show us the advantages and disadvantages of studying an esoteric tradition as a devotee, an activity that brings about unique new insights along with strange new kinds of dissimulation.[147]

More recently, yet another ex-disciple—this time a trained scholar of Tantra—has come forth with further revealing evidence. Sarah Caldwell, a former member of the community who has since gone on to study the Tantric traditions of Kerala, has brought forth still more controversial material on Muktananda and his followers. Caldwell argues that there is a "secret Tantric heart within the Siddha Yoga movement which has been censored and suppressed by later tradition." Muktananda, she thinks, modeled his private life after the great Kashmir Śaivite master Abhinavagupta, including his most esoteric sexual practices. Thus Caldwell hypothesizes that he "was indeed an initiated kaula practitioner, that he aspired to model himself after Abhinavagupta and that he revered the secret teachings of the Kula path as the inner core of his power." Yet this Tantric core was a secret that had to be carefully covered over, concealed beneath intricate layers: "The events of Siddha Yoga's unwritten history replicate a pattern of poorly kept secrecy and multiple religious identities that can be traced back to the tenth century."[148]

Finally, at the 1999 meeting of the American Academy of Religions, a panel was held on the topic "Who Speaks for Siddha Yoga?" which involved both committed defenders of the tradition, like Brooks, and more suspicious critics, like Kripal and Caldwell. Although many of these troubling questions were raised, there appears to have been little rapprochement between the "insider-devotees" and the "outsider-skeptics." On the contrary, it only pointed to the conflicted nature of Tantra itself, which always seems partially concealed and partially unmasked, always the object of both embarrassment and tantalizing allure.

It is not my place here to judge the truth or falsehood of the charges brought against Muktananda; nor do I wish to accuse or acquit his disciple/scholars of censoring his more embarrassing sexual life. I simply want to point to the case of Muktananda as a striking illustration of two of the most important themes running throughout this book: (1) the increasingly close association in the modern imagination, both Indian and American, between Tantra, transgressive sexuality, scandal, and censorship; and (2) the complex, often deeply tangled relationship between scholars of Tantra and their objects of study. Muktananda's is a case in which scholars of Tantra actually seem to be implicated in—or at least accused of, right or wrongly—censoring and concealing the dark secrets of their own guru. In short, the narrative of sexual liberation through Tantra has been accompanied always by its seemingly inevitable counterpart: the narrative of scandal, censorship, violation, and betrayal that lingers behind the most progressive ideals of sexual freedom.

TANTRA.COM: ECSTASY ONLINE AND THE SPIRITUAL LOGIC OF LATE CAPITALISM

> Well, the magic millennium is upon us. Yes, the year 2000 is finally here and the revitalization of an old religion, namely Tantra, may prove to be our world's only saving grace.
>
> Dax Michaels, "The Future of Tantra," www.tantricmassage.com (2001)

> Tantra is like the Internet—expanding exponentially, links everywhere, innovative, cross-cultural, knowing no boundaries, and changing day by day. Information on Tantra . . . is everywhere now. . . . Surf the net . . . check out the scene, and ask yourself, "Isn't this truly a most exciting time? All the barriers are down. Initiation could be but a few clicks away!"
>
> Nik Douglas, *Spiritual Sex* (1997)

If neo-Tantric gurus like Osho and Trungpa embody a remarkable cross-cultural circuit from East to West and back again, then we seem to be witnessing the dissolution of all such geographic boundaries with the advent of new information technologies and the World Wide Web. Amid the ever expanding digital spaces of the Internet, where images and texts circle the globe at mind-boggling speed, the very categories East and West might appear to be collapsing and dissipating into the weird vacuous ether of cyber space. Circulating through a new network of spiritual veins (*nadīs*) and energy centers (*cakras*) comprised of telephone cables and computer terminals, the *śakti* of Tantra is "woven" and "spread out" in a new form through the electronic energy of the World Wide Web. As Douglas put it, Tantra, like the Internet, seems to be "expanding exponentially . . . cross-cultural, knowing no boundaries."

The role of technology in general, and the World Wide Web in particular, is still one of the most poorly understood aspects of contemporary religions. Indeed, the New Age and New Religious movements appear to have capitalized upon the possibilities of the Internet in ways that will take the rest of us decades to catch up to. As a variety of observers have commented, the Internet, like technology in general, opens up vast new possibilities for both oppression and liberation, capitalist exploitation and personal empowerment. "Digital reality contains alternative possibilities towards emancipation and domination."[149] On the one hand, there is no doubt that it is increasingly being used as yet another extension of consumer capitalism, advertising, and big business to all points of the globe and all aspects of human consciousness. At least as it functions today, as we see in the growing proliferation of online superstores like Amazon.com, the primary use of the World Wide Web seems to be for advertising and commercial enterprise rather than for social or spiritual liberation. On the other hand, the Internet and all technology can be used in many creative and subversive ways never imagined by its creators. The Internet, which was originally designed for U.S. military use, is now one of the primary vehicles for the spread of New Age spirituality and the seemingly "subversive" teachings of the Tantras. With its general anonymity, offering the possibility of logging on without any indication of one's gender, race, or physical appearance, the Internet opens remarkable new possibilities for the imagining and reimagining of the self.[150]

So too, with its ability to unite individuals from all points of the globe, irrespective of geographic boundaries, age, sex, or race, it also holds the potential to create new virtual communities, alternative social groups, and even ritual gatherings or new kinds of sacred space in the cyber sphere. Already, we can now enter a wide array of "virtual temples," to experience online ritual encounters with a host of cyber deities. We can even become members of virtual churches, covens, and other alternative communities, allegedly free of the hierarchies and other authority structures that confine mainline religions.

The Tantric cyber surfers have been among the first to exploit the new possibilities of the Internet. As Amy Lavine observes in her study of the changing face of Tibetan Buddhism in America, Vajrayāna Buddhists have skillfully "capitalize[d] on the premium placed on the swift retrieval of information and the constantly moving and relocating nature of American culture," by providing a vast exotic world of sounds, graphics, and icons that allow a "level of access and a vicarious experience of participation unheard of in traditional Tibet."[151] As Rachel McDermott suggests in her study of Kālī, we are witnessing a remarkable global interplay between Indian and Western imaginations, ancient traditions and contemporary surfers of the Internet, mediated by the strange new world of cyber space.[152] In the last few years, the teachings and rituals of Tantra have become among the most widespread of the various alternative spiritualities available online, transmitting what one author calls the "cybernetics of sex and love."[153] Through the seemingly egalitarian medium of the Internet, they profess to offer a more accessible, nonelitist brand of Tantrism, a form of Tantric sex available to anyone regardless of status or education. One need only enter the word "tantra" into any good search engine to generate several hundred sites, bearing titles such as "Sacred Sex: Karessa, Tantra, and Sex Magic," "Extended Orgasm: A Sexual Training Class," "Oceanic Tantra," or "Ceremonial Sensual Pleasuring."

> The enormous variety of sexual-fantasy scenarios offered in the media, over the phone, and on the Internet tells us that nowadays nothing is off limits. . . . Using the information superhighway we can get on with finding out . . . what our sexual fantasies really are and how we want to live them out. We can do this interactively . . . irrespective of country borders. . . . Tantra data on the information superhighway will lead spiritual travelers directly to their goal.[154]

Thus we find a proliferation of new ritual spaces, in which individuals disconnected in physical space can enter virtual temples and participate in online *pūjā*s (worship). A visitor to the "Kali Mandir," for example, is invited to experience a kind of cyber *darśan* (a "visual encounter" with a particular deity), and to perform a virtual *pūjā,* by offering fruits and flowers at the computer screen. One of the most remarkable of these new virtual spaces is the Third Millennium Magic web site, which offers an explicitly late-twentieth-century form of "American Tantra," adapted for a postmodern, globalized, online audience: "American Tantra (tm) is a fresh eclectic weaving of sacred sexual philosophies drawn . . . from around the world, both ancient and modern. . . . In American Tantra (tm) it is vital to embrace our sexuality . . . and celebrate it in every aspect of our daily life."[155]

Ultimately, its advocates claim, the cyber-sexual encounters of the Internet offer truly transformative, even utopian possibilities. As Douglas suggests, they help "reprogram our biocomputer with the spiritual software that tantra offers," rewriting the damaged psychic software of individuals who have been sexually misprogrammed by Western society: "Our bodily 'hardware' is desperately in need of spiritual 'software,' of new spiritual programming. Tantra can best be viewed as an extremely well-tested spiritual software designed specifically for this time, software that, when correctly implanted, imparts world happiness and spiritual liberation in this lifetime."[156]

The goal of this spiritual reprogramming is nothing less than a completely mind-blowing experience of ultimate orgasm—a hyper-real, cyborgasm that utterly transcends the limited sensual pleasure we achieve in ordinary human intercourse. According to an article called "Sexual Energy Ecstasy," reproduced on tantra.com:

> Real Tantric sex blows your mind completely because it takes you beyond all our conceptions of everyday reality. . . . It rips your mind off. . . . The point of Tantric sex is that it will take you out of your head and down into your body. . . . Tantra is about learning to let of go of the mind and discover your supreme self hidden in the heart.[157]

Ultimately, as the American Tantra web site says, the human body itself becomes a kind of terminal in this World Wide Web of flowing energy, a virtual temple of erotic ecstasy, bursting with a "new frequency of living love and light":

> Understanding that our bodies are temples for expressing divinity we can . . . expand, celebrate and share VIBRATIONAL ENGORGEMENT in every cell of our body . . . blending sex and spirit. . . . The benefits we have experienced include: more vitality, physical and spiritual health, positivity and pleasure! (Juice it up, way up!)[158]

Ironically, it is precisely through the Internet, by participating in online ecstasy via modem, mouse, and video screen, that we are said to achieve the ultimate *physical* experience, to achieve the full realization of our bodily and sexual nature.

Perhaps we are witnessing here the birth of a new vision of the human body itself, reconfigured for the digital era. This would seem to be the ultimate fantasy of creating an incorporeal spiritual body, a new cyber self, in which telephone wires become the *nāḍī*s of a virtual subtle corpus, computer terminals become the new *cakra*s or nodes of energy, and the flow of vital *prāṇa* becomes the infinite stream of information transmitted by digital code. As Arthur Kroker suggests, this is perhaps the digital generation's version of the age-old struggle between body and spirit, between the corruptible flesh and the dream of an incorruptible otherworld: "Not something new, digital reality continues anew a very ancient story: the struggle between two irreconcilable elements in the human drama—the unwanted reality of the decay of the flesh and the long-dreamed promised land of escape from the body organic of the pre-technological body. . . . [T]hat's the utopia . . . of digital reality."[159] Yet unlike pessimistic, world-denying cyber movements such as Heaven's Gate, the cyber *tāntrika* seeks a kind of ecstasy that would unite *both* the digital and the physical realms—a cyborgasm that combines the incorruptibility of cyber space with the most this-worldly sensual pleasure in the flesh.

Tantra and the Spiritual Logic of Late Capitalism

> The days of the nations are over, the days of divisions are over, the days of the politicians are over. We are moving in a tremendously new world, a new phase of humanity—and the phase is that there can only be one world now, only one single humanity. And then there will be a tremendous release of energies.
>
> Osho, *Autobiography*

> The Market is becoming the first truly world religion, binding all corners of the globe more and more tightly into a world view and set of values whose religious role we overlook because we insist on seeing them as "secular."
>
> David Loy, "The Religion of the Market" (1997)

Our venture into Tantric cyber space has brought us full circle. We have retraced what Max Müller long ago called "that world-wide circle through which, like an electric current, Oriental thought could run to the West and Western thought return to the East."[160] For we have journeyed from the American appropriation of Tantra, with its redefinition of Tantra as "spiritual sex," to the exportation of "neo-Tantra," which has been packaged anew for a global marketplace and reappropriated by a wide array of spiritual consumers in both the East and the West. In the process, Tantra has undergone a series of important transformations; no longer an esoteric path aimed at the acquisition of power, Tantra not only has been publicized widely, but also sexualized and sensationalized—that is, identified with radically liberating, hyperorgasmic, and often deliciously scandalous sex.

At least as it is portrayed in contemporary popular discourse, Tantra would seem in many ways the ideal religion of and for consumer capitalist society at the start of the millennium. It suggests a remarkable fit with the particular cultural and economic formation that has been variously dubbed "post-industrialism" (Bell), "post-Fordism" (Harvey), or "disorganized capitalism" (Offe).[161] Yet whatever its name, most observers agree, the contemporary global economic system is by no means postcapitalist. On the contrary, it is *hypercapitalist,* or, in Ernest Mandel's terms, a *purer form of capitalism* than any seen before, one which allows for the most powerful and successful application of capitalist principles to all aspects of human life. Since the early 1970s and, above all, since the abandonment of the gold standard and the subsequent "dematerialization" of money, there has been a shift from the "Fordist" economics of modern industrial capitalism to a more pervasive process of "flexible accumulation." In the global marketplace of postmodernity, funds can be transferred and exchanged instantaneously, from any point on the planet, through a network of constantly shifting, increasingly flexible corporate structures and modes of consumption.[162]

At the same time, late capitalism has been accompanied by a series of marked shifts on the cultural level. As Fredric Jameson summarizes it, the "cultural logic of late capitalism" is characterized by a general loss of faith in any grand, unifying view of the world or human history (a death of "metanarratives," to use Lyotard's phrase) and a concomitant sense of intense fragmentation, pluralism, or "heteroglossia," which mirrors the bewildering diversification in consumer society itself.[163] Instead of the construction of any unifying metanarrative, the dominant logic of late capitalism is "pastiche" and "bricolage"—the freewheeling syncretism of diverse elements drawn from disparate historical and cultural eras, patched together solely by the whim of the individual consumer. Today, we "no longer produce monumental works of the modernist type but ceaselessly reshuffle the fragments . . . of older cultural productions, in some new . . . bricolage: metabooks which cannibalize other books."[164] And instead of the ideal of unity, order, or harmony, the late-capitalist aesthetic is one of physical intensity, shock value, immediate gratification, and ecstatic experience. As Terry Eagleton observes, "Its stance toward cultural tradition is one of irreverent pastiche and its contrived depthlessness undermines all metaphysical solemnities . . . by a brutal aesthetics of squalor and shock."[165]

Perhaps the most obvious aspect of late capitalism, however, is the progressive extension of the logic of the marketplace to all aspects of culture. In the "market-like conditions of modern life," as Jürgen Habermas puts it, everything tends to become a commodity that may be bought and sold, from art to politics to religion itself.[166] Now forced to compete in the marketplace alongside other secular businesses, religion tends to become yet another consumer product within the supermarket of values. The believer, meanwhile, is free to choose from a wide array of religious options, to piece together his or her personalized spiritual pastiche:

> Max Weber's metaphor . . . of religion striding into the marketplace of worldly affairs and slamming the monastery door behind, becomes further transformed in modern society with religion placed very much in the consumer marketplace. . . . Individuals [are] able to select form a plurality of suitably packaged bodies of knowledge in the super-market of lifestyles. . . . The tendency in modern societies is for religion to become a private leisure pursuit purchased in the market like any other consumer lifestyle.[167]

Finally, as the logic of the marketplace has spread to all facets of human life, it has also brought about fundamental shifts in our attitudes toward the body, physical pleasure, and desire. As Featherstone, Turner, and others suggest, there has been a basic shift from the early capitalist attitude based on the Protestant work ethic, thriftiness, and innerworldly asceticism, to a late-capitalist attitude based on mass consumption, physical pleasure, and hedonistic enjoyment. In consumer culture the body ceases to be a vessel of sin or an unruly vessel of desires that must be disciplined and mastered—rather, the body is proclaimed as the ultimate source of gratification, enjoyment, and fulfillment: "In the growth of a consumer society with its emphasis on the athletic/beautiful body we see a major transformation of values from an emphasis on the control of the body for ascetic reasons to the manipulation of the body for aesthetic purposes."[168]

All of these general cultural aspects of late capitalism, I would argue, appear in striking form in the various popular appropriations of Tantra. First, as an avowedly "religionless religion" or antireligion, neo-Tantrism rejects all traditional metanarratives and established ideologies, openly embracing the radical pluralism, heteroglossia, and freewheeling pastiche of consumer culture. As Rajneesh explains, Tantra is not an ideology or a grand narrative about the universe: on the contrary it is a nonreligion, an antiphilosophy, whose aim is precisely to deconstruct the ideologies and institutions that bind us to this world: "The Tantric attitude . . . is not an attitude because . . . it has no concepts, it is not a philosophy. It is not a religion, it has no theology. It doesn't believe in words, theories, doctrines. It wants to look at life without any philosophy, without any theory. . . . [I]t is a no-attitude."[169] Or, to quote another popular Tantric guru, Bubba Free John (alias Da Love Ananda or Adi Da), even the teachings of the guru are ultimately empty and worthless. They too are so much "garbage," whose sole aim is to reveal to us the futility of all truths, the emptiness of all spiritual and moral doctrines: "Everything the guru gives you is garbage, and he expects you to throw it away, but you meditate on it. All these precious experiences, all this philosophy . . . none of them is the Divine. They are garbage." "The enlightened person . . . is a seducer, a madman, a hoax, a libertine, a fool, a moralist, a sayer of truths . . . a god. He demonstrates the futility of all things."[170]

Instead of an ideology or master narrative, Tantra is presented as a noninstitutional, universal tradition drawn from the sacred heritage of all cultures. This was already apparent in the early Naropa Institute in Boulder, where Tibetan Tantra mingled freely with Sufi dance, T'ai Ch'i, and the psychology of Gregory Bateson.[171] And it has become even more apparent in recent New Age versions of Tantra, which incorporate everything from ancient Greece and Rome, to Egypt and Mesopotamia, to Native American spirituality and Hebrew Kabbalah. As "simple non-denominational sacred sex for everyday folks," designed for "open-minded sensual beings irrespective of race, gender or faith," Tantra is thus "a way of life drawing inspiration from the realizations of the Enlightened of all traditions."[172] So it is that most neo-tantric authors feel free to draw eclectically from all variety of sacred and secular teachings, creating their own spiritual-sexual pastiche to fit the tastes of their consumers. "The essence of Tantra . . . is not specifically Indian or Tibetan, Hindu or Buddhist. . . . [I]t is as native to the Bronx as to Bengal. . . . [T]here is a Path of Excess which . . . can lead to the heights rather than the depths."[173]

Second, as an offspring of the late-capitalist era, neo-Tantra centers around an aesthetics of intensity, hedonism, and shock. According to Trungpa, Rajneesh, and other neo-Tantric gurus, the ordinary human being is trapped in the dysfunctional patterns of socialization created by mainstream education, politics, and religion: the only way to free us from these destructive patterns is through the intense shock tactics of Tantra—the explicit violation of moral laws through illicit sexuality, indulgence in food, drugs, and wild parties. Their aim is to shatter our usual ways of conceptualizing reality and to project us into the ultimate state of ecstasy beyond all worldly constraints. As Da Love Ananda put it in his characteristically irreverent style,

> The Guru's function is to undermine all this, to make the world show itself. He makes the Goddess pull down her pants and then you see her asshole.
>
> What do I know? . . . No one agrees with me. . . . They all tell me I'm mad. . . . The Goddess used to say, "Yield to me," and I fucked her brains loose. I never listened to anyone.[174]

The aim of Tantra is not to fill our minds with moral codes, rituals, or institutional structures. Rather, it is meant to break down all confining structures through the sheer intensity of physical pleasure, to realize our true selves beyond all moral or institutional restraints: "sex magic is . . . as individual as the persons involved. There are no rules for sex magic. However, there has to be good sex. . . . The idea of 'To thine own self be true' is essential."[175]

Tantra, in these accounts, is thus the only spiritual path that actually accepts and affirms human beings as the creatures they truly are—pleasure-seeking, desiring, sensual creatures, who need to satisfy their hedonistic urges in order to be self-realized and fulfilled individuals: "Tantra is a great yea-sayer," as Rajneesh puts it, "it says yes to everything."[176] Or as another neo-Tantric guru, Swami Nostradamus Virato, proclaims, "The art of Tantra . . . could be called spiritual hedonism, which says 'eat drink and be merry' but with full awareness. . . . Tantra says YES to sex! . . . DO IT NOW! Life!"[177]

Thus, one of the most common themes throughout much recent literature on Tantra is the "Be all that you can be" ethic—the idea that Tantra provides the means of enjoying life to the fullest, of achieving worldly goals, pleasure, and success, as well as spiritual growth. As Alan Watts put it, "Explore the fascination of desire, love and lust to the limit. Accept and enjoy without reservation the ego that you seem to be."[178] As another, more recent New Age *tāntrika* declares, when we embrace the Tantric path we discover our own innermost self, and we realize that our very self is divine: "Tantra wants me to awaken all my potential, to unfold my personality as a whole. . . . *[T]he aim of Tantra is total ecstasy.*"[179]

Perhaps most strikingly, Tantra also appears to have become the ideal religion for late-capitalist society as a specifically *consumer religion*—a form of spirituality that does not deny but actually embraces our material impulses for wealth, financial success, and power. As a variety of observers have noted, the New Age as a whole tends to foster a kind of "consumer approach to religion," offering a wide array of religious products, as readily available as the products on the shelves of Walmart, emphasizing the freedom of the individual spiritual shopper, and championing the union of spiritual realization with material enjoyment. As Feuerstein comments, "the contemporary scene [is] a spiritual supermarket" that caters to the dominant "quick fix consumer mentality" and the desire for instant spiritual and material gratification.[180] As the perfect wedding of *mukti* and *bhukti,* liberation and pleasure, Tantra seems to fit perfectly with this consumer mentality.

As we have seen in the case of Crowley and his disciples, Tantric sex can be used as a practical technique to generate money and financial prosperity. And this use of Tantric sex magic has become an increasingly popular technique in many current forms of neo-Tantra. When we explore the "Tantra: Sex Magic" link on the tantra.com web site, we find that Tantric sex can be used to achieve the most worldly of aims. By focusing the power of orgasm through ritual sex, we can use that awesome sexo-spiritual force to realize any worldly desire:

> The SMRCP [Sex Magic Reality Creation Process] is about maintaining one's focus during orgasm and channeling the energy into creating reality, any reality, whether it's creating a new job, car, experience, relationships, etc.
>
> See, hear, taste, smell and feel the creation as if it's real. . . . What is your life like when you earn $85,000? What does it FEEL like? Make it big, in Technicolor. . . . Do whatever brings you to orgasm . . . masturbation or sex with a supportive partner.[181]

Perhaps the most explicitly consumer-oriented of all the modern Tantric masters was Osho-Rajneesh. Rajneesh made it quite clear that his ideal of the self-realized human being or "Superman" was by no means some otherworldly ascetic, but rather what he called "Zorba the Buddha"—one who combines the healthy materialism of Zorba the Greek with the spiritual realization of the Buddha: "I teach a sensuous religion. I want Gautama the Buddha and Zorba the Greek to come closer and closer; my disciple has to be Zorba-the-Buddha. Man is body-soul together. Both have to be satisfied."[182] Not only was he unopposed to economic success, but he was an open advocate of consumer capitalism. Particularly in its American variety, capitalism is for Rajneesh the natural condition of the human being, for it is the triumph of the powerful few, who are willing to struggle and succeed, over the weak masses, who remain jealous and lazy: "the creation of wealth is the task of genius. . . . Socialism is the jealously of the masses, of the have-nots against the few who succeed in doing something for mankind."[183] As Rajneesh put it, in his typically unapologetic style, "I don't condemn wealth. Wealth is a perfect means which can enhance people in every way and make life rich in all ways. The materially poor can never become spiritual." "People are unequal and a fair world has to give people full freedom to be unequal. Capitalism has grown out of freedom. It is a natural phenomenon."[184]

During his years in the United States, Rajneesh was quite successful in realizing this wedding of capitalism and spirituality, financial prosperity and otherworldly transcendence. And rather remarkably, the newly reborn Osho community in India has become perhaps more successful still, emerging as a universal spiritual enterprise for a new global world order. No small part of the appeal, it would seem, is Osho's blending of spirituality with material prosperity. As he later explained his taste in expensive automobiles and his collection of Rolls-Royces, "People are sad, jealous and thinking that Rolls-Royces don't fit with spirituality. I don't see that there is any contradiction. . . . In fact, sitting in a bullock cart it is very difficult to be meditative; a Rolls-Royce is the best for spiritual growth."[185]

Not surprisingly, the "Just do it" religion of Tantra also comes with a certain price tag. Participation in the art of Tantric loving appears to demand a fairly affluent consumer, who can afford the wide range of books, videos, workshops, and therapies, not to mention the wide line of spiritual-sexual accessories. Thus, online at "Tantra Gift Shop" or at "E-Sensuals Catalogue," one can choose from vast array of Tantric commodities, including books, videos, artworks, herbs, vitamins, incense, aphrodisiacs, and other sexual aids, such as the Goddess Spot G-Spot Stimulator ($49), Lust Dust ($22), Hawaiian Goddess Tantric Massage Oil ($13), Bawdy Butter ($8.50), and even the full Tantric Pleasuring Package ($198).[186]

"AFTER THE ORGY"

> I have a vision for the future where all the necessary sex education will be available for everyone. . . . No one will ever go hungry for sex because there will be sex kitchens all over town serving sex instead of soup. . . . We will learn how to use orgasm to cure disease as some of the ancient Tantrics and Taoists did. . . . In the future, everybody will be so sexually satisfied, there'll be an end to violence, rape and war. We will establish contact with extra-terrestrials and they will be very sexy.
>
> Annie Sprinkle (1996)

> If it were necessary to characterize the state of things I would say that it is after the orgy. The orgy is . . . the explosive moment of modernity, that of liberation in all domains. Political liberation, sexual liberation, liberation of productive forces, liberation of destructive forces. . . . Today everything is liberated . . . we find ourselves before the question: WHAT ARE WE TO DO AFTER THE ORGY?
>
> Jean Baudrillard, *The Transparency of Evil* (1993)

This chapter has only scratched the surface of contemporary appropriations of Tantra in the popular imagination. If space allowed, I could have explored a variety of other neo-Tantric phenomena, such as Robert Svoboda's popular series based on the life and teachings of a modern Aghorī; firsthand accounts by Westerners who have "gone Tantric," like June Campbell and Daniel Odier; Tantra-practicing rock stars (and even bands, in both India and the United States, who call themselves "Tantric"); the rapidly expanding realms of S&M Tantra and gay Tantra (that even claim as advocates respected Tantric scholars like Jeffrey Hopkins); not to mention the various attempts to wed Tantra with Native American, neopagan, and even Christian spiritual practices.[187]

But even from this brief overview, it is not difficult to see why Tantra has become so popular in contemporary popular culture. Nor is it hard to imagine why Tantra has been celebrated as what Nik Douglas calls the "Science of the Future," and even as the "Engine of Political Change" that will reunite humankind during this millennium in a "new spiritual democracy": "The Future of Tantra is like Woman's best Orgasm. . . . It is without limits. . . . Tantra is a vast spiritual experience, oceanic, wondrous and unpredictable."[188] Tantra is a brand of spirituality that can magically unite hedonism and transcendence, self-realization and this-worldly prosperity. As the most radical and transgressive form of spirituality, Tantra (not unlike capitalism itself) oversteps every taboo and shatters every social restriction. Thus performance artists like the notorious Annie Sprinkle—a self-proclaimed "post-porn modernist"—uses her live performances of Tantric sex as a vehicle for liberation from all forms of sexual containment or social taboo.[189] As one Indian American author, Hakim Bey, explains, Tantra is thus the most appropriate path for our own age of radical sexuality, violence, transgression, and power in the Kali yuga of modernity:

> Her age must contain horrors. . . . To go thru CHAOS, to ride it like a tiger, to embrace it (even sexually) & absorb its shakti . . . this is the faith of the Kali yuga. Creative nihilism. For those who follow it she promises enlightenment & even wealth, a share of her temporal *power.* The sexuality & violence serve as metaphors in a poem which acts directly on consciousness. . . . [T]hey can be openly deployed & imbued with a sense of the holiness of *every thing* from ecstasy & wine to garbage & corpses.[190]

As such, this new image of Tantra also fits in well with contemporary attitudes toward sexuality and its liberation—what Jean Baudrillard has aptly dubbed the "culture of premature ejaculation." This is a culture rooted in an imagined dialectic of "repression" and "liberation," or the belief that our sexuality has been suppressed and denied by prudish Victorian values and that we must now free our sexuality through hedonistic enjoyment:

> Ours is a culture of premature ejaculation. More and more, all seduction . . . disappears behind the *naturalized* sexual imperative calling for an immediate relation of a desire. . . .
>
> Nowadays one no longer says: "You've got a soul and you must save it," but "You've got a sexual nature and you must learn how to use it well." . . . "You've got a libido and you must learn how to spend it."[191]

Yet this leaves us with the troubling question of just what is there left to do "after the orgy"—after every taboo has been violated, every prohibition transgressed, and every desire satiated.

I would suggest that the investigation of the contemporary imagining of Tantra has much broader comparative implications. The popular appropriations of Tantra give us some important insights into the many ways in which traditional religions are being adapted, transformed, and exploited in the strange new world of late capitalism. We might also compare, for example, the appropriations of Native American spirituality, Afro-Brazilian movements like Santeria, and even traditional Jewish traditions like Kabbalah (which now claims popular entertainers like Roseanne Barr among its disciples). In each of these cases, we find ancient religious traditions entering more and more into the ever expanding web of global capitalism and consumerism. This process could, of course, be seen as a good and healthy phenomenon, contributing to our awareness of other cultures and leading the way to a more diverse, pluralistic, and tolerant global community. But it could also be seen as quite negative, and even as a form of neocolonialism and cultural imperialism, yet another example of the West's exploitation of the sacred artifacts of other peoples. As Torgovnick points out in her discussion of the fascination with the "primitive" in modern culture, the popular celebration of globalism and pluralism as a carnivalesque liberation is rather naive, to say the least. For it masks the deeper socioeconomic disparity that continues to structure relations between East and West, between First World and Third World; it ignores the forces of neocolonialism and cultural exploitation that continue to rule much of the late-capitalist global marketplace:

> There is a common problematic view in discussions of global culture. . . . The problem is one of carnivalesque rejoicing . . . of believing that contact

> and polyphony are inherently liberating. . . . But carnivals do not last. . . . Behind the festivities are social and economic facts we should not forget.
>
> The problem with the carnival idea . . . is that it ignores the real social and economic cost of the global village. . . . It may sound a discordant note at the carnival, but that note is still heard—daily—in the ghettos and shantytowns of the urban jungle.[192]

However we wish to interpret this phenomenon, it would seem that in this age of increasing pluralism in the late-capitalist world order, we need to practice relentless self-consciousness and self-criticism. We need always to ask ourselves whether we are working toward a genuinely postimperial, pluralistic global community, or whether we are merely absorbing all other, even previously uncolonized, peoples' cultures into the ever expanding network of global capitalism (which some would describe as an even more insidious form of neocolonialism). In other words, to quote Chogyam Trungpa in his work on the widespread disease of "spiritual materialism," we need to ask whether or not "we have simply created a shop, an antique shop."[193]

Conclusion

Reimagining Tantra in Contemporary Discourse

This warning has been given hundreds of times: Don't get into Tantra just like that. . . . It's dangerous. . . . Every Tantric text . . . begins with that warning: Be careful, think twice . . . don't take this carelessly. But interestingly, *the more you put students off, the more interested they become.*

Chogyam Trungpa, *Journey without Goal* (1985)

The twentieth century will undoubtedly have discovered the related categories of exhaustion, excess, the limit and transgression—the strange and unyielding form of these irrevocable movements which consume and consummate us.

Michel Foucault, "A Preface to Transgression," (1963)

At this point, I need to try to tie together the many loose ends and dangling strands that constitute my own genealogy of the tangled threads of Tantra. Obviously, this book cannot claim to be comprehensive or complete. Concerned primarily with the imagining of "Tantra" as a modern category, I have not tried to undertake the far more difficult task of narrating the actual historical development of those particular texts, traditions, practices, and peoples who would later be identified as Tantric. Moreover, as I quickly realized when I began to delve into the contemporary popular literature on Tantra, this is a topic that is too vast for a single book. Thus I have had to leave out an enormous amount of very interesting material. I have not attempted by any means to write a definitive history of Tantra, but rather to tease out and retrace a few of the most important threads that have been woven, tangled, and matted together into the complex snarl that we now call the Tantric traditions.

The imagining of Tantra, it would seem, has turned out to be something more complicated, much more messy, and yet also more interesting than the simple history of an indigenous Indian category or the simple imposition of a Western category onto the passive surface of the exotic Orient. By no means a predictable Saidian narrative of Orientalism, this genealogy of Tantra offers a real challenge to much of the contemporary scholarship in postcolonial and subaltern studies. For Tantra has emerged as a conflicted, contested, and contradictory category, passed back and forth between Indian and Western imaginations, undergoing new transformations in each new historical encounter. It is in this sense that Tantra seems to be analogous, on a conceptual level, to Benjamin's notion of the "dialectical image," as a "critical constellation of past and present," composed not of smooth historical continuities, but rather of "rough and jagged places at which the continuity of the tradition breaks down."[1] As a dialectical category, Tantra is not singular or stable; it is something that is "non-homogeneous" and "fragmented," "which on account of its awkwardness of fit, cracks, and violent juxtapositionings can actively embody both a presentation and counter-presentation of historical time."[2] Rather than a "history" of Tantra, this book has been more like a genealogy (in Foucault's sense) of these many shifting dialectical images of Tantra—an attempt to work backward from our contemporary imagining of Tantra, to retrace the many "accidents, minute deviations, the complete reversals" that have given shape to this complex category in the present.

In simplest form, the imagining of Tantra could be outlined as in figure 14, which is adapted loosely from Benjamin's analysis of the dialectical nature of the commodity.[3] Tantra thus lies at the nexus of a series of conflicting extremes—the archaic past and the modern age of darkness; sexual liberation and sexual depravity; political freedom and political violence—each of which is seized upon in different historical moments.

Perhaps most importantly, we have found that the image of Tantra has progressively shifted from a tradition associated with secrecy, danger, and occult power to one associated primarily with sexual liberation and physical pleasure. At either extreme of this dialectic we have seen, on one hand, the Orientalists' and reformers' horror at Tantric licentiousness and, on the other, the contemporary celebration of Tantric freedom and empow-

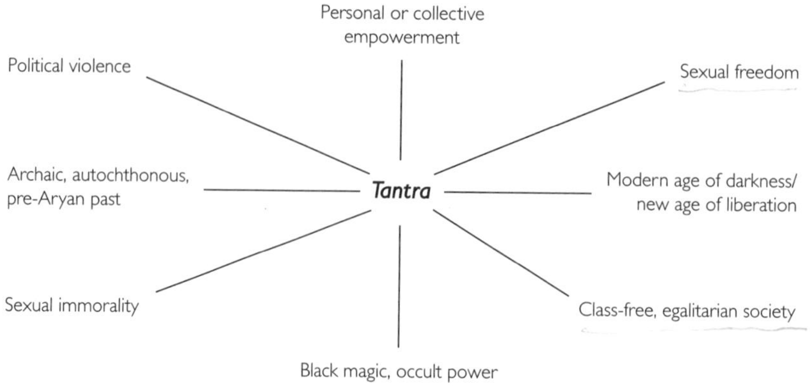

Figure 14. The imagining of Tantra.

erment. As such, this genealogy of Tantra also has turned out to be a political history of the history of religions; for the construction of Tantra has been intimately tied from the outset to particular power formations and political interests—to colonialism and anticolonial revolt; to nationalism and postcolonial identity; to the political investments of scholars of religions; and finally to the global capitalist economy at the turn of the millennium. As an extreme form of Otherness or radical alterity, it has formed a dark mirror against which both Indian and Western authors have imagined their own cultural, religious, and political identities.

"Tantra Yoga: The Practice Everyone's Talking About!" Tantra, Sex, and Neocolonial Angst in Contemporary Rishikesh

> Tantra is a very bad practice. It is a dirty, filthy path. You will never get to heaven by the Tantric path. The *tāntrika* seeks power in this world—he wants *śakti* and he also wants money—but he will not go to heaven.
>
> Nāga Sannyāsī, interviewed in Rishikesh (22 March 2001)

To illustrate some of my concluding thoughts on the strange, contemporary, cross-cultural imagining of Tantra, I will relate some of my observations from my time in Rishikesh, one of the most important holy sites of north India. Although I had spent a good deal of time at various Tantric sites in India and Nepal—such as Tārāpīṭh in West Bengal, Kāmākhyā in Assam, and Kathmandu in Nepal—I found Rishikesh to be one of the most remarkable, because of the weird intersection of East-

Figure 15. An Aghorī and *tāntrika*s in Rishikesh, July 2000. Photo by the author.

ern and Western cultures and the resulting new forms of Tantra.[4] Situated along the Ganges at the base of the Himalayan foothills, Rishikesh has long been a favorite haven for *sādhu*s from all over India. And since the 1960s, with the visit of the Beatles, Donovan, and Mia Farrow to Maharishi Mahesh Yogi's Transcendental Meditation Ashram, it has also become a Mecca for white hippies and spiritual seekers from all over Europe and North America, for Indian *sādhu*s and for white travelers in search of enlightenment and/or cheap hashish (figure 15). For many young American and European travelers, the *sādhus*—and particularly the radical *sādhu*s like the Aghorīs, Nāths, and *tāntrika*s—represent the highest ideals of freedom, self-discovery, and experimental drug use.

Tantra has become one of the most important, yet also controversial, spiritual topics in this ancient holy site. Shortly after my arrival, I was intrigued to see a flyer advertising courses—"Tantra Yoga: The Practice Everyone's Talking About!"—plastered all over town, a little ironic, given the esoteric nature of most Indian Tantric traditions. During my time in Rishikesh, I had the opportunity to interview a wide range of *sādhus*—both Indian yogis and the new breed of white *sādhu*—and came upon a tremendous diversity of opinions regarding Tantra. Thus I met with several Nāth yogis who proudly identified themselves as *tāntrika*s and claimed Tantra to be the highest spiritual path, integrating yoga and *bhoga,* spiritual transcendence and this-worldly enjoyment. Interestingly enough, both the Nāths and the Aghorīs with whom I spoke clearly distinguished the *tāntrika* path from the *aghora* path. In contrast to most Western observers, who often identify the Aghorī as the quintessential *tāntrika,* most of these *sādhu*s identified Tantra as a more restrained path and *aghora* as a more radical, transgressive path (often distinguished as "right hand" from "left hand"). "*Aghora* is the most direct path," one black-clad *sādhu* explained to me, "Tantra is still an indirect path. For the Aghorī, there are no restraints, there is nothing in-between."

Perhaps the majority of *sādhu*s with whom I spoke, however, were generally critical and suspicious of the *tāntrika* path. Thus, one of the older *nāga* (naked) *sannyāsī*s whom I met spoke disparagingly of Tantra as a "filthy path," concerned primarily with the acquisition of worldly power and wealth: "they sleep in urine, they eat anything, they see nothing as unclean." But they will never get to heaven, he assured me. Playing ironically off the usual definition of Tantra as "yoga and *bhoga,*" another older *nāga* defined Tantra simply as "*yoga-bhoga-roga*"—that is, spiritual practice, sensual pleasure, and addiction or disease.

But surely the most intriguing phenomenon in contemporary Rishikesh is the birth of a wholly new kind of *tāntrika*—what we might call the "white *sādhu*" or the "passport *sādhu.*" Bearing *rudrākṣa-mālā*s (rosaries) in one hand and guitars in the other, the white *sādhu*s are young Americans and Europeans who wear their hair in long, tangled dreadlocks, dress in the colored robes of *sannyāsī*s, and blend Rastafarianism and drugs with the *Kāma Sūtra* and Tantric yoga. A strange mixture of Dead Heads and wandering Bāuls, these white *sādhu*s travel from holy site to holy site, clutching their Lonely Planet guide next to their *Bhagavad Gītā,* some in search of enlightenment, some merely in search of cheap hashish. For many of the ones I met in Rishikesh, Tantra was the epitome of everything they sought in India and the opposite of everything they had left behind in the West: freedom in every sense of the word and a kind of bliss that is at once transcendent and yet utterly physical. The Indian *sannyāsī*s in Rishikesh seemed to have mixed reactions to these white *sādhu*s: most viewed them with mild curiosity and guarded interest; some regarded them with utter disdain and reproach; and some actually sought to attract them to live in their ashrams, as a kind of cross-cultural status symbol and emblem of spiritual power.

Probably because of my own long hair and beard, and my female companion, I was occasionally taken to be a white *tāntrika*—and not always in a positive sense. Once as my friend and I were crossing the Lakshman Jhula bridge, a young Ramakrishna monk angrily approached us and, with no apparent provocation, began to verbally abuse us, accusing us of sexual immorality. He proceeded to complain loudly and at great length about the troupes of young Westerners invading India along with their loose sexuality; in his eyes this is simply a new form of colonialism, which only continues the worst kind of imperialism from which India had struggled so long to free itself. No sooner had India driven out the British, who exploited the land economically and politically, then a whole new wave of Western colonizers invaded, who now exploit India's spiritual traditions. He assured us, however, that India would soon be closing its doors to all foreign tourists, with their corrupting immorality, and that the matter was at that very moment being discussed in Parliament.

In sum, what one finds at key spiritual-tourist centers like Rishikesh is a striking example of the dialectical imagining of Tantra—a complex, contradictory figure that lies at the critical intersection between East and West, materialism and spirituality, sexuality and transcendence, cross-cultural dialogue and neo-Orientalist misrepresentation.

Reimagining Tantra: Embodied Tantra and Corporeal Spirituality

> The Supreme Reality has the form of bliss and
> exists within the human body.
> Thus the wise offer the gods the flesh of their
> own bodies.
>
> *Yoginī Tantra* (1.6.53)

> The idea that in order to get clear about the meaning of a general term one had to find the common element in all its applications has shackled philosophical investigations; for it had not only led to no result, but also made the philosopher dismiss as irrelevant *the concrete cases which alone could have helped him to understand the usage of the general term.*
>
> Ludwig Wittgenstein, *The Blue and Brown Books* (1958)

If it is true that Tantra is an imaginary construction, to a large degree a result of the encounter between Indian and Western imaginations over the last two hundred years, a few questions arise: How can we now (or indeed should we even try to) reimagine Tantra in a more useful way in contemporary discourse? Should we abandon the term altogether (as some have proposed we abandon the equally problematic terms "Hinduism" and "religion"), substituting a plurality of more genuinely "indigenous" terms? Or is it still possible to use the term in a more sophisticated, or at least less problematic, form?

There have, of course, been a number of attempts to reimagine Tantra in the past few decades, in both the scholarly and popular imaginations. In American popular culture, as we saw in the last chapter, most authors have presented a form of Tantra that is stripped down and simplified for a contemporary audience—or a form of Tantra divested of the excess baggage that burdens its traditional Indian forms. Most of the neo-*tāntrika*s argue that it is possible to cull the ecstatic, sensual dimensions of Tantric practice, while jettisoning most of the elaborate ritual, hierarchies of knowledge, and the often unsavory elitism and sexism that accompany many traditional forms of Tantra.[5]

This revisioning of Tantra for a popular Western audience has not been limited to popular New Age authors, but has been suggested even by some of the most respected scholars in the academy. Thus Jeffrey Hopkins, one of the foremost authorities on Tibetan Buddhism, has recently come out of the closet and published a gay interpretation of a Tibetan sexual manual. Taking the explicitly *heterosexual* manual, the *Tibetan Arts of Love,* by Gedun Chopel, he has published his own translation of the text from an explicitly *homosexual* perspective; thus we find masculine pronouns substituted for feminine, and male anatomy for female. For Hopkins, Tantric Buddhism is not only a spiritual path that is "sex friendly," making positive use of sexual pleasure "to gain insight into the reality behind appearances," but Tantric techniques can also be adapted in the service of gay spirituality.[6] As Hopkins explains, "Since gay persons need care, support and encouragement from their own community, I felt that in addition to translating . . . a Tibetan heterosexual sex manual, I needed to live up to my responsibilities to my own community. Thus I present a guide to gay sex infused with my perspectives from India and Tibetan culture."[7]

Most modern scholars, however, have reacted strongly against this transformation and popularization of Tantra in American culture, decrying it as a kind of "California Tantra" purveyed by ignorant charlatans who "peddle their shoddy wares."[8] We can see this scholarly denigration of the popularized versions of Tantra already in the work of Agehananda Bharati, who spoke quite critically indeed about the sloppy syncretism and gross misunderstanding that characterize most American forms of pop Tantra. Instead, Bharati argued firmly that the only way for Tantra truly to enter the West would be through solid scholarship and careful historical, linguistic, and textual study.[9] Bharati's advice largely seems to have been followed by most scholars of Tantra over the past three decades. One might well argue that much of the recent scholarship on Tantra has tended to go to the opposite extreme, often bending over backward to prove that Tantra is not in fact simply about sexual indulgence, but is rather a highly philosophical, intellectual, and even elitist enterprise, largely the province of highly educated Brahmans and upper classes. Thus Gupta and Goudriaan argue that Tantra is defined best "not as a popular movement," but as "the outgrowth of the specialized position of an intellectual elite of religious functionaries from the upper classes, as a rule, of Brahmans."[10] As Kripal argues, much recent literature has continued trends in the work of John Woodroffe—above all, his attempt to defend the *tantra*s against the accusation of scandal and immorality, and to redeem them as a sophisticated intellectual system: "Scholarship on Tantra . . . is still working in the legacy of its founder, John Woodroffe, whose work was marked by profound philosophical . . . and moral biases and an apologetic designed to rid Tantra of everything that smacked of superstition, or scandal."[11] In sum, much of the scholarship on Tantra has oscillated erratically between these two extremes—the popular celebration of Tantric freedom, healthy sensuality, and this-worldly affirmation, and the apologetic defense of Tantric philosophy, metaphysics, and mystical speculation.

For my own part, I do think that it is possible—and perhaps now simply *unavoidable* in contemporary discourse—to try to reimagine Tantra in a more useful way. First and foremost, I think it is important to admit that Tantra is an imagined category, in Jonathan Smith's sense of the term: like "religion" itself, it is the result of complex "imaginative acts of comparison and generalization," on the part of both Indian and Western authors. Like "mysticism," Tantra is to a large degree a social construction, a category that is by no means stable or fixed, but that has been "constructed in different ways at different times"; thus the current imagining of the category is only one in a series of constructions, and like the others it is "implicitly bound up with issues of authority and gender."[12]

With Douglas Brooks, I would agree that Tantra cannot be defined "monothetically"—that is, in terms of any one unifying element. Rather, it is best imagined in polythetic terms, by identifying a number of characteristics that share certain family resemblances. Tantra is thus best used, in Smith's sense, as a *tool* or "heuristic device" that we employ in order to organize and interpret a given set of phenomena. Like most categories in the history of religions, however, it is a highly pluralistic and fluid term, in need of ongoing critical examination and redefinition—less a neat and narrowly circumscribed entity than a kind of "messy hodge-podge" or "heap of rubbish."[13] To return to Wittgenstein's metaphor of the thread, Tantra is thus a complex collection of fibers, interlacing strands that have been woven and rewoven throughout history, while also interweaving with the threads of politics, power, gender, and economics. Perhaps more than simply a thread, Tantra might be better described as a great tangled snarl of crisscrossing strands, or even as a great *lint ball,* comprised of fibers and fragments from a wide range of traditions that make up the religious fabrics of Asia.

However, the polythetic definition leaves us with a basic and difficult question: namely, how do we decide when a given phenomenon shares enough of these characteristics to be identified as "Tantra"? How many and which of these family resemblances do we need before we can usefully describe a given phenomenon as "Tantric"? The answer, I would suggest, lies neither in indigenous Indian traditions nor in the imaginary projections of Western scholars. Rather, it arises out of the *historical encounter between* these traditions and the scholars who study them; the category is born through the creative interaction between the scholarly imagination and the object of study. And because both the traditions and the scholars are historically, culturally, and politically situated, the imagining of Tantra will be different in every historical moment and in every new cross-cultural encounter. As Smith reminds us, our imagining of religion and our definition of major categories such as Judaism, Hinduism, and so on, are always conditioned by our own particular *interests,* our theoretical positions and our political agendas.[14] Thus, the specific family resemblances we choose to identify as Tantric will always be tied to our own particular historical positions, normative biases, and political commitments. And for that very reason, we must always remain "relentlessly self-conscious" and self-critical in our imaginings of these academic categories, ever attentive to ways in which we ourselves are bound up in relations of power.[15] However, in contrast to Smith, I would argue that categories like Tantra are never *simply* the creation of the Western scholarly imagination; they are far more complex, joint creations, the ambiguous result of the representation and counter-representation at work between Indian and Western imaginations, reflecting the interests both of practitioners and of interpreters. Understood in this sense, Tantra is not a mere projection of our scholarly fantasies onto the passive mirror of the exotic Other, but is rather a *dialectical relation,* in which both sides are transformed through the encounter and exchange.

Ultimately, as we have seen, the very categories of Occident and Orient, spiritual East and material West, colonized and colonizer, even scholar and practitioner, begin to waver and perhaps to break down altogether. Not only have we encountered a variety of Western devotees of Tantra and Eastern proponents of American neo-Tantra; more and more, as we saw in the cases of Osho and the cyber Tantra of the Internet, there is an increasingly globalized Tantra that renders our categories antiquated and perhaps hermeneutically useless.

I would argue that what is needed most today is a fundamentally *embodied* approach to Tantra—a Tantra encountered "in the flesh." That is to say, we need to look at the peoples and traditions that we wish to identify as "Tantric" in their most material, corporeal forms, placing them firmly within their lived, social, political, and economic contexts. Following Wittgenstein, I would suggest that the abstract general term "Tantra" can be understood only in light of the most *concrete cases*—that is, the real human beings who perform "Tantric" practices. For as Debiprasad Chattopadhyaya, once pointed out, "Unlike the followers of the idealistic systems of philosophy who belittled the importance of the body and dreamt of the liberation of the soul, the Tāntrikas with their supreme emphasis on the material human body *(dehavāda),* conceived liberation only in terms of the . . . culture of the body *(kāya sādhana).*"[16] Thus, as we read in works like the classic Vaiṣṇava-Sahajiyā text, the *Ratnasāra,* "If one knows the truth of the body, he knows the truth of the universe. . . . If one understands the body, he understands the meaning of his own self. . . . From the body, one can know the grandeur of Kṛṣṇa and . . . the essence of Rādhā's love."[17]

By "embodied" Tantra, however, I emphatically do *not* mean that we should make the mistake of fetishizing the body as the center and essence of Tantra—much the way that "sex" has today become the center of most discourse about Tantra.[18] Surely it would be no great improvement merely to appropriate Tantra as yet another example of the obsession with the body in American consumer culture. Rather, by "embodied" I mean not simply the reality of the physical flesh, but also the *embodiedness of actual human agents and their struggles in the messy world of history, politics, economics, and social change.* As June Campbell argues in the remarkable story of her own involvement in Tantric Buddhism, we must resist the temptation toward either "idealisation or denial of the messy aspect" of these traditions.[19] What is most needed now is a study of Tantra seen neither as a seedy cabal of libertines nor as an abstract set of philosophical texts; rather, as Kripal suggests, we need to take Tantra seriously in its *"lived compromises and contradictions,"*[20] as a living, embodied set of traditions, with an enormous diversity of forms in many social and historical contexts.

I would follow the lead of Michel Foucault and his insistence on the fundamentally historical, contextual, constructed, and contested nature of all cultural phenomena, including those that are supposedly transcendent or sacred. Even the most seemingly "natural" categories of sexuality and the body are by no means given facts independent of culture, but are constructions that are intimately tied to historical and material interests; they must therefore be understood "on the basis of the techniques of power that are contemporary with [them]."[21] As Jeremy Carrette has argued, Foucault's work on the body and sexuality has profound implications for the contemporary study of religion. Like sex, the body, and other aspects of human experience, religion needs to be critically grounded in real historical struggles and relations of power: religion, in short, needs to be "taken out of its privileged realm and brought into the body politic and the heart of culture"; for "religious discourse is not some privileged arena free from human prejudice . . . but is rather constructed in and through the ambiguities of human living."[22] Following Foucault, I would argue that the traditions we call Tantric need to be critically examined as forms of *corporeal spirituality*—as "movement[s] that ha[ve] the imprint of a religion which speaks less of a Beyond than of the transformations in this world."[23]

In the past few years, there have been several promising approaches to the study of Tantra, which have tried to situate these traditions more concretely in their lived historical contexts. Kripal's work on Ramakrishna, Caldwell's work on Kālī worship in Kerala, Ronald Davidson's work on Indian Buddhist Tantra, and McDermott's work on Śāktism in Bengal are all important steps in this direction. A few recent authors like David Gordon White and Charles Orzech have also pointed to the important political role of Tantra as a fundamental ideology supporting kingship and royal hierarchies in Tibet, Nepal, China, and India. As White argues, "Until recent times, Tantric ritual constituted a bulwark for the state in the Indianized . . . monarchies of Asia from Nepal to Bali. . . . [I]t has been through royal support . . . that the various Tantric orders have been empowered both to promote their sectarian teachings and to consolidate their socio-economic position."[24] Conversely, White sees the contemporary state of Tantra as a kind of "broken world" that has lost its original political status and royal patronage, now surviving largely on the margins of most Asian cultures.

Yet White's otherwise valuable interpretation of Tantra strikes me as really quite elitist and one-sided, focusing only on the overtly political role of Tantra in state formation and royal power. Instead, I would argue for a much more popular and nonelitist view, taking seriously the non-Sanskritic, lower-class, and nonintellectual forms of living Tantric practice. In addition to the important forms of elite, Brahmanical, and royal Tantra, there is also an equally powerful and arguably far more widespread current of nonelite Tantric practice—what we might call lowbrow, folk, or vernacular Tantra—that has probably always proliferated on the dangerous margins of mainstream Hindu and Buddhist traditions. As we see in the Bāuls, Sahajiyās, and Kartābhajās of Bengal;[25] the teachings of illiterate saints like Bāmākṣepa or Ramakrishna;[26] the shamanic healers and possession cults of Nepal and Ladakh; the radically transgressive Aghorīs of Varanasi; the Nāth yogis throughout India;[27] the various books of pop-Tantric magic for sale throughout Indian bookstalls (figure 16); and now the spread of Tantra to the West—many, and arguably most, of the traditions we call Tantric are nonelite, oriented to the lower classes, and expressed through the crudest of vernacular tongues.[28] Hence, much further work remains to be done in order to ground the traditions that we wish to call Tantric within their embodied, historical, social, and political contexts. Perhaps then we can begin to reimagine this "general term" through its most concrete forms: as a very material, physical, and historical, even if rather messy and problematic, category in the history of religions.

Primitive Passions in a Postmodern World: Tantra and the Problem of Cross-Cultural Understanding

> When touching India, even scholars cannot be impartial. Why? Because India is not a mere subject of academic talk, but is a living force. . . . She is still potentially powerful to impose her ideas upon the world. She is still an antagonist to be reckoned with in the conflict of cultures.
>
> Sir John Woodroffe, *Bharata Shakti* (1921)

To close, I would also like to suggest that this study of Tantra in the history of religions has larger comparative implications for the problem of

Figure 16. Cover illustration for *Tārāpīṭher Bāmābatār*, a popular comic book (Calcutta: Nirmal Book Agency, n.d.).

cross-cultural understanding as a whole. For it raises, in a particularly acute way, the question of whether we are inevitably doomed to misunderstand, misrepresent, and often grossly abuse the cultural traditions of other peoples, or whether it is still possible to transcend these distorted representations and achieve a more genuine, less abusive, less exploitative, human encounter.

Much of the contemporary Western fascination with Tantra, as I argued above, is very similar to our fascination with the idea of the "primitive." As Torgovnick has shown, the West has long defined itself against its Others and opposites, whether in the form of primitives, savages, or exotic Orientals. Yet the primitive has always held a markedly ambivalent role in the Western imagination, at once denigrated as backward, uncivilized, or dangerous, and yet romantically celebrated as more fully in tune with nature, the sacred, and the mystical, ecstatic dimensions of experience. This primitive, ecstatic, and irrational dimension has in some sense always been a fundamental part of the Western imagination. When we turn to the "primitive" in our quest for the oceanic or ecstatic experience, we are in fact searching for a displaced part of ourselves that we have projected onto the exotic Other:

> The West has repeatedly tried to displace . . . the oceanic, severing it from the perceived self and projecting it outward. But the projection has never really worked. The time for denial seems long past. The recognition is overdue that primitivism is much more about us than about them. . . . It is time to realize that the quest for ecstasy is as much a part of Western fears and desires as it is a part of . . . their people.[29]

So too, I would argue, the contemporary fascination with Tantra is to a certain degree the projection of our own fantasies, repressed desires, and longings for ecstasy in the seemingly demystified, desacralized, postmodern world. But this raises the critical question: are we forever doomed to project our own fantasies onto the empty mirror of an exoticized Orient, without ever really achieving a genuine encounter or accurate understanding of other cultural traditions? And what about contemporary Indians and other peoples of Asia? Are they in turn doomed to assimilate our projected images, always conceiving themselves through the terms and categories by which Western authors have already defined them?

In his monumental study of the cross-cultural intellectual exchange between India and Europe, Wilhelm Halbfass seems to have arrived at a fairly pessimistic answer to these questions. What we have witnessed in the modern era, Halbfass believes, is the progressive "Europeanization of the world"—that is, the domination of the globe by Western culture, ideology, and discourse, to such a degree that other cultures can now only define themselves through the categories that have been imposed by the West:

> In the modern planetary system, Eastern and Western "cultures" can no longer meet one another as equal partners. They meet *in* a Westernized world, under conditions shaped by Western ways of thinking.
>
> [F]or the time being there is no escape from the global network of Europeanization and no way to avoid the conceptual and technological ways . . . of communication and interaction which the European tradition has produced.[30]

However, it seems to me that the real danger today is no longer the threat of the "Europeanization" of the world; indeed, it is no longer even the threat of "Americanization." Surely we are now living in a very different sort of global economy, where such boundaries no longer have much meaning. Rather, the threat today is perhaps the spread of consumer capitalism and the domination of the global marketplace over all local economies, polities, and cultural forms—a process of "Coca-colonization" that is no longer dominated by the West, no longer a matter of either "Occidentalization" or "Orientalization," but a far more complex product of transnational capitalism. To many observers, we seem to be living more and more in "one McWorld tied together by communications, information, entertainment and commerce" that remains "caught between Babel and Disneyland."[31] As Aijaz Ahmad has argued, we are perhaps no longer divided into three worlds, nor are we even divided into simple binarisms such as capitalist/precapitalist or modern/premodern. Instead, there is now only one world—that of international capitalism: "One of the many contradictory consequences of decolonization within a largely capitalist framework was that it brought all zones of capital into a single integrated market, entirely dominated by this supreme imperialist power."[32]

Thus many authors are quite cynical and pessimistic about the encounter between East and West in the age of global capitalism. As Gita Mehta argues, India has been subjected to the complete penetration of American mass marketing, and now any encounter between East and West will only result in the worst of both worlds: while India seeks the materialism and technological power of the West, the West seeks the exoticism, eroticism, and cheap drugs of the East. Both end up with empty distorted phantasms reflecting their own repressed desires:

> It is unlikely that either the Occidental or the Easterner has the stamina to survive the exchange of views, yet both insist on trying. . . . [T]he Easterner . . . calls what fascinates him in the West economic necessity, technology, historical imperative. . . . The Occidental . . . calls what fascinates him in the East the transcendence of economics and technology. . . . The Westerner is finding the dialectic of history less fascinating than the endless opportunities for narcissism provided by the wisdom of the East.[33]

Tantra in the style of Osho-Rajneesh, Mehta concludes, is the epitome of this superficial cross-cultural exchange: the result is the neo-Tantric who seeks instant *nirvāṇa* and soda-pop enlightenment: "When East meets West all you get is the neo-Sannyasi, the instant Nirvana. . . . You have the karma, we'll take the Coca-Cola, metaphysical soft drink for a physical one."[34]

In contrast to these bleak and pessimistic visions of "global monoculture" and "Coca-colonization," however, others have suggested the more hopeful possibility of local resistance and indigenous critique. As Marshall Sahlins argues, indigenous peoples are never simply dupes of Western capitalism who passively absorb consumer ideology or the logic of the marketplace without reflection or agency; instead they appropriate, reinterpret, and transform them according to the logic of their own local culture: "Western capitalism has loosed on the world enormous forces of production, coercion and destruction. Yet precisely because they cannot be resisted, the goods of the larger system take on meaningful places in the local scheme of things."[35] Hence, some argue like Pico Ayer that we are witnessing not so much the relentless expansion of capitalism into all corners of the planet, but a more dynamic process of "the spread of America's pop-cultural imperialism throughout the world's ancient civilizations" and the simultaneous "resistances put up against the Coca-colonizing forces."[36]

My own view here is somewhat more complex and ambivalent—at once more optimistic than Halbfass's narrative of inevitable Europeanization of the earth, and yet also more pessimistic than Sahlins's narrative of valiant indigenous resistance against the onslaught of global capitalism. With Sahlins, I would like to highlight, even celebrate, the power of non-Western cultures to appropriate and transform the forces of global capitalism, to adapt them on their own terms, according to their own cultural logic. Yet it seems to me that the rules of the game are still largely conditioned and structured by the logic of the global capitalist market. Thus, any resistance tends to become resistance to the market, a deformation of capitalism, and yet still largely ruled by the laws of the market, still unable to imagine another space outside of global capitalism. And if "resistance" means nothing more than adding an Indian "curry" flavor of Chicken McNuggets to the McDonald's menu, it seems a fairly pathetic form of resistance. (For, as Pierre Bourdieu reminds us, "If in order to resist I have no other recourse than to lay claim to that in the name of which I am dominated, is this resistance? . . . Resistance may be alienating and submission may be liberating. Such is the paradox of the dominated.")[37]

In short, we need to recognize the agency and creativity of other cultures, yet we must also be honest about the hard realities of late capitalism and economic imperialism. It is surely true that indigenous peoples always retain the power to represent and define themselves, often in opposition to the ways in which Western authors would define them; yet it is no less true that today the exchange between cultures takes place largely within the context of a global capitalist marketplace. We must not belittle the fact that those of us in America and Western Europe are often in a position of tremendous economic, political, and military advantage over those whom we study, and that there remains a very real danger of imposing new, perhaps more insidious, forms of cultural imperialism and neocolonialism.

What is most crucial, therefore, is that we recognize not simply that categories like Tantra are imagined ones, and not even simply that they are formed through the cross-cultural interplay between Eastern and Western imaginations. Rather, we must also remember that these imaginings are also tied to real material interests and to historically, economically, and politically *embodied* relations of power. My solution here is not unlike what Michael Taussig has called "mimetic excess"—his own attempt to resolve the intense conflicts and contradictions raised by anthropology in a postcolonial context. Mimetic excess is the acute reflexive awareness of the mimesis that is at work in all cross-cultural representation—"an excess creating reflexive awareness as to the mimetic faculty."[38] This means both that we must be extremely self-critical, ever aware of the potentially destructive effects of our representations of others, and that we must be always open to the creation of new ways to represent both others and ourselves.

Finally, on a more positive note, I would also argue that the recognition that Tantra is an imagined category need not be a cause solely for postmodern despair or postcolonial guilt. Rather, it can also be quite liberating; for it opens the possibility to *reimagine* this category in new and more useful ways. It is in precisely this sense that the encounter with Asian traditions like Tantra can be truly transformative, for both East and West alike. As Woodroffe long ago observed, despite our arrogant claims to global knowledge, we in the West still have a tremendous amount to learn from India—and perhaps above all from Indian religious traditions like Tantra: for "she is still potentially powerful to impose her ideas upon the world. She is still an antagonist to be reckoned with in the conflict of cultures."

As Foucault has more recently suggested, the end of Western colonialism has brought with it not only the threat of new forms of neocolonialism and economic imperialism; in a more positive sense, it has also marked the end of Western intellectual domination, opening new possibilities for the encounter with non-Western ideas. As such it holds the potential for a genuine transformation of both the West and its others through the impact of this encounter:

> European thought finds itself at a turning point. This turning point, on a historical scale, is nothing other than the end of imperialism. The crisis of Western thought is identical to the end of imperialism. . . . For it is the end of the era of Western philosophy. Thus if philosophy of the future exists, it must be born outside Europe or equally born in consequence of meetings and impacts between Europe and non-Europe.[39]

It is just this kind of transformative impact that I would hope we might achieve in our encounter with Tantra, and specifically, with an *embodied Tantra.* This would mean the recognition that both we and those whom we study are historically embodied, socially and politically interested agents, that both we and they continuously reimagine ourselves in relation to real material interests and concerns. Perhaps then we might move beyond an imagining of Tantra as the exotic, erotic "Extreme Orient," and encounter it instead as a rich fabric woven of the many threads of individual peoples, texts, and practices—as a network of traditions that are very much rooted, like we ourselves, "in the flesh."

Notes

PREFACE AND ACKNOWLEDGMENTS

1. Various authors use the terms *Tantra, Tantrism,* and *Tantracism* more or less interchangeably to refer to this category of Asian religions. In this book I use *Tantrism* to refer to the category as it has been constructed as a particular "ism"—an abstract, unified category—in the scholarly imagination. For my own part, however, I prefer to use *Tantra,* which is at least somewhat less burdened with the awkward reifications of academic isms.

2. Jeffrey J. Kripal describes a similar narrative of his own early interest in Tantra in *Roads of Excess, Palaces of Wisdom: Eroticism and Reflexivity in the Study of Mysticism* (Chicago: University of Chicago Press, 2001), p. 152.

3. This research began in 1994 and eventually culminated in my two books *The Economics of Ecstasy: Tantra, Secrecy, and Power in Colonial Bengal* (New York: Oxford University Press, 2001); and *Songs of Ecstasy: Tantric and Devotional Songs from Bengal* (New York: Oxford University Press, 2001).

4. Marianna Torgovnick, *Primitive Passions: Men, Women, and the Quest for Ecstasy* (Chicago: University of Chicago Press, 1998), p. 210; cf. Torgovnick, *Gone Primitive: Savage Intellects, Modern Lives* (Chicago: University of Chicago Press, 1990), p. 8.

5. I found this particularly in areas heavily frequented by Western tourists, such as Rishikesh and Tārāpīṭh, where every third *sādhu* (holy man) invites a young Westerner over to smoke hashish and learn about Tantra. On the "advertisement of secrecy" in Tantric circles, see Hugh B. Urban, "The Torment of Secrecy: Ethical and Epistemological Problems in the Study of Esoteric Traditions," *History of Religions* 37, no. 3 (1998): 209–48; and Robert I. Levy, *Meso-*

cosm: Hinduism and the Organization of Space in a Traditional Newar City in Nepal (Berkeley: University of California Press, 1990), pp. 337 ff.

6. For this critique of Western scholarship on formerly colonized peoples, see Aijaz Ahmad, *In Theory: Classes, Nations, Literatures* (London: Verso, 1992), pp. 34–94; and Bart Moore-Gilbert, ed., *Postcolonial Theory: Contexts, Practices, Politics* (London: Verso, 1997), p. 18.

INTRODUCTION

1. The recent scholarship on Tantra is too vast to cite here in full; the more interesting recent works are: Jeffrey J. Kripal, *Kālī's Child: The Mystical and the Erotic in the Life and Teachings of Ramakrishna* (Chicago: University of Chicago Press, 1998); Sarah Caldwell, *Oh Terrifying Mother: Sexuality, Violence, and the Worship of the Goddess Kālī* (New York: Oxford University Press, 1999); Charles D. Orzech, *Politics and Transcendent Wisdom: The Scripture for Humane Kings in the Creation of Chinese Buddhism* (University Park: Pennsylvania State University Press, 1998); David Gordon White, *The Alchemical Body: Siddha Traditions in Medieval India* (Chicago: University of Chicago Press, 1997); and David Gordon White, ed., *Tantra in Practice* (Princeton, N.J.: Princeton University Press, 2000).

2. Paul Ramana Das and Marilena Silbey, "Celebrating Sacred Sexuality," on the Church of Tantra web site (www.tantra.org/amertan.html). On New Age appropriations of Tantra, see Hugh B. Urban, "The Cult of Ecstasy: Tantrism, the New Age, and the Spiritual Logic of Late Capitalism," *History of Religions* 39, no. 3 (2000): 268–304.

3. "It so happened that it was in texts known as *tantra*s that Western scholars first described doctrines and practices different from those of Brahmanism . . . so the Western experts adopted the word Tantrism for that particular, and for them, repulsive aspect of Indian religion" (André Padoux, "Tantrism: An Overview," in *Encyclopedia of Religion,* vol. 14, ed. Mircea Eliade [New York: Macmillan, 1986], pp. 271–72). For a detailed discussion of Western views of Tantra, see Hugh B. Urban, "The Extreme Orient: The Construction of 'Tantrism' as a Category in the Orientalist Imagination," *Religion* 29 (1999): 123–46.

4. William Ward, *A View of the History, Literature, and Religion of the Hindoos,* vol. 2 (1811; reprint, London: Kingsbury, Parbury, and Allen, 1817), p. 247; J. N. Farquhar, *An Outline of the Religious Literature of India* (Oxford: Oxford University Press, 1920), p. 200.

5. Philip Rawson, *The Art of Tantra* (Greenwich, Conn.: New York Graphics Society, 1973), p. 9; cf. Heinrich Zimmer, *Philosophies of India* (New York: Meridian Books, 1956), p. 576. The most recent argument for the empowering nature of Tantra is Miranda Shaw, *Passionate Enlightenment: Women in Tantric Buddhism* (Princeton, N.J.: Princeton University Press, 1994). As Pratapaditya Pal observes, "We . . . have gone from one extreme to the other. While early scholars were unnecessarily apologetic about some of the sexual . . . practices of Tantra, modern scholars revel in the sexual aspects" (*Hindu Religion and Iconology according to the Tantrasāra* [Los Angeles: Vichitra Press, 1981], p. vi).

6. Douglas Renfrew Brooks, *The Secret of the Three Cities: An Introduction*

to *Hindu Śākta Tantrism* (Chicago: University of Chicago Press, 1990), p. 209; cf. White, *The Alchemical Body,* p. xi.

7. Michel Foucault, *The History of Sexuality,* vol. 1, trans. Robert Hurley (New York: Vintage Books, 1980), pp. 17–49.

8. On the concept of late capitalism, see Fredric Jameson, *Postmodernism; or, The Cultural Logic of Late Capitalism* (Durham, N.C.: Duke University Press, 1991); and Ernest Mandel, *Late Capitalism* (London: New Left Books, 1970).

9. Ronald Inden, *Imagining India* (Oxford: Basil Blackwell, 1990), pp. 263–64. See also Richard King, *Orientalism and Religion: Postcolonial Theory, India, and the Mystic East* (London: Routledge, 1999).

10. On the category of the "exotic," with its fundamental tension between "extraneity and the erotic," see Dorothy M. Figueira, *The Exotic: A Decadent Quest* (Albany: State University of New York Press, 1994).

11. On the dialectical image, see Walter Benjamin, *Illuminations,* ed. Hannah Arendt, trans. Harry Zohn (New York: Schocken Books, 1969), pp. 217–64; and Michael Taussig, *Mimesis and Alterity: A Particular History of the Senses* (London: Routledge, 1993), pp. 177 ff.

12. Herbert V. Guenther, *The Life and Teaching of Nāropa* (New York: Oxford University Press, 1971), p. 102.

13. *Cosmo* quotes Sting on his own Tantric practices: "[Our sex lasts] seven hours and includes dinner and a movie" (Lynn Collins, "The Secret to Tantric Sex," *Cosmopolitan,* May 2000, p. 243).

14. "Chief portion or essence": *Śatapatha Brāhmaṇa* (Benaras: Chowkhamba Sanskrit Series Office, 1964), trans. Julius Eggeling (New Delhi: Motilal Banarsidas, 1963), 12, 14. See Monier Monier-Williams, *A Sanskrit-English Dictionary* (Oxford: Oxford University Press, 1899), p. 436; cf. Chintaharan Chakravarti, *The Tantras: Studies on Their Religion and Literature* (Calcutta: Punthi Pustak, 1963), p. 1.

15. "The word Tantrism assuredly is a Western creation. India traditionally knows only texts called *tantras*" (André Padoux, "A Survey of Tantric Hinduism for the Historian of Religions," review of *Hindu Tantrism,* by Sanjukta Gupta, Teun Goudriaan, and Dirk Jan Hoens, *History of Religions* 20, no. 4 [1981]: 350). See also Padoux, *Vāc: The Concept of the Word in Selected Hindu Tantras* (Albany: State University of New York Press, 1990), pp. 31 ff. John Woodroffe made this point long before in *Shakti and Shākta* (New York: Dover Publications, 1978), pp. 54–55.

16. Swami Nostradamus Virato, "Tantric Sex: A Spiritual Path to Ecstasy," Church of Tantra web site, www.tantra.org.

17. Paul Ramana Das and Marilena Silbey, "Celebrating Sacred Sexuality: American Tantra (tm)," reprinted on the Church of Tantra web site, ibid.

18. Bhagwan Shree Rajneesh, *Tantra: The Supreme Understanding* (Poona: Rajneesh Foundation, 1975), pp. 95, 103.

19. White, introduction to *Tantra in Practice,* p. 5.

20. Benyotosh Bhattacharyya, *An Introduction to Buddhist Esoterism* (Oxford: Oxford University Press, 1932), p. 51.

21. J. Talboys Wheeler, *The History of India from the Earliest Ages* (London: Trübner, 1874), p. 364.

22. Woodroffe, *Shakti and Shākta,* p. 179.

23. Mircea Eliade, *Yoga: Immortality and Freedom* (Princeton, N.J.: Princeton University Press, 1971), pp. 203–5.

24. Rawson, *The Art of Tantra,* p. 9.

25. Others have tried to offer a simpler definition for Tantra; Padoux defines it as the path that "harnesses *kāma*—desire (in every sense of the word) . . . to the service of deliverance" (*Vāc,* p. 40). More recently, White suggests that a working definition is "that Asian body of beliefs and practices which, working from the principle that the universe we experience is nothing other than the concrete manifestation of the divine energy of the godhead that creates and maintains that universe, seeks to ritually appropriate and channel that energy, within the human microcosm, in creative and emancipatory ways" (introduction to *Tantra in Practice,* p. 9). See also Teun Goudriaan and Sanjukta Gupta, *Hindu Tantric and Śākta Literature* (Wiesbaden, Ger.: Otto Harrassowitz, 1981), p. 1.

26. Kripal, *Kālī's Child,* pp. 30–33; Sanjukta Gupta, Teun Goudriaan, and Dirk Jan Hoens, *Hindu Tantrism* (Leiden: E. J. Brill, 1979), pp. 8–9.

27. Brooks, *Secret of the Three Cities,* pp. 53 ff. On the concept of the polythetic definition, see Jonathan Z. Smith, *Imagining Religion: From Babylon to Jonestown* (Chicago: University of Chicago Press, 1982), pp. 1–8.

28. See, for example, my work on the Kartābhajā sect of Bengal, which has a profoundly ambivalent relationship to the category "Tantrism" (*The Economics of Ecstasy: Tantra, Secrecy, and Power in Colonial Bengal* [New York: Oxford University Press, 2001], introduction).

29. Donald S. Lopez, Jr., *Elaborations on Emptiness: Uses of the Heart Sūtra* (Princeton, N.J.: Princeton University Press, 1996), p. 26.

30. Narendra Nath Bhattacharyya, *History of the Tantric Religion: A Historical, Ritualistic and Philosophical Study* (New Delhi: Manohar, 1982), p. v.

31. Brooks, *Secret of the Three Cities,* p. ix.

32. Herbert V. Guenther, *Yuganaddha: The Tantric View of Life* (Varanasi: Chowkhamba Sanskrit Series, 1969), p. 3.

33. Nik Douglas and Penny Slinger, "The Kama Sutra and the Sixty-Four Arts," reproduced on the tantra.com web site.

34. See Urban, "The Cult of Ecstasy," 268–304. Popular books on Tantra include, among many others: Margo Anand, *The Art of Sexual Ecstasy: The Path of Sacred Sexuality for Western Lovers* (Los Angeles: Jeremy P. Tarcher, 1989); John Mumford, *Ecstasy through Tantra* (St. Paul, Minn.: Llewellyn, 1988); Christopher S. Hyatt, *Secrets of Western Tantra: The Sexuality of the Middle Path* (Tempe, Ariz.: New Falcon Publications, 1996). Nik Douglas includes over twenty pages of web sites in the appendix to his *Spiritual Sex: Secrets of Tantra from the Ice Age to the New Millennium* (New York: Pocket Books, 1997), pp. 309 ff.

35. Rachel Fell McDermott, "Kālī's New Frontiers: A Hindu Goddess on the Internet," in *Encountering Kālī: In the Margins, at the Center, in the West,* ed. Jeffrey J. Kripal and Rachel Fell McDermott (Berkeley: University of California Press, 2003), pp. 273–95.

36. Shaw, *Passionate Enlightenment,* pp. 8–9.

37. Eliade, *Yoga,* pp. 202–3. As Zimmer likewise argues, "in the Tantra, we

have another sign of the resurgence of the religiosity of the non-Aryan, pre-Aryan, matriarchal tradition of Dravidian times" (*Philosophies of India,* pp. 568–69).

38. André Van Lysebeth, *Tantra: The Cult of the Feminine* (York Beach, Me.: Samuel Weiser, 1995), p. 53.

39. See Inden, *Imagining India,* pp. 263–64; Richard King, *Orientalism and Religion,* chap. 5.

40. Foucault, *The History of Sexuality,* vol. 1, p. 35; my italics.

41. Ibid., pp. 6–7.

42. White, introduction to *Tantra in Practice,* p. 4.

43. Smith, *Imagining Religion,* p. xi.

44. "In Said's transhistorical formulation, Europe, motivated by a unitary will to inferiorize, created its own identity by establishing the difference of the Orient. . . . The unidirectionality of his approach overlooks the inherent ambivalence of the relationship between the colonizers and colonized" (Figueira, *The Exotic,* p. 3). For a balanced discussion of the criticisms of postcolonial theory, see Bart Moore-Gilbert, ed., *Postcolonial Criticism* (New York: Longman, 1997).

45. See Rosalind O'Hanlon, "Recovering the Subject: Subaltern Studies and Histories of Resistance in Colonial South Asia," *Modern Asian Studies* 22, no. 1 (1988): 189–224; Sara Suleri, *The Rhetoric of British India* (Chicago: University of Chicago Press, 1992). As Anne McClintock argues, postcolonialism is "prematurely celebratory and obfuscatory," for it reifies a singular, monolithic, non-Western Other and in so doing masks subtle forms of neocolonialism (*Imperial Leather: Race, Gender, and Sexuality in the Colonial Context* [New York: Routledge, 1995], p. 13).

46. Benita Parry, "Problems in Current Theories of Colonial Discourse," in *The Post-Colonial Studies Reader,* ed. Bill Ashcroft, Gareth Griffiths, and Helen Tiffin (London: Routledge, 1995), p. 41.

47. McClintock, *Imperial Leather,* p. 15. For similar, more nuanced models, see John D. Kelly, *A Politics of Virtue: Hinduism, Sexuality, and Countercolonial Discourse in Fiji* (Chicago: University of Chicago Press, 1991), p. xiv; see Aiwa Ong, *Spirits of Resistance and Capitalist Discipline: Factory Women in Malaysia* (Albany: State University of New York Press, 1987), pp. 216–17.

48. Aijaz Ahmad, *In Theory: Classes, Nations, Literatures* (New York: Verso, 1992), pp. 34–94. For a discussion of this critique, see Moore-Gilbert, *Postcolonial Theory,* p. 18.

49. See Smith, *Imagining Religion,* pp. xi–xiii.

50. Bruce Lincoln, "Theses on Method," *Method and Theory in the Study of Religion* 8, no. 3 (1996): 225.

51. See Talal Asad, *Genealogies of Religion: Discipline and Reasons of Power in Christianity and Islam* (Baltimore: Johns Hopkins University Press, 1993), introduction.

52. Gustavo Benevides, "Giuseppe Tucci; or, Buddhology in the Age of Fascism," in *Curators of the Buddha: The Study of Buddhism under Colonialism,* ed. Donald S. Lopez, Jr. (Chicago: University of Chicago Press, 1995), p. 162.

53. Richard King, *Orientalism and Religion,* chap. 5. King lucidly examines the "exotic fantasies of Indian religions as deeply mystical, introspective and oth-

erworldly" (p. 142), yet he never mentions Tantra or anything relating to sexuality. I can only conclude that this is because the presence of Tantra would undermine his thesis, namely, that Indian mysticism was imagined as something otherworldly and identified with Vedānta or other philosophical schools. The intense sensuality of Tantra in the Orientalist imagination seems to contradict this thesis. However, I would suggest that Tantra represented, for both Indian and European authors, mysticism in its most degenerate form: a kind of mysticism that had been corrupted with sensual desire and this-worldly power.

54. Marianna Torgovnick, *Gone Primitive: Savage Intellects, Modern Lives* (Chicago: University of Chicago Press, 1990), pp. 247, 246.

55. Wilhelm Halbfass, *India and Europe: An Essay in Understanding* (Albany: State University of New York Press, 1988), p. 173.

56. Debiprasad Chattopadhyaya, *Lokāyata: A Study in Ancient Indian Materialism* (New Delhi: People's Publishing House, 1959), pp. 65–66.

57. Donald S. Lopez, Jr., *Prisoners of Shangri La: Tibetan Buddhism and the West* (Chicago: University of Chicago Press, 1998), p. 44. This is not unlike what Homi Bhabha calls the play of *mimicry* at work between colonizer and colonized—the projection of a Western stereotyped image upon the native, and the manifold ways in which the native mimics, adapts, and deforms that image ("Of Mimicry and Man," in *The Location of Culture,* by Homi Bhabha [London: Routledge, 1984], p. 86).

58. The *pizza effect* refers to a cross-cultural exchange of ideas, through which something comes from one culture (e.g., dough and tomato sauce from Italy), is transformed in another culture (American pizza), and then reimported in a new form by the original culture.

59. Friedrich Max Müller, *Biographical Essays* (New York: Charles Scribner's Sons, 1884), p. 13. On this cross-cultural borrowing between India and the West, see Rachel Fell McDermott, "The Western Kālī," in *Devī: Goddesses of India,* ed. J .S. Hawley and D. M. Wulff (Berkeley: University of California Press, 1996).

60. Walter Benjamin, *Gesammelte Schriften,* vol. 5, ed. Rolf Tiedemann and Hermann Schweppenhauser (Frankfurt: Suhrkamp Verlag, 1972), p. 595.

61. Susan Buck-Morss, *The Dialectics of Seeing: Walter Benjamin and the Arcades Project* (Cambridge: MIT Press, 1989), p. 210: "The dialectical image has as many levels of logic as the Hegelian concept. It is a way of seeing that crystallizes antithetical elements by providing the axes for their alignment." See also Michael Taussig, *Shamanism, Colonialism, and the Wild Man: A Study in Terror and Healing* (Chicago: University of Chicago Press, 1987), p. 442.

62. Taussig, *Mimesis and Alterity,* pp. 65–66. See Walter Benjamin, "On the Mimetic Faculty," in *Reflections,* ed. Peter Demetz, trans. Edmund Jephcott (New York: Schocken Books, 1986), p. 333.

63. Taussig, *Mimesis and Alterity,* pp. 65; see also Torgovnick, *Gone Primitive,* pp. 1–10.

64. Quote from Taussig, *Mimesis and Alterity,* p. 142.

65. Lopez, *Elaborations on Emptiness,* p. 103; cf. Gupta, Goudriaan, and Hoens, *Hindu Tantrism,* p. 5.

66. Padoux, "Hindu Tantrism," p. 275. Probably the best efforts to write

such a history are: Alexis Sanderson, "Śaivism and the Tantric Traditions," in *The World's Religions,* ed. Stewart Sutherland et al. (London: Routledge, 1988), pp. 660–704; and Gupta, Goudriaan, and Hoens, *Hindu Tantrism,* pp. 13–46.

67. On the meanings of *rgyd,* see Lopez, *Elaborations on Emptiness,* pp. 78–104; on the Chinese term *mi-chiao,* see Orzech, *Politics and Transcendent Wisdom,* pp. 135–36n.

68. *Tantrarājatantram,* ed. Arthur Avalon (New Delhi: Motilal Banarsidas, 1981). Cf. *Yoginīhṛdaya Tantra,* ed. Upendranāth Dās (Calcutta: Navabhārata Publishers, 1393 Bengali era [1986]), French trans. André Padoux, *Le Coeur de la yoginī: Yoginīhṛdaya, avec le commentaire Dīpikā d'Amṛtānanda* (Paris: Collège de France, 1994), 1; Punyānandanātha, *Kāmakalāvilāsa,* ed. Arthur Avalon (Madras: Ganesh, 1961), 50f; and SvT. For other narratives of this sort, see Punyānandanātha, *Kāmakalāvilāsa,* 50–53. See also Hélène Brunner, Gerhard Oberhammer, and André Padoux, *Tāntrikābhidhānakośa: Dictionnaire des termes techniques de la littérature hindoue tantrique,* vol. 1 (Wien: Verlag der österreichischen Akademie der Wissenschaften, 2000), pp. 306–7.

69. Eliade, *Yoga:* "The irresistible Tantric advance in the medieval period implies a new victory of the pre-Aryan popular strata" (pp. 201–2); cf. Zimmer, *Philosophies of India;* Narendra Nath Bhattacharyya, *History of the Tantric Religion.* Banikanta Kakati traces the origin of left-handed Tantric rites to the tribal groups of remote and jungly Assam—"a land of natural instincts free from all regimes of self-mortification" (*The Mother Goddess Kāmākhyā* [Guwahati: Publication Board, Assam, 1989], pp. 45–47).

70. Woodroffe, *Shakti and Shākta,* pp. 587–89; see below, chapter 4.

71. Goudriaan and Gupta, *Hindu Tantric and Śākta Literature,* p. 9. See also Padoux, *Vāc,* pp. 33 ff. More recent authors like White suggest that Tantra is the combined result of "shamanic magical" traditions and "speculative and scholastic productions" (introduction to *Tantra in Practice,* p. 18). See also Geoffrey Samuel, *Civilized Shamans: Buddhism in Tibetan Societies* (Washington, D.C.: Smithsonian Institution, 1993).

72. S. N. Das Gupta, cited in Chakravarti, *The Tantras,* pp. 1–2. Īśānaśivagurudeva Miśra derives *tantra* from *tatri,* "to understand," and defines it as the *śāstra* that expounds the six categories of Śaivism (ibid., p. 2). On the etymology of the term, see also see also S. C. Banerji, *A Brief History of Tantra Literature* (Calcutta: Naya Prokash, 1988), p. 1; P. V. Kane, *History of Dharmaśāstra* (Poona: Bhandarkar Oriental Research Institute, 1962), pp. 1031–35; Lopez, *Elaborations on Emptiness,* pp. 78–104.

73. Rama Nath Sharma, ed., *The Aṣṭādhyāyī of Pāṇini* (New Delhi: Munshiram Manoharlal, 1987), 5.2.70, 7.2.9.

74. William K. Mahony, *The Artful Universe: An Introduction to the Vedic Religious Imagination* (Albany: State University of New York Press 1998), pp. 78, 95, 110–11.

75. Wendy Doniger O'Flaherty, trans., *The Rig Veda* (New York: Penguin Books, 1981), p. 32n6. On the sacrifice as an act of "weaving," see Mahony, *The Artful Universe,* p. 111.

76. *Svetāśvatāra Upaniṣad,* in *The Principal Upaniṣads,* trans. Sarvapelli Radhakrishnan (London: Unwin Hyman, 1953), 6.10.

77. *Bṛhadāranyaka Upaniṣad,* in *One Hundred and Eight Upaniṣads,* ed. V. L. S. Panshikar (Varanasi: Vyāsa Prakāśana, 1983), 2.1.20.

78. J. C. Heesterman, *The Broken World of Sacrifice: An Essay in Ancient Indian Ritual* (Chicago: University of Chicago Press, 1993), p. 246n. The Vedic tradition also uses *tantra* as a technical term in the sacrificial ritual, contrasted with *pradhāna.* Whereas *pradhāna* refers to the main offerings, the *tantra*—as the "woof or texture"—comprises the auxiliary acts that remained largely interchangeable among different sacrifices (ibid., p. 61).

79. *Śatapatha Brāhmaṇa,* 14.

80. George Thibaut, trans., *Vedānta Sūtras with the Commentary by Śaṅkarācārya* (New Delhi: Motilal Banarsidas, 1968–71), 2.1.

81. Monier-Williams, *Sanskrit-English Dictionary* (Oxford: Oxford University Press, 1899), p. 436. On *tantra* as *yantra,* see *Agni Purāṇa,* 25.1–3. The Sanskrit dictionary *Amarakośa* defines *tantra* as principle matter, doctrine or *śāstra,* loom or paraphernalia, but does not define it as a certain class of works. Kane concludes that the *tantra*s had not yet been composed by this time (*History of Dharmaśāstra,* p. 1031).

82. P. C. Bagchi, "The Evolution of the Tantras," in *The Cultural Heritage of India,* vol. 4, by P. C. Bagchi (Calcutta: Ramakrishna Mission Institute of Culture, 1953), p. 211.

83. Padoux, "A Survey of Tantrism," p. 350.

84. See Nārāyaṇ Rām Ācārya Kāvyatīrtha, ed., *The Manusmṛti; with the commentary Manvarthamuktāvali of Kullūka* (Bombay: Nirnay Sagar Press, 1946), 2.1.

85. N. A. Deshpande, trans., *Padma Purāṇa* (New Delhi: Motilal Banarsidas, 1990), p. 2087. Similarly, in the *Bhāgavata Purāṇa:* "My worship is threefold—Vedic, Tantric and a synthesis of these two. But of these three, one should offer me worship according to the method of his choice" (BP 11.27.13). Many later texts employ this distinction; see C. Mackenzie Brown, *The Devī Gītā: The Song of the Goddess: A Translation, Annotation, and Commentary* (Albany: State University of New York Press, 1998), 9.3–4, pp. 263–64.

86. For a good discussion of the spread of Tantra in India, see Sanderson, "Śaivism and the Tantric Traditions," p. 661; on its spread throughout Asia, see White, *Tantra in Practice.*

87. Gopinath Kaviraj, *Aspects of Indian Thought* (Burdwan: University of Burdwan, 1966), pp. 175, 216. See E. B. Cowell and A. E. Gough, trans., *The Sarva-Darsana-Samgraha; or, Review of the Different Systems of Hindu Philosophy* (Varanasi: Chowkhamba Sanskrit Series Office, 1978).

88. M. R. Khale, ed., *Bāṇa's Kādambarī (Pūrvabhāga Complete)* (New Delhi: Motilal Banarsidas, 1956), pp. 338–39. Gwendolyn Lane translates *tantra* here simply as "mystical formulas" (*Kādambarī: A Classical Sanskrit Story of Magical Transformations* [New York: Garland Publishing, 1991], p. 226).

89. Goudriaan and Gupta, *Hindu Tantric and Śākta Literature,* p. 21; cf. Adhir Cakravarti, "New Light on Śaiva Tāntrika Texts Known in Ancient Cambodia," *Journal of the Asiatic Society* 15, nos. 1–4 (1973): 1–10.

90. Those on the side of a Buddhist origin for Tantra include Benyotosh Bhattacharyya (*An Introduction to Buddhist Esotericism,* p. 147), while those

on the Hindu side include David Snellgrove, *Indo-Tibetan Buddhism: Indian Buddhists and Their Tibetan Successors* (London: Sirindia, 1987), pp. 152–60. More recently, Alexis Sanderson has argued that the Hindu Mantramārga developed a hierarchy of texts which became the foundation for the later Buddhist fourfold hierarchy of Tantras (see "Śaivism and the Tantric Traditions," pp. 678–79).

91. Alex Wayman dates the text to the fourth or fifth century; however, the most recent editor of the critical edition argues that the formative period of the text was much later, probably the eighth century (Yukei Matsunaga, *The Guhyasamāja Tantra: A New Critical Edition* [Osaka: Toso Shuppan, 1978], p. xxvi); see Alex Wayman, *Yoga of the Guhyasamājatantra: The Arcane Lore of Forty Verses* (New Delhi: Motilal Banarsidas, 1977).

92. "Buddhists were not quite clear as to the specific meaning of the word *tantra*" (Louis de la Vallée Poussin, "Tantrism [Buddhist]," in *Encyclopedia of Religion and Ethics,* vol. 12, ed. James Hastings [New York: Charles Scribner's Sons, 1922], p. 193); cf. Lopez, *Elaborations on Emptiness,* p. 84.

93. "Prabandhaṃ tantram ākhyāta tat prabandham tridhā bhavet / ādhāraḥ prakṛtiś cāiva asaṃhāryaprabheditaḥ / prakṛtiścākṛter hetur asaṃhāryaphalaṃ tathā / ādhāraḥ tad upāyaś ca tribhis tantrārthasaṃgrahaḥ" (this passage is GST 18.5–6 in Benyotosh Bhattacharyya's edition).

94. Wayman, *Yoga of the Guhyasamāja,* p. 61. See also the commentaries by Tsong-kha-pa and Padma dkar-po in Guenther, *Life and Teaching of Nāropa,* p. 114, and *Yuganaddha,* pp. 3–4.

95. David Snellgrove, *The Hevajra Tantra: A Critical Study* (London: Oxford University Press, 1959), v.1, 14.

96. Shashibhushan Dasgupta, *An Introduction to Tantric Buddhism* (Calcutta: University of Calcutta Press, 1958), p. 71.

97. Giuseppe Tucci, *The Religions of Tibet,* trans. Geoffrey Samuel (Berkeley: University of California Press, 1980), p. 262n. Sanderson argues that the Hindu Mantramārga had a similar kind of hierarchical classification ("Śaivism and the Tantric Traditions," pp. 678–79).

98. Lopez, *Elaborations on Emptiness,* p. 93.

99. F. Otto Schrader, *Introduction to the "Pāñcarātra" and the "Ahirbudhnya Saṃhitā"* (Madras: Adyar Library Series, 1916), pp. 2, 146. Other texts classify the body of Pāñcarātra scriptures into four headings*: āgama-siddhānta, mantra-siddhānta, tantra-siddhānta,* and *tantrāntara-siddhānta,* each of which concentrates on particular forms of Viṣṇu and other deities. See Sanjukta Gupta, trans., *Lakṣmī Tantra: A Pañcarātra Text* (Leiden: E. J. Brill, 1972), p. xviii.

100. *Kāmikāgama,* pt. 1, *Pūrvakāmikā,* ed. Svāminātha Śivācārya (Madras: Dakṣiṇabhāratārcakasaṃgha, 1975), 1.29; cf. Mark S. G. Dyczkowski, *The Canon of the Śaivāgamas and the Kubjikā Tantras of the Western Kaula Tradition* (Albany: State University of New York Press, 1988), p. 140n.

101. Goudriaan and Gupta, *Hindu Tantric and Śākta Literature,* p. 18. Many suspect that the Kula may have originated in the Buddhist *tantras*; it holds an important place in early texts like the *Guhyasamāja,* which speaks of the five families (*kula*) of bodhisattvas (see Shashibhushan Dasgupta, *Introduction to Tantric Buddhism,* p. 70).

102. Cf. also *Kaulajñānanirṇaya,* ed. P. C. Bagchi (Varanasi: Prācya Prakāśana, 1986), 2.10.

103. Goudriaan and Gupta, *Hindu Tantric and Śākta Literature,* pp. 13–14. Louise M. Finn, trans., *The Kulacūḍāmaṇi Tantra and the Vāmakeśvara Tantra* (Wiesbaden, Ger.: Otto Harrassowitz, 1986), pp. 74–77.

104. See Cornelia Dimmitt and J. A. B. van Buitenen, *Classical Hindu Mythology: A Reader in the Sanskrit Purāṇas* (Philadelphia: Temple University Press, 1978), pp. 4–5.

105. The most important Bengali compilations are Kṛṣṇānanda Āgamavāgīśa's *Bṛhat-Tantrasāra* (sixteenth century) and Rāmatoṣaṇa's *Prāṇatoṣinī* (eighteenth century). The former offers no clear definition of the term, but speaks only of *tantramantraviśārada* (skill in the *tantras* and *mantras*); the latter uses the term *tantraśāstra,* and also says that *tantra* is a limb of the Vedas (*tantrānām vedāṅgatva*) (Soumyānanda Nāth, ed., *Prāṇatoṣinī* [Calcutta: Navabhārata Publishers, 1991], pp. 5, 65).

106. Trans. Padoux, *Vāc,* p. 58n. On the relations of the Trika, Kula, and Krama systems see K. C. Pandey, *Abhinavagupta: An Historical and Philosophical Study* (Varanasi: Chowkhamba Sanskrit Series Office, 1963), pp. 132–47, 590–611; Navjivan Rastogi, *The Krama Tantricism of Kashmir: Historical and General Sources* (New Delhi: Motilal Banarsidas, 1979); Sanderson, "Śaivism and the Tantric Traditions," pp. 670 ff.

107. Rastogi, *The Krama Tantricism,* p. 32. In many passages (TA 22.40–42; 23.99–100; 26.33–37; 35), *tantra* appears to be identified with the Śaivasiddānta school and as such is inferior to or more "exoteric" than the Kula or Trika. But elsewhere (e.g., TA 35.25–27), *tantra* is contrasted with both *siddānta* and *śākta* (this was pointed out to me by André Padoux, personal communication, 1 June 2001). See also Pandey, *Abhinavagupta,* p. 604.

108. Rastogi, *The Krama Tantricism,* pp. 34–36.

109. Ibid., p. 36n.

110. "Viśvottīrṇamātmatattvam—iti tāntrikāḥ; viśvamayam iti—kulādyāmnāyaniviṣṭāḥ; viśvottīrṇaṃ viśvamayaṃ ca—iti trikādi darśanavidaḥ" (*Pratyabhijñāhṛdayam,* commentary on verse 8); see Jaideva Singh, *The Doctrine of Recognition: A Translation of Pratyabhijñāhṛdayam* (Albany: State University of New York Press, 1990), pp. 61–62.

111. Padoux, personal communication, 1 June 2001.

112. *Kūrma Purāṇa* 1.16.109–20; trans. Wendy Doniger O'Flaherty, in *The Origins of Evil in Hindu Mythology* (Berkeley: University of California Press, 1976), p. 310.

113. David N. Lorenzen, "A Parody of the Kāpālikas in the *Mattavilāsa,*" in *Tantra in Practice,* ed. White, pp. 86–87; cf. Lorenzen, *The Kāpālikas and Kālāmukhas: Two Lost Śaivite Sects* (Berkeley: University of California Press, 1972).

114. Bāṇabhaṭṭa, *Kādambarī,* trans. Lane, *Kādambarī,* p. 227. "He had collected manuscripts containing information about jugglery, mystical formulas and spells [*tantras* and *mantras*]. . . . He had the madness of belief in alchemy. He was obsessed with a yearning to enter the world of the demons" (p. 226).

115. On the concept of the "mother tongues," or vernacular languages, see

A. K. Ramanujan, *Hymns for the Drowning: Poems for Viṣṇu by Nammālvār* (Princeton, N.J.: Princeton University Press, 1981), pp. 126–27.

116. Brooks, *Secret of the Three Cities,* p. 5. For a similar view of Tantra in Nepal, see Robert I. Levy, *Mesocosm: Hinduism and the Organization of a Traditional Newar City in Nepal* (Berkeley: University of California Press, 1990), pp. 298–89.

117. Mahendranāth Gupta, *Śrīśrīrāmakṛṣṇakathāmṛta* (1902; reprint, Calcutta: Kathāmṛta Bhavan, 1987), 4.166.

118. Dāśarathī Rāy, "Kartābhajā," trans. in Hugh B. Urban, *Songs of Ecstasy: Tantric and Devotional Songs from Bengal* (New York: Oxford University Press, 2001), p. 144.

119. See TA and TAV 29.110–11, trans. Lilian Silburn, *Kuṇḍalinī: The Energy of the Depths* (Albany: State University of New York Press, 1988), p. 161; PTv, trans. Singh, *A Trident of Wisdom,* p. 206.

120. White, introduction to *Tantra in Practice,* p. 16.

121. Some schools, such as the Trika of Abhinavagupta, make emission of semen the central act, which repeats the supreme emission of the universe out of Śiva (TA 5.121–24); cf. Paul Eduardo Muller-Ortega, *The Triadic Heart of Śiva: Kaula Tantricism of Abhinavagupta in the Non-Dual Shaivism of Kashmir* (Albany: State University of New York Press, 1989), pp. 110–11; Agehananda Bharati, *The Tantric Tradition* (Garden City, N.Y.: Anchor Books, 1970), p. 265. Many other traditions, however, insist that the semen must not be emitted during intercourse, which is the greatest danger to the yogi: "*maithuna* is never allowed to terminate in an emission of semen" (Eliade, *Yoga,* p. 267). Peter Kvaerne likewise argues that most of the Buddhist Tantric traditions emphasize the sublimation of the semen on an interior plane ("On the Concept of Sahaja in Indian Buddhist Tantric Literature," *Temenos* 11 [1975]: 88–135).

122. On this question, see Sanderson, "Śaivism and the Tantric Traditions," pp. 679–80.

123. On the manipulation and ingestion of sexual fluids, see White, *The Alchemical Body,* pp. 135–40, 184–202; introduction to *Tantra in Practice,* p. 6. Many techniques also involve not just retention of the semen, but the extraction of the vaginal fluids from the partner into the male body. According to the *Haṭha Yoga Pradīpikā,* "The semen that is about to fall into the woman's vagina should be drawn back up. . . . If already fallen he should draw up his own semen [together with the woman's secretions] and preserve it" (Georg Feuerstein, *Tantra: The Path of Ecstasy* [Boston: Shambhala Publications, 1998], p. 233).

124. Agehananda Bharati, "Making Sense out of Tantrism and Tantrics," *Loka: A Journal from Naropa Institute* 2 (1976): 53. Many authors have praised Tantra as an empowerment of women; the most recent proponent of this positive view is Miranda Shaw, *Passionate Enlightenment.* More skeptical scholars see women as tools used for the optimization of male power; see Brooks, *Secret of the Three Cities,* pp. 25–26. For a discussion of the problem in Bengali Tantra, see Urban, *The Economics of Ecstasy,* chaps. 2, 6.

125. Feuerstein, *Tantra,* p. 243; cf. Narendra Nath Bhattacharyya, *History of the Tantric Religion,* p. v.

126. "A *tantra* in the singular can normally refer only to a particular *tantra,*

just as the word *sūtra* can refer to a particular *sūtra*. . . . No one has yet thought of using the word *sūtra* . . . as a general term for non-Tantric Buddhism, for we are well aware of the great variety of literature covered by the term" (Snellgrove, *Indo-Tibetan Buddhism,* p. 173).

127. Grace M. Jantzen, *Power, Gender, and Christian Mysticism* (Cambridge: Cambridge University Press, 1995), p. 12; cf. Richard King, *Orientalism and Religion,* pp. 9 ff.

128. Ludwig Wittgenstein, *Philosophical Investigations,* trans. G. E. M. Anscombe (New York: Macmillan, 1958), p. 32e.

CHAPTER 1. THE GOLDEN AGE OF THE VEDAS

1. Mary Louise Pratt, *Imperial Eyes: Travel Writing and Transculturation* (New York: Routledge, 1992), p. 6.

2. Robin Rhinehart and Tony K. Stewart, "The Anonymous *Āgama Prakāśa:* Preface to a Nineteenth Century Gujarati Polemic," in *Tantra in Practice,* ed. David Gordon White (Princeton, N.J.: Princeton University Press, 2000), p. 272.

3. See Richard King, *Orientalism and Religion: Postcolonial Theory, India, and the Mystic East* (London: Routledge, 1999), p. 128; Bernard Cohn, *An Anthropologist among the Historians, and Other Essays* (Oxford: Oxford University Press, 1990), p. 146; Amal Chatterjee, *Representations of India, 1740–1840: The Creation of India in the Colonial Imagination* (New York: St. Martin's Press, 1998), pp. 8–9.

4. See Richard King, *Orientalism and Religion,* pp. 118–42.

5. Michel Foucault, *The History of Sexuality,* vol. 1, trans. Robert Hurley (New York: Vintage Books, 1978), pp. 144–47.

6. Richard King, *Orientalism and Religion,* p. 98. The term "Hindu" is a Persian adaptation of the Sanskrit *sindhu,* referring to the region of the Indus River Valley. In the late eighteenth century, British authors began using "Hindu" to refer to the religions of the non-Muslim peoples of India. Dermot Killingley suggests that Rāmmohun Roy was probably the first one to use the term, in 1816 (*Rāmmohun Roy in Hindu and Christian Tradition: The Teape Lectures 1990* [Newcastle upon Tyne, Eng.: Grevatt and Grevatt, 1993], p. 60); cf. R. E. Frykenberg, "The Emergence of Modern 'Hinduism' as a Concept and an Institution: A Reappraisal with Special Reference to South India," in *Hinduism Reconsidered,* ed. Gunter D. Sontheimer and Hermann Kulke (New Delhi: Manohar, 1991), p. 31.

7. Cohn, "The Command of Language and the Language of Command," in *Subaltern Studies*, vol. 4, ed. Ranajit Guha (New Delhi: Oxford University Press, 1985), pp. 276, 283–84. See also Gauri Viswanathan, *Masks of Conquest: Literary Study and British Rule in India* (New York: Columbia University Press, 1989).

8. Ronald Inden, *Imagining India* (Oxford: Basil Blackwell, 1990), p. 49.

9. Herbert Risley, *The People of India* (Calcutta: Thacker, Spink, 1908), p. 255.

10. Richard King, *Orientalism and Religion,* pp. 118–42.

11. Thomas R. Trautmann, *Aryans and British India* (Berkeley: University of California Press, 1997), pp. xii–xiii, and chaps. 2–4.

12. Sumanta Banerjee, *The Parlour and the Streets: Elite and Popular Culture in Nineteenth Century Calcutta* (Calcutta: Seagull, 1989), pp. 35–36.

13. David Kopf, "An Historiographical Essay on the Goddess Kālī," in *Shaping Bengali Worlds: Public and Private,* ed. Tony K. Stewart (East Lansing: Asian Studies Center, University of Michigan, 1975), p. 114.

14. See David Gordon White, *The Alchemical Body: Siddha Traditions in Medieval India* (Chicago: University of Chicago Press, 1996), pp. 49–51. For early accounts of *rasayana* and alchemical arts, see Edward Sachau, ed., *Alberuni's India,* vol. 1 (London: Kegan Paul, Trench, and Trübner, 1910), pp. 191–92; François Bernier, *Travels in the Mogul Empire, AD 1656–1668,* trans. Archibald Constable (London: Oxford University Press, 1934), pp. 316–20.

15. James Mill, *The History of British India* (London: J. Madden, 1858), vol. 1. For selections from Dow, Holwell, and others, see Peter Marshall, *The British Discovery of Hinduism in the Eighteenth Century* (Cambridge: Cambridge University Press, 1970). For good discussions of early literature on India, see ibid.; and Kate Teltscher, *India Inscribed: European and British Writing on India, 1600–1800* (New York: Oxford University Press, 1995).

16. William Jones, *The Works of Sir William Jones,* vol. 4 (1799; reprint, New Delhi: Agam Prakashan, 1976), pp. 105–6.

17. Ibid., vol. 3, pp. 383–84.

18. H. T. Colebrooke, *Essays on Hindu Religion and Ancient Indian Literature,* vol. 2 (1837; reprint, New Delhi: Cosmo Publications, 1977), pp. 185–86.

19. Colebrooke, "On the Religious Ceremonies of the Hindus," in *Miscellaneous Essays* (London: Trübner, 1837), p. 111. See also David Kopf, *British Orientalism and the Bengal Renaissance: The Dynamics of Modernization, 1773–1835* (Berkeley: University of California Press 1969), pp. 41–42.

20. Abbé Dubois, *Hindu Manners, Customs, and Ceremonies* (Oxford: Clarendon Press, 1906).

21. Ibid., p. 9.

22. Ibid., pp. 286–88.

23. William Ward, *A View of the History, Literature, and Religion of the Hindoos,* vol. 2 (London: Kingsbury, Parbury, and Allen, 1817), pp. lxxvi, xlix, xiii, xlii, xxii.

24. Ibid., vol. 1, p. 247; cf. pp. li–lv.

25. Ibid., p. 247.

26. H. H. Wilson, *Essays and Lectures, Chiefly on the Religion of the Hindus* (London: Trübner, 1846), pp. 257–58. As Arthur Avalon observes, "Since Wilson's time all who have dealt with the Tantras . . . adopted second-hand the accounts given by him and Ward" (*Principles of Tantra: The Tantratattva of Śrīyukta Śiva Candra Vidyārṇava Bhaṭṭācārya Mahodaya,* vol. 1 [Madras: Ganesh, 1960], p. 4).

27. H. H. Wilson, *Religious Sects of the Hindus,* ed. Ernst R. Rost (Calcutta: Susil Gupta, 1858), p. 140.

28. Monier Monier-Williams, *Hinduism* (London: Society for Promoting Christian Knowledge, 1894), pp. 122–23. Somewhat earlier, in 1874, J. Talboys Wheeler spoke of the "so-called Tantric religion," in which "nudity is worshipped in Bacchanalian orgies which cannot be described" (*The History of India from the Earliest Age* [London: Trübner, 1874], p. 364).

29. Monier-Williams, *Hinduism,* p. 116.

30. Ibid., p.130.

31. Quoted in Avalon, *Principles of Tantra,* p. 5. As J. N. Farquhar put it, "The observances are foul beyond description, always involving promiscuity and often incest" (*Modern Religious Movements in India* [New York: Macmillan, 1915], p. 304).

32. Edmond Demaitre, *The Yogis of India* (London: Geoffrey Bless, 1937), pp. 222–23. Similar accounts can be found in a variety of other authors. According to August Barth, "a Śākta of the left hand is almost always a hypocrite and a superstitious debauchee" (*The Religions of India* [London: Kegan Paul, 1891], pp. 199–200).

33. Eugene Burnouf, *Introduction à l'histoire du Bouddhisme Indien* (Paris: Maisonneuve, 1844), p. 523. Similar narratives of primitive Buddhism and Tantric decline were used by Indian authors. As Rajendralala Mitra comments, "Practices are enjoined which are at once the most revolting and horrible that human depravity could think of and compared to which the worst specimens of Holiwell Street literature . . . would appear absolutely pure" (*The Sanskrit Buddhist Literature of Nepal* [1882; reprint, New Delhi: Cosmo Publications, 1981], p. 261).

34. L. Austine Waddell, *Tibetan Buddhism: With Its Mystic Cults, Symbolism, and Mythology, and in Its Relation to Indian Buddhism* (1895; reprint, New York: Dover Publications, 1972), pp. 4–5. See also Louis de la Vallé Poussin, "Tantrism [Buddhist]," in *Encyclopedia of Religion and Ethics,* vol. 12, ed. James Hastings (New York: Charles Scribner's Sons, 1922), pp. 194–95.

35. Waddell, *Tibetan Buddhism,* p. 1.

36. Ibid., pp. ix.

37. Ibid., p. 573.

38. Gustav Oppert, *On the Original Inhabitants of Bharatavarsa* (London: A. Constable, 1893), pp. 553–54. For Friedrich Max Müller's influential account of "Aryan civilization" and its distinction from the "Dravidian" peoples, see *Lectures on the Science of Language* (New York: Charles Scribner's Sons, 1864), chaps. 7, 9, 11.

39. Isaac Taylor, *The Origin of the Aryans: An Account of the Prehistoric Ethnology and Civilisation of Europe* (London: Walter Scott, 1889), p. 212. Similar narratives are repeated by Indologists like Arthur A. Macdonell and Arthur Barriedale Keith, *Vedic Index of Names and Subjects* (London: John Murray, 1912), pp. 247–71.

40. Inden, *Imagining India,* p. 119. See also Trautmann, *Aryans and British India,* chap. 2.

41. Jeffrey Weeks, *Sex, Politics, and Society: The Regulation of Society since 1800* (London: Longman, 1989), pp. 6–7.

42. Michel Foucault, quoted in Robert Wuthnow et al., eds., *Cultural Analysis: The Work of Peter L. Berger, Mary Douglas, Michel Foucault, and Jürgen Habermas* (Boston: Routledge and Kegan Paul, 1984), pp. 171–72.

43. Steven Kern, *The Culture of Love: Victorians to Moderns* (Cambridge, Mass.: Harvard University Press 1992), pp. 334–35.

44. John Maynard, "Victorian Discourses on Sexuality and Religion," *University of Hartford Studies in Literature* 19 (1987): 61.

45. Patricia Anderson, *When Passion Reigned: Sex and the Victorians* (New York: Basic Books, 1995), pp. 17–18.

46. See David Arnold, *Colonizing the Body: State Medicine and Epidemic Disease in Nineteenth Century India* (Berkeley: University of California Press, 1993).

47. Anne McClintock, *Imperial Leather: Race, Gender, and Sexuality in the Colonial Context* (New York, Routledge, 1995), p. 14. See Edward Said, *Orientalism* (New York: Alfred A. Knopf, 1979), p. 23.

48. Robert Orme, *Historical Fragments of the Moghul Empire* (1782; reprint, New Delhi: Associated Publishing House, 1982), p. 306. As Katherine Mayo later described it in her classic, *Mother India,* the Indian is characterized by a basic kind of effeminate "slave mentality," which is "ever the flaccid subject of foreign rule," due to the "devitalizing character of Hindu religion" (*Mother India* [New York: Harcourt, Brace, 1928], p. 29).

49. George MacMunn, *The Underworld of India* (London: Jarrolds Publishers, 1933), p. 96. As Mayo described it, the Indian character is from the earliest age corrupted by premature sexual stimulation, excessive masturbation, and other moral evils. At the very age "when the Anglo-Saxon is just coming into the full glory of manhood," the Indian is so drained and debilitated by sexual indulgences that he is left "poor and sick and his hands too weak to hold the reins of Government" (*Mother India,* p. 38). See also Kenneth Ballhatchet, *Race, Sex, and Class under the Raj: Imperial Attitudes and Policies, 1793–1905* (New York: St. Martin's Press, 1980), p. 5.

50. Lewis D. Wurgaft, *The Imperial Imagination: Magic and Myth in Kipling's India* (Middletown, Conn: Wesleyan University Press, 1983), p. 49. See also Jenny Sharpe, *Allegories of Empire: The Figure of Women in the Colonial Text* (Minneapolis: University of Minnesota Press, 1993).

51. Miranda Shaw, *Passionate Enlightenment: Women in Tantric Buddhism* (Princeton, N.J.: Princeton University Press, 1994), pp. 8–9. On the British denigration of the *devadāsī* tradition, see Frédérique Apffel Marglin, *Wives of the God-King: The Devadāsīs of Puri* (New York: Oxford University Press, 1985).

52. John Campbell Oman, *The Mystics, Ascetics, and Saints of India* (London: T. F. Urwin, 1903), p. 165. Likewise, as Barend Faddegon commented in 1940, "We may regard Śāktism as an epidemic and social neurosis; as such it is not without significance for neurology" ("Brahmanisme en Hindoeisme," in *De Godsdiensten der Wereld,* vol. 1, ed. G. van der Leeuw [Amsterdam: H. Meulenhoff, 1940], p. 333).

53. Foucault, *The History of Sexuality,* vol. 1, p. 145.

54. Wilhelm Halbfass, *India and Europe: An Essay in Understanding* (Albany: State University of New York Press, 1988), p. 173.

55. Prem Lata, *Swami Dayānanda Sarasvatī* (New Delhi: Sumit Publications, 1990), p. 199.

56. Chiranjiva Bharadwaja, trans., *The Light of Truth; or, An English Translation of the Satyarth Prakash of Swami Dayanand Saraswati* (1927; reprint, Madras: Arya Samaj, 1932), p. 319.

57. *The Autobiography of Swāmī Dayānand Saraswatī,* ed. K. C. Yadav (New Delhi: Manohar, 1976), pp. 29–30.

58. Reprinted in Rhinehart and Stewart, "The Anonymous *Āgama Prakāśa,*" pp. 277, 281.

59. Ibid., pp. 267–68.

60. Ibid., pp. 269–70.

61. On the concept of the "counter-Bengal-Renaissance," see Hugh B. Urban, *The Economics of Ecstasy: Tantra, Secrecy, and Power in Colonial Bengal* (New York: Oxford University Press, 2001), chap. 2.

62. David Kopf, *The Brahmo Samaj and the Shaping of the Modern Indian Mind* (Princeton, N.J.: Princeton University Press, 1979), p. xiii. The quote at the start of this section, and the epigraph, come from Rāmmohun Roy, "A Defence of Hindoo Theism," in *The English Works of Raja Rāmmohun Roy,* vol. 1, ed. J. C. Ghose (New Delhi: Cosmo Publications, 1982), p. 98.

63. Friedrich Max Müller, *Biographical Essays* (New York: Charles Scribner's Sons, 1884), p. 13.

64. Kopf, *British Orientalism,* p. 9.

65. Halbfass, *India and Europe,* p. 203. See also Tapan Raychaudhuri, *Europe Reconsidered: Perceptions of the West in Nineteenth Century Bengal* (New Delhi: Oxford University Press, 1988), pp. 3–4.

66. Ashis Nandy, *At the Edge of Psychology: Essays in Politics and Culture* (New Delhi: Oxford University Press, 1980), p. 23.

67. S. K. De, *Bengali Literature in the Nineteenth Century* (Calcutta: Firma KLM, 1962), p. 516.

68. Rāmmohun Roy, "An Abridgment of the Vedānta," in *Sources of Indian Tradition,* ed. T. de Bary (New York: Columbia University Press, 1958), p. 573.

69. Letter to A. Duff, in Sophia Collet, *The Life and Letters of Raja Rāmmohun Roy* (Calcutta: D. K. Biswas, 1962), p. 280.

70. Kopf, *The Brahmo Samaj,* p. 265; cf. Rāmmohun Roy, "A Defence of Hindoo Theism," p. 99.

71. Farquhar, *Modern Religious Movements in India,* p. 31.

72. Nandy, *At the Edge of Psychology,* p. 9.

73. Rāmmohun Roy, "A Defence of Hindoo Theism," p. 99.

74. Ernest Payne, *The Śāktas: An Introductory and Comparative Study* (New York: Garland Publishing, 1979), p. 55. Here I will use Arthur Avalon translation, *Tantra of the Great Liberation: Mahānirvāṇa Tantra* (New York: Dover Publications, 1979). For a more detailed discussion of this text, see Hugh B. Urban, "The Strategic Uses of an Esoteric Text: *The Mahānirvāṇa Tantra,*" *South Asia* 18, no. 1 (1995): 55–81.

75. John Woodroffe, *Shakti and Shākta* (New York: Dover Publications, 1978), p. 594.

76. See Urban, "Strategic Uses," pp. 55–81; J. Duncan M. Derrett, "A Juridical Fabrication of Early British India: The *Mahānirvāṇa Tantra,*" in Derrett, *Essays in Classical and Modern Indian Law* (Leiden: E. J. Brill, 1977), pp. 197–242.

77. S. C. Banerji, *Tantra in Bengal* (New Delhi: Manohar Publications, 1992), p. 106.

78. Avalon, preface to the *Tantra of the Great Liberation,* p. xii.

79. Ernest Payne, *The Śāktas,* p. 55.

80. On the Tantric image of Kālī and its later transformations, see Jeffrey J.

Kripal and Rachel Fell McDermott, eds., *Encountering Kālī: In the Margins, at the Center, in the West* (Berkeley: University of California Press, 2003); on changing images of Kālī in the colonial era, see Hugh B. Urban, "India's Darkest Heart: Kālī in the Colonial Imagination," in the same volume; also Kopf, "An Historiographical Essay," pp. 12–15.

81. Rachel Fell McDermott, *Mother of My Heart, Daughter of My Dreams: Transformations of Kālī and Umā in the Devotional Poetry of Bengal* (New York: Oxford University Press, 2001).

82. Wendy Doniger O'Flaherty, ed., *Textual Sources for the Study of Hinduism* (Chicago: University of Chicago Press, 1989), p. 134.

83. June McDaniel, *The Madness of the Saints: Ecstatic Religion in Bengal* (Chicago: University of Chicago Press, 1989), p. 104.

84. Woodroffe, *Shakti and Shākta,* p. 594.

85. Derrett, "A Juridical Fabrication," p. 206.

86. See Banerji, *Tantra in Bengal,* p. 108.

87. Ibid., pp. 110 ff.

88. Derrett, "A Juridical Fabrication," p. 208.

89. Ibid., pp. 225, 214.

90. Ibid., p. 224.

91. De, *Bengali Literature,* pp. 513, 503. "It is probable that Hariharananda initiated Rammohun into Tantrik belief. This appears . . . from Debendranath Thakur's testimony . . . that he made a disciple of Hariharananda . . . who informed him that Rammohun . . . was a Tantrik Brahman Avadhuta" (ibid.).

92. Rāmmohun Roy, quoted in Halbfass, *India and Europe,* p. 343.

93. Derrett, "A Juridical Fabrication," p. 230. See also McDaniel, *The Madness of the Saints,* pp. 103–4.

94. Because Hariharānanda's commentary on the text contains a number of errors and misreadings, it seems unlikely that he composed the text himself (Derrett, "A Juridical Fabrication," p. 201).

95. B. N. Dasgupta, *The Life and Times of Rajah Rāmmohun Roy* (New Delhi: Ambika, 1980), p. 154.

96. Jonathan Z. Smith, *Imagining Religion: From Babylon to Jonestown* (Chicago: University of Chicago Press, 1982), p. 98.

97. David Haberman, "On Trial: The Love of the Sixteen Thousand Gopīs," *History of Religions* 33, no. 1 (1993): 67–68.

98. Benyotosh Bhattacharyya, *An Introduction to Buddhist Esoterism* (Oxford: Oxford University Press, 1932), p. 32.

99. Ibid., pp. 172, 165.

CHAPTER 2. SACRIFICING WHITE GOATS TO THE GODDESS

1. See Francis Hutchins, *The Illusion of Permanence* (Princeton, N.J.: Princeton University Press, 1967), pp. x–xii; Thomas Metcalf, *The Aftermath of Revolt: India, 1857–1870* (Princeton, N.J.: Princeton University Press, 1964). For a classic account of the Indian Mutiny see Colin Campbell, *Narrative of the Indian Revolt, from Its Outbreak to the Capture of Lucknow* (London: G. Vickers, 1858).

2. Indra Sinha, *The Great Book of Tantra: Translations and Images from Classic Indian Texts with Commentary* (Rochester, Vt.: Destiny Books, 1993), p. 11.

3. Michael Taussig, *Shamanism, Colonialism, and the Wild Man: A Study in Terror and Healing* (Chicago: University of Chicago Press, 1987), p. 134.

4. Nicholas Thomas, *Colonialism's Culture: Anthropology, Travel, and Government* (Princeton, N.J.: Princeton University Press, 1994), p. 15.

5. M. Paul Dare, *Indian Underworld: A First-hand Account of Hindu Saints, Sorcerers, and Superstitions* (New York: E. P. Dutton, 1940), p. 56. See also Augustus Somerville, *Crime and Religious Beliefs in India* (Calcutta: Thacker, Spink, 1931).

6. Richard King, *Orientalism and Religion: Postcolonial Theory, India, and the Mystic East* (London: Routledge, 1999), p. 97.

7. Lewis D. Wurgaft, *The Imperial Imagination: Magic and Myth in Kipling's India* (Middletown, Conn: Wesleyan University Press, 1983), p. 6. For a comprehensive account from the British perspective, see Colin Campbell, *Narrative of the Indian Revolt.*

8. Valentine Chirol, *Indian Unrest* (London: Macmillan, 1910), pp. 29–30.

9. Friedrich Max Müller, *Biographical Essays* (New York: Charles Scribner's Sons, 1884), p. 49.

10. See Thomas Coburn, *Devī Mahātmya: The Crystallization of the Goddess Tradition* (New Delhi: Motilal Banarsidas, 1984), p. 110; Wendell Charles Beane, *Myth, Cult, and Symbols in Śākta Hinduism: A Study of the Indian Mother Goddess* (Leiden: E. J. Brill, 1977), chap. 2.

11. James Preston, *The Cult of the Goddess: Social and Religious Change in a Hindu Temple* (New Delhi: Vikas, 1980) p. 63; cf. David Kinsley, *The Sword and the Flute: Kālī and Kṛṣṇa, Dark Visions of the Terrible and the Sublime in Hindu Mythology* (Berkeley: University of California Press, 1975), p. 108.

12. William Ward, *A View of the History, Literature, and Religion of the Hindoos*, vol. 1 (London: Kingsbury, Parbury, and Allen, 1817), pp. xcvi, xxxvii.

13. Reverend Alexander Duff, *Indian and Indian Missions, Including the Gigantic System of Hinduism, both in Theory and Practice* (1839; reprint, New Delhi: Swati, 1988), p. 265.

14. John Campbell Oman, *The Brahmans, Theists, and Mystics of India* (Philadelphia: George W. Jacob, 1903), p. 10.

15. Oman, *Brahmans, Theists, and Mystics,* p. 11. See also Katherine Mayo's gory description of a wild, bloody, almost orgiastic goat sacrifice to Kālī, which opens her widely read *Mother India* (New York: Harcourt, Brace, 1928), pp. 15–16.

16. Caleb Wright, *India and Its Inhabitants* (St. Louis: J. A. Brainerd, 1860), p. 225.

17. Chirol, *Indian Unrest,* pp. 102–3.

18. Taussig, *Shamanism,* p. 104.

19. William Ward, *A View of the History,* p. 151.

20. For a good discussion of the Thuggee in relation to British rule, see Radhika Singha, "'Providential' Circumstances: The Thuggee Campaign of the 1830s and Legal Innovation," *Modern Asian Studies* 27, no. 1 (1993): 83–146.

Amal Chatterjee seems to think the Thuggee narrative was largely the product of the British imagination, much as the narratives of heresy and witchcraft during the European Middle Ages were largely the product of the Inquisition (*Representations of India, 1740–1840: The Creation of India in the Colonial Imagination* [New York: St. Martin's Press, 1998], pp. 125–44).

21. See Humes, "Wrestling with Kālī: South Asian and British Constructions of the Dark Goddess," in *Encountering Kālī: In the Margins, at the Center, in the West,* ed. Jeffrey J. Kripal and Rachel Fell McDermott (Berkeley: University of California Press, 2003), pp. 145–68; Hugh B. Urban, "India's Darkest Heart: Kālī in the Colonial Imagination," in the same volume. See also Javed Majeed, "Meadows Taylor's *Confessions of a Thug:* The Anglo-Indian Novel as Genre in the Making," in *Writing India, 1757–1990: The Literature of British India,* ed. Bart Moore-Gilbert (Manchester: Manchester University Press, 1996), pp. 86–110.

22. Richard Sherwood, quoted in W. H. Sleeman, *The Thugs or Phansigars of India: Comprising a History of the Rise and Progress of That Extraordinary Fraternity of Assassins* (Philadelphia: Carey and Hart, 1839), pp. 13, 18

23. James Sleeman, *Thug; or, A Million Murders* (London: Sampson, Low, Marston, 1926), p. 117. On the life and work of Sleeman, see Francis Tuker, *The Yellow Scarf: The Story of the Life of Thuggee Sleeman* (London: J. M. Dent and Sons, 1961); *Selected Records Collected from the Central Provinces and Berar Secretariat Relating to the Suppression of Thuggee* (Nagpur: Government Printing, 1939).

24. George Bruce, *The Stranglers: The Cult of Thuggee and Its Overthrow in British India* (London: Longman's, 1968), p. 124.

25. Philip Meadows Taylor, *Confessions of a Thug* (1839; reprint, Oxford: Clarendon Press, 1984), pp. 5–6.

26. Amal Chatterjee, *Representations of India,* pp. 133–34.

27. George MacMunn, *The Underworld of India* (London: Jarrolds Publishers, 1933), p. 214. See W. H. Sleeman, *Ramaseeana; or, A Vocabulary of the Peculiar Language Used by the Thugs, with an Introduction and Appendix, Descriptive of the System Pursued by That Fraternity and of the Measures Which Have Been Adopted by the Supreme Government of India for Its Suppression* (Calcutta: Military Orphan Press, 1836); reprinted in *The Thugs or Phansigars of India,* compiled from the documents published by Captain W. H. Sleeman (Philadelphia: Carey and Hart, 1839).

28. James Sleeman, *Thug,* p. 18; cf. Tuker, *The Yellow Scarf,* p. 87.

29. Homi Bhabha, "The Other Question: Difference, Discrimination, and the Discourse of Colonialism," in *Literature, Politics, and Theory,* ed. Francis Barker, Peter Hulme, Margaret Iverson, and Diana Loxley (London: Methuen, 1986), p. 156.

30. See Edward Thornton, *Illustrations of the History and Practices of the Thugs* (London: Nattali and Bond, 1837); Philip Meadows Taylor, *Confessions of a Thug.* On Taylor's *Confessions,* see Majeed, "Meadows Taylor's *Confessions of a Thug.*"

31. Sherwood, reprinted in W. H. Sleeman, *The Thugs or Phansigars,* p. 27.

32. David Annan, "Thuggee," in *Secret Societies,* ed. Norman MacKenzie (New York: Holt, Rhinehart, and Winston, 1967), p. 76, summarizing Richard

Sherwood, "Of the Murderers Called Phansigars," *Madras Literary Gazette* (1816).

33. Wright, *India and Its Inhabitants,* p. 129.

34. W. H. Sleeman to Francis Curwen Smith, June 1830, in Bruce, *The Stranglers,* p. 78. On this point, see Singha, "'Providential' Circumstances," which argues that the British campaign to suppress the Thuggee in the 1830s was a key part of the state's changing role in the territories, justifying the need for a more pervasive legal and police apparatus (pp. 90–118).

35. Bruce, *The Stranglers,* p. 6.

36. John Malcolm, governor of Bombay, cited in Bruce, *The Stranglers,* p. 8.

37. James Sleeman, *Thug,* p. 109; cf. Thornton, *Illustrations,* p. 4.

38. F. C. Smith to H. T. Prinsep, 19 November 1830, in *Selected Records Collected from the Central Provinces,* p. 53.

39. "Measures of the Government for the Suppression of Thuggee," in W. H. Sleeman, *The Thugs or Phansigars of India,* pp. 66–67.

40. James Sleeman, *Thug,* p. 102. For a good discussion of Act 30, see Singha, "'Providential' Circumstances," pp. 90–118. As W. H. Sleeman commented, "Thug approvers whose evidence we required were employed in all parts of India . . . [but] it was difficult to bring all whose evidence was necessary at the tribals to the courts of the district in which the murder was perpetrated. . . . To obviate all these difficulties separate courts were formed, with permission to receive whatever evidence they might think likely to prove valuable, attaching to each portion . . . whatever weight it might seem to deserve" (*Rambles and Reflections of an Indian Official* [1844; reprint, Oxford: Oxford University Press, 1915], pp. 88–89).

41. James Sleeman, *Thug,* p. 29.

42. MacMunn, *The Underworld of India,* pp. 214, 218.

43. The Earl of Ronaldshay, *The Heart of Aryavarta: A Study of the Psychology of Indian Unrest* (London: A. Constable, 1925), p. 92.

44. Justice S. A. T. Rowlatt et al., *Report of Committee Appointed to Investigate Revolutionary Conspiracies in India* (London: His Majesty's Stationary Office, 1918), par. 30; see also Ernest Payne, *The Śāktas: An Introductory and Comparative Study* (New York: Garland Publishing, 1979), p. 101.

45. MacMunn, *The Underworld of India,* p. 239.

46. Ibid., p. 218.

47. Ibid., pp. 101, 209–10. See also the chapter "Sex Symbolism" in the Earl of Ronaldshay's *The Heart of Aryavarta.*

48. See Bill Ashcroft, Gareth Griffiths, Helen Tiffin, *The Empire Writes Back: Theory and Practice in Post-Colonial Literatures* (London: Routledge, 1989), p. 33.

49. Susan Buck-Morss, *The Dialectics of Seeing: Walter Benjamin and the Arcades Project* (Cambridge, Mass.: MIT Press, 1989), p. 116.

50. Ibid., p. 219. See also Walter Benjamin, *Gesammelte Schriften,* vol. 5, ed. Rolf Tiedemann and Hermann Schweppenhauser (Frankfurt: Suhrkamp Verlag, 1972), p. 595; Buck-Morss, "Benjamin's *Passagenwerk,*" *New German Critique* 29 (1983): 211–40.

51. See Benjamin, "On the Mimetic Faculty," in *Reflections,* ed. Peter Demetz, trans. Edmund Jephcott (New York: Schocken Books, 1986), pp. 333–36; Michael Taussig, *Mimesis and Alerity: A Particular History of the Senses* (London: Routledge, 1993), pp. 19–20, 177.

52. Taussig, *Shamanism,* pp. 230, 391.

53. Taussig, *Mimesis and Alterity,* pp. 177–82.

54. Sumit Sarkar, *The Swadeshi Movement in Bengal, 1903–1908* (New Delhi: People's Publishing House, 1973), pp. 314, 400. Sarkar provides a good outline of the Swadeshi movement, and divides it into four classes: (1) the moderates; (2) the trend toward self-development without inviting an immediate political clash (constructive Swadeshi); (3) political extremism using extended boycott or passive resistance; and (4) terrorism (p. 33).

55. K. R. Srinivasa Iyengar, *Sri Aurobindo* (Calcutta: Arya Publishing House, 1950), p. 177. See Arun Chandra Guha, *Aurobindo and Jugantar* (Calcutta: Sāhitya Saṃsad, 1978); Peter Heehs, "Aurobindo Ghose and Revolutionary Terrorism," *South Asia* 15, no. 2 (1992): 47–69; and *The Bomb in Bengal: The Rise of Revolutionary Terrorism in India, 1900–1910* (New Delhi: Oxford University Press, 1993); Robert N. Minor, *The Religious, the Spiritual, and the Secular: Auroville and Secular India* (Albany: State University of New York Press, 1999), pp. 20–23.

56. Sri Aurobindo, cited in Arun Chandra Guha, *Aurobindo and Jugantar,* p. 21.

57. As Heehs argues, the term "Jugantar" was originally applied by the government to the group surrounding Barin Ghose and the staff of the *Jugantar* paper; later it came to refer to the loose federation of secret societies in various parts of Bengal that stood apart from the Dacca Anushilan. The phrase "Jugantar Party" did not come into general use until after 1915 (*The Bomb in Bengal,* p. 243). As Aurobindo's brother Barin put it, "Very few among my countrymen, except the government, know that Aurobindo had been the father the revolutionary cult in Bengal" (Barindra Kumar Ghose, *Sri Aurobindo as I Understand Him,* cited in Heehs, "Aurobindo Ghose," p. 53).

58. Letter of 13 July 1911, published in *Sri Aurobindo: Archives and Research* 1, no. 2 (1977): 84. Sometime around 1902, Aurobindo had come into contact with a mysterious brotherhood led by a figure named Thakur Saheb, that claimed to have existed since the time of the mutiny. Its purpose was to prepare a national insurrection. See Barindra Kumār Ghoṣe, *Agnijug* (Calcutta: Book Publishing, 1355 Bengali era [1948]), p. 38; Heehs, *The Bomb and Bengal,* p. 43.

59. Keshub Choudhuri, *The Mother and Passionate Politics* (Calcutta: Vidyodaya Library, 1979), p. 56. On Aurobindo's use of Tantric elements in both his political and spiritual works, see Kees Bolle, *The Persistence of Religion: An Essay on Tantrism and Sri Aurobindo's Philosophy* (Leiden: E. J. Brill, 1971), pp. 79–102. "The Dacca Anushilan . . . had a complicated system of primary *(adya)* and final *(antya)* vows, all emphasising total subordination to the leader, secrecy and readiness to do anything for the samiti. . . . The neo-tantric rituals affected by the revolutionary groups . . . struck a chord in the folk memory of Bengal" (Sarkar, *The Swadeshi Movement in Bengal,* pp. 313, 314).

60. Heehs, *The Bomb and Bengal,* pp. 111–12.

61. Peter Heehs, *Sri Aurobindo: A Brief Biography* (New Delhi: Oxford: University Press, 1989), p. 53.

62. Ibid., p. 54.

63. Sri Aurobindo Ghose, *Bande Mataram: Early Political Writings* (Pondicherry: Sri Aurobindo Ashram Press, 1972), pp. 652, 659–60.

64. Cited in Iyengar, *Sri Aurobindo,* p. 225; cf. Minor, *The Religious,* p. 20.

65. Heehs, *Sri Aurobindo,* p. 37.

66. Cited in Arun Chandra Guha, *Aurobindo and Jugantar,* p. 19. Lieutenant Governor Baker described Aurobindo as "an active generator of revolutionary sentiment. He is imbued with a semi-religious fanaticism . . . and I attribute the spread of seditious doctrines to him personally in a greater degree than to any other individual . . . in India" (Baker to Minto, 10 April 1910; cited in Guenter Lewy, *Religion and Revolution* [New York: Oxford University Press, 1974], p. 292).

67. *Jugantar,* cited in Chirol, *Indian Unrest,* p. 92. On the revolutionary wing of the nationalists, see Leonard Gordon, *Bengal: The Nationalist Movement, 1876–1940* (New York: Columbia University Press, 1973).

68. See Bankimcandra Caṭṭopādhyāy, *Ānandamaṭh: Racanār Preranā o Parināma, tatsaha Bankimacandrer Ānanda maṭher Prathama Saṃskāraner Phatokapi,* ed. Cittarañjan Bandyopādhyāy (Calcutta: Ānanda, 1983). As we will see in chapter 3, there are many conflicting interpretations of *Ānandamaṭh;* while some see it as primarily anti-Muslim propaganda, which defends the need for just British rule, others argue that it was an originally anti-British text that was censored in order to protect the author's place as a British civil servant.

69. Choudhuri, *The Mother and Passionate Politics,* p. 39.

70. Bankim Chandra Chatterjee, *The Abbey of Bliss* (Ānandamaṭh), trans. Nares Chandra Sen-Gupta (Calcutta: Cherry Press, n.d.), pp. 40–41.

71. Quoted in Iyengar, *Sri Aurobindo,* p. 180. See Aurobindo's translation of "Bande Mataram" in V. Rangarajan, *Vande Mataram* (Madras: Sisiter Nivedita Academy, 1977), p. xv.

72. Kumari Jayawardena, *The White Woman's Other Burden: Western Women and South Asia during British Colonial Rule* (New York: Routledge, 1995), p. 210.

73. Lewy, *Religion and Revolution,* p. 292.

74. Leonard Gordon, *Bengal,* p. 113. "It is our mission to purge barbarism . . . out of humanity and to Aryanise the world" (Aurobindo Ghose, "Bhawani Mandir," in *Bande Mataram,* p. 66).

75. Ghose, "Bhawani Mandir," pp. 61–62.

76. Ibid., p. 65.

77. Ibid., p. 64. On this "search for martial Indianness," see Ashis Nandy, *The Intimate Enemy: Loss and Recovery of Self under Colonialism* (New Delhi: Oxford University Press, 1983), p. 7.

78. Nandy, *The Intimate Enemy,* p. 52.

79. Bipanchandra Pal, cited in Choudhuri, *The Mother and Passionate Politics,* p. 53; cf. Ernest Payne, *The Śāktas,* p. 104.

80. Sri Aurobindo Ghose, "The Wheat and the Chaff," *Bande Mataram Daily* (23 April 1908), in *Bande Mataram,* p. 873.

81. Sri Aurobindo Ghose, "Bhavani Bharati, Mother of India," *Sri Aurobindo: Archives and Research* 9 (1985): 134, 149–51.

82. *Jugantar,* quoted in Choudhuri, *The Mother and Passionate Politics,* p. 46. As the radical newspaper *Sandhya* stated in 1907, "This bomb is called Kālī Ma's boma . . . it must be kept in every house. . . . A son is wanted from every family who must practice the virtues of the *Kshatriya.* Let them play with Kālī Ma's boma" (Heehs, *The Bomb and Bengal,* p. 117).

83. Choudhuri, *The Mother and Passionate Politics,* p. 50; Nandy, *The Intimate Enemy,* p. 92.

84. See Nandy, *The Intimate Enemy,* p. 52.

85. See Heehs, *Sri Aurobindo,* p. 130.

86. Sri Aurobindo Ghose, *The Hour of God* (Pondicherry: Sri Aurobindo Ashram Press, 1973), p. 366.

87. Partha Chatterjee, *The Nation and Its Fragments: Colonial and Postcolonial Histories* (Princeton, N.J.: Princeton University Press, 1993), pp. 117, 59.

88. Heehs, *Sri Aurobindo,* pp. 34–35. As Aurobindo puts it, "The most vital issue of the age is whether the future progress of humanity is to be governed by the modern economic and materialist mind of the West or by a nobler pragmatism . . . enlightened by spiritual culture. . . . The hope of the world lies . . . in the flooding out of the light of Asia in the Occident" (*The Supramental Manifestation and Other Writings* [Pondicherry: Sri Aurobindo Ashram Press, 1972], p. 326).

89. Heehs, *Sri Aurobindo,* p. 152.

90. Wilhelm Halbfass, *India and Europe: An Essay in Understanding* (Albany: State University of New York Press, 1988), p. 249.

91. See Aurobindo Ghose, *The Mother* (Pondicherry: Sri Aurobindo Ashram Press, 1929); Kireet Joshi, *Sri Aurobindo and the Mother* (New Delhi: Motilal Banarsidas, 1989), pp. 24 ff. See also K. R. Srinivasa Iyengar, *On the Mother: The Character of Her Manifestation and Ministry* (Pondicherry: Sri Aurobindo International Centre, 1994).

92. Sri Aurobindo Ghose, *Sri Aurobindo on Himself and the Mother* (Pondicherry: Sri Aurobindo Asram Press, 1953), p. 431; cf. Joshi, *Sri Aurobindo and the Mother,* p. 106. On the "the deification and transformation of Mira Richards into the Mother," see Jayawardena, *White Woman's Other Burden,* p. 214.

93. Aurobindo, cited in Satprem, *Mother; or, The Divine Materialism* (Madras: Macmillan India, 1977), p. 1.

94. Heehs, *Sri Aurobindo,* p. 133; cf. letter of 26 March 1926, in *Sri Aurobindo Circle* 32 (1976): 25–26.

95. Joshi, *Sri Aurobindo and the Mother,* p. 97.

96. Ghose, *The Mother,* p. 24.

97. Nandy, *The Intimate Enemy,* p. 85.

98. Partha Chatterjee, *The Nation,* pp. 6–11; cf. Halbfass, *India and Europe,* p. 250.

99. Halbfass, *India and Europe,* p. 369.

100. Ranajit Guha, "On Some Aspects of the Historiography of Colonial India," in *Subaltern Studies,* vol. 1, *Writings on South Asian History and Society,*

ed. Ranajit Guha (1982; reprint, New Delhi: Oxford University Press, 1994), p. 7. See also Partha Chatterjee, *The Nation,* pp. 6–11.

101. Ranajit Guha, "The Prose of Counter-Insurgency," in *Subaltern Studies,* vol. 2, *Writings on South Asian History and Society,* ed. Ranajit Guha (1982; reprint, New Delhi: Oxford University Press, 1994): "The specificity of rebel consciousness had eluded radical historiography as well. . . . In this a-historical view of the history of insurgency all moments of consciousness are assimilated to the ultimate and highest moment of the series—to an Ideal Consciousness. . . . Since the Ideal is supposed to be 100 percent secular in character, the devotee tends to look away when confronted with the evidence of religiosity . . . or explain it away as a clear but well-intentioned fraud perpetrated by enlightened leaders on their moronic followers" (p. 39). On this point, see also Saurabh Dube, *Untouchable Pasts: Religion, Identity, and Power among a Central Indian Community, 1780–1950* (Albany: State University of New York Press, 1998); and Hugh B. Urban, *The Economics of Ecstasy: Tantra, Secrecy, and Power in Colonial Bengal* (New York: Oxford University Press, 2001), chaps. 4, 7.

CHAPTER 3. INDIA'S DARKEST HEART

1. Marie Louise Pratt, *Imperial Eyes: Travel Writing and Transculturation* (New York: Routledge, 1992), p. 6. On this point, see also Bart Moore-Gilbert, ed., *Writing India, 1757–1990: The Literature of British India* (Manchester: Manchester University Press, 1996), pp. 5–6.

2. David N. Lorenzen, "A Parody of the Kāpālikas in the *Mattavilāsa,*" in *Tantra in Practice,* ed. David Gordon White (Princeton, N.J.: Princeton University Press, 2000), p. 87. See also Hugh B. Urban, "The Remnants of Desire: Sacrificial Violence and Sexual Transgression in the Cult of the Kāpālikas and in the Writings of Georges Bataille," *Religion* 25 (1995): 67–90.

3. Lorenzen, "A Parody of the Kāpālikas," p. 87.

4. Sita Krishna Nambiar, trans., *Prabodhacandrodaya of Kṛṣṇa Miśra* (New Delhi: Motilal Banarsidas, 1971), 3.12–13. See also Bhavabhūti's *Mālatī-Mādhava,* French trans. G. Strehly (Paris: Ernest Leroux, 1885), p. 119.

5. *Prabodhacandrodaya,* 3.16.

6. Timothy Brennan, "The National Longing for Form," in *The Post-Colonial Studies Reader,* ed. Bill Ashcroft, Gareth Griffiths, and Helen Tiffin (New York: Routledge, 1995), pp. 172–73; cf. Homi Bhabha, ed., *Nation and Narration* (London: Routledge, 1990); Firdous Azim, *The Colonial Rise of the Novel* (New York: Routledge, 1993).

7. Benita Parry, *Delusions and Discoveries: Studies on India in the British Imagination, 1880–1930* (London: Allen Lane, 1972), p. 87. On "the notion of India as a locus of exotic sexual energies," see M. Keith Booker, *Colonial Power, Colonial Texts: India in the Modern British Novel* (East Lansing: Asian Studies Center, University of Michigan, 1997), p. 176. See also Nancy L. Paxton, *Writing under the Raj: Gender, Race, and Rape in the British Colonial Imagination, 1830–1947* (New Brunswick, N.J.: Rutgers University Press, 1999).

8. On the role of the *devadāsī* in the British imagination, see Paxton, *Writing under the Raj,* p. 84. As Parry comments, "The Tantric tradition . . . was fre-

quently invoked by the British as evidence of India's depravity and intimacy with the forces of darkness. The rites of this system gave expression to inclinations which were rigorously suppressed in Imperial Britain. . . . Indians were feared not only as subjects who had once rebelled . . . but as perverts threatening to . . . seduce the white world" (*Delusions and Discoveries,* p. 149).

9. Flora Annie Steel, "On the Second Story," in *In the Permanent Way* (London: Heinemann, 1898), p. 309.

10. In 1876, Burton and his collaborator, Arbuthnot, undertook a project of translating various Oriental works, primarily erotica, to be released under the guise of an Oriental publishing house known as the Kama Shastra Society. The most important texts they translated were the *Anaṅga Raṅga* and the *Kāma Sūtra,* the latter appearing in 1883. Originally, the *Kāma Sūtra* was intended only for private circulation, but it was soon pirated and published in Paris and Brussels (Edward Rice, *Captain Sir Richard Francis Burton: The Secret Agent Who Made the Pilgrimage to Mecca, Discovered the Kāma Sūtra, and Brought the Arabian Nights to the West* [New York: Charles Scribner's Sons, 1990], pp. 444–47).

11. Rice, *Captain Sir Richard Francis Burton,* p. 65. "Burton's life was passed in a ceaseless quest for the kind of secret knowledge labeled broadly as Gnosis by which he hoped to uncover the very source of existence. . . . This search led him to investigate the Kabbalah, alchemy . . . and the erotic way called Tantra" (ibid., p. 3).

12. Richard F. Burton, trans., *Vikram and the Vampire; or, Tales of Hindu Devilry* (1870; reprint, New York: Dover Publications, 1969), preface. For the original Sanskrit text, see Heinrich Uhle, ed., *Die Vetālapañcaviṃśatikā in den Recension des Śivadāsa und eines Ungenannten* (Leipzig: F. A. Brockhaus, 1881).

13. Rice, *Captain Sir Richard Francis Burton,* p. 59.

14. Burton, *Vikram and the Vampire,* pp. 82–83.

15. Uhle, *Die Vetālapañcaviṃśatikā,* pp. 14–15.

16. I. A. R. Wylie, *The Daughter of Brahma* (Indianapolis: Bobbs-Merrill, 1912), p. 390.

17. F. E. F. Penny, *The Swami's Curse* (London: Heinemann, 1929), p. 48.

18. Elizabeth Sharpe, *The Secrets of the Kaula Circle: A Tale of Fictitious People. . . .* (London: Luzac, 1936), p. 45.

19. Ibid., pp. 14–15.

20. Ibid., pp. 46–47.

21. On Crowley and his relation to Tantra, see Hugh B. Urban, "The Omnipotent Oom: Tantra and Its Impact on Modern Western Esotericism," *Esoterica: The Journal of Esoteric Studies* 3 (2001): 218–59; Lawrence Sutin, *Do What Thou Wilt: A Life of Aleister Crowley* (New York: St. Martin's Press, 2000).

22. Elizabeth Sharpe, *Secrets of the Kaula Circle,* pp. 48–49.

23. Ibid., p. 56.

24. Parry, *Delusions and Discoveries,* pp. 100–106. On Steel's life, see her autobiography, *The Garden of Fidelity: Being the Autobiography of Flora Annie Steel, 1847–1929* (London: Macmillan, 1930); Nancy L. Paxton, "Feminism under the Raj: Complicity and Resistance in the Writings of Flora Annie Steel and Annie Besant," *Women's Studies International Forum* 13 (Spring 1990): 333–46.

25. Nancy L. Paxton, "Disembodied Subjects: English Women's Autobiography under the Raj," in *De/Colonizing the Subject: The Politics of Gender in Women's Autobiography,* ed. Sidonie Smith and Julia Watson (Minneapolis: University of Minnesota Press, 1992), p. 401.

26. Paxton, "Disembodied Subjects," p. 404.

27. Flora Annie Steel, "A Maiden's Prayer," in *The Indian Scene,* by Flora Annie Steel (London: E. Arnold, 1933), p. 626.

28. Ibid., p. 630.

29. Flora Annie Steel, *The Law of the Threshold* (New York: Macmillan, 1924), pp. 1–2.

30. Ibid., p. 9. On Bernard, see Urban, "The Omnipotent Oom," pp. 218–59; and chapter 6, below.

31. Steel, *The Law of the Threshold,* p. 44.

32. Ibid., p. 47.

33. Ibid., p. 37.

34. Ibid.

35. Parry, *Delusions and Discoveries,* p. 129.

36. Lewis D. Wurgaft, *The Imperial Imagination: Magic and Myth in Kipling's India* (Middletown, Conn: Wesleyan University Press, 1983), p. 56.

37. Parry, *Delusions and Discoveries,* p. 99.

38. Pramod Kumār Caṭṭopādhyāy, *Tantrābhilāṣīr Sādhusaṅga,* vol. 1 (Calcutta: Viśvavanī Prakāśinī 1963), p. 233. There are many similar travel narratives centering around *tāntrik* themes, such as Nigūṛhānanda, *Sarpatāntriker Sandhāne* (Calcutta: Karuṇā Prakāśanī, 1980).

39. Pramod Kumār Caṭṭopādhyāy, vol. 1, *Tantrābhilāṣīr Sādhusaṅga,* p. 237.

40. Ibid., p. 243. The narrator's last fading sight is a vision of the *tāntrikas* embracing, as if they were Śiva, Parvatī, and the other gods playing in their Himalayan abode.

41. Azim, *The Colonial Rise,* p. 3. On the rise of the novel as a new genre in Bengal, see Dusan Zbavitel, *Bengali Literature* (Wiesbaden: Otto Harrassowitz, 1976), pp. 238–45.

42. See Wilhelm Halbfass, *India and Europe: An Essay in Understanding* (Albany: State University of New York Press, 1988), pp. 243–45. There is a large body of literature on Bankim; see especially: Tapan Raychaudhuri, *Europe Reconsidered: Perceptions of the West in Nineteenth Century Bengal* (New Delhi: Oxford University Press, 1988); Sudipta Kaviraj, *The Unhappy Consciousness: Bankimchandra Chattopadhyay and the Formation of Nationalist Discourse in India* (New Delhi: Oxford University Press, 1995); Sisir Kumar Das, *The Artist in Chains: The Life of Bankimchandra Chatterji* (New Delhi: New Statesman, 1984); Sunil Kumar Banerjee, *Bankim Chandra: A Study of His Craft* (Calcutta: Firma KLM, 1969).

43. Raychaudhuri, *Europe Reconsidered,* p. 132. For a good discussion of Bankim's complex nationalism, see Sudipta Kaviraj, *The Unhappy Consciousness,* pp. 131–57; Partha Chatterjee, *Nationalist Thought and the Colonial World: A Derivative Discourse?* (Minneapolis: University of Minnesota Press, 1993), pp. 75 ff.

44. Halbfass, *India and Europe,* pp. 243–44.

45. Bankimcandra Caṭṭopādhyāy, "Letter on Hinduism," quoted in Partha Chatterjee, *Nationalist Thought,* p. 75.
46. Halbfass, *India and Europe,* p. 339; cf. Sudipta Kaviraj, *The Unhappy Consciousness,* pp. 141–43.
47. Bankimcandra Caṭṭopādhyāy, *Kapālakuṇḍalā* (1866; reprint, Calcutta: Taptī Publishing, 1966), p. 10.
48. Ibid., pp. 87–88.
49. Ibid., pp. 84–85.
50. For the original edition of the text, see Bankimcandra Caṭṭopādhyāy, *Ānandamaṭh: Racanār Preranā o Parināma, tatsaha Bankimacandrer Ānanda maṭher Prathama Saṃskāraner Phatokapi,* ed. Cittarañjan Bandyopādhyāy (Calcutta: Ānanda, 1983).
51. Das, *The Artist in Chains,* p. 140.
52. Bankim Chandra Chatterjee, *The Abbey of Bliss* (Ānandamaṭh), trans. Nares Chandra Sen-Gupta (Calcutta: Cherry Press, n.d.), p. 41.
53. Trans. Sri Aurobindo, in V. Rangarajan, *Vande Mataram* (Madras: Sister Nivedita Academy, 1977), p. xv.
54. Raychaudhuri, *Europe Reconsidered,* p. 119.
55. Bankim Chandra Chatterjee, *The Abbey of Bliss,* pp. 198–99, 199, 200.
56. Trans. Sunil Kumar Banerjee, *Bankim Chandra,* p. 118. See also Das, *The Artist in Chains,* p. 137.
57. J. C. Ghose, *Bengali Literature* (New York: AMS Press, 1978), p. 160. See also M. K. Haldar, *Foundations of Nationalism in India: A Study of Bankimchandra Chatterjee* (New Delhi: Ajanta Publications, 1989), p. 101.
58. J. C. Ghose, *Bengali Literature,* p. 161.
59. Das, *The Artist in Chains,* p. 139.
60. Raychaudhuri, *Europe Reconsidered,* p. 132.
61. Ibid., p. 134.
62. David Kopf, *The Brahmo Samaj and the Shaping of the Modern Indian Mind* (Princeton, N.J.: Princeton University Press, 1979), p. 287; cf. Leonard Gordon, *Bengal: The Nationalist Movement, 1876–1940* (New York: Columbia University Press, 1974), pp. 85–89.
63. Rabindranoth Tagore, *Letters to a Friend,* ed. C. F. Andrews (New York: Macmillan, 1929), p. 111. Tagore compared the revolutionaries to people who had taken a drink and made alcohol an end in itself (Leonard Gordon, *Bengal,* pp. 157–58); see also Mary Lago, *Rabindranath Tagore* (Boston: Twayne Publishers, 1976), p. 34.
64. Kopf, *The Brahmo Samaj,* p. 301; see also Rabindranoth Tagore, *Nationalism* (London: Macmillan, 1950), pp. 16–17.
65. Anita Desai, introduction to Rabindranoth Tagore, *The Home and the World,* trans. Surendranath Tagore (London: Macmillan, 1967), p. 17. See also Krishna Dutta and Andrew Robinson, *Rabindranath Tagore: The Myriad-Minded Man* (New York: St. Martin's Press, 1995), p. 194.
66. Dutta and Robinson, *Rabindranath Tagore,* p. 193.
67. Desai, introduction to Tagore, *The Home and the World,* pp. 10–11.
68. Kopf, *The Brahmo Samaj,* p. 306.
69. Tagore, *The Home and the World,* p. 160.

70. Ibid., pp. 120–21. As Bimala likewise remarks, "fascination must be supplied to me in bodily shape by my country. She must have some visible symbol casting its spell upon my mind. I would make my country a Person, and call her Mother, Goddess, Durga—for whom I would redden the earth with sacrificial offerings" (ibid., p. 38).

71. Ibid., pp. 122–23.

72. Ibid., p. 39.

73. Ibid., pp. 80–81.

74. Ibid., p. 123.

75. Ibid., p. 177.

76. Brennan, "The National Longing for Form," p. 172.

77. Homi Bhabha, "Dissemination: Time, Narrative and the Margins of the Modern Nation," in *Nation and Narration,* ed. Homi Bhabha (London: Routledge, 1990), p. 3.

78. Ernest Gellner, *Nations and Nationalism* (Oxford: Basil Blackwell, 1983), p. 56.

79. Moore-Gilbert, *Writing India,* p. 25.

80. Bhabha, introduction to *Nation and Narration,* p. 4.

81. John Masters, *The Deceivers* (London: Penguin, 1955). On Masters, see Avtar Singh Bhullar, *India, Myth and Reality: Images of India in the Fiction by English Writers* (New Delhi: Ajanta Publications, 1985), pp. 121–22.

CHAPTER 4. DEODORIZED TANTRA

1. Sumit Sarkar, *An Exploration of the Ramakrishna Vivekananda Tradition* (Shimla: Indian Institute of Advanced Study, 1993), p. 45.

2. Kathleen Taylor has argued persuasively that Arthur Avalon is not simply a pseudonym assumed by Woodroffe for his Tantric publications; rather, Avalon is actually the joint persona of Woodroffe (who knew little Sanskrit) and the Bengali translator with whom he collaborated ("Arthur Avalon: The Creation of a Legendary Orientalist," in *Myth and Mythmaking,* ed. Julia Leslie [Richmond, Eng.: Curzon Press, 1996], pp. 151–61); see also her paper "Arthur Avalon among the Orientalists: Sir John Woodroffe and Tantra" (paper presented at Oxford University, 2001); and her book, *Sir John Woodroffe, Tantra, and Bengal: "An Indian Soul in a European Body"?* (Richmond, Eng.: Curzon Press, 2001).

3. See Jeffrey J. Kripal, *Kālī's Child: The Mystical and the Erotic in the Life and Teachings of Ramakrishna* (Chicago: University of Chicago Press, 1998), pp. 21–31.

4. Wilhelm Halbfass, *India and Europe: An Essay in Understanding* (Albany: State University of New York Press, 1988), p. 369.

5. Sue Curry Jansen, *Censorship: The Knot That Binds Knowledge and Power* (New York: Oxford University Press, 1988). On censorship, see also Hugh B. Urban, *The Economics of Ecstasy: Tantra, Secrecy, and Power in Colonial Bengal* (New York: Oxford University Press, 2001), introduction, chaps. 3 and 6.

6. Kathleen Taylor, "Arthur Avalon among the Orientalists."

7. Vasanta Kumār Pāl, "Tantrācārya Śivacandra," *Himādri* (Agrahāyan 1372 Bengali era, Pauṣ 1373 Bengali era [1965–66]). On Woodroffe's involvement in

Tantra, see Bhupendranath Datta, *Swami Vivekananda: Patriot, Prophet* (Calcutta: Navabhārata Publishers, 1954), pp. 309–12.

8. Kathleen Taylor, "Arthur Avalon: The Creation," pp. 151–61.

9. Ibid., p. 158.

10. Ibid., pp. 157, 161.

11. John Woodroffe, *Shakti and Shākta* (1918; reprint, New York: Dover Publications, 1978), p. x.

12. Harold Begbie, quoted in John Woodroffe, *India: Culture and Society* (1922; reprint, New Delhi, Life and Light, 1978), p. 157; Woodroffe, *Shakti and Shākta,* p. xii.

13. Woodroffe, *Shakti and Shākta,* p. 71.

14. Arthur Avalon, *Principles of Tantra: The Tantratattva of Śrīyukta Śiva Candra Vidyārṇava Bhaṭṭācārya Mahodaya* (Madras: Ganesh, 1960), p. 31.

15. Ibid., p. 5.

16. Woodroffe, *Shakti and Shākta,* p. 1.

17. Ibid., pp. 63, 365.

18. Ibid., pp. 587, 589.

19. Ibid., p. 3; cf. Halbfass, *India and Europe,* p. 400.

20. John Woodroffe, *Bharata Shakti: Essays and Addresses on Indian Culture* (Madras: Ganesh, 1921), p. 103.

21. M. P. Pandit, introduction to John Woodroffe, *The World as Power* (Madras: Ganesh, 1974), pp. vi–vii. "The Primary doctrine of Advaita Vedānta is Unity. . . . All are connected, one with the other. . . . [P]ractical Science is charged with the same mission. Railways, steamers, aeroplanes, the telegraph, the telephone, all help establish the idea of the unity of mankind, to foster a wide view of the universe" (Woodroffe, *The World as Power,* p. 4). See also Kathleen Taylor, *Sir John Woodroffe,* pp. 194–96.

22. Woodroffe, *The World as Power,* p. 91.

23. Arthur Avalon, introduction to Avalon, trans., *Tantra of the Great Liberation: Mahānirvāṇa Tantra* (New York: Dover Publications, 1979), p. cxix.

24. Woodroffe, *Shakti and Shākta,* p. 134.

25. Ibid., p. 594.

26. Avalon, *Principles of Tantra,* p. 63; cf. Kathleen Taylor, *Sir John Woodroffe,* pp. 187–89.

27. Kathleen Taylor, "Arthur Avalon among the Orientalists." See also her *Sir John Woodroffe,* pp. 40–60.

28. Kathleen Taylor, "Arthur Avalon among the Orientalists."

29. Woodroffe, *Bharata Shakti,* pp. xx, xxvi.

30. Ibid., p. xxx.

31. Woodroffe, *Is India Civilized? Essays on Indian Culture* (Madras: Ganesh, 1919), p. 345.

32. Ibid., p. vii.

33. Ibid., p. 344.

34. Woodroffe, *Bharata Shakti,* p. xliii.

35. Ibid., pp. 51–52.

36. Kathleen Taylor rejects the idea that Woodroffe was a secret revolutionary behind a public facade of conformity. Instead, she suggests that he was an

extremely complex individual who lived in an age when it was not unusual to hold views that might today seem contradictory (personal communication, May 5, 2001).

37. Woodroffe, *Shakti and Shākta,* p. 730.

38. As Halbfass puts it, "The Hinduism which Ramakrishna exemplifies . . . appears as an open, yet in itself complete framework of encounter and reconciliation with other traditions" (*India and Europe,* pp. 227–28).

39. Kripal, *Kālī's Child*, pp. 24–33; see also Narasimha Sil, "Vivekānanda's Rāmakṛṣṇa: An Untold Story of Mythmaking and Propaganda," *Numen* 40 (1993): 38–62.

40. Mahendranāth Gupta, *Śrīśrīrāmakṛṣṇakathāmṛta* (1902; reprint, Calcutta: Kathāmṛta Bhavan, 1987), 4.166.

41. Ibid., 3.33.

42. Swami Nikhilananda, *The Gospel of Sri Ramakrishna* (New York: Ramakrishna-Vivekananda Center, 1942), p. 21. See also LP 1.197–216. As an early biographer, Satyacaran Mitra, commented, "Although Ramakrishna Paramahaṃsa also practiced *sādhanas* of other traditions, the tradition of Tantra was his preeminent tradition. . . . Ramakrishna Paramahaṃsa was a fierce *tāntrika*" (*Śrī Śrī Rāmakṛṣṇa Paramahaṃsa: Jīvana o Upadeśa* [Calcutta: Great India Press, 1897], p. 72). On the role of Tantra in Ramakrishna's life, see Sarkar, *An Exploration,* pp. 45 ff.; John Rosselli, "Sri Ramakrishna and the Educated Elite of Late Nineteenth Century Bengal," *Contributions to Indian Sociology* 12, no. 2 (1978): 195–212; Walter G. Neeval, "Sri Ramakrishna: At Play in His Mother's Mansion," in *Hindu Spirituality: Postcolonial and Modern,* ed. K. R. Sundararajan and Bithaka Mukerji (New York: Crossroad, 1997), p. 291.

43. Akṣaykumār Sen, *Śrī Śrī Rāmakṛṣṇa Puṅthi* (Calcutta: Udbodhan Kāryālay, 1976), p. 116. As the master recalled, "The Brahmani guided me through all the exercises mentioned in the sixty-four Tantric works. Most of these are extremely difficult Sadhanas, which cause many a devotee to . . . sink into moral degradation" (*Sayings of Sri Ramakrishna* [Mylapore: Sri Ramakrishna Math, 1949], p. 311).

44. Kripal, *Kālī's Child,* p. 5.

45. Nikhilananda, *The Gospel of Sri Ramakrishna,* p. 123.

46. Swami Saradananda, *Sri Ramakrishna the Great Master* (Mylapore: Sri Ramakrishna Math, 1952), p. 227.

47. Christopher Isherwood, *Ramakrishna and His Disciples* (London: Methuen, 1965), p. 102.

48. Kripal, *Kālī's Child,* p. 32. See also Kripal, "Mystical Homoeroticism, Reductionism, and the Reality of Censorship: A Response to Gerald James Larson," *Journal of the American Academy of Religion* 66, no. 3 (1998): 627–35.

49. Jeffrey J. Kripal, "On the Fearful Art of Writing Left-Handed: Some Personal and Theoretical Reflections on Translating the *Kathāmṛta* into American English," in *In the Flesh: Eros, Secrecy, and Power in the Vernacular Tantric Traditions of India*, ed. Hugh B. Urban, Glen A. Hayes, and Paul Muller-Ortega (Albany: State University of New York Press, in progress).

50. Narasimha Sil, "The Question of Ramakrishna's Homosexuality," *The Statesman,* 31 January 1997, pp. 10–13.

51. Kripal, "On the Fearful Art." There have been a number of critical reviews of *Kālī's Child;* see Swami Atmajnananda, "Scandals, Cover-ups, and Other Imagined Occurrences in the Life of Ramakrishna: An Examination of Jeffrey Kripal's *Kālī's Child,*" *International Journal of Hindu Studies* 1, no. 2 (1997): 401–20; Gerald Larson, "Polymorphic Sexuality, Homoeroticism, and the Study of Religion," *Journal of the American Academy of Religion* 65, no. 3 (1997): 655–65. For a more positive review, see Hugh B, Urban, review of *Kālī's Child: The Mystical and the Erotic in the Life and Teachings of Ramakrishna,* by Jeffrey J. Kripal, *Journal of Religion* 78, no. 2 (1998): 318–20.

52. Narasimha Sil, *Rāmakṛṣṇa Paramahaṃsa: A Psychological Profile* (Leiden: E. J. Brill, 1991), p. 8.

53. Rāmacandra Datta, *Śrīśrīrāmakṛṣṇa Paramahaṃsadever Jīvanavṛttānta* (1890; reprint, Calcutta: Jogodyan, Kakurgachi, 1935). As Rosselli comments, Saradananda was "plainly embarrassed by the Tantric episode" in his *Līlāprasaṇga* ("Sri Ramakrishna and the Educated Elite," p. 203).

54. Swami Vivekananda, *The Complete Works of Swami Vivekananda,* vol. 5 (Calcutta: Advaita Ashram, 1984), letter 22; italics in the original. See Sil, "Vivekānanda's Rāmakṛṣna," p. 50.

55. Kripal, "On the Fearful Art."

56. On Vivekananda's spiritual nationalism, see Paul Hacker, "Vivekananda's Religious Nationalism," in *Philology and Confrontation: Paul Hacker on Traditional and Modern Vedānta,* ed. Wilhelm Halbfass (Albany: State University of New York Press, 1995), pp. 319–33. There is a vast literature on Vivekananda, most of it written from an uncritical devotional perspective. See, for example, Marie L. Burke, *Swami Vivekananda in the West: New Discoveries* (Calcutta: Advaita Ashram, 1983–87). Among the few more critical discussions of the Swami are: Sarkar, *An Exploration;* Narasingha Sil, "Swami Vivekananda in the West: The Legend Reinterpreted," *South Asia* 18, no. 1 (1995): 1–53; and *Swami Vivekananda: A Reassessment* (Selinsgrove, Pa.: Susquehanna University Press, 1997); Thomas Bryson, "The Hermeneutics of Religious Syncretism: Swami Vivekananda's Practical Vedānta" (Ph.D. diss., Divinity School, University of Chicago, 1992); Tapan Raychaudhuri, *Europe Reconsidered: Perceptions of the West in Nineteenth Century Bengal* (New Delhi: Oxford University Press, 1988), pp. 237–315; William Radice, ed., *Swami Vivekananda and the Modernization of Hinduism* (New Delhi: Oxford University Press, 1998).

57. Hacker, quoted in Halbfass, *India and Europe,* p. 228; cf. Tapan Raychaudhuri, "Swami Vivekananda's Construction of Hinduism," in *Swami Vivekananda and the Modernization of Hinduism,* pp. 2 ff.

58. Hacker, "Vivekananda's Religious Nationalism," p. 321.

59. Vivekananda, *Complete Works,* vol. 3, pp. 267–68.

60. Sister Nivedita, *The Master as I Saw Him* (Calcutta: Udbodhan Office, 1948), p. 56.

61. Kripal, *Kālī's Child,* pp. 26–27.

62. Vivekananda, *Complete Works,* vol. 3, p. 190.

63. Swami Tapasyananda, ed., *The Nationalistic and Religious Lectures of Swami Vivekananda* (Madras: Sri Ramakrishna Math, 1985), pp. 118–19. On

this point see Lise McKean, *Divine Enterprise: Gurus and the Hindu Nationalist Movement* (Chicago: University of Chicago Press, 1996), p. 285.

64. McKean, *Divine Enterprise,* pp. 282–83; cf. Halbfass, *India and Europe,* p. 231.

65. Sil, "Swami Vivekānanda in the West," p. 3; cf. Sil, *Swami Vivekananda,* pp. 151–67. As Svāmī Sadaśivānanda recalls, "Speaking of Napoleon, he himself had become like Napoleon. It was as if he himself were directing the fight of Jena and Austerlitz. . . . We have won the battle—we have conquered, he cried in joy" (Svāmī Abhedānanda, *Svāmījīr Padaprānte (Svāmī Vivekānander Sannyāsī-Śiṣyaganer Jīvanacarita)* [Calcutta: Udbhodhan Kāryālay, 1398 Bengali era (1991)], pp. 411–12).

66. "It is fitting that, whenever there is a spiritual adjustment it should come from the Orient. . . . [W]hen the Oriental wants to learn about machine making, he should sit at the feet of the Occidental and learn from him. When the Occident wants to learn about the spirit, about God . . . he must sit at the feet of the Orient" (Vivekananda, *Complete Works,* vol. 4, p. 156; cf. Halbfass, *India and Europe,* p. 233).

67. Vivekananda, *Complete Works,* vol. 3, pp. 148 ff. A severe critique of the West appears in his short work, *The East and the West* (New York: Vedanta Society, 1909).

68. Vivekananda, in Memphis, Tenn., January 1885, cited in Rajagopal Chattopadhyaya, *Swami Vivekananda in the West* (Houston: Rajagopal Chattopadhyaya, 1993), p. iii.

69. See Sil, "Swami Vivekānanda in the West," p. 15. "India alone was to be of all lands the land of toleration and spirituality. . . . For us Hindus this truth has been the very backbone of our national existence" (Vivekananda, *Complete Works,* vol. 3, pp. 186 ff.).

70. Burke, *Swami Vivekananda in the West,* vol. 1, pp. 445–46; cf. Sil, *Swami Vivekananda,* pp. 61–62.

71. Burke, *Swami Vivekananda in the West,* vol. 1, pp. 32–33.

72. Ibid., p. 31.

73. Vivekananda, *Complete Works,* vol. 6, p. 190.

74. *Letters of Swami Vivekananda,* ed. Swami Mumukshananda (Calcutta: Advaita Ashram, 1964), p. 25. As Kripal comments, "Ramakrishna's incarnation and its perennialist message were understood as the answers that would deliver India from the yoke of an oppressive and spiritually sterile culture, Western civilization. . . . The West is depicted as a demon that only the Goddess Kālī can slay" (*Kālī's Child,* pp. 39–40).

75. Halbfass, *India and Europe,* p. 229. "Although he is concerned with a self-assertion of Hinduism based upon Hinduism's own premises, the way in which he returns to these sources is mediated by his encounter with the West and shaped by Western models" (ibid., pp. 238–39).

76. "In Vivekananda's hands, Orientalist notions of India as otherworldly and mystical were embraced and praised as India's special gift to mankind. Thus the very discourse that succeeded in alienating, subordinating and controlling India was used by Vivekananda as a religious clarion for the Indian people to unite under the banner of a universalistic . . . Hinduism" (Richard King, *Orien-*

talism and Religion: Postcolonial Theory, India, and the Mystic East [London: Routledge, 1999], p. 93).

77. Halbfass, *India and Europe,* p. 232.

78. Vivekananda, *Complete Works,* vol. 5, p. 67, and vol. 4, p. 407. On Vivekananda's appropriation of missionary strategies, see Bryson, "Hermeneutics of Religious Syncretism," pp. 293–99; Halbfass, *India and Europe,* pp. 228–29.

79. Halbfass, *India and Europe,* p. 242.

80. Ibid., p. 235; cf. Vivekananda, *Complete Works,* vol. 3, p. 457.

81. Vivekananda, *Complete Works,* vol. 6, p. 226.

82. Ibid., p. 313.

83. Ibid., vol. 7, p. 494; my italics.

84. Agehananda Bharati, *The Ochre Robe: An Autobiography* (Santa Barbara, Calif.: Ross-Erikson Publishers, 1980), p. 244.

85. Kumari Jayawardena, *The White Woman's Other Burden: Western Women and South Asia during British Colonial Rule* (New York: Routledge, 1995), p. 186; cf. Hacker, "Vivekananda's Religious Nationalism," pp. 322–25.

86. Partha Chatterjee, *The Nation and Its Fragments: Colonial and Postcolonial Histories* (Princeton, N.J.: Princeton University Press, 1993), p. 76.

87. Ibid., p. 102.

88. Richard King, *Orientalism and Religion,* p. 107. "Our vigor, our strength, nay our national life is in our religion" (Vivekananda, *Complete Works,* vol. 5, p. 37).

89. Vivekananda, *Complete Works,* vol. 7, p. 174.

90. Ibid., vol. 3, p. 340.

91. Halbfass, *India and Europe,* p. 235.

92. Vivekananda, *Complete Works,* vol. 3, p. 458; cf. ibid., vol. 4, p. 336.

93. Ibid., vol. 7, pp. 215–16.

94. Sil, "Vivekānanda's Rāmakṛṣṇa," p. 42.

95. Vivekananda, *Complete Works,* vol. 7, p. 262.

96. Kripal, *Kālī's Child,* p. 171.

97. Bryson, "Hermeneutics of Religious Syncretism," p. 283.

98. Rosselli, "Sri Ramakrishna and the Educated Elite," p. 207.

99. Vivekananda, *Complete Works,* vol. 8, letter 90.

100. Nivedita, *The Master as I Saw Him,* pp. 251, 47.

CHAPTER 5. RELIGION FOR THE AGE OF DARKNESS

1. Jung merits a note here. He was quite interested in certain aspects of Tantra, such as *maṇḍala*s and *kuṇḍalinī* yoga, to which he devoted a number of publications. Jung saw in *maṇḍala*s and in *kuṇḍalinī* examples of his idea of the "process of individuation," or the integration of the Self. See *The Psychology of Kundalini Yoga* (Princeton, N.J.: Princeton University Press, 1996), and *Mandala Symbolism* (Princeton, N.J.: Princeton University Press, 1972). However, he was also critical of Indian yoga as an essentially otherworldly and thus imbalanced worldview, unsuitable for Westerners. On Jung's connection to Tantra see Harold G. Coward, *Jung and Eastern Thought* (Albany: State University of New York Press, 1985), pp. 110 ff.

2. D. N. Bose and Haralal Haldar, *Tantras: Their Philosophy and Occult Secrets* (Calcutta: Oriental Publishing, 1956), pp. 6–7. See also Gopīnāth Kavirāj, *Tāntrik Sādhana o Siddānta* (Burdwan: Burdwan University Press, 1376 Bengali era [1969]).

3. On the concept of esocentrism, see Steven M. Wasserstrom, *Religion after Religion* (Princeton, N.J.: Princeton University Press, 1999), pp. 37–38, 45–49; Hugh B. Urban, "Syndrome of the Secret: Eso-centrism and the Work of Steven M. Wasserstrom," *Journal of the American Academy of Religion* 69, no. 2 (2001): 439–49.

4. For good discussions of the political history of the history of religions in this century, see Wasserstrom, *Religion after Religion,* pp. 127–52; Russell T. McCutcheon, *Manufacturing Religion: The Discourse on Sui Generis Religion and the Politics of Nostalgia* (New York: Oxford University Press, 1997).

5. Gustavo Benavides, "Giuseppe Tucci; or, Buddhology in the Age of Fascism," in *Curators of the Buddha: The Study of Buddhism under Colonialism,* ed. Donald S. Lopez, Jr. (Chicago: University of Chicago Press, 1995). Tucci's work on Tantric Buddhism has been very influential; see his *The Religions of Tibet,* trans. Geoffrey Samuel (Berkeley: University of California Press, 1980). Jeffrey J. Kripal, *Roads of Excess, Palaces of Wisdom: Eroticism and Reflexivity in the Study of Mysticism* (New York: Seven Bridges Press, 2001), pp. 207–50. Born Leopold Fischer in 1923, Bharati was accepted into Hinduism at age sixteen by an Indian in Vienna; during the war, he was drafted into the German army and served in the Indian Legion. He later joined the Ramakrishna Mission, but was frustrated by its prudery. He left the order and later entered the Dasnami sect in 1951, where he was given the new name Agehananda Bharati. He then taught at various universities in India and the United States, including the University of Washington. Bharati's life is recounted in his autobiography, *The Ochre Robe: An Autobiography* (Santa Barbara, Calif.: Ross-Erickson Publishers, 1980); he also wrote one of the most influential works on Tantra: *The Tantric Tradition* (Garden City, N.Y.: Anchor Books, 1970).

6. Benavides, "Giuseppe Tucci," pp. 162, 178–79. On this general trend among European intellectuals of this generation, see Arno Mayer, *The Persistence of the Old Regime: Europe to the Great War* (New York: Pantheon Books, 1981); Steven M. Wasserstrom, "The Lives of Baron Evola," *Alphabet City* 4 (1995): 84–90.

7. Heinrich Zimmer, *Philosophies of India* (New York: Meridian Books, 1956), p. 576.

8. Herbert Nette, "An Epitaph for Heinrich Zimmer," in *Heinrich Zimmer: Coming into His Own,* ed. Margaret H. Case (Princeton, N.J.: Princeton University Press, 1994), p. 21. For his biography, see his essay "Some Biographical Remarks on Henry R. Zimmer," appendix to *Artistic Form and Yoga in the Sacred Images of India* (Princeton, N.J.: Princeton University Press, 1984).

9. Maya Rauch "Heinrich Zimmer from a Daughter's Perspective," in *Heinrich Zimmer: Coming into His Own,* ed. Margaret H. Case (Princeton, N.J.: Princeton University Press, 1994), p. 18.

10. Nette, "Epitaph for Heinrich Zimmer," p. 24.

11. Zimmer, "Some Biographical Remarks," p. 248.

12. Case, introduction to *Heinrich Zimmer,* pp. 4–5. See Zimmer's *Ewiges Indien: Leitmotive indischen Daseins* (Potsdam, Ger.: Müller and Kiepenheuer, 1930).

13. Zimmer, "Some Biographical Remarks," p. 250.

14. Ibid.

15. Heinrich Zimmer, quoted in Nette, "Epitaph for Heinrich Zimmer," p. 30.

16. Case, introduction to *Heinrich Zimmer,* p. 9. On Zimmer's admiration for Jung, see "The Impress of Dr. Jung on My Profession," in ibid., pp. 43–47.

17. Nette, "Epitaph for Heinrich Zimmer," p. 23; cf. Zimmer, "On the Significance of the Indian Tantric Yoga," in *Spiritual Disciplines: Papers from the Eranos Yearbooks*, ed. Joseph Campbell (New York: Pantheon Books, 1960), p. 284.

18. Zimmer, *Artistic Form and Yoga,* p. 22.

19. Zimmer, *Philosophies of India,* p. 578.

20. Ibid., p. 601.

21. Ibid., pp. 601, 602.

22. First quote from Roger Eatwell, *Fascism: A History* (Harmondsworth, Eng.: Penguin Books, 1995), p. 318. See also Stanley Payne, *A History of Fascism, 1914–1945* (Madison: University of Wisconsin Press, 1995), p. 113n; Wasserstrom, "Lives of Baron Evola"; Franco Ferraresi, "Julius Evola: Tradition, Reaction, and the Radical Right," *Archives européennes de sociologie* 28 (1987): 107–51. Second quote from Guido Stucco, introduction to Julius Evola, *The Yoga of Power: Tantra, Shakti, and the Secret Way,* trans. Guido Stucco (1968; reprint, Rochester, N.Y.: Inner Traditions, 1992), p. 216n16. See also Steven M. Wasserstrom, "Eliade and Evola," in *The Unknown, Remembered Gate: Religious Experience and Hermeneutical Reflection,* ed. Elliot R. Wolfson and Jeffrey J. Kripal (New York: Seven Bridges Press, forthcoming).

23. Stucco, introduction to *The Yoga of Power,* p. x.

24. See Thomas Sheehan, "*Diventare Dio:* Julius Evola and the Metaphysics of Fascism," *Stanford Italian Review* 6 (1986): 279–92.

25. Julius Evola, *Revolt against the Modern World* (Rochester, N.Y.: Inner Traditions, 1995).

26. Thomas Sheehan, "Myth and Violence: The Fascism of Julius Evola and Alain de Benoist," *Social Research* 48 (1981): 51.

27. Richard Drake, "Julius Evola and the Ideological Origins of the Radical Right in Contemporary Italy," in *Political Violence and Terror: Motifs and Motivations,* ed. Peter H. Merkl (Berkeley: University of California Press, 1986).

28. Evola, *The Yoga of Power,* p. 15.

29. Ibid., p. 190; cf. Julius Evola, *The Metaphysics of Sex* (1969; reprint, New York: Inner Traditions, 1983), p. 117.

30. Stucco, introduction to *The Yoga of Power,* pp. xv, xii–xiii.

31. Julius Evola, *René Guénon: A Teacher for Modern Times,* trans. Guido Stucco (Edmonds, Wa.: Holmes Publishing, 1994), p. 21; cf. Roger Griffin, ed., *Fascism* (Oxford: Oxford University Press, 1955), p. 317.

32. Evola, *The Yoga of Power,* pp. 2, 3–4.

33. Ibid., p. 3.

34. Evola, *The Metaphysics of Sex,* p. 273.
35. Ibid., pp. 6–7.
36. Evola, *The Yoga of Power,* p. 54.
37. Stucco, introduction to ibid., p. xiv.
38. Julius Evola, "East and West. The Gordion Knot," review of *Der gordische Knoten,* by Ernst Jünger, *East and West* 5 (1954–55): 94, 98.
39. Evola, *The Metaphysics of Sex,* p. 62.
40. Ibid., pp. 64, 61.
41. Evola, *The Yoga of Power,* pp. 187–88.
42. Ibid., p. 189.
43. Ibid., pp. 60–61.
44. On Evola's "deep and continuing impact on the ideology of the extreme right," see Sheehan, "Myth and Violence."
45. Eliade's connections with Evola are only now beginning to be explored. Eliade himself wrote a long unpublished manuscript on Evola in 1928 (see Mac Linscott Ricketts, *Mircea Eliade: The Romanian Roots,* vol. 2 [New York: Columbia University Press, 1988], p. 849). See Wasserstrom, "Eliade and Evola"; Philippe Baillet, "Julius Evola et Mircea Eliade (1927–1974): Une Amitié manquée," *Les Deux Etendards* (1988): 45–55.
46. John David Cave, *Mircea Eliade's Vision for a New Humanism* (New York: Oxford University Press, 1993), p. 10.
47. On Codreanu and the Legion, see Nicholas M. Nagy-Talavera, *The Green Shirts and the Others: A History of Fascism in Hungary and Romania* (Stanford, Calif.: Hoover Institution, 1970), pp. 250 ff.
48. Mircea Eliade, *Images and Symbols: Studies in Religious Symbolism* (New York: Sheed and Ward, 1969), p. 19.
49. For critical views of Eliade's politics, see Ivan Strenski, *Four Theories of Myth in the Twentieth Century: Cassirer, Eliade, Lévi-Strauss, and Malinowski* (Iowa City: University of Iowa Press, 1987); Leon Volovici, *Nationalist Ideology and Antisemitism: The Case of Romanian Intellectuals in the 1930s* (Oxford: Oxford University Press, 1991); Daniel Dubuisson, *Mythologies du XXe siècle (Dumézil, Lévi-Strauss, Eliade)* (Lille, Fr.: Presses Universitaires de Lille, 1993); Adriana Berger, "Fascism and Religion in Romania," *Annals of Scholarship* 6, no. 4 (1989): 455–65; Wasserstrom, *Religion after Religion.* For a more sympathetic view, see Bryan S. Rennie, *Reconstructing Eliade: Making Sense of Religion* (Albany: State University of New York Press, 1996).
50. Rennie, *Reconstructing Eliade,* p. 143. The clearest statement of Eliade's support for the Legion appeared in his 1937 article, "Why I Believe in the Victory of the Legionary Movement": "The Legionary movement will lead not only to the restoration of the virtues of our people, to a valorous, dignified and powerful Romania; it will also create a new man attuned to a new type of life in Europe" (quoted in Volovici, *Nationalist Ideology and Antisemitism,* p. 84).
51. See Ricketts, *Mircea Eliade,* pp. 882 ff.; cf. Dubuisson, *Mythologies du XXe siècle,* pp. 221 ff., 292 ff.
52. Virgil Ierunca, "The Literary Work of Mircea Eliade," in *Myths and Symbols: Studies in Honor of Mircea Eliade,* ed. Joseph M. Kitagawa and Charles H. Long (Chicago: University of Chicago Press, 1969), p. 344.

53. Mircea Eliade, *The Forbidden Forest* (Noaptea de sânziene), trans. Mac Linscott Ricketts and Mary Park Stevenson (South Bend, Ind.: University of Notre Dame Press, 1978), p. 214.

54. Strenski, *Four Theories of Myth,* p. 94. See also Wasserstrom, "Eliade and Evola."

55. Guilford Dudley, III, *Religion on Trial: Mircea Eliade and His Critics* (Philadelphia: Temple University Press, 1977), p. 148.

56. Strenski, *Four Theories of Myth,* p. 77.

57. Mircea Eliade, *The Quest: History and Meaning in Religion* (Chicago: University of Chicago Press, 1969), p. 62.

58. Strenski, *Four Theories of Myth,* p. 121. As Wasserstrom argues, "For Eliade and Evola, the initiatic secret of the New Man . . . was the practice of spiritual sex, specifically the rite of Maithuna, the Tantric sexual retention of semen" ("Eliade and Evola," p. 33).

59. Eliade, *The Quest,* preface.

60. Mircea Eliade, *The Sacred and the Profane: The Nature of Religion* (New York: Harcourt Brace, 1959), p. 203; cf. Eliade, *Myths, Dreams and Mysteries: The Encounter between Contemporary Faiths and Archaic Realities* (London: Harvill Press, 1960), p. 237.

61. Eliade, *The Quest,* preface; cf. *Images and Symbols,* preface.

62. Strenski, *Four Theories of Myth,* p. 83.

63. Mircea Eliade, *Rites and Symbols of Initiation: The Mysteries of Birth and Rebirth* (New York: Harper and Row, 1958), p. 105.

64. Mircea Eliade, *Yoga: Immortality and Freedom* (Princeton, N.J.: Princeton University Press, 1971), pp. 201–2.

65. Eliade, *Sacred and the Profane,* p. 172.

66. Eliade, *Yoga,* pp. 202–3.

67. Ibid., p. 259.

68. Mircea Eliade, *History of Religious Ideas,* vol. 1, *From the Stone Age to the Eleusinian Mysteries* (Chicago: University of Chicago Press, 1976), p. xvi.

69. Mircea Eliade, *Journal,* vol. 3, 1970–78 (Chicago: University of Chicago Press, 1989), pp. 8–9.

70. Ibid., vol. 4, 1979–85, p. 2.

71. Mircea Eliade, *Patterns in Comparative Religion* (London: Sheed and Ward, 1958), p. 419.

72. Shashibhusan Dasgupta, *Obscure Religious Cults, as a Background to Bengali Literature* (Calcutta: Firma KLM, 1962), p. xxiii.

73. See Ajit Mookerjee, *Tantra Asana: A Way to Self-Realization* (New York: George Wittenborn, 1971), p. 35.

74. Kaviraj is the author of a large number of Tantric works, including: Gopīnāth Kavirāj, *Tantra o Āgamaśāstrer Digdarśana* (Calcutta: Calcutta Sanskrit College Researches, 1963); *Tāntrik Sāhitya* (Lucknow: Hindī Samiti, 1972). For discussions of his work, see Arlene Mazak, "Gopinath Kaviraj's Synthetic Understanding of Kuṇḍalinī Yoga in Relation to the Nondualistic Hindu Tantric Traditions" (Ph.D. diss., Department of South Asian Languages and Civilizations, University of Chicago, 1994); Kalidas Bhattacharyya, *Gopinath Kaviraj's Thoughts: Towards a Systematic Study* (Calcutta: University of Calcutta Press,

1982); G. C. Pande, *Mahamahopadhyaya Gopinath Kaviraj* (New Delhi: Sahitya Akademi, 1989).

75. Pande, *Mahamahopadhyaya Gopinath Kaviraj*, p. 11.

76. Ibid., p. 9.

77. Ram Chandra Adhikari, "Shiva Shakti Yoga," in *Life and Philosophy of Gopinath Kaviraj* (Calcutta: University of Calcutta Press, 1981), p. 92. See Gopinath Kaviraj, "Śākta Philosophy," in *Aspects of Indian Thought* (University of Burdwan), pp. 175–76.

78. See Gopinath Kaviraj, "Śākta Philosophy," p. 175.

79. Gopinath Kaviraj, "Nyāya-Vaiśeṣika Philosophy," in *Aspects of Indian Thought*, p. 76.

80. See Manoranjan Basu, *Fundamentals of the Philosophy of the Tantras* (Calcutta: Mira Basu Publishers, 1986), p. 63.

81. Basu, *Fundamentals*, p. 631. See Gopīnāth Kavirāj, *Akhaṇḍa Mahāyoger Pathe* (Calcutta: Mahesh Library, 1975); *Akhaṇḍa Mahāyoga: Mūla Lekhak Gopīnāth Kavirāj* (Varanasi: Akhaṇḍa Mahāyoga Saṅgha, 1978).

82. Mazak, "Gopinath Kaviraj's Synthetic Understanding," p. 413.

83. Ibid., p. 429. See Gopīnāth Kavirāj, *Akhaṇḍa Mahāyoger Pathe.*

84. Basu, *Fundamentals*, p. 633.

85. Mazak, "Gopinath Kaviraj's Synthetic Understanding," pp. 429–30. See Gopīnāth Kavirāj, "Deha aur karma," in *Tāntrik Vāṅmay meṅ Śāktadṛṣṭi* (Patna: Bihar Rāṣṭrabhāṣā Pariṣad, 1963), pp. 221–22.

86. N. H. Chandrashekara, "Akhanda Mahayoga of Pt Gopinath Kaviraj ji," reprinted online at www.geocities.com/amvaranasi/amyoga.htm. For Kaviraj's view of Śakti see "Mahāśakti—Śrī Śrī Mā," in *Tāntrik Vāṅmay meṅ Śāktadṛṣṭi*, pp. 173 ff.

87. Mazak, "Gopinath Kaviraj's Synthetic Understanding," p. 438.

88. Gopinath Kaviraj, *Selected Writings of M. M. Gopinath Kaviraj* (Varanasi: M. M. Gopinath Kaviraj Centenary Celebrations Committee, 1990), p. 225.

89. Debiprasad Chattopadhyaya, *Lokāyata: A Study in Ancient Indian Materialism* (New Delhi: People's Publishing House, 1959), pp. xiii, xvi.

90. On the early growth of communism in Bengal, see David Laushey, *Bengal Terrorism and the Marxist Left: Aspects of Regional Nationalism in India, 1905–1942* (Calcutta: Firma KLM, 1975); T. J. Nossiter, *Marxist State Governments in India: Politics, Economics, and Society* (London: F. Pinter, 1988). On M. N. Roy, whom some have called the "apocalyptic hero of Indian Communism," see Bhabani Sen Gupta, *Communism in Indian Politics* (New York: Columbia University Press, 1972), pp. 10–11 (source of preceding quote).

91. Nossiter, *Marxist State Governments*, p. 21.

92. Ibid., p. 143. On Marxism in Bengal, see Laushey, *Bengal Terrorism;* Sen Gupta, *Communism in Indian Politics*, pp. 152–71. Anjali Ghosh, *Peaceful Transition to Power: A Study of Marxist Political Strategies in West Bengal, 1967–1777* (Calcutta: Firma KLM, 1981).

93. Narendra Nath Bhattacharyya, personal communication, May 28, 2001. I am very grateful to Dr. Bhattacharyya for his willingness to answer a series of questions about his life, work, and attitudes toward Tantra.

94. Ibid. Most of Bhattacharyya's most important works were during or

shortly after the rise of Marxism to power in Bengal: *Indian Mother Goddess* (Calcutta: Indian Studies, 1971); *Bhāratavarṣer Rājanaitika Itihāsa* (Calcutta: Firma KLM, 1974); *History of the Śākta Religion* (New Delhi: Munshiram Manoharlal, 1974; reprint, New Delhi: Munshiram Manoharlal, 1996); and *History of the Tantric Religion: A Historical, Ritualistic, and Philosophical Study* (New Delhi: Manohar, 1982).

95. Narendra Nath Bhattacharyya, *Indian Mother Goddess,* p. 3.

96. Narendra Nath Bhattacharyya, *History of the Tantric Religion,* p. viii. Bhattacharyya clearly cites James, Briffault, and others as his inspirations (*History of the Śākta Religion,* p. xii).

97. Narendra Nath Bhattacharyya, *Indian Mother Goddess,* p. 5.

98. Narendra Nath Bhattacharyya, *History of the Tantric Religion,* p. ix.

99. Ibid., p. 171.

100. Narendra Nath Bhattacharyya, *Indian Mother Goddess,* p. 115.

101. Narendra Nath Bhattacharyya, *History of the Śākta Religion,* p. 1.

102. Narendra Nath Bhattacharyya, *History of the Tantric Religion,* pp. x–xi; cf. p. 34.

103. Ibid., pp. 125.

104. Ibid., p. 31; cf. p. 34.

105. Ibid., p. 14.

106. Ibid., p. 210.

107. Ibid., p. 302.

108. Narendra Nath Bhattacharyya, *History of the Śākta Religion,* pp. 156, 157.

109. Ibid., p. 164.

110. Ibid., p. 165.

111. Debiprasad Chattopadhyaya, *Lokāyata,* pp. xiii–xiv.

112. See M. N. Roy, *Reason, Romanticism, and Revolution* (Calcutta: Renaissance Publications, Ltd., 1955), p. 294.

113. Narendra Nath Bhattacharyya, *History of the Śākta Religion,* reprint ed., p. 206; cf. *History of the Tantric Religion,* reprint ed., pp. 26 ff.; and *Religious Culture of North-Eastern India* (New Delhi: Manohar, 1995).

114. Erich Neumann argues, "It is in India that the Terrible Mother has been given its most grandiose form," as Kālī, "dark all-devouring time." As such, the image of Kālī represents a much-needed therapy for the psyche of Western man who is "one-sidedly patriarchal" and has lost the archetypal power of the feminine (*The Great Mother: An Analysis of an Archetype* [Princeton, N.J.: Princeton University Press, 1955], p. 150). On Jung and his ambivalent relation to Tantra, see note 1, above.

115. Joseph Campbell, *The Masks of God,* vol. 2, *Oriental Mythology* (New York: Viking Press, 1962), p. 165.

CHAPTER 6. THE CULT OF ECSTASY

1. Lynn Collins, "The Secret to Tantric Sex," *Cosmopolitan,* May 2000, p. 240. "Tantra is the exotic art of prolonging your passion play to reach new levels of lusty satisfaction. . . . Inspired by the sexual success of these ancient love

teachings . . . *Cosmo* came up with its own turbo-charged version of Tantra" (ibid.).

2. Georg Feuerstein, *Tantra: The Path of Ecstasy* (Boston: Shambhala Publications, 1998), p. xiv. See also Agehananda Bharati, "The Future (if Any) of Tantrism," *Loka: A Journal from Naropa Institute* 1 (1975): 129.

3. Angus McLaren, *Twentieth-Century Sexuality: A History* (Oxford: Basil Blackwell, 1999), p. 1.

4. Michel Foucault, *Religion and Culture,* ed. Jeremy R. Carrette (New York: Routledge, 1999), p. 117.

5. The term *sexuality* first entered the English vocabulary through an 1892 translation of Richard von Krafft-Ebing's classic work on sexual deviance (McLaren, *Twentieth-Century Sexuality,* p. 224n).

6. Agehananda Bharati, *The Tantric Tradition* (Garden City, N.Y.: Anchor Books, 1970), p. 298.

7. Helena Petrovna Blavatsky, *Collected Writings,* vol. 11, comp. and ed. Boris De Zirkoff (Madras: Theosophical Publishing House, 1950–73), p. 29. See also A. P. Sinnett, *Esoteric Buddhism* (London: Trübner, 1884).

8. See Edward Rice, *Captain Sir Richard Francis Burton: The Secret Agent Who Made the Pilgrimage to Mecca, Discovered the Kāma Sūtra, and Brought the Arabian Nights to the West* (New York: Charles Scribner's Sons, 1990), pp. 444–47.

9. Dr. Charles Potter, *World Telegram,* 7 May 1931, cited in William Seabrook, *Witchcraft: Its Power in the World Today* (New York: Harcourt, Brace, 1940), p. 359. As Monica Randall comments, "The media followed his every move. . . . [N]eighbors accused him of hosting orgies and abducting virgins to sacrifice to his elephants" (*Phantoms of the Hudson Valley: The Glorious Estates of a Lost Era* [Woodstock, N.Y.: Overlook Press, 1995], p. 78).

10. For a more developed discussion of Bernard, see Hugh B. Urban, "The Omnipotent Oom: Tantra and Its Impact on Modern Western Esotericism," *Esoterica: The Journal of Esoteric Studies* 3 (2001): 218–59. Contemporary news reports include: "Oom: Omnipotent Doctor Bernard Makes News Again," *Newsweek,* 1 July 1933, p. 22; John Lardner, "Out of a Book," *Newsweek,* 19 May 1939, p. 24; Eckert Goodman, "The Guru of Nyack: The True Story of Father India, the Omnipotent Oom," *Town and Country,* April 1941, pp. 50, 53, 92–93, 98–100; "The Ascent of Peter Coon," *Newsweek,* 10 October 1955, pp. 53–56; Kenneth R. MacCalman, "Impressions of Dr. Bernard and the C.C.C. as Viewed by a Nyack On-Looker," *South of the Mountains* 14, no. 4 (1970): 2–8. There is also some scholarly literature on Bernard, such as: J. Gordon Melton, "Pierre Bernard," in *Biographical Dictionary of American Cult and Sect Leaders* (New York: Garland Publishing, 1986), pp. 32–33, 138; Gary L. Ward, "Pierre Arnold Bernard (Tantrik Order in America)," in *Religious Leaders of America: A Biographical Guide to Founders and Leaders of Religious Bodies, Churches, and Spiritual Groups in North America,* ed. J. Gordon Melton (Detroit: Gale Research, 1991), pp. 39–40; Paul Sann, *Fads, Follies, and Delusions of the American People* (New York: Bonanza Books, 1967).

11. Nik Douglas, *Spiritual Sex: Secrets of Tantra from the Ice Age to the New Millennium* (New York: Pocket Books, 1997), pp. 192–93.

12. Quoted in ibid., p. 195.
13. *International Journal of the Tantrik Order* 5, no. 1 (1906): 96–97.
14. Quoted in Sann, *Fads, Follies, and Delusions,* p. 190.
15. Douglas, *Spiritual Sex,* p. 195.
16. Pierre Arnold Bernard, *Life: at the Clarkstown Country Club* (Nyack: Clarkstown Country Club, 1935). Bernard's estate contained thirty-four buildings, including a temple and a theater, dancing elephants, a gorilla named Gonzo, a tiger, a leopard, and enough birds to fill an aviary (Randall, *Phantoms of the Hudson Valley,* pp. 81 ff.).
17. Leslie Shepherd, "Bernard, Pierre," in *The Encyclopedia of Occultism and Parapsychology,* vol. 1, ed. Leslie Shepherd (Detroit: Gale Research, 1961), p. 104.
18. *Town and Country,* April 1941, quoted in Douglas, *Spiritual Sex,* p. 198.
19. Charles Boswell, "The Great Fuss and Fume over the Omnipotent Oom," *True: The Man's Magazine* (January 1965): 32.
20. *International Journal of the Tantrik Order,* quoted in Sann, *Fads, Follies, and Delusions,* p. 190. "The principal rites of Tantrik worshippers take place in secret. . . . This secrecy is in accordance with the Tantrik precept . . . 'One should guard the Kaula system from uninitiated beasts . . . just as one guards money . . . from thieves'" (*International Journal of the Tantrik Order,* 5, no. 1 [1906]: 27).
21. Sann, *Fad, Follies, and Delusions,* p. 189.
22. Boswell, "Great Fuss and Fume," p. 32.
23. *International Journal of the Tantrik Order* 5, no. 1 (1906): 105.
24. Seabrook, *Witchcraft,* pp. 356–57.
25. "Tantrik Worship: The Basis of Religion," *International Journal of the Tantrik Order* 5, no. 1 (1906): 71. "Sex worship as a religion . . . constitutes the basis of all that is sacred, holy and beautiful" (ibid., pp. 35–36).
26. Ibid., p. 71.
27. Boswell, "Great Fuss and Fume," p. 33.
28. Quoted in Francis King, *Sexuality, Magic, and Perversion* (Secaucus, N.J.: Citadel, 1971), p. 155.
29. Douglas, *Spiritual Sex,* p. 197.
30. Boswell, "Great Fuss and Fume," p. 85.
31. Sann, *Fad, Follies, and Delusions,* p. 190.
32. Boswell, "Great Fuss and Fume," p. 91.
33. Francis King, *Sexuality, Magic, and Perversion,* pp. 170–71.
34. John Patrick Deveney, *Paschal Beverly Randolph: A Nineteenth Century American Spiritualist, Rosicrucian, and Sex Magician* (Albany: State University of New York Press, 1997), pp. 211 ff. Some speculate that Randolph encountered Tantric practices in the course of his wanderings, though there is no real evidence of this (Douglas, *Spiritual Sex,* p. 85).
35. Franklin Rosemont, foreword to Deveney, *Paschal Beverly Randolph,* p. xv.
36. Deveney, *Paschal Beverly Randolph,* pp. 218–19.
37. Paschal Beverly Randolph, *The Mysteries of Eulis* (1860), in ibid., pp. 339–40. "At the moment his seminal glands open, his nostrils expand, and while the seed is going from his soul to her womb he breathes one of two atmospheres,

either fetid damnation from the border spaces or Divine Energy from heavens" (ibid.).

38. See Randolph, *The Mysteries of Eulis,* in Deveney, *Paschal Beverly Randolph,* p. 337. Randolph lists over a hundred uses for sexual magic, from winning money to domestic happiness to "the grand secret of life prolongation" (ibid., pp. 319–25).

39. Paschal Beverly Randolph, *Magia Sexualis* (Paris: Robert Telin, 1931), pp. 76–78.

40. Paschal Beverly Randolph, *Eulis! The History of Love: Its Wondrous Magic, Chemistry, Rules, Laws, Modes, and Rationale; Being the Third Revelation of Soul and Sex* (Toledo, Ohio: Randolph Publishing, 1974), p. 126. "No real magic power can or will descend into the soul of either except in the mighty moment, the orgasmal instant of BOTH—not one alone! for then and then only do the mystic doors of the SOUL OPEN TO THE SPACES" (*The Ansairetic Mystery,* in Deveney, *Paschal Beverly Randolph,* p. 314).

41. Deveney, *Paschal Beverly Randolph,* p. 252.

42. Kellner claims to have been initiated by the Arab fakir Soliman ben Aifha and the Indian yogis Bhima Sen Pratap and Sri Mahatma Agamya Guru Paramahamsa, from whom he learned "the mysteries of yoga and the philosophy of the left-hand path which he called sexual magic" (John Symonds, *The Magic of Aleister Crowley* [London: Frederick Muller, 1958], p. 95). On Reuss and his knowledge of Tantra, see A. R. Naylor, ed., *Theodor Reuss and Aleister Crowley: O.T.O. Rituals and Sexmagick* (Thames, Eng.: Essex House, 1999). Peter-Robert Koenig argues that the OTO was not founded by Kellner but was formed after his death under Reuss's leadership ("Spermo Gnostics and the OTO," OTO Phenomenon web site, www.cyberlink.ch/~koenig/ spermo.htm). See also Koenig, "The OTO Phenomenon," *Theosophical History* 4, no. 3 (1992): 92–98.

43. Many of Randolph's ideas on sex magic were transmitted to Germany through a little-known but extremely influential occult group known as the Hermetic Brotherhood of Luxor, begun in the 1880s. Drawing heavily on Randolph's sexual teaching, the Hermetic Brotherhood of Luxor warned against the dangerous excesses of sexual magic, which can lead men to madness or suicide (Joscelyn Godwin, Christian Chanel, and John Patrick Deveney, *The Hermetic Brotherhood of Luxor: Initiatic and Historical Documents of an Order of Practical Occultism* [York Beach, Me.: Samuel Weiser, 1995], pp. 213–78; Joscelyn Godwin, *The Theosophical Enlightenment* [Albany: State University of New York Press, 1994], pp. 258 ff., 347–61).

44. *Oriflamme* (1912): 18, in R. Swinburne Clymer, *The Rosicrucian Fraternity in America: Authentic and Spurious Organizations,* vol. 2 (Quakertown, Pa.: Rosicrucian Foundation, n.d.), p. 541.

45. Francis King, *The Magical World of Aleister Crowley* (New York: Coward, McCann, and Geoghegan, 1978), p. 79. On homosexual rites, see Peter-Robert Koenig's chapter "Anal Intercourse and the O.T.O.," in *Das OTO-Phaenomen: An Agony in 22 Fits,* trans. (by author) online, OTO Phenomenon web site, www.home.sunrise.ch/~prkoenig/phenomen.htm.

46. Francis King, *Magical World,* p. 79. See also Godwin, *The Theosophical Enlightenment,* pp. 255–56.

47. Francis King, *Magical World,* p. 100. Crowley's main texts on sex magic include: *Of the Nature of the Gods; Liber Agape—the Book of the Unveiling of the Sangraal de Arte Magica;* and *Of the Homunculus,* most of which are included in Francis King, ed., *The Secret Rituals of the O.T.O.* (New York: Samuel Weiser, 1973).

48. Lawrence Sutin, *Do What Thou Wilt: A Life of Aleister Crowley* (New York: St. Martin's Press, 2000), p. 1.

49. Aleister Crowley, "The Temple of Solomon the King," *Equinox* 1, no. 4 (1910): 161. On Crowley's Tantric influences, see Sutin, *Do What Thou Wilt,* pp. 92, 127.

50. Sutin, *Do What Thou Wilt,* p. 141.

51. Douglas, *Spiritual Sex,* p. 208; Elizabeth Sharpe, *The Secrets of the Kaula Circle: A Tale of Fictitious People. . . .* (London: Luzac, 1936), pp. 48–49.

52. Aleister Crowley, *The Confessions of Aleister Crowley* (1968; reprint, New York: Hill and Wang, 1970), p. 767. On Crowley's sex magic and its relation to the OTO, see Koenig, "Spermo-Gnostics and the O.T.O.": "Crowley's VIIIth degree unveiled . . . that masturbating on a sigil of a demon or meditating upon the image of a phallus would bring power or communication with a divine being. . . . The IXth degree was labeled heterosexual intercourse where the sexual secretions were sucked out of the vagina and when not consumed . . . put on a sigil to attract this or that demon to fulfill the pertinent wish."

53. Aleister Crowley, "The Law of Liberty: A Tract of Therion, Issued by the Ordo Templi Orientis," reproduced in Clymer, *Rosicrucian Fraternity in America,* vol. 2, p. 572.

54. Francis King, *Magical World,* p. 82. A detailed record of the Paris workings is contained in two manuscripts, *The Book of High Magick Art* and the *Esoteric Record,* compiled by Victor Neuberg.

55. "The orgasm of coitus (as also the effect of drugs) led to openings of consciousness toward the supersensual. . . . The technique . . . was that of excess; through pain or pleasure, sex or intoxication, it was necessary to attain condition of exhaustion taken to the extreme limit" (Julius Evola, *The Metaphysics of Sex* [1969; reprint, New York: Inner Traditions, 1983], pp. 264, 266).

56. Sutin, *Do What Thou Wilt,* pp. 244 ff.

57. Symonds, *The Magic of Aleister Crowley,* pp. 141–42.

58. Aleister Crowley, *The Vision and the Voice* (London: Simpkin, Marshall, Hamilton, Kent, 1911), pp. 385–86. On the creation of alchemical androgynes, see Hugh B. Urban, "Birth Done Better: Conceiving the Immortal Fetus in India, China, and Renaissance Europe," in *Notes on a Mandala: Essays in Honor of Wendy Doniger,* ed. Laurie Patton, pp. 25–56 (New York: Seven Bridges Press, 2003).

59. Sutin, *Do What Thou Wilt,* p. 239.

60. Ibid., p. 274.

61. There is a vast array of such books, for example: Christopher S. Hyatt and Lon Milo Duquette, *Sex Magic, Tantra, and Tarot: The Way of the Secret*

Lover (Tempe, Ariz.: New Falcon Publications, 1991); Christopher S. Hyatt and S. Jason Black, *Tantra without Tears* (Tempe, Ariz.: New Falcon Publications, 2000); Donald Michael Kraig, Linda Falorio, and Tara Nema, *Modern Sex Magick: Secrets of Erotic Spirituality* (St. Paul, Minn.: Llewellyn, 1998).

62. Jeffrey Weeks, *Sex, Politics, and Society: The Regulation of Society since 1800* (London: Longman, 1989), p. 255; cf. Foucault, *Religion and Culture*, pp. 57 ff.

63. Omar Garrison, *Tantra: The Yoga of Sex* (New York: Julian Press, 1964), pp. xxviii, xxvi.

64. Douglas, *Spiritual Sex*, pp. 219, 221.

65. Allen Ginsberg, *Indian Journals, March 1962–May 1963* (San Francisco: City Lights Books, 1970), p. 93. On Ginsberg's relationship with Trungpa, see Barry Miles, *Ginsberg: A Biography* (New York: Simon and Schuster, 1989), pp. 440–44, 466–75.

66. Ginsberg, *Indian Journals*, p. 80.

67. Ibid., pp. 13–14.

68. Alan Watts, "Tantra," *Loka: A Journal from Naropa Institute* 1 (1975): 57.

69. Michael York, *The Emerging Network: A Sociology of New Age and New Religious Movements* (Lanham, Md.: Rowman and Littlefield, 1995), p. 34. A variety of authors have attempted to provide definitions—or at least typologies—of the chaotic body of phenomena known as "New Age." See Robert S. Ellwood, *Religious and Spiritual Groups in Modern America* (Englewood, N.J.: Prentice-Hall, 1988), pp. 14–15; James Lewis, "Approaches to the Study of the New Age Movement," in *Perspectives on the New Age*, ed. James Lewis and J. Gordon Melton (Albany: State University of New York Press, 1992); Wouter J. Hanegraaff, *New Age Religion and Western Culture: Esotericism in the Mirror of Secular Thought* (New York: State University of New York Press, 1998), pp. 1–21.

70. Paul Heelas, *The New Age Movement: The Celebration of the Self and the Sacralization of Modernity* (Oxford: Basil Blackwell, 1996), p. 169.

71. Sondra Ray, *How to Be Chic, Fabulous, and Live Forever* (Berkeley, Calif.: Celestial Arts, 1986).

72. Sanaya Roman and Duane Packer, *Creating Money* (New York: H. J. Kramer, 1988), p. 18.

73. Heelas, *The New Age Movement*, p. 68; cf. Paul Heelas, "Cults for Capitalism: Self Religions, Magic, and the Empowerment of Business," in *Religion and Power, Decline and Growth: Sociological Analyses of Religion in Britain, Poland, and the Americas*, ed. Peter Gee and John Fulton (Twickenham, Eng.: British Sociological Association, 1991), pp. 27 ff. York comments: "Many New Agers . . . are adamant that the capitalist profit motive is fully compatible with New Age ideals" (*The Emerging Network*, p. 40).

74. Howard Zitko, *New Age Tantra Yoga: The Cybernetics of Sex and Love* (Tuscon: World University Press, 1974), p. xix.

75. Douglas, *Spiritual Sex*, pp. 17, 345; cf. André Van Lysebeth, *Tantra: The Cult of the Feminine* (York Beach, Me.: Samuel Weiser, 1995), xiii.

76. Nik Douglas, "New Tantric Order," Tantra Works web site, www.tantraworks.com/tantrausa2.html#NTO.

77. Online advertisement for Douglas, *Spiritual Sex,* Tantra Works web site, www.tantraworks.com.

78. Christopher S. Hyatt, *Secrets of Western Tantra: The Sexuality of the Middle Path* (Tempe, Ariz.: New Falcon Publications, 1996), p. 22.

79. Margo Anand, *The Art of Sexual Ecstasy: The Path of Sacred Sexuality for Western Lovers* (Los Angeles: Jeremy P. Tarcher, 1989), p. 44.

80. Douglas, *Sexual Secrets,* quoted in ibid., p. 41.

81. Van Lysbeth, *Tantra,* p. 53; cf. Vicki Noble, *Shakti Woman: Feeling Our Fire, Healing Our World: The New Female Shamanism* (San Francisco: HarperSanFrancisco, 1991).

82. As Dax Michaels argues, "By controlling sexual activity . . . the Church would insure the filling of their ranks with a growing supply of indoctrinated Catholics. . . . Only through the usage of Tantric erotic synergy can we again regain our feelings of being connected to ourselves, our mother earth and each other" (Tantric Massage web site, www.tantricmassage.com/tantric-overview.html). Many lesbians have appropriated Tantra in similar ways. As Diane Mariechild suggests, "Erotic love between women can be a celebration of and an initiation into the female creative spirit. . . . When we open to the great feminine, the holy space that is the foundation of the world, making love becomes sacred" ("Lesbian Sacred Sexuality," Church of Tantra web site, www.tantra.org/lesbian.html).

83. Foucault, *Religion and Culture,* p. 57.

84. Bhagwan Shree Rajneesh, *From Sex to Superconsciousness* (Bombay: Jeevan Jagruti Kendra, 1971), p. 39.

85. See Chogyam Trungpa, *Born in Tibet* (Baltimore: Penguin Books, 1971). See also Donald S. Lopez, *Prisoners of Shangri-La: Tibetan Buddhism and the West* (Chicago: University of Chicago Press, 1998), pp. 76–81; Rita M. Gross, *Soaring and Settling: Buddhist Perspectives on Contemporary Social and Religious Issues* (New York: Continuum, 1998), pp. 60 ff.

86. Georg Feuerstein, *Holy Madness: The Shock Tactics and Radical Teachings of Crazy-Wise Adepts, Holy Fools, and Rascal Gurus* (New York: Paragon House, 1990), p. 73.

87. See Amy Lavine, "Tibetan Buddhism in America: The Development of American Vajrayāna," in *The Faces of Buddhism in America,* ed. Charles S. Prebish and Kenneth K. Tanaka (Berkeley: University of California Press, 1998), p. 103.

88. Feuerstein, *Holy Madness,* p. 73.

89. Richard Grossinger, *Waiting for the Martian Express Cosmic Visions, Earth Warriors, Luminous Dreams* (Berkeley, Calif.: North Atlantic Books, 1989), p. 19; cf. Rick Fields, *How the Swans Came to the Lake: A Narrative History of Buddhism in America* (Boston: Shambhala Publications, 1986), p. 310.

90. Chogyam Trungpa, *First Thought, Best Thought: 108 Poems* (Boulder, Colo.: Shambhala Publications, 1973), p. 7.

91. Chogyam Trungpa, *Cutting through Spiritual Materialism* (Berkeley, Calif.: Shambhala Publications, 1973), p. 107.

92. Stephen T. Butterfield, *The Double Mirror: A Skeptical Journey into Tibetan Buddhism* (Berkeley, Calif.: North Atlantic Books, 1994), p. 7.

93. Ibid., p. 107.

94. Trungpa, *Journey without Goal: The Tantric Wisdom of the Buddha* (Boston: Shambhala, 1985), pp. 25, 53.

95. Butterfield, *The Double Mirror,* p. 140.

96. Feuerstein, *Holy Madness,* p. 75; Merwin's story is told by him in Miles, *Ginsberg: A Biography,* pp. 466–70.

97. Butterfield, *The Double Mirror,* p. 110.

98. Ibid., p. 100.

99. Ibid., p. 140.

100. Miles, *Ginsberg,* p. 525; cf. Butterfield, *The Double Mirror,* p. 185.

101. Jeffrey Weeks, *Sexuality and its Discontents: Meanings, Myths, Modern Sexualities* (London: Routledge and Kegan Paul, 1985), pp. 23, 24.

102. Douglas, *Spiritual Sex,* p. 15.

103. For Rajneesh's biography, see Hugh B. Urban "Zorba the Buddha: Capitalism, Charisma, and the Cult of Bhagwan Shree Rajneesh," *Religion* 26 (1996): 161–82; Lewis Carter, *Charisma and Control in Rajneeshpuram: The Role of Shared Values in the Creation of a Community* (Cambridge: Cambridge University Press, 1990); Susan J. Palmer and Arvind Sharma, eds., *The Rajneesh Papers: Studies in a New Religious Movement* (New Delhi: Motilal Banarsidas, 1993). More popular accounts include: Yati, *The Sound of Running Water: A Photobiography of Bhagwan Shree Rajneesh* (Poona: Rajneesh Foundation, 1980); Hugh Milne, *Bhagwan: The God That Failed* (New York: St. Martin's Press, 1986); James Gordon, *The Golden Guru: The Strange Journey of Bhagwan Shree Rajneesh* (New York: Viking Press, 1987). There is also the posthumously published *Autobiography of a Spiritually Incorrect Mystic* (New York: St. Martin's Press, 2000).

104. Feuerstein, *Holy Madness,* p. 65.

105. Quoted in Hugh Milne, *Bhagwan: The God That Failed* (New York: St. Martin's Press, 1986), p. 192.

106. The Rajneesh movement had a remarkably successful business structure, which developed a complicated system of parent companies and subsidiaries, extending through a range of secular and spiritual enterprises. Three separated but interlocking organizations were formed: the Ranch Church (RFI) was managed through the Rajneesh Investment Corporation (RIC) and the Rajneesh Neo-Sannyasin International Corporation (RNSIC), allowing the movement to transfer funds fluidly and easily, while paying as little taxes as possible. Meanwhile, the Rajneesh Church spread worldwide in a proliferation of ancillary businesses—not only spiritual institutes and meditation centers, but also secular businesses like restaurants, discotheques, and cleaning services. See Urban, "Zorba the Buddha," pp. 174–78; and Carter, *Charisma and Control,* pp. 77 ff.

107. Carter, *Charisma and Control,* pp. 225, 237.

108. Bob Mullan, *Life as Laughter: Following Bhagwan Shree Rajneesh* (Boston: Routledge, 1983), p. 44.

109. Rajneesh, cited in Kate Strelley, *The Ultimate Game* (San Francisco: Harper and Row, 1987), pp. 71–72.

110. Feuerstein, *Holy Madness,* p. 67.

111. Bhagwan Shree Rajneesh, *Tantra: The Supreme Understanding* (Poona: Rajneesh Foundation, 1975), pp. 55, 56.

112. Sannyasin informant, cited in Carter, *Charisma and Control,* p. 48. As Osho puts it, "You are certainly brainwashed, I use a dry-cleaning machine. . . . And what is wrong with being brainwashed? Wash it every day, keep it clean. . . . It is just an up-to-date religious laundry" (*Autobiography,* pp. 133–34).

113. Osho, *Tantric Transformation* (Shaftesbury, Eng.: Element Books, 1978), p. 4.

114. Ibid., pp. 6–7.

115. Rajneesh, *Tantra: The Supreme Understanding,* pp. 93, 157.

116. Ibid., pp. 190, 98–99.

117. Bhagwan Shree Rajneesh, *Yoga: The Alpha and the Omega* (Poona: Rajneesh Foundation, 1981), pp. 157, 21. See Susan J. Palmer, "Lovers and Leaders in a Utopian Commune," in Palmer and Sharma, *The Rajneesh Papers,* p. 127.

118. Rajneesh, *Tantra: The Supreme Understanding,* p. 100.

119. Feuerstein, *Holy Madness,* p. 70.

120. Rajneesh, *Tantra: The Supreme Understanding,* p. 100.

121. Bhagwan Shree Rajneesh, *The Goose Is Out* (Poona: Rajneesh Foundation, 1982), p. 286.

122. Swami Anand Jina, "The Work of Osho Rajneesh: A Thematic Overview," in Palmer and Sharma, *The Rajneesh Papers,* p. 54.

123. Osho, "Osho, Never Born, Never Died," www.sannyas.net/osho02.htm.

124. Osho, "Osho Times," www.osho.com/main.cfm?area=magazine.

125. Osho, *Autobiography,* p. 132.

126. Ibid., pp. 268–69.

127. Appendix to ibid., p. 294; cf. Sharma and Palmer, epilogue to *The Rajneesh Papers,* p. 161.

128. I am indebted to Sarah Caldwell for sharing her work and personal experience with the Siddha Yoga movement. See her article "The Heart of the Secret: A Personal and Scholarly Encounter with Shakta Tantrism in Siddha Yoga," in *The Unknown, Remembered Gate: Religious Experience and Hermeneutical Reflection,* ed. Elliot R. Wolfson and Jeffrey J. Kripal (New York: Seven Bridges Press, forthcoming).

129. Swami Muktananda, *Secret of the Siddhas* (South Fallsburg, N.Y.: SYDA Foundation, 1994), p. 1.

130. Douglas Renfrew Brooks, introduction to Douglas Renfrew Brooks, Swami Durgananda, Paul E. Muller-Ortega, William K. Mahoney, Constantina Rhodes Bailly, and S. P. Sabharathnam, *Meditation Revolution: A History and Theology of the Siddha Yoga Lineage* (South Fallsburg, N.Y.: Agama Press, 1997), p. xxxv.

131. Swami Muktananda *The Perfect Relationship: The Guru and the Disciple* (South Fallsburg, N.Y.: SYDA Foundation, 1985), p. 14.

132. Muktananda, cited in William Rodarmor, "The Secret Life of Swami Muktananda," reproduced at the "Leaving Siddha Yoga" web site, www.cyberpass .net/truth/secret.htm.

133. Douglas Renfrew Brooks, "The Canons of Siddha Yoga: The Body of Scripture and the Form of the Guru," in Brooks et al., *Meditation Revolution,* pp. 334, 327.

134. Swami Muktananda, *The Play of Consciousness (Chitshakti Vilas)* (New York: Harper and Row, 1978), p. 91.

135. Ibid., p. 92.

136. Ibid., p. 99.

137. Ibid., p. 105.

138. Muktananda, *The Perfect Relationship,* p. 14.

139. Lis Harris, "O Guru, Guru, Guru," *The New Yorker,* 14 November 1994, p. 96.

140. Rodarmor, "Secret Life of Swami Muktananda."

141. Ibid.

142. Harris, "O Guru, Guru, Guru," p. 97.

143. Caldwell, "Heart of the Secret," p. 21.

144. Harris, "O Guru, Guru, Guru," p. 108.

145. Thurman, quoted in ibid., p. 97.

146. Jeffrey J. Kripal, "Inside-Out, Outside-In: Existential Place and Academic Practice in the Study of North American Guru-Traditions," *Religious Studies Review* 25, no. 3 (1999): 236–37.

147. Ibid., p. 236.

148. Caldwell, "Heart of the Secret," p. 22, 37.

149. Arthur Kroker and Marilouise Kroker, *Hacking the Future: Stories for the Flesh-eating 90s* (New York: St. Martin's Press, 1996), p. 78. One of the few studies of religion and cyber space is Erik Davis, *Techgnosis: Myth, Magic, and Mysticism in the Age of Information* (New York: Harmony Books, 1998).

150. Jenny Terry and Melodie Calvert, introduction to *Processed Lives: Gender and Technology in Everyday Life* (New York: Routledge, 1997), p. 7.

151. Lavine, "Tibetan Buddhism in America," p. 113.

152. Rachel Fell McDermott, "Kālī's New Frontiers: A Hindu Goddess on the Internet," in *Encountering Kālī: In the Margins, at the Center, in the West,* ed. Jeffrey J. Kripal and Rachel Fell McDermott (Berkeley: University of California Press, forthcoming), p. 30.

153. Zitko, *New Age Tantra Yoga,* pp. xv–xx.

154. Douglas, *Spiritual Sex,* p. 323. Douglas includes an appendix that lists twenty pages of online sex magic.

155. Paul Ramana Das and Marilena Silbey, "Third Millennium Magic," Third Millennium Magic web site, www.3mmagic.com.

156. Douglas, *Spiritual Sex,* pp. 307–8, 19.

157. David Ramsdale and Ellen Ramsdale, "Sexual Energy Ecstasy," Tantra web site, www.tantra.com.

158. Paul Ramana Das and Marilena Silbey, "American Tantra's Top 5 Techniques!" Third Millennium Magic web site, www.3mmagic.com/at_main.html.

159. Kroker and Kroker, *Hacking the Future,* p. 33.

160. Friedrich Max Müller, *Biographical Essays* (New York: Charles Scribner's Sons, 1884), p. 13.

161. On the concept of late capitalism, see Fredric Jameson, *Postmodernism; or, The Cultural Logic of Late Capitalism* (Durham, N.C.: Duke University Press 1991); and "Postmodernism; or, The Cultural Logic of Late Capitalism," *New Left Review* 146 (1984): 53–93; Daniel Bell, *The Coming of Post-Industrial So-*

ciety (New York: Basic Books, 1973); Claus Offe, *Disorganized Capitalism* (Oxford: Oxford University Press, 1985); David Harvey, *The Condition of Postmodernity* (London: Blackwell Publishers, 1989); Mike Featherstone, "The Body in Consumer Culture," in *The Body: Social Process and Cultural Theory,* ed. Mike Featherstone, Mike Hepworth, Brian S. Turner (London: Sage Publications, 1991).

162. For a good discussion of the differences between modern or "Fordist" capitalism, which predominated up to the 1970s, and late or post-Fordist capitalism, see Harvey, *The Condition of Postmodernity,* pp. 291–98.

163. Frederic Jameson, "Postmodernism and Consumer Society," in *The Anti-Aesthetic: Essays on Postmodern Culture,* ed. Hal Foster (New York: New Press, 1998), p. 99; cf. Terry Eagleton, "Awakening from Modernity," *Times Literary Supplement,* 20 February 1987, p. 194; Jean-François Lyotard, *The Postmodern Condition: A Report on Knowledge* (Minneapolis: University of Minnesota Press, 1984).

164. Jameson, *Postmodernism,* p. 96.

165. Eagleton, "Awakening from Modernity," p. 194.

166. Jürgen Habermas, "Legitimation Problems in the Modern State," in *Communication and the Evolution of Society,* by Jürgen Habermas (Boston: Beacon Press, 1974), pp. 178–206.

167. Mike Featherstone, *Consumer Culture and Postmodernism* (London: Sage, 1991), pp. 112–13.

168. Bryan S. Turner, *Regulating Bodies: Essays in Medical Sociology* (London: Routledge, 1992), pp. 164–65, 47.

169. Rajneesh, *Tantra: The Supreme Understanding,* p. 96.

170. Bubba Free John, *Garbage and the Goddess: The Last Miracles and Final Spiritual Instructions of Bubba Free John* (Lower Lake, Calif.: Dawn Horse Press, 1974), p. 104; *The Knee of Listening: The Early Life and Radical Spiritual Teachings of Bubba Free John* (Middletown, Calif.: Dawn Horse Press, 1978), p. 270.

171. As Chogyam Trungpa put it, "There is enormous individualism in terms of the doctrines and teachings that are presented. All of them are valid" ("Sparks," *Loka: A Journal from Naropa Institute* 1 [1975]: 19).

172. Nik Douglas, *Tantra Yoga* (New Delhi: Munshiram Manoharlal, 1971), p. 93.

173. Francis King, *Tantra: The Way of Action* (Rochester, N.Y.: Destiny Books, 1990), pp. 128–29.

174. Free John, *Garbage and the Goddess,* pp. 106–7.

175. Don Webb, "A Sex Magic Primer," www.altx.com/interzones/violet/sex.magic.html.

176. Rajneesh, *Tantra: The Supreme Understanding,* p. 95.

177. Swami Nostradamus Virato, "Tantric Sex: A Spiritual Path to Ecstasy," Church of Tantra web site, www.tantra.org.

178. Watts, "Tantra," p. 56; cf. David Ramsdale and Ellen Ramsdale, *Energy Ecstasy: A Practical Guide to Lovemaking Secrets of the East and West* (New York: Bantam Books, 1993), p. 23.

179. Van Lysebeth, *Tantra,* pp. 347, 139.

180. Feuerstein, *Holy Madness,* pp. 108–9.

181. Jeffrey Tye, "Tantra: Sex Magic," Church of Tantra web site, www.tantra.org/sexmagic.html.

182. Rajneesh, quoted in Vasant Joshi, *The Awakened One: The Life and Work of Bhagwan Shree Rajneesh* (San Francisco: Harper and Row, 1982), p. 1.

183. Mullan, *Life as Laughter,* p. 48.

184. Bhagwan Shree Rajneesh, cited in Laurence Grafstein, "Messianic Capitalism," *The New Republic,* 20 February 1984, p. 14; *Beware of Socialism!* (Rajneeshpuram, Oreg.: Rajneesh Foundation International, 1984), pp. 15, 19.

185. Osho, *Autobiography,* p. 157.

186. From the Tantra web site, www.tantra.com/tantra2/product1.html.

187. Robert E. Svoboda, *Aghora: At the Left Hand of God* (Calcutta: Rupa, 1986), and *Aghora II: Kundalini* (Calcutta: Rupa, 1993). See June Campbell, *Traveller in Space: In Search of Female Identity in Tibetan Buddhism* (New York: George Braziller, 1996); and Daniel Odier, *Tantric Quest: An Encounter with Absolute Love* (Rochester, N.Y.: Inner Traditions, 1997). Campbell provides a sobering and critical perspective on the role of women in Tantric Buddhism; Odier's is a far more romantic tale of self-discovery through Tantric practice. Jeffrey Hopkins has published a translation of the Tibetan heterosexual erotic manual, *Tibetan Arts of Love,* by Gedun Chopel, which he has rewritten from an explicitly gay point of view (*Sex, Orgasm, and the Mind of Clear Light* [Berkeley, Calif.: North Atlantic Books, 1998]). The most interesting example of the use of Tantra for S&M purposes is Fakir Musafar, who argues that both Tantra and S&M use extreme sex as means of inducing ecstatic states (interview with Fakir Musafar, by Kristine Ambrosia and Joseph Lanza, in *Apocalypse Culture,* ed. Adam Parfrey [Los Angeles: Feral House, 1990]). The first epigraph for this section comes from an April 1996 interview with Annie Sprinkle, by Gary Morris, on the Bright Lights Films web site, www.brightlightsfilm.com/16/annie.html.

188. Douglas, *Spiritual Sex,* pp. 345–46.

189. Annie Sprinkle, *Post-Porn Modernist* (San Francisco: Cleis Press, 1998), p. 193.

190. Hakim Bey, "Instructions for the Kali Yuga," in *Apocalypse Culture,* ed. Adam Parfrey, p. 87.

191. Jean Baudrillard, *Forget Foucault* (New York: Semiotext[e], 1987), pp. 23–24.

192. Marianna Torgovnick, *Gone Primitive: Savage Intellects, Modern Lives* (Chicago: University of Chicago Press, 1990), pp. 40, 41.

193. Trungpa, *Cutting through Spiritual Materialism,* p. 15.

CONCLUSION

1. Susan Buck-Morss, *The Dialectics of Seeing: Walter Benjamin and the Arcades Project* (Cambridge, Mass.: MIT Press, 1989), p. 249, paraphrasing Benjamin.

2. Michael Taussig, *Shamanism, Colonialism, and the Wild Man: A Study in Terror and Healing* (Chicago: University of Chicago Press, 1987), p. 443.

3. See Buck-Morss, *The Dialectics of Seeing*, pp. 210–12. The commodity "lies at the intersection of petrified nature and transitory nature, waking and dream, natural history and historical nature, mythic history (phantasmagoria) and mythic nature (Symbol)" (ibid., p. 211).

4. On Kāmākhyā, see Hugh B. Urban, "The Path of Power: Impurity, Kingship, and Sacrifice in Assamese Tantra," *Journal of the American Academy of Religion* 69, no. 4 (2001): 777–816.

5. Margo Anand, *The Art of Sexual Ecstasy: The Path of Sacred Sexuality for Western Lovers* (Los Angeles: Jeremy P. Tarcher, 1989), p. 7. Even Georg Feuerstein, who is quite critical of popular Tantra, holds out the hope for a new form of Tantra for a new age: "If Tantra can recruit enough authentic Western practitioners, it could have an important role to play in the birthing of a civilization that is dedicated to the welfare of all people" (*Tantra: The Path of Ecstasy* [Boston: Shambhala Publications, 1998], p. 273).

6. Jeffrey Hopkins, *Sex, Orgasm, and the Mind of Clear Light* (Berkeley, Calif.: North Atlantic Books, 1998), pp. 71–72.

7. Ibid., p. xii.

8. See Feuerstein, *Tantra*, p. xiv; quote from David Gordon White, *Tantra in Practice* (Princeton, N.J.: Princeton University Press, 2000), p. 5.

9. Agehananda Bharati, *The Tantric Tradition* (Garden City, N.Y.: Anchor Books, 1970), p. 299.

10. Teun Goudriaan and Sanjukta Gupta, *Hindu Tantric and Śākta Literature* (Wiesbaden, Ger.: Otto Harrasowitz, 1981), p. 9. Likewise, Padoux argues that Tantra is "in no way popular" but is "the work of Brahmins, expressing the ideology of the higher classes" ("A Survey of Tantrism for the Historian of Religions," review of *Hindu Tantrism*, by Sanjukta Gupta, Teun Goudriaan, and Dirk Jan Hoens, *History of Religions* 20, no. 4 [1981]: 353).

11. Jeffrey J. Kripal, *Kālī's Child: The Mystical and the Erotic in the Life and Teachings of Ramakrishna* (Chicago: University of Chicago Press, 1998), p. 28.

12. Grace M. Jantzen, *Power, Gender, and Christian Mysticism* (Cambridge: Cambridge University Press, 1995), p. 12.

13. Jonathan Z. Smith, *Imagining Religion: From Babylon to Jonestown* (Chicago: University of Chicago Press, 1982), p. 18.

14. See ibid., p. 51. As Bruce Lincoln argues, "Scholars are no different from other human beings. They exist within a time, a place and a social institution, and their speech, thought and interests originate in, reflect and engage these givens of their own experience" (*Death, War, and Sacrifice: Studies in Ideology and Practice* [Chicago: University of Chicago Press, 1991], pp. xvi–xvii).

15. Smith, *Imagining Religion*, p. xi; cf. Richard King, *Orientalism and Religion: Postcolonial Theory, India, and the Mystic East* (London: Routledge, 1999), p. 210.

16. Debiprasad Chattopadhyaya, *Lokāyata: A Study in Ancient Indian Materialism* (New Delhi: People's Publishing House, 1959), p. 358.

17. Quoted in Shashibhushan Dasgupta, *Obscure Religious Cults, as a Background to Bengali Literature* (Calcutta: Firma KLM, 1968), pp. 140–41n.

18. On the fetishization of the body in late capitalist society, see Mike Feath-

erstone, "The Body and Consumer Culture," in *The Body: Social Process and Cultural Theory,* ed. Mike Featherstone, Mike Hepworth, and Bryan S. Turner (London: Sage Publications, 1991).

19. June Campbell, *Traveller in Space: In Search of Female Identity in Tibetan Buddhism* (New York: George Braziller, 1996), p. 171. Campbell provides a fascinating insider's view of the role of female partners in Tantric practice, a role that is often far from empowering or liberating.

20. Kripal, *Kālī's Child,* p. 29; my italics.

21. Michel Foucault, *The History of Sexuality,* vol. 1, trans. Robert Hurley (New York: Vintage Books, 1978), p. 150.

22. Jeremy R. Carrette, *Foucault and Religion: Spiritual Corporeality and Political Spirituality* (London: Routledge, 2000), pp. xi, 146.

23. Michel Foucault, "Le chef mythique de la révolte de l'Iran," in *Dits et écrits, 1948–1988,* vol. 3, ed. Daniel Defert and Francois Ewald (Paris: Gallimard, 1994), p. 716.

24. White, introduction to *Tantra in Practice,* p. 32. On the political role of Tantra, see also Charles D. Orzech, *Politics and Transcendent Wisdom: The Scripture for Humane Kings in the Creation of Chinese Buddhism* (University Park: Pennsylvania State University Press, 1998); Urban, "The Path of Power"; David Snellgrove, "The Notion of Divine Kingship in Tantric Buddhism," in *The Sacral Kingship: Contributions to the Central Theme of the Eighth International Congress for the History of Religions* (Leiden: E. J. Brill, 1959); Michel Strickmann, *Mantras et mandarins: Le Bouddhisme tantrique en Chine* (Paris: Gallimard, 1996).

25. There is a large body of literature on the Bāuls and Sahajiyās; see, for example, Edward C. Dimock, *The Place of the Hidden Moon: Erotic Mysticism in the Vaiṣṇava-Sahajiyā Tradition of Bengal* (Chicago: University of Chicago Press, 1966); Carol Salomon, "Bāul Songs," in *Religions of India in Practice,* ed. Donald S. Lopez, Jr. (Princeton, N.J.: Princeton University Press, 1995); and Glen A. Hayes, "Vaiṣṇava Sahajiyā Traditions," in the same volume. On the Kartābhajās, see Hugh B. Urban, *The Economics of Ecstasy: Tantra, Secrecy, and Power in Colonial Bengal* (New York: Oxford University Press, 2001); and Urban, ed. and trans., *Songs of Ecstasy: Tantric and Devotional Songs from Bengal* (New York: Oxford University Press, 2001).

26. On Ramakrishna, see Kripal, *Kālī's Child.* On Bāmākṣepa, see Malcolm McLean, "Eating Corpses and Raising the Dead: The Tantric Madness of Bāmākṣepa," in *In the Flesh: Eros, Secrecy and Power in the Vernacular Tantric Traditions of India,* ed. Hugh B. Urban, Glen A. Hayes, and Paul Muller-Ortega (Albany: State University of New York, in progress).

27. On possession in Nepal and Ladakh, see John T. Hitchcock and Rex L. Jones, eds., *Spirit Possession in the Nepal Himalayas* (Warminster, Eng.: Aris and Phillips, 1976); Robert I. Levy, *Mesocosm: Hinduism and the Organization of a Traditional Newar City in Nepal* (Berkeley: University of California Press, 1990). On the Nāths, see David Gordon White, *The Alchemical Body: Siddha Traditions in Medieval India* (Chicago: University of Chicago Press, 1996). On the Aghorīs, see Jonathan Parry, "Sacrificial Death and the Necrophagous Ascetic," in *Death and the Regeneration of Life,* ed. Maurice Bloch and Jonathan

Parry (New York: Cambridge University Press, 1982); for a more popular account, see Svoboda's *Aghora* series.

28. Vernacular Tantric traditions is the focus of the volume that I coedited with Glen A. Hayes and Paul Muller-Ortega, *In the Flesh.*

29. Marianna Torgovnick, *Primitive Passions: Men, Women, and the Quest for Ecstasy* (Chicago: University of Chicago Press, 1998), pp. 219.

30. Wilhelm Halbfass, *India and Europe: An Essay in Understanding* (Albany: State University of New York Press, 1988), pp. 339–40, 441–42.

31. Benjamin Barber, *Jihad vs. McWorld: How Globalism and Tribalism Are Reshaping the World* (New York: Ballantine Books, 1992), p. 4. See also Aijaz Ahmad, *In Theory: Classes, Nations, Literatures* (New York: Verso, 1992); Arjun Appadurai, "Disjuncture and Difference in the Global Cultural Economy," in *The Globalization Reader,* ed. Frank J. Lechner and John Boli (London: Blackwell Publishers, 2000), pp. 322–30.

32. Ahmad, *In Theory,* p. 21.

33. Gita Mehta, *Karma Cola: Marketing the Mystic East* (New York: Simon and Schuster, 1979), p. 102.

34. Ibid., p. 103.

35. Marshall Sahlins, "Cosmologies of Capitalism: The Trans-Pacific Sector of 'The World System,'" *Proceedings of the British Academy* 74 (1988): 4. A similar argument is made in John Comaroff and Jean Comaroff, eds., *Modernity and Its Malcontents: Ritual and Power in Postcolonial Africa* (Chicago: University of Chicago Press, 1993), pp. xi–xii.

36. Pico Iyer, *Video Night in Kathmandu, and Other Reports from the Not-So-Far East* (New York: Alfred A. Knopf, 1988), p. 5.

37. Pierre Bourdieu, *In Other Words: Essays toward a Reflexive Sociology* (Stanford, Calif.: Stanford University Press, 1990), p. 155. Some authors seem more hopeful about this sort of local adaptation of the global market: "Countries still have great leeway in structuring their own polities; the same television program means different things to different audiences; McDonald's adapts its menu and marketing to local tastes" (Lechner and Boli, *The Globalization Reader,* p. 2).

38. Michael Taussig, *Mimesis and Alterity: A Particular History of the Senses* (London: Routledge, 1993), pp. 254–55.

39. Michel Foucault, "Michel Foucault and Zen," in Foucault, *Religion and Culture,* ed. Jeremy R. Carrette (New York: Routledge, 1999), p. 113.

Bibliography

WORKS IN SANSKRIT, BENGALI, AND HINDI

Abhedānanda, Svāmī. *Svāmījīr Padaprānte (Svāmī Vivekānander Sannyāsī-Śiṣyaganer Jīvanacarita)*. Calcutta: Udbhodhan Kāryālay, 1398 Bengali era (1991).

Āgamavāgīśa, Kṛṣṇānanda. *Bṛhat-Tantrasāra*. Ed. Śrīrasikamohana Caṭṭopādhyāya. Calcutta: Navabhārata Publishers, 1996.

Bhaṭṭācārya, Narendranāth. *Bhāratavarṣer Rājanaitika Itihāsa*. Calcutta: Firma KLM, 1974.

Bhattacharya, Benyotosh, ed. *The Guhyasamāja Tantra*. Baroda: Oriental Institute, 1931.

Brahmānanda, Śrī. *Sarvva Manaskāmanā Siddhi Pustaka*. Calcutta: Rajendra Library, n.d.

Bṛhadāranyaka Upaniṣad. In *One Hundred and Eight Upaniṣads*, ed. V. L. S. Panshikar. Varanasi: Vyāsa Prakāśana, 1983.

Caṭṭopādhyāy, Bankimcandra. *Ānandamaṭh: Racanār Preranā o Parināma, tatsaha Bankimacandrer Ānanda maṭher Prathama Saṃskāraner Phatokapi*. Ed. Cittarañjan Bandyopādhyāy. Calcutta: Ānanda, 1983.

———. *Bankim Racanāvalī*. Calcutta: Sāhitya Saṃsad, 1372 Bengali era (1965).

———. *Kapālakuṇḍalā*. 1866. Reprint, Calcutta: Taptī Publishing, 1966.

Caṭṭopādhyāy, Pramod Kumār. *Tantrābhilāṣīr Sādhusaṅga*. Calcutta: Viśvavanī Prakāśanī, 1963.

Daṇḍisvāmī Dāmodara Āśram, ed. *Jñānārṇavatantram*. Calcutta: Navabhārata Publishers, 1389 Bengali era (1982).

Dās, Jyotirlāl, ed. *Nīlatantram*. Calcutta: Navabhārata Publishers, 1388 Bengali era (1981).

Datta, Mahendranāth. *Śrīmat Vivekānanda Svāmījīr Jīvaner Granthāvalī*. Calcutta: Mahendra Publishing Committee, 1393–95 Bengali era (1986–88).

Datta, Rāmacandra. *Śrīśrīrāmakṛṣṇa Paramahaṃsadever Jīvanavṛttānta*. 1890. Reprint, Calcutta: Jogodyan, Kakurgachi, 1935.

Ghoṣe, Barinda Kumār. *Agnijug*. Calcutta: Book Publishing, 1355 Bengali era (1948).

Gokhale, G. S., ed. *Jñānārṇavatanta*. Poona: Ānandāśrama Series, 1952.

Gupta, Mahendranāth. *Śrīśrīrāmakṛṣṇakathāmṛta*. 1902. Reprint, Calcutta: Kathāmṛta Bhavan, 1987.

Kaulajñānanirṇaya. Ed. P. C. Bagchi. Varanasi: Prācya Prakāśana, 1986.

Kavirāj, Gopīnāth. *Akhaṇḍa Mahāyoga: Mūla Lekhak Gopīnāth Kavirāj*. Varanasi: Akhaṇḍa Mahāyoga Saṅgha, 1978.

———. *Akhaṇḍa Mahāyoger Pathe*. Calcutta: Mahesh Library, 1975.

———. *Tantra o Āgamaśāstrer Digdarśana*. Calcutta: Calcutta Sanskrit College Researches, 1963.

———. *Tāntrik Sādhana o Siddānta*. Burdwan: Burdwan University Press, 1376 Bengali era (1969).

———. *Tāntrik Sāhitya*. Lucknow: Hindī Samiti, 1972.

———. *Tāntrik Vāṅmay meṅ Śāktadṛṣṭi*. Patna: Bihar Rāṣṭrabhāṣā Pariṣad, 1963.

Krishnamacharya, V., ed. *Ahirbudhnyasaṃhitā*. Adyar: Adyar Library Series, 1966.

Maheśvarānanda. *Mahārthamañjarī*. Ed. V. V. Dvivedi. Varanasi: Sanskrit University Press, 1972.

Mitra, Satyacaran. *Śrī Śrī Rāmakṛṣṇa Paramahaṃsa: Jīvana o Upadeśa*. Calcutta: Great India Press, 1897.

Nāth, Soumānanda, ed. *Rudrayāmala (Uttaratantram)*. Calcutta: Navabhārata Publishers, 1997.

Nigūṛhānanda. *Sarpatāntriker Sandhāne*. Calcutta: Karuṇā Prakāśanī, 1980.

Pāl, Vasanta Kumār. "Tantrācārya Śivacandra." *Himādri* (Agrahāyan 1372 Bengali era, Pauṣ 1373 Bengali era [1965–66]).

Piṅgalāmatam. 123 fols. MSS 376 B. 1174. Durbar Library, Nepal.

Punyānandanātha. *Kāmakalāvilāsa*. Ed. Arthur Avalon. Madras: Ganesh, 1961.

Rāmatoṣaṇa. *Prāṇatoṣinī*. Ed. Soumyānanda Nāth. Calcutta: Navabhārata Publishers, 1991.

Śatapatha Brāhmaṇa. Benaras: Chowkhamba Sanskrit Series Office, 1964. Trans. Julius Eggeling. New Delhi: Motilal Banarsidas, 1963.

Sen, Akṣaykumār. *Śrī Śrī Rāmakṛṣṇa Puṅthi*. Calcutta: Udbodhan Kāryāyal, 1976.

Sharma, Rama Nath, ed. *The Aṣṭādhyāyī of Pāṇini*. New Delhi: Munshiram Manoharlal, 1987.

Shastri, Biswanarayan, ed. *See below, under "Yoginī Tantra."*

Śivācārya, Svāminātha, ed. *Kāmikāgama*. Pt. 1, *Pūrvakāmikā*. Madras: Dakṣiṇabhāratārcakasaṃgha, 1975.

Svetāśvatāra Upaniṣad. In *The Principal Upaniṣads,* trans. Sarvapelli Radhakrishnan. London: Unwin Hyman, 1953.

Tantrarājatantram. Ed. Arthur Avalon. New Delhi: Motilal Banarsidas, 1981.

Uhle, Heinrich, ed. *Die Vetālapañcaviṃśatikā in den Recension des Śivadāsa und eines Ungenannten.* Leipzig: F. A. Brockhaus, 1881.

Yoginīhṛdaya Tantra. Ed. Upendranāth Dās. Calcutta: Navabhārata Publishers, 1393 Bengali era (1986). French trans. André Padoux, *Le Coeur de la yoginī: Yoginīhṛdaya, avec le commentaire Dīpikā d'Amṛtānanda.* Paris: Collège de France, 1994.

Yoginī Tantra. Ed. Biswanarayan Shastri. New Delhi: Bharatīya Vidyā Prakāśana, 1982.

Yonī Tantra. Ed. J. A. Schoterman. New Delhi: Manohar, 1980.

WORKS IN ENGLISH AND OTHER LANGUAGES

Adhikari, Ram Chandra. "Shiva Shakti Yoga." In *Life and Philosophy of Gopinath Kaviraj.* Calcutta: University of Calcutta Press, 1981.

Ahmad, Aijaz. *In Theory: Classes, Nations, Literatures.* New York: Verso, 1992.

Anand, Margo. *The Art of Sexual Ecstasy: The Path of Sacred Sexuality for Western Lovers.* Los Angeles: Jeremy P. Tarcher, 1989.

Anderson, Patricia. *When Passion Reigned: Sex and the Victorians.* New York: Basic Books, 1995.

Annan, David. "Thuggee." In *Secret Societies,* ed. Norman MacKenzie, pp. 64–83. New York: Holt, Rhinehart, and Winston, 1967.

Appadurai, Arjun. "Disjuncture and Difference in the Global Cultural Economy." In *The Globalization Reader,* ed. Frank J. Lechner and John Boli, pp. 322–30. London: Blackwell Publishers, 2000.

Arnold, David. *Colonizing the Body: State Medicine and Epidemic Disease in Nineteenth Century India.* Berkeley: University of California Press, 1993.

Asad, Talal. *Genealogies of Religion: Discipline and Reasons of Power in Christianity and Islam.* Baltimore: Johns Hopkins University Press, 1993.

Ashcroft, Bill, Gareth Griffiths, and Helen Tiffin. *The Empire Writes Back: Theory and Practice in Post-Colonial Literatures.* London: Routledge, 1989.

———, eds. *The Post-Colonial Studies Reader.* London: Routledge, 1995.

Atmajnananda, Swami. "Scandals, Cover-ups, and Other Imagined Occurrences in the Life of Ramakrishna: An Examination of Jeffrey Kripal's *Kālī's Child. International Journal of Hindu Studies* 1, no. 2 (1997): 401–20.

Avalon, Arthur. *Principles of Tantra: The Tantratattva of Śrīyukta Śiva Candra Vidyārṇava Bhaṭṭācārya Mahodaya.* Madras: Ganesh, 1960.

——, trans. *Tantra of the Great Liberation: Mahānirvāṇa Tantra.* New York: Dover Publications, 1979.

Azim, Firdous. *The Colonial Rise of the Novel.* New York: Routledge, 1993.

Bagchi, P. C. "The Evolution of the Tantra." In *The Cultural Heritage of India,* by P. C. Bagchi. Calcutta: Ramakrishna Mission Institute of Culture, 1953.

———. *Studies in the Tantras.* Calcutta: University of Calcutta Press, 1975.

Baillet, Philippe. "Julius Evola et Mircea Eliade (1927–1974): Une Amitié manquée." *Les Deux Etendards* (1988): 45–55.

Ballhatchet, Kenneth. *Race, Sex, and Class under the Raj: Imperial Attitudes and Policies, 1793–1905.* New York: St. Martin's Press, 1980.

Bandyopadhyay, Panchkori. *Sāhitya.* Reproduced in *Principles of Tantra: The*

Tantratattva of Śrīyukta Śiva Candra Vidyārṇava Bhaṭṭācārya Mahodaya, by Arthur Avalon. Madras: Ganesh, 1960.

Banerjee, Sumanta. *The Parlour and the Streets: Elite and Popular Culture in Nineteenth Century Calcutta.* Calcutta: Seagull, 1989.

Banerjee, Sunil Kumar. *Bankim Chandra: A Study of His Craft.* Calcutta: Firma KLM, 1969.

Banerji, S. C. *A Brief History of Tantra Literature.* Calcutta: Naya Prokash, 1988.

———. *Tantra in Bengal.* New Delhi: Manohar Publications, 1992.

Barber, Benjamin. *Jihad vs. McWorld: How Globalism and Tribalism Are Reshaping the World.* New York: Ballantine Books, 1992.

Barth, August. *The Religions of India.* London: Kegan Paul, 1891.

Barthes, Roland. *Empire of Signs.* Trans. Richard Howard. New York: Hill and Wang, 1982.

Basu, Manoranjan. *Fundamentals of the Philosophy of the Tantras.* Calcutta: Mira Basu Publishers, 1986.

Baudrillard, Jean. *Forget Foucault.* New York: Semiotext(e), 1987.

———. *Simulations.* New York: Semiotext(e), 1988.

———. *The Transparency of Evil: Essays on Extreme Phenomena.* London: Verso, 1993.

Beane, Wendell Charles. *Myth, Cult, and Symbols in Śākta Hinduism: A Study of the Indian Mother Goddess.* Leiden: E. J. Brill, 1977.

Bell, Daniel. *The Coming of Post-Industrial Society.* New York: Basic Books, 1973.

Benevides, Gustavo. "Giuseppe Tucci; or, Buddhology in the Age of Fascism." In *Curators of the Buddha: The Study of Buddhism under Colonialism,* ed. Donald S. Lopez, Jr., pp. 161–96. Chicago: University of Chicago Press, 1995.

Benjamin, Walter. *Gesammelte Schriften.* 7 vols. Ed. Rolf Tiedemann and Hermann Schweppenhauser. Frankfurt: Suhrkamp Verlag, 1972.

———. *Illuminations.* Ed. Hannah Arendt. Trans. Harry Zohn. New York: Schocken Books, 1969.

———. *Reflections.* Ed. Peter Demetz. Trans. Edmund Jephcott. New York: Schocken Books, 1986.

Berger, Adriana. "Fascism and Religion in Romania." *Annals of Scholarship* 6, no. 4 (1989): 455–65.

Bernard, Pierre Arnold, ed. *International Journal of the Tantrik Order* 5, no. 1 (1906).

———. *Life: At the Clarkstown Country Club.* Nyack, N.Y.: Clarkstown Country Club, 1935.

Bernier, François. *Travels in the Mogul Empire,* AD 1656–1668. Trans. Archibald Constable. London: Oxford University Press, 1934.

Bey, Hakim. "Instructions for the Kali Yuga." In *Apocalypse Culture,* ed. Adam Parfrey, pp. 84–87. Los Angeles: Feral House, 1990.

Bhabha, Homi. "Dissemination: Time, Narrative and the Margins of the Modern Nation." In *Nation and Narration,* ed. Homi Bhabha, pp. 291–322. London: Routledge, 1990.

———. "Of Mimicry and Man." In *The Location of Culture,* by Homi Bhabha. London: Routledge, 1984.

———. "The Other Question: Difference, Discrimination, and the Discourse of

Colonialism." In *Literature, Politics, and Theory,* ed. Francis Barker, Peter Hulme, Margaret Iverson, and Diana Loxley, pp. 148–72. London: Methuen, 1986.
———, ed. *Nation and Narration.* London: Routledge, 1990.
Bharadwaja, Chiranjiva, trans. *The Light of Truth; or, An English Translation of the Satyarth Prakash of Swami Dayanand Saraswati.* 1927. Reprint, Madras: Arya Samaj, 1932.
Bharati, Agehananda. "The Future (if Any) of Tantrism." *Loka: A Journal from Naropa Institute* 1 (1975): 126–30.
———. "Making Sense out of Tantrism and Tantrics." *Loka: A Journal from Naropa Institute* 2 (1976): 52–55.
———. *The Ochre Robe: An Autobiography.* Santa Barbara, Calif.: Ross-Erikson Publishers, 1980.
———. *The Tantric Tradition.* Garden City, N.Y.: Anchor Books, 1970.
Bhattacharya, Brajamadhava. *The World of Tantra.* New Delhi: Munshiram Manoharlal, 1988.
Bhattacharyya, Benyotosh. *An Introduction to Buddhist Esoterism.* Oxford: Oxford University Press, 1932.
Bhattacharyya, Kalidas. *Gopinath Kaviraj's Thoughts: Towards a Systematic Study.* Calcutta: University of Calcutta Press, 1982.
Bhattacharyya, Narendra Nath. *History of the Śākta Religion.* New Delhi: Munshiram Manoharlal, 1974. Reprint, New Delhi: Munshiram Manoharlal, 1996.
———. *History of the Tantric Religion: A Historical, Ritualistic, and Philosophical Study.* New Delhi: Manohar, 1982. Reprint, New Delhi: Manohar, 1999.
———. *Indian Mother Goddess.* Calcutta: Indian Studies, 1971.
———. *Religious Culture of North-Eastern India.* New Delhi: Manohar, 1995.
Bhavabhūti. *Mālatī-Mādhava.* French trans. G. Strehly. Paris: Ernest Leroux, 1885.
Bhullar, Avtar Singh. *India, Myth and Reality: Images of India in the Fiction by English Writers.* New Delhi: Ajanta Publications, 1985.
Blavatsky, Helena Petrovna. *Collected Writings.* 14 vols. Comp. and ed. Boris De Zirkoff. Madras: Theosophical Publishing House, 1950–73.
Boehmer, Ellekem, ed. *Empire Writing: An Anthology of Colonial Literature, 1870–1918.* New York: Oxford University Press, 1998.
Bolle, Kees. *The Persistence of Religion: An Essay on Tantrism and Sri Aurobindo's Philosophy.* Leiden: E. J. Brill, 1971.
Booker, M. Keith. *Colonial Power, Colonial Texts: India in the Modern British Novel.* East Lansing: Asian Studies Center, University of Michigan, 1997.
Bose, D. N., and Hiralal Haldar. *Tantras: Their Philosophy and Occult Secrets.* Calcutta: Oriental Publishing, 1956.
Bose, Manindra Mohan. *The Post-Caitanya Sahajiā Cult of Bengal.* Calcutta: University of Calcutta Press, 1930.
Boswell, Charles. "The Great Fuss and Fume over the Omnipotent Oom." *True: The Man's Magazine* (January 1965): 31, 32, 85, 91.
Bourdieu, Pierre. *In Other Words: Essays toward a Reflexive Sociology.* Stanford, Calif.: Stanford University Press, 1990.
Brennan, Timothy. "The National Longing for Form." In *The Post-Colonial Stud-*

ies Reader, ed. Bill Ashcroft, Gareth Griffiths, and Helen Tiffin. London: Routledge, 1995.

Briffault, Robert. *The Mothers: The Matriarchal Theory of Social Origins.* New York: H. Fertig, 1993.

Brooks, Douglas Renfrew. *Auspicious Wisdom: The Texts and Traditions of Śrīvidyā Śākta Tantrism in South India.* Albany: State University of New York Press, 1992.

———. "The Canons of Siddha Yoga: The Body of Scripture and the Form of the Guru." In *Meditation Revolution: A History and Theology of the Siddha Yoga Lineage,* by Douglas Renfrew Brooks, Swami Durgananda, Paul E. Muller-Ortega, William K. Mahoney, Constantina Rhodes Bailly, and S. P. Sabharathnam, 277–346. South Fallsburg, N.Y.: Agama Press, 1997.

———. "Encountering the Hindu 'Other': Tantrism and the Brahmans of South India." *Journal of the American Academy of Religion* 60, no. 3 (1992): 405–36.

———. *The Secret of the Three Cities: An Introduction to Hindu Śākta Tantrism.* Chicago: University of Chicago Press, 1990.

Brooks, Douglas Renfrew, Swami Durgananda, Paul E. Muller-Ortega, William K. Mahoney, Constantina Rhodes Bailly, and S. P. Sabharathnam. *Meditation Revolution: A History and Theology of the Siddha Yoga Lineage.* South Fallsburg, N.Y.: Agama Press, 1997.

Brown, C. Mackenzie. *The Devī Gītā: The Song of the Goddess: A Translation, Annotation, and Commentary.* Albany: State University of New York Press, 1998.

Bruce, George. *The Stranglers: The Cult of Thuggee and Its Overthrow in British India.* London: Longman, 1968.

Brunner, Hélène, Gerhard Oberhammer, and André Padoux. *Tāntrikābhidhānakośa: Dictionnaire des termes techniques de la littérature hindoue tantrique.* Wien: Verlag der österreichischen Akademie der Wissenschaften, 2000.

Bryson, Thomas. "The Hermeneutics of Religious Syncretism: Swami Vivekananda's Practical Vedānta." Ph.D. diss., Divinity School, University of Chicago, 1992.

Buck-Morss, Susan. "Benjamin's *Passagenwerk.*" *New German Critique* 29 (1983): 211–40.

———. *The Dialectics of Seeing: Walter Benjamin and the Arcades Project.* Cambridge, Mass.: MIT Press, 1989.

Burke, Marie L. *Swami Vivekananda in the West: New Discoveries.* 6 vols. Calcutta: Advaita Ashram, 1983–87.

Burnouf, Eugene. *Introduction à l'histoire du Bouddhisme Indien.* Paris: Maisonneuve, 1844.

Burton, Richard F., trans. *The Kama Sutra: The Classic Hindu Treatise on Love and Social Conduct.* New York: E. P. Dutton, 1963.

———, trans. *Vikram and the Vampire; or, Tales of Hindu Devilry.* 1870. Reprint, New York: Dover Publications, 1969.

Butterfield, Stephen T. *The Double Mirror: A Skeptical Journey into Tibetan Buddhism.* Berkeley, Calif.: North Atlantic Books, 1994.

Cakravarti, Adhir. "New Light on Śaiva Tāntrika Texts Known in Ancient Cambodia." *Journal of the Asiatic Society* 15, nos. 1–4 (1973): 1–10.

Caldwell, Sarah. "The Heart of the Secret: A Personal and Scholarly Encounter with Shakta Tantrism in Siddha Yoga." In *The Unknown, Remembered Gate: Religious Experience and Hermeneutical Reflection,* ed. Elliot R. Wolfson and Jeffrey J. Kripal. New York: Seven Bridges Press, forthcoming.

———. *Oh Terrifying Mother: Sexuality, Violence, and the Worship of the Goddess Kālī.* New York: Oxford University Press, 1999.

Campbell, Colin. *Narrative of the Indian Revolt, from Its Outbreak to the Capture of Lucknow.* London: G. Vickers, 1858.

Campbell, Joseph. *The Masks of God.* Vol. 2, *Oriental Mythology.* New York: Viking Press, 1962.

Campbell, June. *Traveller in Space: In Search of Female Identity in Tibetan Buddhism.* New York: George Braziller, 1996.

Carrette, Jeremy R. *Foucault and Religion: Spiritual Corporeality and Political Spirituality.* London: Routledge, 2000.

Carter, Lewis. *Charisma and Control in Rajneeshpuram: The Role of Shared Values in the Creation of a Community.* Cambridge: Cambridge University Press, 1990.

Case, Margaret H., ed. *Heinrich Zimmer: Coming into His Own.* Princeton, N.J.: Princeton University Press, 1994.

Cave, John David. *Mircea Eliade's Vision for a New Humanism.* New York: Oxford University Press, 1993.

Chakravarti, Chintaharan. *The Tantras: Studies on Their Religion and Literature.* Calcutta: Punthi Pustak, 1963.

Chakravarti, Kshitish Chandra. *Lectures on Hindu Religion, Philosophy, and Yoga.* Calcutta: U. C. Shome, 1893.

Chandrashekara, N. H. "Sri Gopinath Kaviraj Ji's Life Philosophy: Akhanda Mahayoga." In *Life and Philosophy of Gopinath Kaviraj,* pp. 14–20. Calcutta: University of Calcutta Press, 1981.

Chatterjee, Amal. *Representations of India, 1740–1840: The Creation of India in the Colonial Imagination.* New York: St. Martin's Press, 1998.

Chatterjee, Bankim Chandra. *The Abbey of Bliss* (Ānandamaṭh). Trans. Nares Chandra Sen-Gupta. Calcutta: Cherry Press, n.d.

———. *Ānandamaṭh.* Trans. Basanta Koomar Roy. New Delhi: Orient Paperbacks, 1992.

Chatterjee, Partha. *The Nation and Its Fragments: Colonial and Postcolonial Histories.* Princeton, N.J.: Princeton University Press, 1993.

———. *Nationalist Thought and the Colonial World: A Derivative Discourse?* Minneapolis: University of Minnesota Press, 1993.

Chattopadhyaya, Debiprasad. *Lokāyata: A Study in Ancient Indian Materialism.* New Delhi: People's Publishing House, 1959.

Chattopadhyaya, Rajagopal. *Swami Vivekananda in the West.* Houston: Rajagopal Chattopadhyaya, 1993.

Choudhuri, Haridas. *Sri Aurobindo and the Life Divine.* San Francisco: Cultural Integration Fellowship, 1973.

Choudhuri, Keshub. *The Mother and Passionate Politics.* Calcutta: Vidyodaya Library, 1979.

Chirol, Valentine. *Indian Unrest.* London: Macmillan, 1910.

Clymer, R. Swinburne. *The Rosicrucian Fraternity in America: Authentic and Spurious Organizations.* Quakertown, Pa.: Rosicrucian Foundation, n.d.

Coburn, Thomas. *Devī Mahātmya: The Crystallization of the Goddess Tradition.* New Delhi: Motilal Banarsidas, 1984.

Cohen, Chapman. *Religion and Sex: Studies in the Pathology of Religious Development.* London: Foulis, 1919.

Cohn, Bernard. *An Anthropologist among the Historians, and Other Essays.* Oxford: Oxford University Press, 1990.

———. "The Command of Language and the Language of Command." In *Subaltern Studies,* vol. 4, ed. Ranajit Guha, pp. 276–329. New Delhi: Oxford University Press, 1985.

Colebrooke, H. T. *Essays on Hindu Religion and Ancient Indian Literature.* 1837. Reprint, New Delhi: Cosmo Publications, 1977.

———. *Miscellaneous Essays.* London: W. H. Allen, 1837.

Coleman, Charles. *The Mythology of the Hindoos.* London: Parbury, Allen, 1832.

Collet, Sophia. *The Life and Letters of Rāmmohun Roy.* Calcutta: D. K. Biswas, 1962.

Collins, Lynn. "The Secret to Tantric Sex." *Cosmopolitan,* May 2000.

Comaroff, John, and Jean Comaroff, eds. *Modernity and Its Malcontents: Ritual and Power in Postcolonial Africa.* Chicago: University of Chicago Press, 1993.

Coward, Harold. *Jung and Eastern Thought.* Albany: State University of New York Press, 1985.

Cowell, E. B., and A. E. Gough, trans. *The Sarva-Darsana-Samgraha; or, Review of the Different Systems of Hindu Philosophy.* Varanasi: Chowkhamba Sanskrit Series Office, 1978.

Crowley, Aleister. *The Book of Lies, Which Is Also Falsely Called, Breaks.* London: Wieland, 1913.

———. *The Confessions of Aleister Crowley.* 1968. Reprint, New York: Hill and Wang, 1970.

———. "The Temple of Solomon the King." *Equinox* 1, no. 4 (1910): 43–118.

———. *The Vision and the Voice.* London: Simpkin, Marshall, Hamilton, Kent, 1911.

Dare, M. Paul. *Indian Underworld: A First-hand Account of Hindu Saints, Sorcerers, and Superstitions.* New York: E. P. Dutton, 1940.

Das, Sisir Kumar. *The Artist in Chains: The Life of Bankimchandra Chatterji.* New Delhi: New Statesman, 1984.

Dasgupta, B. N. *The Life and Times of Rajah Rammohun Roy.* New Delhi: Ambika, 1980.

Dasgupta, Shashibhushan. *An Introduction to Tantric Buddhism.* Calcutta: University of Calcutta Press, 1958.

———. *Obscure Religious Cults, as a Background to Bengali Literature.* Calcutta: Firma KLM, 1962.

Datta, Bhupendranath. *Swami Vivekananda: Patriot, Prophet.* Calcutta: Navabhārata Publishers, 1954.

Davidson, Ronald M. *Indian Esoteric Buddhism: A Social History of the Tantric Movement.* New York: Columbia University Press, 2002.

Davis, Erik. *Techgnosis: Myth, Magic, and Mysticism in the Age of Information.* New York: Harmony Books, 1998.

De, S. K. *Bengali Literature in the Nineteenth Century.* Calcutta: Firma KLM, 1962.

Demaitre, Edmond. *The Yogis of India.* London: Geoffrey Bless, 1937.

Derrett, J. Duncan M. *Essays in Classical and Modern Indian Law.* Leiden: E. J. Brill, 1977.

Deshpande, N. A., trans. *Padma Purāṇa.* New Delhi: Motilal Banarsidas, 1990.

Deveney, John Patrick. *Paschal Beverly Randolph: A Nineteenth Century American Spiritualist, Rosicrucian, and Sex Magician.* Albany: State University of New York Press, 1997.

Dimmitt, Cornelia, and J. A. B. van Buitenen. *Classical Hindu Mythology: A Reader in the Sanskrit Purāṇas.* Philadelphia: Temple University Press, 1978.

Dimock, Edward C. *The Place of the Hidden Moon: Erotic Mysticism in the Vaiṣṇava-Sahajīyā Cult of Bengal.* Chicago: University of Chicago Press, 1966.

Douglas, Nik. *Spiritual Sex: Secrets of Tantra from the Ice Age to the New Millennium.* New York: Pocket Books, 1997.

———. *Tantra Yoga.* New Delhi: Munshiram Manoharlal, 1971.

Drake, Richard. "Julius Evola and the Ideological Origins of the Radical Right in Contemporary Italy." In *Political Violence and Terror: Motifs and Motivations,* ed. Peter H. Merkl, pp. 61–89. Berkeley: University of California Press, 1986.

Dube, Saurabh. *Untouchable Pasts: Religion, Identity, and Power among a Central Indian Community, 1780–1950.* Albany: State University of New York Press, 1998.

Dubois, Abbé. *Hindu Manners, Customs, and Ceremonies.* Oxford: Clarendon Press, 1906.

Dubuisson, Daniel. *Mythologies du XXe siècle (Dumézil, Lévi-Strauss, Eliade).* Lille, Fr.: Presses Universitaires de Lille, 1993.

Dudley, Guilford, III. *Religion on Trial: Mircea Eliade and His Critics.* Philadelphia: Temple University Press, 1977.

Duff, Reverend Alexander. *A Description of the Durgā and Kālī Festival Celebrated in Calcutta at an Expense of Three Million Dollars.* Troy, N.Y.: C. Wright, 1846.

———. *India and Indian Missions, Including the Gigantic System of Hinduism, both in Theory and Practice.* 1839. Reprint, New Delhi: Swati, 1988.

Dutta, Krishna, and Andrew Robinson. *Rabindranath Tagore: The Myriad-Minded Man.* New York: St. Martin's Press, 1995.

Dyczkowski, Mark S. G. *The Canon of the Śaivāgamas and the Kubjikā Tantras of the Western Kaula Tradition.* Albany: State University of New York Press, 1988.

———. *The Doctrine of Vibration: An Analysis of the Doctrines and Practices of Kashmir Shaivism.* Albany: State University of New York Press, 1987.

Eagleton, Terry. "Awakening from Modernity." *Times Literary Supplement,* 20 February 1987, p. 194.

Eatwell, Roger. *Fascism: A History.* Harmondsworth, Eng.: Penguin Books, 1995.

Eliade, Mircea. *Autobiography.* Vol. 1, *Journey East, Journey West.* Chicago: University of Chicago Press, 1981.

———. *The Forbidden Forest* (Noaptea de sânziene). 1954. English ed., trans. Mac Linscott Ricketts and Mary Park Stevenson. South Bend, Ind.: University of Notre Dame Press, 1978.

———. *History of Religious Ideas.* Vol. 1, *From the Stone Age to the Eleusinian Mysteries.* Chicago: University of Chicago Press, 1976.

———. *Huliganii.* Bucharest: Edituria Nationala-Ciornei, 1935.

———. *Images and Symbols: Studies in Religious Symbolism.* New York: Sheed and Ward, 1969.

———. *Journal.* Vols. 3 and 4, 1970–78 and 1979–85. Chicago: University of Chicago Press, 1989.

———. *Myths, Dreams, and Mysteries: The Encounter between Contemporary Faiths and Archaic Realities.* London: Harvill Press, 1960.

———. *No Souvenirs.* New York: Harper and Row, 1977.

———. *Patterns in Comparative Religion.* London: Sheed and Ward, 1958.

———. *The Quest: History and Meaning in Religion.* Chicago: University of Chicago Press, 1969.

———. *Rites and Symbols of Initiation: The Mysteries of Birth and Rebirth.* New York: Harper and Row, 1958.

———. *The Sacred and the Profane: The Nature of Religion.* New York: Harcourt, Brace, 1959.

———. *Yoga: Immortality and Freedom.* Princeton, N.J.: Princeton University Press, 1971.

Ellwood, Robert S. *Religious and Spiritual Groups in Modern America.* Englewood, N.J.: Prentice-Hall, 1988.

Evola, Julius. "East and West: The Gordion Knot." Review of *Der gordische Knoten,* by Ernst Jünger. *East and West* 5 (1954–55): 94–98.

———. *The Metaphysics of Sex.* 1969. Reprint, New York: Inner Traditions, 1983.

———. *René Guénon: A Teacher for Modern Times.* Trans. Guido Stucco. Edmonds, Wash.: Holmes Publishing, 1994.

———. *Revolt against the Modern World.* Rochester, N.Y.: Inner Traditions, 1995.

———. "What Tantrism Means to Modern Western Civilization." *East and West* 1 (1950): 28–32.

———. *The Yoga of Power: Tantra, Shakti, and the Secret Way.* Trans. Guido Stucco. 1968. Reprint, Rochester, N.Y.: Inner Traditions, 1992.

Faddegon, Barend. "Brahmanisme en Hindoeisme." In *De Godsdiensten der Wereld,* vol. 1, ed. G. van der Leeuw, pp. 330–89. Amsterdam: H. Meulenhoff, 1940.

Farquhar, J. N. *Modern Religious Movements in India.* New York: Macmillan, 1915.

———. *An Outline of the Religious Literature of India.* Oxford: Oxford University Press, 1920.

Featherstone, Mike. "The Body in Consumer Culture." In *The Body: Social Process and Cultural Theory,* ed. Mike Featherstone, Mike Hepworth, and Bryan S. Turner, pp. 170–92. London: Sage Publications, 1991.

———. *Consumer Culture and Postmodernism.* London: Sage, 1991.
Ferraresi, Franco. "Julius Evola: Tradition, Reaction, and the Radical Right." *Archives européennes de sociologie* 28 (1987): 107–51.
Feuerstein, Georg. *Holy Madness: The Shock Tactics and Radical Teachings of Crazy-Wise Adepts, Holy Fools, and Rascal Gurus.* New York: Paragon House, 1990.
———. *Tantra: The Path of Ecstasy.* Boston: Shambhala Publications, 1998.
Fields, Rick. *How the Swans Came to the Lake: A Narrative History of Buddhism in America.* Boston: Shambhala Publications, 1986.
Figueira, Dorothy M. *The Exotic: A Decadent Quest.* Albany: State University of New York Press, 1994.
Finn, Louise M., trans. *The Kulacūḍāmaṇi Tantra and the Vāmakeśvara Tantra.* Wiesbaden, Ger.: Otto Harrassowitz, 1986.
Foucault, Michel. "Le chef mythique de la révolte de l'Iran." In *Dits et écrits, 1948–1988,* vol. 3, ed. Daniel Defert and François Ewald. Paris. Gallimard, 1994.
———. *Discipline and Punish: The Birth of the Prison.* Trans. Alan Sheridan. New York: Vintage Books, 1980.
———. *The Foucault Reader.* Ed. Paul Rabinow. New York: Pantheon Books, 1984.
———. *The History of Sexuality.* Vol. 1. Trans. Robert Hurley. New York: Vintage Books, 1978.
———. *The History of Sexuality.* Vol. 2, *The Use of Pleasure.* Trans. Robert Hurley. New York: Vintage Books, 1986.
———. *Power/Knowledge: Selected Interviews and Other Writings.* Ed. and trans. Colin Gordon. New York: Random House, 1977.
———. *Religion and Culture.* Ed. Jeremy R. Carrette. New York: Routledge, 1999.
Free John, Bubba (Adi Da, Da Love Ananda). *Garbage and the Goddess: The Last Miracles and Final Spiritual Instructions of Bubba Free John.* Lower Lake, Calif.: Dawn Horse Press, 1974.
———. *The Knee of Listening: The Early Life and Radical Spiritual Teachings of Bubba Free John.* Middletown, Calif.: Dawn Horse Press, 1978.
Freud, Sigmund. *The Standard Edition of the Complete Psychological Writings of Sigmund Freud.* Ed. James Strachey. 24 vols. London: Hogarth Press, 1953–74.
Frykenberg, R. E. "The Emergence of Modern 'Hinduism' as a Concept and an Institution: A Reappraisal with Special Reference to South India." In *Hinduism Reconsidered,* ed. Gunter D. Sontheimer and Hermann Kulke, pp. 29–50. New Delhi: Manohar, 1991.
Garrison, Omar. *Tantra: The Yoga of Sex.* New York: Julian Press, 1964.
Gellner, Ernest. *Nations and Nationalism.* Oxford: Basil Blackwell, 1983.
Ghose, Sri Aurobindo. "Bhavani Bharati, Mother of India." *Sri Aurobindo: Archives and Research* 9 (1985): 130–51.
———. "Bhawani Mandir." In *Bande Mataram: Early Political Writings.* Pondicherry: Sri Aurobindo Ashram Press, 1972.
———. *The Hour of God.* Pondicherry: Sri Aurobindo Ashram Press, 1973.
———. *The Mother.* Pondicherry: Sri Aurobindo Ashram Press, 1929.

———. *Sri Aurobindo on Himself and the Mother*. Pondicherry: Sri Aurobindo Asram Press, 1953.

———. *The Supramental Manifestation and Other Writings*. Pondicherry: Sri Aurobindo Ashram Press, 1972.

Ghose, I. C., ed. *The English Works of Rāja Rāmmohun Roy*. New Delhi: Cosmo Publications, 1982.

Ghose, J. C. *Bengali Literature*. New York: AMS Press, 1978.

Ghosh, Anjali. *Peaceful Transition to Power: A Study of Marxist Political Strategies in West Bengal, 1967–1777*. Calcutta: Firma KLM, 1981.

Ginsberg, Allen. *Indian Journals, March 1962–May 1963*. San Francisco: City Lights Books, 1970.

Girardot, Norman. *Imagination and Meaning: The Scholarly and Literary Worlds of Mircea Eliade*. New York: Seabury Press, 1982.

Gnoli, Raniero, trans. (from Sanskrit). *Luce delle sacre scritture (Tantrāloka) di Abhinavagupta*. Turin: Unione Tipografico-Editrice Torinese, 1972.

Godwin, Joscelyn. *The Theosophical Enlightenment*. Albany: State University of New York Press, 1994.

Godwin, Joscelyn, Christian Chanel, and John Patrick Deveney. *The Hermetic Brotherhood of Luxor: Initiatic and Historical Documents of an Order of Practical Occultism*. York Beach, Me.: Samuel Weiser, 1995.

Goodman, Eckert. "The Guru of Nyack: The True Story of Father India, the Omnipotent Oom." *Town and Country*, April 1941, pp. 50, 53, 92–93, 98–100.

Gordon, James *The Golden Guru: The Strange Journey of Bhagwan Shree Rajneesh*. New York: Viking Press, 1987.

Gordon, Leonard. *Bengal: The Nationalist Movement, 1876–1940*. New York: Columbia University Press, 1973.

Goudriaan, Teun, and Sanjukta Gupta. *Hindu Tantric and Śākta Literature*. Wiesbaden, Ger.: Otto Harrasowitz, 1981.

Grafstein, Laurence. "Messianic Capitalism." *The New Republic*, 20 February 1984, pp. 14–15.

Gross, Rita M. *Soaring and Settling: Buddhist Perspectives on Contemporary Social and Religious Issues*. New York: Continuum, 1998.

Grossinger, Richard. *Waiting for the Martian Express: Cosmic Visions, Earth Warriors, Luminous Dreams*. Berkeley, Calif.: North Atlantic Books, 1989.

Guenther, Herbert V. *The Life and Teaching of Nāropa*. New York: Oxford University Press, 1971.

———. *The Tantric View of Life*. Berkeley, Calif.: Shambhala Publications, 1972.

———. *Yuganaddha: The Tantric View of Life*. Varanasi: Chowkhamba Sanskrit Series Office, 1969.

Guha, Arun Chandra. *Aurobindo and Jugantar*. Calcutta: Sāhitya Saṃsad, 1978.

Guha, Ranajit. "On Some Aspects of the Historiography of Colonial India." In *Subaltern Studies*, vol. 1, *Writings on South Asian History and Society*, ed. Ranajit Guha, pp. 1–8. 1982. Reprint, New Delhi: Oxford University Press, 1994.

———. "The Prose of Counter-Insurgency." In *Subaltern Studies*, vol. 2, *Writings on South Asian History and Society*, ed. Ranajit Guha. New Delhi: Oxford University Press, 1983.

Gupta, Bhabani Sen. *Communism in Indian Politics.* New York: Columbia University Press, 1972.
Gupta, Sanjukta, trans. *Lakṣmī Tantra: A Pāñcarātra Text.* Leiden: E. J. Brill, 1972.
Gupta, Sanjukta, Teun Goudriaan, and Dirk Jan Hoens, *Hindu Tantrism.* Leiden: E. J. Brill, 1979.
Haberman, David. "On Trial: The Love of the Sixteen Thousand Gopīs." *History of Religions* 33, no. 1 (1993): 44–70.
Habermas, Jürgen. *Communication and the Evolution of Society.* Boston: Beacon Press, 1974.
Hacker, Paul. *Philology and Confrontation: Paul Hacker on Traditional and Modern Vedānta.* Ed. Wilhelm Halbfass. Albany: State University of New York Press, 1995.
Halbfass, Wilhelm. *India and Europe: An Essay in Understanding.* Albany: State University of New York Press, 1988.
Haldar, M. K. *Foundations of Nationalism in India: A Study of Bankimchandra Chatterjee.* New Delhi: Ajanta Publications, 1989.
Hanegraaff, Wouter J. *New Age Religion and Western Culture: Esotericism in the Mirror of Secular Thought.* Albany: State University of New York Press, 1998.
Hardiman, David. *The Coming of the Devi: Adivasi Assertion in Western India.* New Delhi: Oxford University Press, 1995.
Harris, Lis. "O Guru, Guru, Guru." *The New Yorker,* 14 November 1994, pp. 92–107.
Harvey, David. *The Condition of Postmodernity.* London: Blackwell Publishers, 1989.
Hayes, Glen A. "Vaiṣṇava Sahajiyā Traditions." In *Religions of India in Practice,* ed. Donald S. Lopez, Jr., 333–51. Princeton, N.J.: Princeton University Press, 1995.
Heehs, Peter. "Aurobindo Ghose and Revolutionary Terrorism." *South Asia* 15, no. 2 (1992): 47–69.
———. *The Bomb in Bengal: The Rise of Revolutionary Terrorism in India, 1900–1910.* New Delhi: Oxford University Press, 1993.
———. *Nationalism, Terrorism, Communalism: Essays in Modern Indian History.* New Delhi: Oxford University Press, 1998.
———. *Sri Aurobindo: A Brief Biography.* New Delhi: Oxford University Press, 1989.
Heelas, Paul. "Cults for Capitalism: Self Religions, Magic, and the Empowerment of Business." In *Religion and Power, Decline and Growth: Sociological Analyses of Religion in Britain, Poland, and the Americas,* ed. Peter Gee and John Fulton, pp. 25–50. Twickenham, Eng.: British Sociological Association, 1991.
———. *The New Age Movement: The Celebration of the Self and the Sacralization of Modernity.* Oxford: Basil Blackwell, 1996.
Heesterman, J. C. *The Broken World of Sacrifice: An Essay in Ancient Indian Ritual.* Chicago: University of Chicago Press, 1993.
Hegel, G. W. F. *Lectures on the Philosophy of Religion.* 1827. Reprint, ed.

O. Hodgson. Trans. R. F. Brown, P. C. Hodgson, and J. M. Stewart, with H. S. Harris. Berkeley: University of California Press, 1984.

Herbert, Thomas. *A Relation of Some Yeares Travaile.* London: R. Everingham, 1634.

Hitchcock, John T., and Rex L. Jones, eds. *Spirit Possession in the Nepal Himalayas.* Warminster, Eng.: Aris and Phillips, 1976.

Hockley, William Browne. *The English in India: A Novel.* London: H. S. King, 1828.

Hodgen, Margaret. *Early Anthropology in the Sixteenth and Seventeenth Centuries.* Philadelphia: University of Pennsylvania Press, 1964.

Hopkins, Edward Washburn. *The Religions of India.* Boston and London: Ginn, 1895.

Hopkins, Jeffrey. *Sex, Orgasm, and the Mind of Clear Light.* Berkeley, Calif.: North Atlantic Books, 1998.

Humes, Cynthia Ann. "Wrestling with Kālī: South Asian and British Constructions of the Dark Goddess." In *Encountering Kālī: In the Margins, at the Center, in the West,* ed. Jeffrey J. Kripal and Rachel Fell McDermott. Berkeley: University of California Press, 2003.

Hutchins, Francis. *The Illusion of Permanence.* Princeton, N.J.: Princeton University Press, 1967.

Hyatt, Christopher S. *Secrets of Western Tantra: The Sexuality of the Middle Path.* Tempe, Ariz.: New Falcon Publications, 1996.

Hyatt, Christopher S., and S. Jason Black. *Tantra without Tears.* Tempe, Ariz.: New Falcon Publications, 2000.

Hyatt, Christopher S., and Lon Milo Duquette. *Sex Magic, Tantra, and Tarot: The Way of the Secret Lover.* Tempe, Ariz.: New Falcon Publications, 1991.

Ierunca, Virgil. "The Literary Work of Mircea Eliade." In *Myths and Symbols: Studies in Honor of Mircea Eliade,* ed. Joseph M. Kitagawa and Charles H. Long, pp. 343–64. Chicago: University of Chicago Press, 1969.

Inden, Ronald. *Imagining India.* London: Blackwell Publishers, 1990.

Isherwood, Christopher. *Ramakrishna and His Disciples.* London: Methuen, 1965.

Iyengar, K. R. Srinivasa. *On the Mother: The Character of Her Manifestation and Ministry.* Pondicherry: Sri Aurobindo International Centre, 1994.

———. *Sri Aurobindo.* Calcutta: Arya Publishing House, 1950.

Iyer, Pico. *Video Night in Kathmandu, and Other Reports from the Not-So-Far East.* New York: Alfred A. Knopf, 1988.

Jacoby, Russel. "Marginal Returns: The Problem with Post-Colonial Theory." *Lingua Franca* (September–October 1995): 30–38.

James, E. O. *The Cult of the Mother Goddess.* New York: Praeger, 1959.

Jameson, Fredric. "Postmodernism and Consumer Society." In *The Anti-Aesthetic: Essays on Postmodern Culture,* ed. Hal Foster, pp. 111–25. New York: New Press, 1998.

———. "Postmodernism; or, The Cultural Logic of Late Capitalism." *New Left Review* 146 (1984): 53–93.

———. *Postmodernism; or, The Cultural Logic of Late Capitalism.* Durham, N.C.: Duke University Press, 1991.

Jansen, Sue Curry. *Censorship: The Knot That Binds Power and Knowledge.* New York: Oxford University Press, 1988.
Jantzen, Grace M. *Power, Gender, and Christian Mysticism.* Cambridge: Cambridge University Press, 1995.
Jayawardena, Kumari. *The White Woman's Other Burden: Western Women and South Asia during British Colonial Rule.* New York: Routledge, 1995.
Jina, Swami Anand. "The Work of Osho Rajneesh: A Thematic Overview." In *The Rajneesh Papers: Studies in a New Religious Movement,* ed. Susan J. Palmer and Arvind Sharma. New Delhi: Motilal Banarsidas, 1993.
Jones, William. *The Works of Sir William Jones.* 13 vols. 1799. Reprint, New Delhi: Agam Prakashan, 1976.
Joshi, Kireet. *Sri Aurobindo and the Mother.* New Delhi: Motilal Banarsidas, 1989.
Joshi, Vasant. *The Awakened One: The Life and Work of Bhagwan Shree Rajneesh.* San Francisco: Harper and Row, 1982.
"Jugantar." 1905. Bengali journal. Quoted in Keshub Choudhuri, *The Mother and Passionate Politics.* Calcutta: Vidyodaya Library, 1979.
Jung, C. G. *Mandala Symbolism.* Trans. R. F. C. Hull. Princeton, N.J.: Princeton University Press, 1972.
———. *The Psychology of Kundalini Yoga.* Ed. Sonu Shamdasani. Princeton, N.J.: Princeton University Press, 1996.
Kakati, Banikanta. *The Mother Goddess Kāmākhyā.* Guwahati: Publication Board, Assam, 1989.
Kane, P. V. *History of Dharmaśāstra.* Poona: Bhandarkar Oriental Research Institute, 1962.
Kaviraj, Gopinath. *Aspects of Indian Thought.* Burdwan: University of Burdwan Press, 1966.
———. *Selected Writings of M. M. Gopinath Kaviraj.* Varanasi: M. M. Gopinath Kaviraj Centenary Celebrations Committee, 1990.
Kaviraj, Sudipta. *The Unhappy Consciousness: Bankimchandra Chattopadhyay and the Formation of Nationalist Discourse in India.* New Delhi: Oxford University Press, 1995.
Kāvyatīrtha, Nārāyaṇ Rām Ācārya, ed. *The Manusmṛti; with the Commentary Manvarthamuktāvali of Kullūka.* Bombay: Nirnay Sagar Press, 1946.
Kelly, John D. *A Politics of Virtue: Hinduism, Sexuality, and Countercolonial Discourse in Fiji.* Chicago: University of Chicago Press, 1991.
Kern, Steven. *The Culture of Love: Victorians to Moderns.* Cambridge, Mass.: Harvard University Press 1992.
Khale, M. R., ed. *Bāṇa's Kādambarī (Pūrvabhāga Complete).* New Delhi: Motilal Banarsidas, 1956.
Killingley, Dermot. *Rāmmohun Roy in Hindu and Christian Tradition: The Teape Lectures 1990.* Newcastle upon Tyne, Eng.: Grevatt and Grevatt, 1993.
King, Francis. *The Magical World of Aleister Crowley.* New York: Coward, McCann, and Geoghegan, 1978.
———. *Tantra: The Way of Action.* Rochester, N.Y.: Destiny Books, 1990.
———. *Sexuality, Magic, and Perversion.* Secaucus, N.J.: Citadel, 1971.

———, ed. *The Secret Rituals of the O.T.O.* New York: Samuel Weiser, 1973.
King, Richard. *Orientalism and Religion: Postcolonial Theory, India, and the Mystic East.* London: Routledge, 1999.
Kinsley, David. *The Sword and the Flute: Kālī and Kṛṣṇa, Dark Visions of the Terrible and the Sublime in Hindu Mythology.* Berkeley: University of California Press, 1975.
Kitagawa, Joseph M., and Charles H. Long, eds. *Myths and Symbols: Studies in Honor of Mircea Eliade.* Chicago: University of Chicago Press, 1969.
Koenig, Peter-Robert. "Anal Intercourse and the O.T.O." In *Das OTO-Phaenomen: An Agony in 22 Fits.* Trans. online, www.home.sunrise.ch/~prkoenig/phenomen.htm.
———. *Der Grosse Theodor Reuss Reader.* Munich: Arbeitsgemeinschaft für Religions und Weltanschauungsfragen, 1997.
———. "The OTO Phenomenon." *Theosophical History* 4, no. 3 (1992): 92–98.
———. "Spermo Gnostics and the OTO." OTO Phenomenon web site, www.cyberlink.ch/~koenig/ spermo.htm.
Kopf, David. *The Brahmo Samaj and the Shaping of the Modern Indian Mind.* Princeton, N.J.: Princeton University Press, 1979.
———. *British Orientalism and the Bengal Renaissance: The Dynamics of Modernization, 1773–1835.* Berkeley: University of California Press, 1969.
———. "An Historiographical Essay on the Goddess Kālī." In *Shaping Bengali Worlds: Public and Private,* ed. Tony K. Stewart, pp. 112–27. East Lansing: Asian Studies Center, University of Michigan, 1975.
Kraig, Donald Michael, Linda Falorio, and Tara Nema. *Modern Sex Magick: Secrets of Erotic Spirituality.* St. Paul, Minn.: Llewellyn, 1998.
Kripal, Jeffrey J. "On the Fearful Art of Writing Left-Handed: Some Personal and Theoretical Reflections on Translating the *Kathāmṛta* into American English." In *In the Flesh: Eros, Secrecy, and Power in the Vernacular Tantric Traditions of India*, ed. Hugh B. Urban, Glen A. Hayes, and Paul Muller-Ortega. Albany: State University of New York Press, forthcoming.
———. "Inside-Out, Outside-In: Existential Place and Academic Practice in the Study of North American Guru Traditions." Review of *Meditation Revolution: A History and Theology of the Siddha Yoga Lineage,* by Douglas Renfrew Brooks, Swami Durgananda, Paul E. Muller-Ortega, William K. Mahoney, Constantina Rhodes Bailly, and S. P. Sabharathnam. *Religious Studies Review* 25, no. 3 (1999): 233–38.
———. *Kālī's Child: The Mystical and the Erotic in the Life and Teachings of Ramakrishna.* Chicago: University of Chicago Press, 1998.
———. "Mystical Homoeroticism, Reductionism, and the Reality of Censorship: A Response to Gerald James Larson." *Journal of the American Academy of Religion* 66, no. 3 (1998): 627–35.
———. *Roads of Excess, Palaces of Wisdom: Eroticism and Reflexivity in the Study of Mysticism.* Chicago: University of Chicago Press, 2001.
Kripal, Jeffrey J., and Rachel Fell McDermott, eds. *Encountering Kālī: In the Margins, at the Center, in the West.* Berkeley: University of California Press, 2003.

Kroker, Arthur, and Marilouise Kroker. *Hacking the Future: Stories for the Flesh-eating 90s.* New York: St. Martin's Press, 1996.
Kvaerne, Peter. "On the Concept of Sahaja in Indian Buddhist Tantric Literature." *Temenos* 11 (1975): 88–135.
Lago, Mary. *Rabindranath Tagore.* Boston: Twayne Publishers, 1976.
Lane, Gwendolyn, trans. *Kādambarī: A Classical Sanskrit Story of Magical Transformations.* New York: Garland Publishing, 1991.
Larson, Gerald. "Polymorphic Sexuality, Homoeroticism, and the Study of Religion." *Journal of the American Academy of Religion* 65, no. 3 (1997): 655–65.
Lata, Prem. *Swami Dayānanda Sarasvatī.* New Delhi: Sumit Publications, 1990.
Laushey, David. *Bengal Terrorism and the Marxist Left: Aspects of Regional Nationalism in India, 1905–1942.* Calcutta: Firma KLM, 1975.
Lavine, Amy. "Tibetan Buddhism in America: The Development of American Vajrayāna." In *The Faces of Buddhism in America,* ed. Charles S. Prebish and Kenneth K. Tanaka, pp. 99–116. Berkeley: University of California Press, 1998.
Levy, Robert I. *Mesocosm: Hinduism and the Organization of a Traditional Newar City in Nepal.* Berkeley: University of California Press, 1990.
Lewis, James, and J. Gordon Melton, eds. *Perspectives on the New Age.* Albany: State University of New York Press, 1992.
Lewy, Guenter. *Religion and Revolution.* New York: Oxford University Press, 1974.
Lincoln, Bruce. *Death, War, and Sacrifice: Studies in Ideology and Practice.* Chicago: University of Chicago Press, 1991.
———. "Theses on Method." *Method and Theory in the Study of Religion* 8, no. 3 (1996): 225–28.
Lopez, Donald S., Jr. *Elaborations on Emptiness: Uses of the Heart Sūtra.* Princeton, N.J.: Princeton University Press, 1996.
———. *Prisoners of Shangri La: Tibetan Buddhism and the West.* Chicago: University of Chicago Press, 1998.
Lorenzen, David N. *The Kāpālikas and Kālāmukhas: Two Lost Śaivite Sects.* Berkeley: University of California Press, 1972.
———. "A Parody of the Kāpālikas in the *Mattavilāsa.*" In *Tantra in Practice,* ed. David Gordon White, pp. 81–96. Princeton, N.J.: Princeton University Press, 2000.
Loy, David. "The Religion of the Market." *Journal of the American Academy of Religion* 65, no. 2 (1997): 275–90.
Lyotard, Jean-François. *The Postmodern Condition: A Report on Knowledge.* Minneapolis: University of Minnesota Press, 1984.
MacCalman, Kenneth R. "Impressions of Dr. Bernard and the C.C.C. as Viewed by a Nyack On Looker." *South of the Mountains* 14, no. 4 (1970): 2–8.
Macdonell, Arthur A., and Arthur Barriedale Keith. *Vedic Index of Names and Subjects.* London: John Murray, 1912.
MacMunn, George. *The Religions and Hidden Cults of India.* New York: Macmillan, 1932.
———. *The Underworld of India.* London: Jarrolds Publishers, 1933.
MacNicol, Nicol. *Indian Theism, from the Vedic to the Mohammedan Period.* New Delhi: Munshiram Manoharlal, 1914.

Mahony, William K. *The Artful Universe: An Introduction to the Vedic Religious Imagination.* Albany: State University of New York Press, 1998.

Majeed, Javed. "Meadows Taylor's *Confessions of a Thug:* The Anglo-Indian Novel as Genre in the Making." In *Writing India, 1757–1990: The Literature of British India,* ed. Bart Moore-Gilbert. Manchester: Manchester University Press, 1996.

Majumdar, R. C. *History of the Freedom Movement in India.* Calcutta: Firma KLM, 1962.

Mandel, Ernest. *Late Capitalism.* London: New Left Books, 1970.

Marglin, Frédérique Apffel. *Wives of the God-King: The Devadāsīs of Puri.* New York: Oxford University Press, 1985.

Marshall, Peter. *The British Discovery of Hinduism in the Eighteenth Century.* Cambridge: Cambridge University Press, 1970.

Martin, Reverend E. Osborn. *The Gods of India: A Brief Description of Their History, Character and Worship.* London: E. M. Dent, 1913.

Marx, Karl, and Friedrich Engels. *Werke.* Berlin: Dietz Verlag, 1960.

Masters, John. *The Deceivers.* London: Penguin, 1955.

Mathur, Anurag. *The Inscrutable Americans.* New Delhi: Rupa, 1999.

Matsunaga, Yukei. *The Guhyasamāja Tantra: A New Critical Edition.* Osaka: Toso Shuppan, 1978.

Mayer, Arno. *The Persistence of the Old Regime: Europe to the Great War.* New York: Pantheon Books, 1981.

Maynard, John. "Victorian Discourses on Sexuality and Religion." *University of Hartford Studies in Literature* 19 (1987).

Mayo, Katherine. *Mother India.* New York: Harcourt, Brace, 1928.

Mazak, Arlene. "Gopinath Kaviraj's Synthetic Understanding of Kuṇḍalinī Yoga in Relation to the Nondualistic Hindu Tantric Traditions." Ph.D. diss., Department of South Asian Languages and Civilizations, University of Chicago, 1994.

McClintock, Anne. *Imperial Leather: Race, Gender, and Sexuality in the Colonial Context.* New York: Routledge, 1995.

McCutcheon, Russell T. *Manufacturing Religion: The Discourse on Sui Generis Religion and the Politics of Nostalgia.* New York: Oxford University Press, 1997.

McDaniel, June. *The Madness of the Saints: Ecstatic Religion in Bengal.* Chicago: University of Chicago Press, 1989.

McDermott, Rachel Fell. "Kālī's New Frontiers: A Hindu Goddess on the Internet." In *Encountering Kālī: In the Margins, at the Center, in the West,* ed. Jeffrey J. Kripal and Rachel Fell McDermott. Berkeley: University of California Press, 2003.

———. *Mother of My Heart, Daughter of My Dreams: Transformations of Kālī and Umā in the Devotional Poetry of Bengal.* New York: Oxford University Press, 2001.

———. "The Western Kālī." In *Devī: Goddesses of India,* ed. J. S. Hawley and D. M. Wulff. Berkeley: University of California Press, 1996.

McKean, Lise. *Divine Enterprise: Gurus and the Hindu Nationalist Movement.* Chicago: University of Chicago Press, 1996.

McLaren, Angus. *Twentieth-Century Sexuality: A History.* Oxford: Basil Blackwell, 1999.
McLean, Malcolm. "Eating Corpses and Raising the Dead: The Tantric Madness of Bāmākṣepa." In *In the Flesh: Eros, Secrecy, and Power in the Vernacular Tantric Traditions of India,* ed. Hugh B. Urban, Glen A. Hayes, and Paul Muller-Ortega. Albany: State University of New York Press, in progress.
Mehta, Gita. *Karma Cola: Marketing the Mystic East.* New York: Simon and Schuster, 1979.
Melton, J. Gordon. *Biographical Dictionary of American Cult and Sect Leaders.* New York: Garland Publishing, 1986.
———, ed. *New Age Encyclopedia.* Detroit: Gale Research, 1990.
Metcalf, Thomas. *The Aftermath of Revolt: India, 1857–1870.* Princeton, N.J.: Princeton University Press, 1964.
Miles, Barry. *Ginsberg: A Biography.* New York: Simon and Schuster, 1989.
Mill, James. *The History of British India.* 9 vols. London: J. Madden, 1858.
Milne, Hugh. *Bhagwan: The God That Failed.* New York: St. Martin's Press, 1986.
Minor, Robert N. *The Religious, the Spiritual, and the Secular: Auroville and Secular India.* Albany: State University of New York Press, 1999.
Mitchell, J. Murray, and William Muir. *Two Old Faiths: Essays on the Religion of the Hindus and the Mohammedans.* New York: Chautauqua Press, 1891.
Mitra, Rajendralala. *The Sanskrit Buddhist Literature of Nepal.* 1882. Reprint, New Delhi: Cosmo Publications, 1981.
Mitter, Partha. *Art and Nationalism in Colonial India, 1850–1922.* Cambridge: Cambridge University Press, 1994.
Monier-Williams, Monier. *Brahmanism and Hinduism.* New York: Macmillan, 1891.
———. *Hinduism.* London: Society for Promoting Christian Knowledge, 1894.
———. *A Sanskrit-English Dictionary.* Oxford: Oxford University Press, 1899.
Mookerjee, Ajit. *Tantra Asana: A Way to Self-Realization.* New York: George Wittenborn, 1971.
———. *The Tantric Way: Art, Science, Ritual.* Boston: New York Graphics Society, 1977.
Moore-Gilbert, Bart, ed. *Postcolonial Criticism.* New York: Longman, 1997.
———, ed. *Postcolonial Theory: Contexts, Practices, Politics.* London: Verso, 1997.
———, ed. *Writing India, 1757–1990: The Literature of British India.* Manchester: Manchester University Press, 1996.
Moreland, W. H. *A Short History of India.* New York: MacKay, 1936.
Muktananda, Swami. *From the Finite to the Infinite.* South Fallsburg, N.Y.: SYDA Foundation, 1994.
———. *The Perfect Relationship: The Guru and the Disciple.* South Fallsburg, N.Y.: SYDA Foundation, 1985.
———. *The Play of Consciousness (Chitshakti Vilas).* New York: Harper and Row, 1978.
———. *Secret of the Siddhas.* South Fallsburg, N.Y.: SYDA Foundation, 1994.
Mullan, Bob. *Life as Laughter: Following Bhagwan Shree Rajneesh.* Boston: Routledge, 1983.

Müller, Friedrich Max. *Lectures on the Science of Language.* New York: Charles Scribner's Sons, 1864.

———. *Biographical Essays.* New York: Charles Scribner's Sons, 1884.

Muller-Ortega, Paul Eduardo. *The Triadic Heart of Śiva: Kaula Tantricism of Abhinavagupta in the Non-Dual Shaivism of Kashmir.* Albany: State University of New York Press, 1989.

Mumford, John. *Ecstasy through Tantra.* St. Paul, Minn.: Llewellyn, 1988.

Nagy-Talavera, Nicholas M. *The Green Shirts and the Others: A History of Fascism in Hungary and Romania.* Stanford, Calif.: Hoover Institution, 1970.

Nambiar, Sita Krishna, trans. *Prabodhacandrodaya of Kṛṣṇa Miśra.* New Delhi: Motilal Banarsidas, 1971.

Nandy, Ashis. *At the Edge of Psychology: Essays in Politics and Culture.* New Delhi: Oxford University Press, 1980.

———. *The Intimate Enemy: Loss and Recovery of Self under Colonialism.* New Delhi: Oxford University Press, 1983.

Naylor, A. R., ed. *Theodor Reuss and Aleister Crowley, O.T.O. Rituals and Sexmagick.* Thames, Eng.: Essex House, 1999.

Needleman, Jacob. *The New Religions.* New York: Crossroad, 1970.

Neeval, Walter G. "Sri Ramakrishna: At Play in His Mother's Mansion." In *Hindu Spirituality: Postcolonial and Modern,* ed. K. R. Sundararajan and Bithaka Mukerji, pp. 283–98. New York: Crossroad, 1997.

Nette, Herbert. "An Epitaph for Heinrich Zimmer." In *Heinrich Zimmer: Coming into His Own,* ed. Margaret H. Case, pp. 21–30. Princeton, N.J.: Princeton University Press, 1994.

Neumann, Erich. *The Great Mother: An Analysis of an Archetype.* Princeton, N.J.: Princeton University Press, 1955.

Nikhilananda, Swami, trans. *The Gospel of Sri Ramakrishna.* New York: Ramakrishna-Vivekananda Center, 1942.

Nivedita, Sister. *The Master as I Saw Him.* Calcutta: Udbodhan Office, 1948.

Noble, Vicki. *Shakti Woman: Feeling Our Fire, Healing Our World: The New Female Shamanism.* San Francisco: HarperSanFrancisco, 1991.

Nossiter, T. J. *Marxist State Governments in India: Politics, Economics, and Society.* London: F. Pinter, 1988.

O'Connor, June. *The Quest for Political and Spiritual Liberation: A Study in the Thought of Sri Aurobindo Ghose.* Rutherford, N.J.: Dickinson University Press, 1977.

Odier, Daniel. *Tantric Quest: An Encounter with Absolute Love.* Rochester, N.Y.: Inner Traditions, 1997.

Offe, Claus. *Disorganized Capitalism.* Oxford: Oxford University Press, 1985.

O'Flaherty, Wendy Doniger. *The Origins of Evil in Hindu Mythology.* Berkeley: University of California Press, 1976.

———, ed. *Textual Sources for the Study of Hinduism.* Chicago: University of Chicago Press, 1989.

———, trans. *The Rig Veda.* New York: Penguin Books, 1981.

O'Hanlon, Rosalind. "Recovering the Subject: Subaltern Studies and Histories of Resistance in Colonial South Asia." *Modern Asian Studies* 22, no. 1 (1988): 189–224.

Oman, John Campbell. *The Brahmans, Theists, and Mystics of India.* Philadelphia: George W. Jacob, 1903.
———. *The Mystics, Ascetics, and Saints of India.* London: T. F. Urwin, 1903.
Ong, Aiwa. *Spirits of Resistance and Capitalist Discipline: Factory Women in Malaysia.* Albany: State University of New York Press, 1987.
Oppert, Gustav. *On the Original Inhabitants of Bharatavarsa.* London: A. Constable, 1893.
Orme, Robert. *Historical Fragments of the Moghul Empire.* 1782. Reprint, New Delhi: Associated Publishing House, 1982.
Orzech, Charles D. *Politics and Transcendent Wisdom: The Scripture for Humane Kings in the Creation of Chinese Buddhism.* University Park: Pennsylvania State University Press, 1998.
Osho. *Autobiography of a Spiritually Incorrect Mystic.* New York: St. Martin's Press, 2000.
———. *The Tantric Transformation.* Shaftesbury, Eng.: Element Books, 1978.
Padoux, André. "A Survey of Tantrism for the Historian of Religions." Review of *Hindu Tantrism,* by Sanjukta Gupta, Teun Goudriaan, and Dirk Jan Hoens. *History of Religions* 20, no. 4 (1981): 345–60.
———. "Tantrism: An Overview." In *Encyclopedia of Religion,* vol. 14, ed. Mircea Eliade, pp. 272–74. New York: Macmillan, 1986.
———. *Vāc: The Concept of the Word in Selected Hindu Tantras.* Albany: State University of New York Press, 1990.
Pal, Pratapaditya. *Hindu Religion and Iconology According to the Tantrasāra.* Los Angeles: Vichitra Press, 1981.
Palmer, Susan J. "Lovers and Leaders in a Utopian Commune." In *The Rajneesh Papers: Studies in a New Religious Movement,* ed. Susan J. Palmer and Arvind Sharma, pp. 103–36. New Delhi: Motilal Banarsidas, 1993.
Palmer, Susan J., and Arvind Sharma, eds. *The Rajneesh Papers: Studies in a New Religious Movement.* New Delhi: Motilal Banarsidas, 1993.
Pande, G. C. *Mahamahopadhyaya Gopinath Kaviraj.* New Delhi: Sahitya Akademi, 1989.
Pandey, K. C. *Abhinavagupta: An Historical and Philosophical Study.* Varanasi: Chowkhamba Sanskrit Series Office, 1963.
Parfrey, Adam, ed. *Apocalypse Culture.* Los Angeles: Feral House, 1990.
Parry, Benita. *Delusions and Discoveries: Studies on India in the British Imagination, 1880–1930.* London: Allen Lane, 1972.
Parry, Jonathan. "Sacrificial Death and the Necrophagous Ascetic." In *Death and the Regeneration of Life,* ed. Maurice Bloch and Jonathan Parry, pp. 74–110. New York: Cambridge University Press, 1982.
Paxton, Nancy L. "Disembodied Subjects: English Women's Autobiography under the Raj." In *De/Colonizing the Subject: The Politics of Gender in Women's Autobiography,* ed. Sidonie Smith and Julia Watson, pp. 387–409. Minneapolis: University of Minnesota Press, 1992.
———. "Feminism under the Raj: Complicity and Resistance in the Writings of Flora Annie Steel and Annie Besant." *Women's Studies International Forum* 13 (Spring 1990): 333–46.
———. *Writing under the Raj: Gender, Race, and Rape in the British Colonial*

Imagination, 1830–1947. New Brunswick, N.J.: Rutgers University Press, 1999.
Payne, Ernest. *The Śāktas: An Introductory and Comparative Study.* New York: Garland Publishing, 1979.
Payne, Stanley. *A History of Fascism, 1914–1945.* Madison: University of Wisconsin Press, 1995.
Penny, F. E. F. *The Swami's Curse.* London: Heinemann, 1929.
Poussin, Louis de la Vallé. "Tantrism [Buddhist]." In *Encyclopedia of Religion and Ethics,* vol. 12, ed. James Hastings, pp. 193–97. New York: Charles Scribner's Sons, 1922.
Powell, Violet. *Flora Annie Steel: Novelist of India.* London: Heinemann, 1981.
Pratt, James Bissett. *India and Its Faiths: A Traveler's Record.* Boston: Houghton Mifflin, 1915.
Pratt, Marie Louise. *Imperial Eyes: Travel Writing and Transculturation.* New York: Routledge, 1992.
Preston, James. *The Cult of the Goddess: Social and Religious Change in a Hindu Temple.* New Delhi: Vikas, 1980.
Purani, A. B. *The Life of Sri Aurobindo.* Pondicherry: Sri Aurobindo Ashram Press, 1978.
Radice, William, ed. *Swami Vivekananda and the Modernization of Hinduism.* New Delhi: Oxford University Press, 1998.
Rajneesh, Bhagwan Shree. *Beware of Socialism!* Rajneeshpuram, Oreg.: Rajneesh Foundation International, 1984.
———. *From Sex to Superconsciousness.* Bombay: Jeevan Jagruti Kendra, 1971.
———. *The Goose Is Out.* Poona: Rajneesh Foundation International, 1982.
———. *Tantra: The Supreme Understanding.* Poona: Rajneesh Foundation, 1975.
———. *Tantra Spirituality and Sex.* Rajneeshpuram, Oreg.: Rajneesh Foundation International, 1983.
———. *Yoga: The Alpha and the Omega.* Poona: Rajneesh Foundation, 1981.
Ramakrishna, Sri. *Sayings of Sri Ramakrishna.* Mylapore: Sri Ramakrishna Math, 1949.
Ramanujan, A. K. *Hymns for the Drowning: Poems for Viṣṇu by Nammālvār.* Princeton, N.J.: Princeton University Press, 1981.
Ramsdale, David, and Ellen Ramsdale. *Energy Ecstasy: A Practical Guide to Lovemaking Secrets of the East and West.* New York: Bantam Books, 1993.
Randall, Monica. *Phantoms of the Hudson Valley: The Glorious Estates of a Lost Era.* Woodstock, N.Y.: Overlook Press, 1995.
Randolph, Paschal Beverly. *The Ansairetic Mystery: A New Revelation Concerning Sex!* Toledo, Ohio: Toledo Sun, Liberal Printing House, n.d. (ca. 1873).
———. *Eulis! The History of Love: Its Wondrous Magic, Chemistry, Rules, Laws, Modes, and Rationale; Being the Third Revelation of Soul and Sex.* Toledo, Ohio: Randolph Publishing, 1974.
———. *Magia Sexualis.* Paris: Robert Telin, 1931.
Rangarajan, V. *Vande Mataram.* Madras: Sister Nivedita Academy, 1977.
Rastogi, Navjivan. *Introduction to the Tantrāloka.* New Delhi: Motilal Banarsidas, 1987.

———. *The Krama Tantricism of Kashmir: Historical and General Sources.* New Delhi: Motilal Banarsidas, 1979.
Rauch, Maya. "Heinrich Zimmer from a Daughter's Perspective." In *Heinrich Zimmer: Coming into His Own,* ed. Margaret H. Case, pp. 15–20. Princeton, N.J.: Princeton University Press, 1994.
Rawson, Philip, *The Art of Tantra.* Greenwich, Conn.: New York Graphics Society, 1973.
Ray, Sondra. *How to Be Chic, Fabulous, and Live Forever.* Berkeley, Calif.: Celestial Arts, 1986.
Raychaudhuri, Tapan. *Europe Reconsidered: Perceptions of the West in Nineteenth Century Bengal.* New Delhi: Oxford University Press, 1988.
———. "Swami Vivekananda's Construction of Hinduism." In *Swami Vivekananda and the Modernization of Hinduism,* ed. William Radice, pp. 1–16. New Delhi: Oxford University Press, 1998.
Rennie, Bryan S. *Reconstructing Eliade: Making Sense of Religion.* Albany: State University of New York Press, 1996.
Rhinehart, Robin, and Tony K. Stewart. "The Anonymous *Āgama Prakāśa:* Preface to a Nineteenth Century Gujarati Polemic." In *Tantra in Practice,* ed. David Gordon White, pp. 266–84. Princeton, N.J.: Princeton: University Press, 2000.
Rice, Edward. *Captain Sir Richard Francis Burton: The Secret Agent Who Made the Pilgrimage to Mecca, Discovered the Kāma Sūtra, and Brought the Arabian Nights to the West.* New York: Charles Scribner's Sons, 1990.
Ricketts, Mac Linscott. *Mircea Eliade: The Romanian Roots.* 2 vols. New York: Columbia University Press, 1988.
Risley, Herbert. *The People of India.* Calcutta: Thacker, Spink, 1908.
Robbins, Trina. *Eternally Bad: Goddesses with Attitude.* Berkeley, Calif.: Conari Press, 2001.
Roman, Sanaya, and Duane Packer. *Creating Money.* New York: H. J. Kramer, 1988.
Ronaldshay, Earl of. *The Heart of Aryavarta: A Study of the Psychology of Indian Unrest.* London: A. Constable, 1925.
Rosselli, John. "Sri Ramakrishna and the Educated Elite of Late Nineteenth Century Bengal." *Contributions to Indian Sociology* 12, no. 2 (1978): 195–212.
Rowlatt, Justice S. A. T., et al. *Report of Committee Appointed to Investigate Revolutionary Conspiracies in India.* London: His Majesty's Stationary Office, 1918.
Roy, M. N. *Reason, Romanticism, and Revolution.* Calcutta: Renaissance Publications, 1955.
Roy, Rāmmohun. "An Abridgment of the Vedānta." In *Sources of Indian Tradition,* ed. T. de Bary, pp. 573–75. New York: Columbia University Press, 1958.
———. *Brief Remarks Regarding Modern Encroachment on the Ancient Rights of Females.* Calcutta: Sadharan Brahmo Samaj, 1922.
———. *The English Works of Raja Rammohun Roy.* Ed. J. C. Ghose. New Delhi: Cosmo Publications, 1982.
———. *The Precepts of Jesus, the Guide to Peace and Happiness.* Calcutta: Baptist Mission Press, 1820.

Sachau, Edward, ed. *Alberuni's India*. London: Kegan Paul, Trench, and Trübner, 1910.

Sahlins, Marshall. "Cosmologies of Capitalism: The Trans-Pacific Sector of the World System." *Proceedings of the British Academy* 74 (1988): 1–51.

Said, Edward. *Orientalism*. New York: Alfred A. Knopf, 1979.

"The Śāktas: Their Characteristic and Practical Influence in Society." *Calcutta Review* 24, no. 47 (1855): 66–67.

Salomon, Carol. "Bāul Songs." In *Religions of India in Practice,* ed. Donald S. Lopez, Jr., pp. 187–208. Princeton, N.J.: Princeton University Press, 1995.

Samuel, Geoffrey. *Civilized Shamans: Buddhism in Tibetan Societies*. Washington, D.C.: Smithsonian Institution, 1993.

Sanderson, Alexis. "Maṇḍala and Āgamic Identity in the Trika of Kashmir." In *Mantras et diagrammes rituels dans l'hindouisme,* pp. 169–207. Paris: Editions du CNRS, 1986.

———. "Purity and Power among the Brahmans of Kashmir." In *The Category of the Person: Anthropology, Philosophy, History,* ed. Michael Carrithers, Steven Collins, and Steven Lukes, pp. 190–216. Cambridge: Cambridge University Press, 1985.

———. "Śaivism and the Tantric Traditions." In *The World's Religions,* ed. Stewart Sutherland et al., pp. 660–704. London: Routledge, 1988.

Sann, Paul. *Fads, Follies, and Delusions of the American People*. New York: Bonanza Books, 1967.

Saradananda, Swami. *Sri Ramakrishna the Great Master.* Mylapore: Sri Ramakrishna Math, 1952.

Saraswatī, Swāmī Dayānanda. *The Autobiography of Swāmī Dayānand Saraswatī.* Ed. K. C. Yadav. New Delhi: Manohar, 1976.

———. *The Light of Truth; or, An English Translation of the "Satyartha Prakasha."* Trans. Chiranjivan Bharadwaja. 1927. Reprint, Madras: Arya Samaj, 1932.

Sarkar, Sumit. *An Exploration of the Ramakrishna-Vivekananda Tradition.* Simla: Indian Institute of Advanced Study, 1993.

———. *The Swadeshi Movement in Bengal, 1903–1908.* New Delhi: People's Publishing House, 1973.

Satprem. *The Mother; or, The Divine Manifestation.* Madras: Macmillan India, 1977.

Schrader, F. Otto. *Introduction to the "Pāñcarātra" and the "Ahirbudhnya Saṃhitā."* Madras: Adyar Library Series, 1916.

Seabrook, William. *Witchcraft: Its Power in the World Today*. New York: Harcourt, Brace, 1940.

Selected Records Collected from the Central Provinces and Berar Secretariat Relating to the Suppression of Thuggee. Nagpur: Government Printing, 1939.

Sharpe, Elizabeth. *Secrets of the Kaula Circle: A Tale of Fictitious People. . . .* London: Luzac, 1936.

Sharpe, Jenny. *Allegories of Empire: The Figure of Women in the Colonial Text.* Minneapolis: University of Minnesota Press, 1993.

Shastri, H. P. *A Catalogue of Palm-Leaf and Selected Paper Manuscript belonging to the Durbar Library, Nepal.* Calcutta, Baptist Mission Press, 1905–15.

Shaw, Miranda. *Passionate Enlightenment: Women in Tantric Buddhism.* Princeton, N.J.: Princeton University Press, 1994.
Sheehan, Thomas. "*Diventare Dio:* Julius Evola and the Metaphysics of Fascism." *Stanford Italian Review* 6 (1986): 279–92.
———. "Myth and Violence: The Fascism of Julius Evola and Alain de Benoist." *Social Research* 48 (1981): 45–73.
Shepherd, Leslie, ed. *The Encyclopedia of Occultism and Parapsychology.* 2 vols. Detroit: Gale Research, 1961.
Sil, Narasimha. "The Question of Ramakrishna's Homosexuality." *The Statesman,* 31 January 1997, pp. 10–13.
———. *Rāmakṛṣṇa Paramahaṃsa: A Psychological Profile.* Leiden: E. J. Brill, 1991.
———. *Swami Vivekananda: A Reassessment.* Selinsgrove, Pa.: Susquehanna University Press, 1997.
———. "Swami Vivekananda in the West: The Legend Reinterpreted." *South Asia* 18, no. 1 (1995): 1–53.
———. "Vivekānanda's Rāmakṛṣṇa: An Untold Story of Mythmaking and Propaganda." *Numen* 40 (1993): 38–62.
Silburn, Lilian. *Kuṇḍalinī: The Energy of the Depths.* Albany: State University of New York Press, 1988.
Silburn, Lilian, and André Padoux, trans. *Abhinavagupta: La Lumière sur les tantras, chapitres 1 à 5 du "Tantrāloka."* Paris: Collège de France, 1998.
Singh, Jaideva. *The Doctrine of Recognition: A Translation of Pratyabhijñāhṛdayam.* Albany: State University of New York Press, 1990.
Singha, Radhika. "'Providential' Circumstances: The Thuggee Campaign of the 1830s and Legal Innovation." *Modern Asian Studies* 27, no. 1 (1993): 83–146.
Sinha, Indra. *The Great Book of Tantra: Translations and Images from Classic Indian Texts with Commentary.* Rochester, Vt.: Destiny Books, 1993.
Sinnett, A. P. *Esoteric Buddhism.* London: Trübner, 1884.
Sleeman, James. *Thug; or, A Million Murders.* London: Sampson, Low, Marston, 1926.
Sleeman, W. H. *Ramaseeana; or, A Vocabulary of the Peculiar Language Used by the Thugs, with an Introduction and Appendix, Descriptive of the System Pursued by That Fraternity and of the Measures Which Have Been Adopted by the Supreme Government of India for Its Suppression.* Calcutta: Military Orphan Press, 1836. Reprinted in *The Thugs or Phansigars of India,* compiled from the documents published by Captain W. H. Sleeman. Philadelphia: Carey and Hart, 1839.
———. *Rambles and Reflections of an Indian Official.* 1844. Reprint, Oxford: Oxford University Press, 1915.
———. *The Thugs or Phansigars of India: Comprising a History of the Rise and Progress of That Extraordinary Fraternity of Assassins.* Philadelphia: Carey and Hart, 1839.
Smith, Jonathan Z. *Imagining Religion: From Babylon to Jonestown.* Chicago: University of Chicago Press, 1982.
Snellgrove, David. *Indo-Tibetan Buddhism: Indian Buddhists and Their Tibetan Successors.* London: Sirindia, 1987.

———. "The Notion of Divine Kingship in Tantric Buddhism." In *The Sacral Kingship: Contributions to the Central Theme of the Eighth International Congress for the History of Religions,* pp. 204–18. Leiden: E. J. Brill, 1959.

Somerville, Augustus. *Crime and Religious Beliefs in India.* Calcutta: Thacker, Spink, 1931.

Sprinkle, Annie. *Post-Porn Modernist.* San Francisco: Cleis Press, 1998.

Steel, Flora Annie. *On the Face of the Waters.* 1896. Reprint, London: Heinemann, 1985.

———. *The Garden of Fidelity: Being the Autobiography of Flora Annie Steel, 1847–1929.* London: Macmillan, 1930.

———. *The Law of the Threshold.* New York: Macmillan, 1924.

———. "A Maiden's Prayer." In *The Indian Scene,* by Flora Annie Steel. London: E. Arnold, 1933.

———. *In the Permanent Way.* London: Heinemann, 1898.

Strelley, Kate. *The Ultimate Game: The Rise and Fall of Bhagwan Shree Rajneesh.* San Francisco: Harper and Row, 1987.

Strenski, Ivan. *Four Theories of Myth in the Twentieth Century: Cassirer, Eliade, Lévi-Strauss, and Malinowski.* Iowa City: University of Iowa Press, 1987.

Suleri, Sara. *The Rhetoric of English India.* Chicago: University of Chicago Press, 1992.

Sutin, Lawrence. *Do What Thou Wilt: A Life of Aleister Crowley.* New York: St. Martin's Press, 2000.

Svoboda, Robert E. *Aghora: At the Left Hand of God.* Calcutta: Rupa, 1986.

———. *Aghora II: Kundalini.* Calcutta: Rupa, 1993.

Symonds, John. *The Magic of Aleister Crowley.* London: Frederick Muller, 1958.

Tagore, Rabindranath. *The Home and the World.* Trans. Surendranath Tagore. 1926. Reprint, London: Macmillan, 1967.

———. "Letters from an On-Looker." *Modern Review* 27, no. 1 (1919): 1–13.

———. *Letters to a Friend.* Ed. C. F. Andrews. New York: Macmillan, 1929.

———. *Nationalism.* London: Macmillan, 1950.

Tapasyananda, Swami, ed. *The Nationalistic and Religious Lectures of Swami Vivekananda.* Madras: Sri Ramakrishna Math, 1985.

Taussig, Michael. *Mimesis and Alterity: A Particular History of the Senses.* London: Routledge, 1993.

———. *Shamanism, Colonialism, and the Wild Man: A Study in Terror and Healing.* Chicago: University of Chicago Press, 1987.

Taylor, Isaac. *The Origin of the Aryans: An Account of the Prehistoric Ethnology and Civilisation of Europe.* London: Walter Scott, 1889.

Taylor, Kathleen. "Arthur Avalon: The Creation of a Legendary Orientalist." In *Myth and Mythmaking,* ed. Julia Leslie, pp. 144–63. Richmond, Eng.: Curzon Press, 1996.

———. "Arthur Avalon among the Orientalists: Sir John Woodroffe and Tantra." Paper presented at Oxford University, 2001.

———. *Sir John Woodroffe, Tantra, and Bengal: "An Indian Soul in a European Body"?* Richmond, Eng.: Curzon Press, 2001.

Taylor, Philip Meadows. *Confessions of a Thug.* 1839. Reprint, Oxford: Clarendon Press, 1984.

Teltscher, Kate. *India Inscribed: European and British Writing on India, 1600–1800*. New York: Oxford University Press, 1995.
Terry, Jennifer, and Melodie Calvert, eds. *Processed Lives: Gender and Technology in Everyday Life*. New York: Routledge, 1997.
Thibaut, George, trans. *Vedānta Sūtras with the Commentary by Śaṅkarācārya*. New Delhi: Motilal Banarsidas, 1968–71.
Thomas, Nicholas. *Colonialism's Culture: Anthropology, Travel, and Government*. Princeton, N.J.: Princeton University Press, 1994.
Thornton, Edward. *Illustrations of the History and Practices of the Thugs*. London: Nattali and Bond, 1837.
Torgovnick, Marianna. *Gone Primitive: Savage Intellects, Modern Lives*. Chicago: University of Chicago Press, 1990.
———. *Primitive Passions: Men, Women, and the Quest for Ecstasy*. Chicago: University of Chicago Press, 1998.
Trautmann, Thomas R. *Aryans and British India*. Berkeley: University of California Press, 1997.
Trungpa, Chogyam. *Born in Tibet*. Baltimore: Penguin Books, 1971.
———. *Cutting through Spiritual Materialism*. Berkeley, Calif.: Shambhala Publications, 1973.
———. *First Thought, Best Thought: 108 Poems*. Boulder, Colo.: Shambhala Publications, 1973.
———. *Journey without Goal: The Tantric Wisdom of the Buddha*. Boston: Shambhala Publications, 1985.
———. "Sparks." *Loka: A Journal from Naropa Institute* 1 (1975): 19–20.
Tucci, Giuseppe. *The Religions of Tibet*. Trans. Geoffrey Samuel. Berkeley: University of California Press, 1980.
———. *The Theory and Practice of the Maṇḍala: With Special Reference to the Modern Psychology of the Unconscious*. Trans. Alan H. Brodrick. London: Rider, 1969.
Tuker, Francis. *The Yellow Scarf: The Story of the Life of Thuggee Sleeman*. London: J. M. Dent and Sons, 1961.
Turner, Bryan S. *Regulating Bodies: Essays in Medical Sociology*. London: Routledge, 1992.
Urban, Hugh B. "Birth Done Better: Conceiving the Immortal Fetus in India, China, and Renaissance Europe." In *Notes on a Mandala: Essays in Honor of Wendy Doniger*, ed. Laurie Patton, pp. 25–56. New York: Seven Bridges Press, 2003.
———. "The Cult of Ecstasy: Tantrism, the New Age, and the Spiritual Logic of Late Capitalism." *History of Religions* 39, no. 3 (2000): 268–304.
———. *The Economics of Ecstasy: Tantra, Secrecy, and Power in Colonial Bengal*. New York: Oxford University Press, 2001.
———. "The Extreme Orient: The Construction of 'Tantrism' as a Category in the Orientalist Imagination." *Religion* 29 (1999): 123–46.
———. "India's Darkest Heart: Kālī in the Colonial Imagination." In *Encountering Kālī: In the Margins, at the Center, in the West*, ed. Jeffrey J. Kripal and Rachel Fell McDermott. Berkeley: University of California Press, 2003.
———. "The Marketplace and the Temple: Economic Metaphors and Religious

Meanings in the Folk Songs of Colonial Bengal." *Journal of Asian Studies* 60, no. 4 (2001): 1085–1114.

———. "The Omnipotent Oom: Tantra and Its Impact on Modern Western Esotericism." *Esoterica: The Journal of Esoteric Studies* 3 (2001): 218–59.

———. "The Path of Power: Impurity, Kingship, and Sacrifice in Assamese Tantra." *Journal of the American Academy of Religion* 69, no. 4 (2001): 777–816.

———. "The Remnants of Desire: Sacrificial Violence and Sexual Transgression in the Cult of the Kāpālikas and in the Writings of Georges Bataille." *Religion* 25 (1995): 67–90.

———. Review of *Kālī's Child: The Mystical and the Erotic in the Life and Teachings of Ramakrishna*, by Jeffrey J. Kripal. *Journal of Religion* 78, no. 2 (1998): 318–20.

———. "The Strategic Uses of an Esoteric Text: *The Mahānirvāṇa Tantra*." *South Asia* 18, no. 1 (1995): 55–81.

———. "Syndrome of the Secret: Eso-centrism and the Work of Steven M. Wasserstrom." *Journal of the American Academy of Religion* 69, no. 2 (2001): 439–49.

———. "The Torment of Secrecy: Ethical and Epistemological Problems in the Study of Esoteric Traditions." *History of Religions* 37, no. 3 (1998) : 209–48.

———. "Zorba the Buddha: Capitalism, Charisma, and the Cult of Bhagwan Shree Rajneesh." *Religion* 26 (1996): 161–82.

———, ed. and trans. *Songs of Ecstasy: Tantric and Devotional Songs from Bengal.* New York: Oxford University Press, 2001.

Urban, Hugh B., Glen A. Hayes, and Paul Muller-Ortega, eds. *In the Flesh: Eros, Secrecy, and Power in the Vernacular Tantric Traditions of India.* Albany: State University of New York Press, in progress.

Van Lysebeth, André. *Tantra: The Cult of the Feminine.* York Beach, Me.: Samuel Weiser, 1995.

van Woerkens, Martine. *The Strangled Traveler: Colonial Imaginings and the Thugs in India.* Chicago: University of Chicago Press, 2002.

Viswanathan, Gauri. *Masks of Conquest: Literary Study and British Rule in India.* New York: Columbia University Press, 1989.

Vivekananda, Swami. *The Complete Works of Swami Vivekananda.* 8 vols. Calcutta: Advaita Ashram, 1984.

———. *The East and the West.* New York: Vedanta Society, 1909.

———. *Letters of Swami Vivekananda.* Ed. Swami Mumukshananda. Calcutta: Advaita Ashram, 1964.

Volovici, Leon. *Nationalist Ideology and Antisemitism: The Case of Romanian Intellectuals in the 1930s.* Oxford: Oxford University Press, 1991.

Waddell, L. Austine. *Tibetan Buddhism: With Its Mystic Cults, Symbolism, and Mythology, and in Its Relation to Indian Buddhism.* Originally published as *The Buddhism of Tibet; or, Lamaism.* London: W. H. Allen, 1895. Reprint, New York: Dover Publications, 1972.

Ward, Gary L. "Pierre Arnold Bernard (Tantrik Order in America)." In *Religious Leaders of America: A Biographical Guide to Founders and Leaders of Religious Bodies, Churches, and Spiritual Groups in North America,* ed. J. Gor-

don Melton, pp. 39–40. Detroit: Gale Research, 1991.
Ward, William. *A View of the History, Literature, and Religion of the Hindoos*. 3 vols. 1811. Reprint, London: Kingsbury, Parbury, and Allen, 1817.
Wasserstrom, Steven M. "Eliade and Evola." In *The Unknown, Remembered Gate: Religious Experience and Hermeneutical Reflection*, ed. Elliot R. Wolfson and Jeffrey J. Kripal. New York: Seven Bridges Press, forthcoming.
———. "The Lives of Baron Evola." *Alphabet City* 4 (1995): 84–90.
———. *Religion after Religion*. Princeton, N.J.: Princeton University Press, 1999.
Watts, Alan. "Tantra." *Loka: A Journal from Naropa Institute* 1 (1975): 55–57.
Wayman, Alex. *Buddhist Tantra: Light on Indo-Tibetan Esotericism*. New York: Samuel Weiser, 1973.
———. *Yoga of the "Guhyasamājatantra": The Arcane Lore of Forty Verses*. New Delhi: Motilal Banarsidas, 1977.
Weeks, Jeffrey. *Sex, Politics, and Society: The Regulation of Society since 1800*. London: Longman, 1989.
———. *Sexuality and Its Discontents: Meanings, Myths, and Modern Sexualities*. London: Routledge and Kegan Paul, 1985.
Wheeler, J. Talboys. *The History of India from the Earliest Age*. London: Trübner, 1874.
White, David Gordon. *The Alchemical Body: Siddha Traditions in Medieval India*. Chicago: University of Chicago Press, 1996.
———. *The Kiss of the Yoginī: "Tantric Sex" in Its South Asian Contexts*. Chicago: University of Chicago Press, 2003.
———. "Tantric Sects and Tantric Sex: The Flow of Secret Tantric Gnosis." In *Rending the Veil: Concealment and Secrecy in the History of Religions*, ed. Elliot R. Wolfson, pp. 249–70. New York: Seven Bridges Press, 1999.
———, ed. *Tantra in Practice*. Princeton, N.J.: Princeton University Press, 2000.
Wilson, H. H. *Essays and Lectures, Chiefly on the Religion of the Hindus*. London: Trübner, 1846. Originally published in *Asiatic Researches* (1828, 1832).
———. *Religious Sects of the Hindus*. Ed. Ernst R. Rost. Calcutta: Susil Gupta, 1858.
Wittgenstein, Ludwig. *Philosophical Investigations*. Trans. G. E. M. Anscombe. New York: Macmillan, 1958.
———. *Preliminary Studies for the "Philosophical Investigations," Generally Known as the Blue and Brown Books*. Oxford: Basil Blackwell, 1958.
Woodroffe, John. *Bharata Shakti: Essays and Addresses on Indian Culture*. Madras: Ganesh, 1921.
———. *India: Culture and Society*. 1922. Reprint, New Delhi: Life and Light, 1978.
———. *Introduction to Tantra Śāstra*. 1913. Reprint, Madras: Ganesh, 1973.
———. *Is India Civilized? Essays on Indian Culture*. Madras: Ganesh, 1919.
———. Papers of Sir John Woodroffe, Atal Behari Ghose, and Lama Kazi Dawasamdup. MSS Eur. F285, fol. 2. British Museum, London.
———. *Shakti and Shākta*. 1918. Reprint, New York: Dover Publications, 1978.
———. *The World as Power*. Madras, Ganesh, 1974.
Wright, Caleb. *India and Its Inhabitants*. St. Louis: J. A. Brainerd, 1860.

Wurgaft, Lewis D. *The Imperial Imagination: Magic and Myth in Kipling's India.* Middletown, Conn: Wesleyan University Press, 1983.

Wuthnow, Robert, et al., eds., *Cultural Analysis: The Work of Peter L. Berger, Mary Douglas, Michel Foucault, and Jürgen Habermas.* Boston: Routledge and Kegan Paul, 1993.

Wylie, I. A. R. *The Daughter of Brahma.* Indianapolis: Bobbs-Merrill, 1912.

Yati. *The Sound of Running Water: A Photobiography of Bhagwan Shree Rajneesh.* Poona: Rajneesh Foundation, 1980.

York, Michael. *The Emerging Network: A Sociology of New Age and New Religious Movements.* Lanham, Md.: Rowman and Littlefield, 1995.

Zbavitel, Dusan. *Bengali Literature.* Wiesbaden, Ger.: Otto Harrassowitz, 1976.

Zimmer, Heinrich. *Artistic Form and Yoga in the Sacred Images of India.* Princeton, N.J.: Princeton University Press, 1984.

———. *Ewiges Indien: Leitmotive indischen Daseins.* Potsdam, Ger.: Müller and Kiepenheuer, 1930.

———. "Indische Mythen als Symbole: Zwei Vorträge." In *Eranos Jahrbuch, 1934,* vol. 2, pp. 97–151. Zurich: Rhein, 1935.

———. *Philosophies of India.* New York: Meridian Books, 1956.

———. "On the Significance of the Indian Tantric Yoga." In *Spiritual Disciplines: Papers from the Eranos Yearbooks,* ed. Joseph Campbell, pp. 3–58. New York: Pantheon Books, 1960.

Zitko, Howard. *New Age Tantra Yoga: The Cybernetics of Sex and Love.* Tuscon: World University Press, 1974.

Index

Compositor: Integrated Composition Systems
Text: 10/13 Sabon
Display: Sabon
Printer and Binder: Maple-Vail Manufacturing Group